Armed Only with Faith

Armed Only with Faith

*The Civil War Correspondence
of Chaplain William Lyman Hyde,
112th New York Infantry*

WILLIAM LYMAN HYDE

Edited by Jim Quinlan

Foreword by
Major General Donald L. Rutherford

McFarland & Company, Inc., Publishers
Jefferson, North Carolina

All photographs are from the editor's collection unless otherwise noted.

Frontispiece: William L. Hyde enrolled at Albany, New York, and served as the sole chaplain of the Chautauqua Regiment during the Civil War.

LIBRARY OF CONGRESS CATALOGUING-IN-PUBLICATION DATA

Hyde, William L. (William Lyman), 1819–1896, author.
Armed only with faith : the Civil War correspondence of Chaplain William Lyman Hyde, 112th New York Infantry / William Lyman Hyde ; edited by Jim Quinlan ; foreword by Major General Donald L. Rutherford.
    p.   cm.
Includes bibliographical references and index.

ISBN 978-0-7864-9991-5 (softcover : acid free paper) ♾
ISBN 978-1-4766-2253-8 (ebook)

1. Hyde, William L. (William Lyman), 1819–1896—Correspondence. 2. United States. Army. New York Infantry Regiment, 112th (1862–1865) 3. United States—History—Civil War, 1861–1865—Personal narratives. 4. New York (State)—History—Civil War, 1861–1865—Personal narratives. 5. Soldiers—New York (State)—Chautauqua County—Correspondence. 6. Chautauqua County (N.Y.) Biography. I. Quinlan, Jim (Genealogist), editor. II. Title.

E523.5112th .H94 2015   973.7'447092—dc23   [B]   2015033246

BRITISH LIBRARY CATALOGUING DATA ARE AVAILABLE

© 2015 Jim Quinlan. All rights reserved

No part of this book may be reproduced or transmitted in any form or by any means, electronic or mechanical, including photocopying or recording, or by any information storage and retrieval system, without permission in writing from the publisher.

Front cover: William Lyman Hyde portrait (Chautauqua County Historical Society, Westfield, New York)

Printed in the United States of America

McFarland & Company, Inc., Publishers
Box 611, Jefferson, North Carolina 28640
www.mcfarlandpub.com

To
the Chaplain Corps,
honoring
those who have gone in harm's way
armed only with faith

Table of Contents

Foreword by Major General Donald L. Rutherford   1

Preface   3

Introduction   5

1. **1862**   7
2. **1863**   13
3. **1864**   61
4. **1865**   188

Appendices:
   A. Mortuary Records   233
   B. Dear Chaplain Hyde   241
   C. The Union Soldier   256
   D. Ships Referenced by Hyde   261

Chapter Notes   265

References and Sources   277

Index   279

Foreword

by Major General Donald L. Rutherford

The passage of time changes many things, but it cannot change the heart's yearning for freedom and transcendence. Chaplain William Hyde relied upon this yearning, this faith, to sustain him as he sought to serve God and country as the regimental chaplain of the 112th New York Infantry, the Chautauqua Regiment. While this book is about faith, it is also about the actions that faith inspires: commitment to one's fellow soldiers, service to those who suffer, and the sacrifice that is all too often necessary so that the experiment that is our republic may continue.

When one looks into the steady gaze of Chaplain William Hyde's photograph, it is easy to conjure up images of a prophet following a distant god of wrath and judgment. If we reduce the beliefs of his generation, a generation that passed through the flames of war, to a caricature, then we rob both them and us of an authentically lived faith, a faith that provided the resilience necessary to sustain a suffering and shattered nation. Instead, in his words and the words of the Chautauqua soldiers, we find this chaplain embodying the same virtues embraced by our chaplains and chaplain assistants today: to nurture the living, to care for the wounded, and to honor the fallen. In these pages you will encounter the shadow of stern discipline, stoic resolve, and uncompromising dedication to duty, but it is soon overcome by the blinding dawn of love for God, love for country, and love for soldiers. Chaplain Hyde did not build his vocation upon the false jingoism of a shallow and self-serving patriot. His answer to God's call came from the deep and abiding longing to serve despite the sacrifices required.

The importance of this collection reaches far beyond the boundaries of faith, for it provides both the amateur and professional historian with a snapshot of what life was truly like for the common soldier, a perspective often overlooked amidst the battles and egos that swirled around the Civil War. For every Grant and Lee, there were thousands of men like William Hyde swept up and borne upon the tides of circumstance. His letters, diary and other writings remind us that this particular war was fought by citizen soldiers, representing entire communities, who were ready to rally to the sound of the trumpet. America was changing; men and women of merit, skill, and entrepreneurial spirit were replacing the old class of established families and landed gentry. While the Revolutionary War was led by the aristocracy, this war would be fought and won by the common man, who, along with their communities, stepped forward to wager their lives to preserve the freedom and hope of a still new republic.

In an age of tweets, emojis, and six-second videos, Chaplain Hyde reacquaints us with the beauty of the well-written word. He tells us that war is, "a terrible Moloch, within whose brazen mouth all forms of misery and woe mingle, and by whose devastating power the fondest ties that link heart to heart, the sweetest scenes of domestic bliss, the noblest aspirations of manliness are alike consumed." His diaries reacquaint us with the oft forgotten power and resonance of phrase and diction, of how this generation of men and women reflected upon their age and its challenges, and of the beauty and the horror that the soldier often discovers—simultaneously—as he gazes across the battlefield. This work brings humanity to the people and the units who have drifted into legend and obscurity. It reminds us of the heritage that all Americans share and the obligations we owe to the past generations who have so dearly purchased our liberty.

I want to personally thank Mr. Quinlan for his efforts to bring this project to fruition. To borrow a phrase from the era, it surely was divine providence that brought the collection of Chaplain Hyde's letters and journals into his possession. His expertise in chronicling and summarizing these works has produced a very readable and accessible book. I know his efforts will continue to shape chaplains, historians, and the public in the years ahead.

As I reflect upon the Chaplain Hyde's legacy, I am reminded that, despite the chaplain corps' growing diversity and number, we have far more in common with him and each other than we realize. We can proudly stand hand in hand with him to continue to provide the Constitutionally mandated religious support that our citizen soldiers deserve and our nation expects.

Pro Deo et Patria
Donald L. Rutherford
Chaplain (Major General) U.S. Army

The views expressed in this Foreword are my own and do not necessarily represent the views of the Department of Defense or the U.S. Army.

Major General Donald L. Rutherford became the 23rd Army Chief of Chaplains in 2011, after more than 20 years of active service in the Chaplain Corps. He served in operations Desert Shield, Desert Storm, Hurricane Andrew Relief, Desert Thunder and Iraqi Freedom, and is the recipient of numerous military awards. He is a native of Kinderhook, New York.

Preface

During the summer of 1989, I attended a Civil War relic and memorabilia show in Gettysburg, Pennsylvania with my good friend Bob Cammaroto. Having always been interested in military history and in particular the American Civil War, I was amazed to see the vast number of original artifacts that had survived the test of time. As Bob and I took in all the treasures, we came across a dealer who specialized in selling soldier's letters and documents. Hidden amongst his many binders, I found one with a label identifying the contents as letters from the 112th New York Infantry. There, before my eyes, were ninety-nine original, war-dated letters written by Chaplain William L. Hyde. Thinking it would be a shame for these letters to be sold separately and scattered throughout the country, I decided to purchase the entire lot. I planned to write an article about Chaplain Hyde and the 112th New York Infantry when I retired from the Marine Corps.

Through the years, I continued to add to my ever-growing Hyde collection. Some of the acquisitions were by design, others fate. Shortly after my initial purchase of the Hyde letters, I was contacted and asked if I would be interested in purchasing Hyde's 1863 diary. Needless to say, I was very interested. Later, while visiting my son in Park City, Utah, I found Hyde's war chronicle of 1862–1865 in a local antique store. How the documents found their way to Utah, remains a mystery. Later, I obtained Hyde's war journals and chaplain reports from yet another Civil War memorabilia dealer. It became apparent, I was destined to edit Hyde's war correspondence and tell his story.

William Hyde joined the Chautauqua Regiment during its formative period and remained with the regiment until it mustered out in 1865. Although he did not assault the trenches at Petersburg or scale the earthen mounds of Fort Fisher, he did bear personal witness to the horrors of war. After many skirmishes between the 112th and Confederate forces, Hyde would be found among the injured, dressing soldier's wounds, assisting regimental surgeons in amputation procedures or providing comfort and prayer to the dying.

He was dutiful in writing his wife and two sons during the course of the war. He continually expressed his love and devotion to his family and longed for the day when the war's end would enable him to return home. A prolific writer, his personal insight into the regiment, the army and the war, provided a vivid description of the routine and hardship of soldiering and the tragedy of war.

As dedicated to the men of the 112th as he was to his family, his letters are full of instances exhibiting his concern for the spiritual and general welfare of the common soldier. He fulfilled his duties as religious leader as well as that of confidante to the men. Soldiers felt at ease with the chaplain in discussing personal, family and religious issues. So much so, the enlisted men would present him with a horse to show their gratitude.

Chaplain Hyde ensured the families of those left behind in Chautauqua County were kept abreast of the regiment's undertakings. He frequently corresponded with newspaper editors, providing firsthand accounts of the regiment's activities. He kept the home front informed with timely casualty lists and was often the first to write a family about the wounding or death of their loved one. Some of the letters Hyde received from grieving families, thanking him for his kindness, are included in Appendix B.

Hyde had the foresight to preserve much of his personal correspondence. The materials used to tell his story come primarily from his own hand. His faithful letters to Francis Hyde, "My dear Wife," his 1863 diary, war dated chaplain and mortuary reports, and letters sent to the editors of newspapers give insight into what he witnessed and experienced during the great rebellion on a daily basis. His journals, chronicle, regimental history and speeches to veterans groups provide the reader with additional insight into Hyde's war experiences.

I organized this book chronologically; each year has its own dedicated chapter. The source of each correspondence entry is cited (e.g., Diary, Chronicle, Journal, Newspaper, etc.) with the exception of letters, which are self-evident. Unless otherwise noted, Hyde is the author of all sources. Many dates have multiple sources, showing Hyde often recorded daily events in more than one piece of correspondence. For consistency, source precedence for correspondence entries is: chronicle, diary, journal, and letter.

Editing was done with a conscious effort not to detract from Hyde's original thoughts or writing style. Although Hyde was notorious for writing run-on sentences and lengthy paragraphs, I made only minimal changes to punctuation and paragraph structure when necessary for clarification or ease of reading. Additionally, correction or consistency in spelling of names and locations were made for accuracy. Abbreviations were spelled out and brackets were inserted when a word was illegible or an additional word was needed to make the sentence intelligible. The chaplain often recorded his daily recollections in the late hours of the day or while rushing to catch the mail runner. I trust he will understand that in my editing I am trying to be the aide he did not have the luxury of enjoying at the time.

It would have been extremely difficult to put Chaplain Hyde's story to paper without the assistance of many individuals and organizations. My sincere gratitude to Bob Cammaroto, Roger Hunt, Henry Deeks, Ron Coddington, Jan Wade and Don Ryberg for their friendship, insight and knowledge pertaining to the 112th New York Infantry and the American Civil War. I want to publicly thank the hard working people at the National Archives; the Library of Congress; the United States Army Research Center at Carlisle, Pennsylvania; Emory University, Atlanta, Georgia; Navarro College, Corsicana, Texas; and the staff of the following New York libraries and historical centers: the New York State Library in Albany; Fenton History Center in Jamestown, especially Norman Carlson and Karen Livsey; Chautauqua County Historical Society in Westfield, especially John Paul Wolfe; Patterson Library in Westfield, especially Nancy N. Ensign; Daniel A. Reed Library at the State University of New York in Fredonia, especially Cynthia Yochym; James Prendergast Library in Jamestown; Dunkirk Historical Society and Museum in Dunkirk; and the Yorker Museum in Sherman. They provided invaluable assistance in providing additional Hyde materials for my research.

Lastly, transcribing Hyde's correspondence and editing this book was a herculean task and could not have been accomplished without the dedicated assistance of Clair Marie, Sheila Vaughan and my devoted wife, Candace. They have my heartfelt appreciation.

Introduction

By September 1862, America had been at war with itself for approximately eighteen months. The fierce fighting at Manassas, bloodletting at Shiloh and horrific carnage at Antietam, only reinforced the sentiment that there would be no early end to the conflict. The reality of a protracted war hovered over the nation like an ominous storm cloud. Civilians anguished over the lists of military casualties published daily in northern papers as President Lincoln repeatedly pressed the states for more volunteers to fill the army's depleting ranks.

Enthusiastically, the citizens of New York again responded to the president's call to arms. Captain Frederick Phisterer recorded in his account of *New York in the War of the Rebellion, 1861–1865* that overall, New York provided 298 regiments (infantry, artillery, cavalry and engineers) to the Union cause.[1]

In the case of Chautauqua County, located on the far southwestern edge of the state, its patriotic citizens rallied to the army recruiting centers to enlist. Many Chautauqua men unreservedly filled the ranks of at least nineteen state regiments. When the governor specifically asked for volunteers for the formation of a new infantry regiment-the 112th, the response was immediate. Men from all walks of life, throughout Chautauqua and neighboring counties, enlisted into Union service with the regiment for a period of three years. So great was the response from Chautauqua County alone, that the regiment took the title "The Chautauqua Regiment." On September 11, 1862, the 112th was mustered into Federal service. The regiment was organized to include ten infantry companies and a field and staff element. This element included a colonel, lieutenant colonel, major, adjutant, sergeant major, surgeon, assistant surgeon and chaplain.

Selected to command the regiment was Jeremiah C. Drake, a resident of Westfield, a small town within Chautauqua County. At the outbreak of war, Drake left the ministry of a Baptist church and was commissioned a captain to command a company in the 49th New York Infantry Regiment. Just three days prior to the bloodiest one-day battle of the war—Antietam—Drake mustered out of the 49th for promotion to colonel and took command of the 112th.

Earlier in 1861, the War Department's Adjutant General's Office addressed the appointment of chaplains within the army. It stated "That there shall be allowed to each regiment one chaplain, who shall be appointed by the regimental commander on the vote of the field officers and company commanders on duty with the regiment at the time the appointment shall be made. The chaplain so appointed must be a regular ordained minister of a Christian denomination, and shall receive the pay and allowances of a captain of cavalry, and shall be required to report to the colonel commanding the regiment to which he is attached, at the end of each quarter, the moral and religious condition of the regiment, and such suggestions as may conduce to the social happiness and moral improvement of the troops."[2]

On October 10, 1862, J. B. Stonehouse, Acting Assistant Adjutant General informed the recruiting officer in Albany, New York, that the governor requested the Reverend William L. Hyde be mustered into the service of the United States as Chaplain of the 112th New York State Volunteers for a period of three years.[3]

Hyde's appointment as chaplain met with the approval of Colonel Drake and the officers of the 112th. He rapidly assimilated to a soldier's life and absorbed himself in the duties of regimental chaplain. So highly thought of by the officers and enlisted men, the regiment's adjutant wrote the following to the *Jamestown Journal*:

> The selection of the Reverend Mr. Hyde, formerly of Dunkirk, as chaplain, has proved to be a very judicious and fortunate one. He is universally liked and is very active in the discharge of his duties, he is untiring in his devotion to the sick and moves about in a quiet, unassuming way with a pleasant smile and kind word to all. He seems to comprehend the duties of a chaplain, believing that they do not consist merely in an outward display on Sunday and close confinement during the week, but every day alike and each day increased efforts to accomplish something that will tend to the good of the boys. His influence is being felt and he is respected by all.[4]

William Lyman Hyde was born in Bath, Maine, on December 27, 1819, and was the son of Captain Henry and Maria Hyde. Graduating from Bowdoin College in Brunswick, Maine, in 1842, he realized he had an internal calling to the church. After attending seminary, he was ordained a minister in 1849. In 1852, while still living in Maine, he married Francis Elizabeth Rice and they would have two surviving sons (Henry Warren and Frederick William) and after the war, adopt a daughter (Elizabeth Clover). In 1856, Hyde moved his family to Dunkirk, New York, for an opportunity to serve as a Presbyterian pastor. He remained there until enlisting into military service with the 112th Regiment in October 1862.

From October 1862 until June of 1865, Hyde tramped over rebel soil in Virginia, South Carolina, Florida and North Carolina. For nearly thirty-two months he served as the regimental chaplain, tending to the spiritual and moral needs of the Chautauqua Regiment until being mustered out with the regiment at the end of hostilities.

Upon returning to civilian life, Hyde served as a pastor in Ripley and later Sherman, New York. In 1874, Hyde switched his profession from preaching to teaching. He first held a position as high school principal in Ovid, Seneca County, and later taught at a private school in Jamestown, Chautauqua County.

Hyde never forgot his service with the Chautauqua Regiment. In 1866 he wrote the *History of the One Hundred and Twelfth Regiment New York Volunteers*. It remains the only regimental history ever written regarding the 112th Infantry. While living in Jamestown, he remained a very active member of the Grand Army of the Republic. He volunteered and served as the chaplain for the James M. Brown Post and in 1896 he was elected as honorary chaplain of the Grand Encampment, Department of New York, Grand Army of the Republic.[5]

The following pages tell the story of William L. Hyde's military service with the 112th during the War of the Rebellion. This is his story, in his own words.

1

1862

By September of 1862, Ulysses S. Grant had already earned his nickname of "Unconditional Surrender" for his capture of Forts Henry and Donelson in Tennessee. Former United States Secretary of War Jefferson Davis was inaugurated as the first President of the Confederacy. The first naval duel between ironclad ships was fought between the USS Monitor and the CSS Virginia. President Lincoln presented his Emancipation Proclamation to his cabinet and the country was in its second year of the war.

On September 12th, only one day after being mustered into active service, the Chautauqua Regiment boarded trains and left the Empire State for the seat of war. Briefly stopping in the District of Columbia, the regiment received orders from the War Department to proceed to Fortress Monroe in Hampton, Virginia, whereupon it was directed to immediately proceed to Suffolk, Virginia to serve as part of Colonel Robert S. Foster's Provisional Brigade.[1]

Friday, September 12th

Left Jamestown. (Chronicle)

Wednesday, September 17th

Arrived at Suffolk. (Chronicle)

Monday, September 22nd

100 men detailed to start for Deserted House to Summerton Road. (Chronicle)

Tuesday, September 23rd

Major General J. J. Peck assumes command.[2] (Chronicle)

Robert S. Foster commanded the 13th Indiana Infantry during the Shenandoah Valley campaign of 1862 and commanded Union elements in Virginia, South Carolina and Florida. He served as a member of the military commission that tried the Lincoln conspirators (courtesy Library of Congress).

Wednesday, September 24th

6th Massachusetts, 112th New York and 130th New York Provisional Brigade, Colonel R. S. Foster, 13th Indiana Infantry. Detail of 250 privates, 7 noncommissioned, 4 commissioned officers. (Chronicle)

Friday, September 26th

For fatigue 15 men with descriptive lists to serve in Howard's Battery.[3] (Chronicle)

Saturday, September 27th

450 men and 7 officers to fatigue work. 12 men detailed to serve in Follett's Battery.[4] (Chronicle)

Monday, September 29th

All men under arms at reveille (5 o'clock) to continue 30 minutes. (Chronicle)

Ulysses S. Grant was General in Chief of the Armies of the United States and ordered the devastating Union assaults at Cold Harbor, Virginia, in 1864. He served as eighteenth president of the United States.

Thursday, October 2nd

Colonel Drake, October 1, school of instruction ordered. Sent protest to Governor Morgan against detailing men to serve in batteries against their will.[5] (Chronicle)

Wednesday, October 8th

Major Carpenter reached regiment.[6] (Chronicle)

Friday, December 5th

Wessells' Brigade leaves.[7] Change camp vicinity Fort McLellan. (Chronicle)

Tuesday, December 16th

Private, Company C, sentenced to 6 months hard labor and forfeit $10 a month for 6 months for taking from an open barrel 3 onions. Order of Brigadier General Vogdes.[8] (Chronicle)

Thursday, December 18th

Suffolk, Va
December 18th 1862

Editors [Dunkirk] Union[9]:

It is well known that there has been a very serious amount of sickness and a very large number of deaths in this regiment since it left Chautauqua County last September.

Some of the best men in the regiment, beloved by their comrades here, and ornaments

Camp Suffolk, Virginia. Group photograph of members of the 112th at Camp Suffolk during the winter of 1862–1863. Chaplain Hyde is the eleventh adult from the right, wearing a bowler style hat with hand on hip. Colonel John Smith is the eighth from the right, facing right with folded arms (courtesy U.S. Army Heritage and Education Center [USAHEC]).

to society at home, and men of high-toned character, and noble, patriotic impulses have thus, in a manner far different from their aspirations when they entered the service at the call of their country, been called to give up their lives and to leave behind them desolated homes, the deep anguish of bereaved mother, the loneliness and the bitterness of widowhood, the sighs and helplessness of the orphan. War is a terrible Moloch, within whose brazen mouth all forms of misery and woe mingle, and by whose devastating power the fondest ties that link heart to heart, the sweetest scenes of domestic bliss, the noblest aspirations of manliness are alike consumed.[10]

Around those who die upon the field of battle a certain halo of glory gathers. They were actors in the strife, they dared and struggled nobly. They struck the blow for their country's preservation and gave their lives as a sacrifice. We mark them high upon the record of the worthy and with the sadness which we feel in their loss, there is a certain pride mingled because the world regards death upon the field of battle as glorious. While such are remembered gratefully, how often are those who went forth with as noble aspirations and as ardent desires to dare and to do for their imperiled country but who stricken down by disease, waste away and die in the hospital, forgotten except by their immediate family and friends. There is nothing poetic and thrilling in such a death, therefore their lives are regarded as wasted, and they are dropped from remembrances. There is certainly gross injustice in this. In entering the service they could not choose the manner of death, should death come. Their lives are as truly a gift to the cause as they would have been if the bullet, rather than the fever, and the glorious strife, rather than the lingering weakness, had been their lot.

It is from a desire to rectify this injustice and to do honor to those who have deserved so well of their country, that I have prepared these brief sketches of the dead of the 112th Regiment. Hurried from the place of its formation before it was fairly organized after a very tedious journey, it was cast without a shelter upon the borders of the Dismal Swamp, a region highly malarious, exposed to a wilting ... [this portion of the article is illegible] ... without shelter upon the cold ground to breathe in an infected air at the most sickly season of the year. Is it astonishing that so many have died; is it not, rather, wondered that the mortality has not been greater?

1. The first man of the regiment who died: Alba H. Duncan of Stockton, a member of Company I. He was taken sick on the journey here and on the arrival of the regiment, was sent back to the hospital on Craney Island. He returned in about two weeks, was able to do only the lightest duty, soon he was again taken down with malarial fever which turned into inflammation of the bowels. He died October 7th, after four days sickness, aged 24 years. He was a man of excellent character and promised to make an excellent soldier.

2. Ira A. Knowlton, Company C, son of William Knowlton, of Arkwright, died October 13th, disease typhoid fever. He was a good, faithful man, but was taken sick soon after coming here and did but very little duty. He was a single man, aged 24 years.

3. Daniel M. Waite, Company D, of Clymer, aged 30 years, leaves a wife and one child. He was taken sick on the passage hither and had never been able to do any duty. Died of marasmus, October 19th.

4. F. W. Daniels, Company F, of Panama, son of George B. Daniels, aged 19. He was a fine boy. Soon after reaching here, he was taken sick and died of dysentery, October 20th.

5. H. W. Smith, Company B, of Stockton. He was a good soldier and well beloved in the company. Died of dysentery, October 21st, aged 19.

6. Andre W. Matteson, Company E, of Ripley, son of Victor M. Matteson, died of typhoid fever, October 22nd, aged 20. He was orderly sergeant of the company, highly esteemed by officers and men.

7. R. A. Rockwell, Company K, of Villenova, aged 24. He leaves a family to mourn his loss. Soon after coming here, he was taken down with typhoid fever and lingering, died October 22nd.

8. Albert Losee, Company K, of Cherry Creek, son of Clark Losee, a youth of fine promise. He died of typhoid fever, October 23rd, aged 18.

9. Warham S. Foot, Company K, of Forestville, died October 27th of fever terminating in dysentery. He leaves a wife and one child to mourn his loss. Aged 21.

10. Harvey Potter, Company G, of Centerville, son of John Potter, a quiet, resolute boy, always prompt; he promised well. In his youthful prime, he died, rapidly sinking after he was taken. His disease was typhoid fever, followed by hemorrhaging of the bowels. Aged 18 years.

11. Frank L. Wilson, Company G, of Westfield, sergeant. A young man universally beloved, an enterprising mechanic, he gave up a good business to enter upon his country's service. He was prompt and faithful in every duty till disease arrested him. For more than a week, that fell disease, typhoid fever, assailed his vigorous constitution. His sickness was borne with Christian composure. His death was beautiful; when he could no longer recognize through delirium the friend who had watched over him, a picture of his young wife and his mother, which he had kept near him through his sickness, was opened and held up to his gaze. His lately vacant eye was at once fixed and with eagerness, he seized the case with both hands, drew it to his heart, where it lay till he breathed his last. He died November 3rd, aged 25.

12. John G. Mayborn, Company H, of Sherman, aged 27. Died of typhoid fever November 10th. He leaves a wife and two children. He had never been able to do any duty. Soon after coming here he was sent to the hospital on Craney Island. On his return he was feeble, typhoid set in, death came after a lingering sickness. He was an excellent man.

13. Marcus Vanness, Company H, of Sherman, corporal. He was a fine looking soldier, tall and muscular; apparently one of the most powerful men in the regiment. His constitution had been shattered by a severe fever a year ago and he had not at any time while with us, his usual health. He was while on guard at one of the fortifications, taken suddenly and

violently with inflammation of the bowels and died in a few hours, on November 10th, aged 32. He leaves a wife to mourn his loss.

14. D. M. Smith, Company I, of Stockton, aged 31 years. He was an enterprising and thrifty farmer, enlisted with two other brothers, one of whom preceded him to the grave. A valuable man and a prompt soldier, after a short run of typhoid fever, he calmly met the summons which called him to higher duty in realms where there is no strife. He died on November 14th and leaves a wife and two children.

15. Hugh O. Jones, Company B, of Sinclairville. He died of homesickness; long constant, depressing, no efforts could avail to shake it from him. He lay day after day and sighed for his cottage home, where were his wife and five children dependent on his labor for their support. A Welshman by birth, a quiet and exemplary man, died November 14th, aged 42.

16. David Hogins, Company D, of Busti, died November 18th of measles, the first death from this disease. He had, however, when the measles set in, a very severe inflammation of the lungs. He was a single man, son of Amos Hogins of Ashville. By his own exertions, he had accumulated a comfortable property. His energy and promptness made him a valuable soldier, age 30.

17. Charles E. Teed, Company I, of Cassadaga. A widowed mother and numerous connections mourn his untimely loss. He was a fine, active, cheerful boy; prompt in every duty and perhaps fell a victim to his determination to accompany the regiment on a long and arduous march when he had better remain in camp. The measles came out during the march, lying on the ground at night they were checked, and on his return, inflammation of the brain set in and soon ended his life. Died November 23rd, aged 18.

18. William Chamberlim, Company B, of Brockton, corporal, son of [blank] Chamberlim. He was a young man of that energy and tact which would have enabled him to make his mark on any calling, and his social virtues were such as belong to the finest molded of our race. Beautiful in life and in death, he is a loss to his regiment as well as to those who in the home of his love, are so deeply bereaved. Died November 23rd, aged 19.

19. Theron Reed, Company B, of Laona, corporal. Mr. Reed was a native of the state of Maine, where his parents still reside. Mr. Reed came into our county during the summer of 1861 to engage in manufacturing. In partnership with Hiram Thompson, he leased the Holmes bedstead factory, at Laona. Both partners enlisted last summer in the 112th. He was a man of a fine vigorous constitution, energetic and enterprising. While many were stricken down with sickness, he went through every exposure unharmed and often boasted of his power of endurance. For more than a month after he was first taken, no harm was felt in regard to him, but after the fever was subdued, the exhaustion of the nervous system was so complete that he could not be rallied. His disease was typhoid fever. Aged 25.

20. Hollister H. Peck, Company F, of Westfield, corporal. Peck was a young man of not very vigorous constitution, yet many such have endured the draft of military life better than others who seemed made of iron. He was greatly beloved in his native village and by his comrades. In his case, the typhoid fever was attended by a singular affliction of the brain, so that he was not rational after he was taken to the hospital. The disease made such rapid progress that in two days his valuable life was ended. Died December 4th, aged 26.

21. Malcom W. Gage, Company C, Hanover, son of Charles B. Gage, died of measles completed with typhoid fever. Age 18. He had been an invalid most of the time after he came into the regiment.

22. Paul Squimer, Company G, of Dunkirk, son-in-law of Peter Krayer, born in Holland. At an early age was brought over to this country. He was educated in our public schools, and was learning the trade of carpenter with Mr. A. W. Murray, when he enlisted last summer. He enjoyed camp life and learned the duties of a soldier readily, always prompt and efficient, he had the respect of his officers and was liked by his comrades. He took cold, during the march to the Blackwater the middle of November, from exposure.

After this, he could only do light duty part of the time. Typhoid fever set in and he died December 4th, aged 18 years.

23. Russell H. Dean, Company A, of Jamestown, son of Jesse Dean. His system was much debilitated by frequent attacks of illness incident to the climate so that he was frequently relieved of duty. Taken down with measles, complicated with typhoid. He was hurried to the grave. Died December 16th, age 18.

24. Walter S. Risley, son of Lyman of Panama, died December 17th, aged 22. He was for some time sick with typhoid, but recovered. While yet suffering from the consequent prostration, measles set in and ended his life. While in health, he was prompt and efficient as a soldier, and was highly esteemed by his comrades.

25. Lester C. Merriman, Company G, of Sheridan, volunteered after the regiment reached Suffolk, to join Follett's Artillery Battery. He was soon attacked by typhoid fever and died. He leaves behind a wife and two children. Died, age 21.

26. Conrad Benz, of the Independent Company Sharpshooters, died November 2nd of hemorrhage of bowels. He was a Swede by birth, enlisted at Jamestown.[11]

27. John Lawson, of the same company, died December 19th, age 18, of typhoid fever. He was also a Swede. His parents still live in Carroll. This company has been very fortunate in losing only two of their number.

Thus twenty-seven of those who left Jamestown in seeming vigor have finished their military career without the slightest experience of the battlefield. Disease wasted them. But they did well in giving themselves to so glorious a cause and let their memory be honored by those for whose sake they went forth and in whose behalf they have thus laid down their lives.

There is still a large amount of sickness in the regiment; measles, fever and rheumatism are the prevailing forms. Almost fifty are in the measles hospital—all doing well. The fever hospital has about 30 cases, all convalescing. There are many about quarters disabled by slight ailments and rheumatism.

Since I last wrote, the regiment has changed camp. After General Wessells left for North Carolina, General Foster was sent to guard that part of the port where Wessells' Brigade was located. It was a sad change for the boys to leave their nice new quarters for the old smoky tents of those old regiments, but with some grumbling which we all know is the priceless privilege of every true American, they had to stand it.

Wishing all my old friends a Happy New Year, I will close this letter.

Chaplain [Hyde]

Sunday, December 28th

Spinola's Brigade leaves.[12] Move tents from 1st campground. (Chronicle)

Monday, December 29th

Busy in remodeling camp. (Chronicle)

> *In mid–November, the regiment participated in a series of sorties in the vicinities of Franklin, Zuni and locations around the Blackwater River area of Virginia. Although the brigade did encounter small numbers of Confederate troops, the 112th was never heavily engaged in 1862. As the year ended, the Chautauqua Regiment reluctantly continued to pull fatigue duty in order to strengthen Suffolk's defensive positions and when the opportunity presented itself, companies conducted formation and weapon drills.*

2

1863

By the dawn of the New Year, the Nation was entering into its third year of civil war. During January of 1863, President Lincoln issued the Emancipation Proclamation. In the west, Generals Grant and Sherman continued to strengthen their forces, while they slowly and systematically tightened the noose around the Confederate forces defending Vicksburg. In the east, the Army of the Potomac, once again, changed command. After Burnside's disaster at Fredericksburg, Lincoln decided to take his chances with General Joseph Hooker. Hooker in turn, would lose command that summer after a devastating defeat at Chancellorsville by the hands of Robert E. Lee and Stonewall Jackson. In the South, Chaplain Hyde and the 112th found themselves assigned to the 2nd Provisional Brigade as part of the Union army in defense of Suffolk, VA.[1]

Thursday, January 1st

Rode horseback most of the day. Then rode to this camp of mounted rifles.[2] It was a gloomy day to me. I thought much of home. (Diary)

Saturday, January 3rd

Funeral in 6th Massachusetts in morning. Spent pleasant evening with Chaplain Whitaker, 11th Pennsylvania Cavalry.[3] He received a box from home while we took tea. (Diary)

Sunday, January 4th

Preached in the afternoon to a large audience in the Methodist church

Ambrose E. Burnside. During early 1862, he conducted a successful expedition against North Carolina's coastal area and received command of the Army of the Potomac, only to lose it after his failure at Fredericksburg, Virginia.

where we are hereafter to occupy for afternoon service. Evening prayer meeting quartermaster tent. (Diary)

Monday, January 5th

Left at 9 am for Drummond Lake. Thru canal. House at lake. Lake itself, evening moonlight excursion. Negro singing. Sleeping. (Diary)

Tuesday, January 6th

Mary Hunt started for home about 10. Rain. Reached home 4 o'clock. Letter from Doctor Rogers.[4] Chaplain Hanson said he sent my box with other packages certified for him.[5] Called on Powers.[6] He was in a deep distress of mind. Hope by conversation and prayer he was comforted. (Diary)

Thursday, January 8th

Regiment went on reconnaissance towards Franklin. (Chronicle)

Regiment left on an expedition at 6 o'clock am, cold and lowery day. Spent most of day with the sick. Letter from wife in evening. Mason died.[7] (Diary)

Friday, January 9th

Spent most of the day in the hospitals. Had precious interview with Powers and Davis.[8] Afternoon called on Captain Curtis and Lieutenant Andrews.[9] Rode Boyd's horse downtown.[10] (Diary)

Saturday, January 10th

Regiment returned about midnight, dark rainy muddy, a very severe march. (Chronicle)

Morning. Occupied with the arrangements for funeral of Otis A. Mason. Funeral at noon. Evening in my tent writing. About 10, regiment returned in drenching rain. (Diary)

Sunday, January 11th

Preached to thin audience in pm, Psalms 119:11.[11] Regiment worn out with march. Went to colored church. Evening I spent with lieutenant colonel and wrote to wife.[12] (Diary)

Monday, January 12th

Surgeon J. R. Thomas having resigned on account of feeble health leaves the regiment.[13] (Chronicle)

Edson Boyd enrolled at Jamestown, New York, as assistant surgeon with the 112th New York Volunteers. He was discharged for disability on November 9, 1863.

Rode down to headquarters. Doctor Thomas left. We gave him a paper signed by all the field and staff expressing regards. Lieutenant colonel received notice his resignation accepted. Lieutenant colonel pictures taken. Supped with Boyd. (Diary)

Tuesday, January 13th

Rode. Did not do much. Spent evening with lieutenant colonel. Heard of Louis Colman's death.[14] Bought articles, see memo of lieutenant colonel. (Diary)

Wednesday, January 14th

Lieutenant Colonel Redington left having resigned. (Chronicle)

Lieutenant Colonel Redington went home, having resigned. I tore down his tent in preparation to moving it. Jule began to take care of my horse.[15] Evening sick, terrible night. (Diary)

Thursday, January 15th

Sick all day. Better evening. Nervous fever. Night awful wind and rain, tents almost blown down. Had tea sent from hospital. (Diary)

Jeffery R. Thomas enrolled at Jamestown, New York, as assistant surgeon with the 112th New York Volunteers. He was discharged for disability on December 20, 1862.

Friday, January 16th

Better today. Though weak. Stormy day. Did not go to other camp til night. Stopped with boys in the sergeant's tent, Company B. (Diary)

Saturday, January 17th

Bright pleasant day. Wrote letters morning and evening. Afternoon had my tent walled. Got box from Chaplain Hanson's. Contained hat, etc. Wrote to home journal. (Diary)

Sunday, January 18th

Morning in hospitals. Visited all but the stockade. Afternoon preached up "whatsoever a man soweth that shall he also reap."[16] Went to colored church. Evening retired early. Letter to wife. (Diary)

Monday, January 19th

Spent the day in moving from the other camp. Slept in new quarters at night. Received letters. (Diary)

Tuesday, January 20th

Spent day in fixing up quarters. Several left for Chautauqua. Mr. Kessel arrested for interfering in [medical] department. Violent storm at night. (Diary)

Wednesday, January 21st

Forenoon spent fixing up. Afternoon rode to provost marshal. Evening wrote and read. Wrote lieutenant colonel. (Diary)

Thursday, January 22nd

Raining. Spent the day among the sick boys. (Diary)

Friday, January 23rd

Raw and chilly. Spent the day in arranging and distributing tracts, paper and religious books for the boys. (Diary)

Saturday, January 24th

Crosgrove in the hospital, very bad, probably will not live.[17] He was in a most delightful state of mind. I know that my Redeemer liveth in us since by faith.[18] 5 years Jesus precious savior. (Diary)

Sunday, January 25th

Crosgrove died 9 am. We sang and prayed in the hospital. Attended church. Whitaker preached, "for thou shall die or not live."[19] Then I preached on the "Peace be still."[20] After went to hospitals. Evening wrote wife. (Diary)

Monday, January 26th

Service at 9 at hospital. Crosgrove taken to cars. Saw Cobb he was anxious.[21] Charley Norton told me he was awakened by remarks in hospital.[22] Rode in pm with Palmeter.[23] Changed my saddle with Whitaker. (Diary)

Tuesday, January 27th

Rainy morning, moved [illegible]. Afternoon made chair. Evening read, visited Colonel Drake. (Diary)

Wednesday, January 28th

Rainy. Made saddlecloth. Visited hospital. (Diary)

Ammon B. Cobb enlisted at Pomfret, New York, as a private in Company I, 112th New York Volunteers. Wounded in action at Chapin's Farm, Virginia, he transferred to the 3rd New York Infantry on June 13, 1865.

Thursday, January 29th

Paymaster. Received $77.88. Had building hauled from other camp for my horse and went over to see Cobb. Two companies of our regiment were ordered out at midnight to report to Colonel Dobbs.[24] (Diary)

Friday, January 30th

Battle of Deserted Farm, 2 companies, B and C. Watson killed.[25] (Chronicle)
The rest of our regiment ordered to scene of conflict.[26] (Diary)

> **Editor's note:** *After the action at the Deserted Farm, Hyde wrote a letter home to a Dr. Wright, describing the death of Sergeant Watson.*[27]

Companies B and C of our regiment had orders last evening (29th) to form at midnight and report to Colonel Dobbs of the 13th Indiana, as a part of a reconnoitering force, it being understood that the enemy had crossed the Blackwater and were entrenching themselves about 8 miles from here. About 4 o'clock this morning, I was awakened by the most incessant artillery firing I ever heard, and at breakfast time the remainder of the regiment were ordered to form in column and march in the same direction immediately. I know there had been serious work.

About 9, rumors began to come in that there had been a severe battle. I started out to share with our dear boys the dangers and be where I could aid and comfort the wounded. After a ride of an hour and a half, I found the regiment 9 miles distant from Suffolk occupying the battlefield of the morning—as a reserved force, Corcoran having driven the Rebels forward and being then in pursuit.[28] On my way I met three ambulances with the wounded and dead. Soon I came along where was a group of men and one accosted me, "Chaplain," said he, "there lies poor Watson." I went towards him and uncovered the face. It was him indeed—all that was mortal of him, but so pale and cold, with the same placid, resolute face. I then uncovered the right leg, and what a sight! A cannon ball had ploughed into the flesh and tore from above the knee to the thigh, and a frightful wound it was.

Over Watson my heart yearned. I thought of him as I had seen him in our Sabbath gatherings and at our little prayer meetings; of his true and manly patriotism—of his gentle and unobtrusive goodness—of his warm yet quiet piety. Nobly gifted Watson! Chautauqua has not many such gifts to lay upon the altar of our afflicted country. When he was killed the regiment was lying on the ground as reserve support to artillery. Warren Smith, of Captain Scott's Company, was slightly wounded at the battle of the Blackwater.[29]

Suffolk, Va
January 30th 1863

Messrs. Editors:

Knowing the interest felt by your readers in the 112th, I venture to write you and them. Jamestown naturally feels warmly toward the 112th. The representatives of many of its most honored families, and also of the best bone and muscle of the place are in it.

You will be glad to learn that the regiment is slowly, but surely, recovering from the terrible ordeal of exposure, in a most unhealthy locality, which it passed through on its first arrival upon the borders of the Dismal Swamp. The week ending the 27th, it was 129. The week ending January 3rd, 132. There are still, as the figures show, a large number of sick in the regiment; but most are slightly sick. All forms of disease are much more manageable than two months ago.[30]

There has been a marked improvement in the condition and management of the hospitals. There are three buildings used as hospitals, and one large hospital tent. One of these is a two story house painted white, once the residence of a Rebel family that could not appreciate the good but powerful neighbors who came from the north and pitched their tents in their cornfields and so fled. The house relieved of the shame of sheltering so much of wickedness as a southern Rebel's skin covers, is now honored by being the principal hospital building of one of the noblest regiments in the service of the Union. It is, however, too small, having only one large and one small room above and below; no closets, or pantry, or any of those conveniences deemed essential in the humblest northern dwelling. The chimneys are on the outside, as is the almost universal custom. In this building there are 24 patients, mostly convalescents from fever, though two are yet very sick. The other building near it is a long stockade house, one story high, and about 80 feet long. The regiment is principally indebted for it to the earnest endeavors of Major Carpenter, Captain J. F. Smith and Sergeant Sherwin.[31] It is divided into three compartments, one of which is used for storing away hospital clothing. There are huge fireplaces in each of these rooms. The building is hardly tight enough about the roof, which is covered with the only kind of shingles that can be obtained, called shakes, split from pine logs six or eight feet in length, and not shaven. It is enough to give one the shakes to look through the cracks in them at the open sky, and think what the poor boys may suffer in some driving storm. With some old canvas, however, which we hope soon to obtain, they can be made very comfortable in stormy and cold, as they are now in pleasant weather.

These rooms are kept neat and tidy by competent and careful nurses, and I am glad to say, that the sick in them are all improving rapidly. A little further on is a very large canvas tent, warmed also by a fireplace, in which six patients are well accommodated and well cared for. Some of your readers will no doubt shiver at the idea of sick boys being kept in a tent in the winter, but with a smooth board floor and a good large fireplace, this tent is far from being an objectionable place in which to be sick. Some of the most desperate cases of fever have been successfully treated here, and the patients in the tent get well quite as rapidly as in wooden buildings.

I would pass over, entirely, the measles hospital, which is quite aside from the camp, on the road to Suffolk, were it not for the great improvement in it within two weeks. It is a forbidding-looking, unpainted two story house, one half seemingly calculated for summer and the other for winter, for there is only a chimney on one side, and no provision for warming the other half of the dwelling. Before it was used for its present purpose, the boys from some of the camps about had stolen the windows out of the summer side, evidently thinking that people who can live without fireplaces can live without windows. Sash have been prepared to replace those stolen, but the impossibility of getting glass here and the multitudinous red tape through which requisitions are run, have prevented this being of any use, so parts of sash are used in two rooms, and the rest of the windows covered up. Small stoves, with pipes running out of what were windows, warm these rooms. We hope from the manifest improvement of the patients, that these rooms will soon be vacated, and all the measles patients accommodated in the winter side of the building, where above and below are large fireplaces.

It was in this building that Russell Dean, of Company A, died.[32] Poor boy; he came in here with measles, typhoid fever soon set in, and made a complication which his not very vigorous constitution could not stand. I shall not soon forget the strong grasp of his hand, and the kind attention he gave me, as I attempted, bending over him, to whisper in his ear words of Christian consolation, and to point his waning eye to the Savior of the soul. This is the first and only death, which has occurred in Company A. Company F, also recruited in Jamestown, has lost only two. The last who died, was Gilman Bartlett.[33] He had lived in Wisconsin for a time, but with his wife returned last year to Warren County, Pa. His wife died and was buried the last summer at Sugar Grove, and when his regiment was forming, he enlisted, as two brothers had previously done in other regiments, to aid the cause of his imperiled country. He was never very vigorous, and the camp fever, when it seized him, soon wasted his life. In his pocket was found a letter from his aged father, now living in Cattaraugus County, received about the time he was taken sick, telling him that one of his brothers had died in the hospital at Alexandria, and he feared the other had died or was killed and begging him to come home and stay with him, for he was an old man and this was the only son left. His last request to his attending physician was that he might be "taken home and laid by the side of his dear wife." After his death, Captain Mathews immediately caused his body to be embalmed and sent word to his friends, that they might come and receive it.[34]

The Sharpshooters have a beautiful camping ground, which they have improved by building very tasteful log houses on two sides of a square. Their ground is a slight bluff on the banks of the Nansemond near the South Quay Road. Their hospital is in a large house upon the ground. There are none at present very sick, the health of the company is generally good. They have buried two of their number. The last died December 20, of camp fever. His name was John Lawson, of the town of Carroll, where his father still lives.[35] The other was a Swede by birth, a nation that has given to our republic many vigorous men, and one of the greatest geniuses of the age, John Ericsson.[36]

Lawson was very kindly and tenderly cared for, everything surrounding him was favorable to his recovery, but all in vain. It is a sad fact to contemplate, that thirty-one of those who came out from the homes of Chautauqua last fall have already fallen; and let us remember that their lives are as truly given to their country, as though they had fallen on the field of battle. I presume that before this reaches you the box sent by the ladies of Jamestown will be brought up from Norfolk. For a week past the trains have been wholly absorbed in the changes of troops. When it comes, the presence here of two of your excellent ladies, is an assurance that its contents will be well applied to the comfort of the boys. Already the ladies here have made the hearts of many a weary sufferer glad by their acts of kindness and words of sympathy. We need now good reading for the convalescents. Magazines not too old, pictorial papers, good books that have seen service and have been packed away, if gathered up and sent to me will at once be set about doing good. Some cheap checker boards, dominoes, or other harmless games for their amusement would serve to while away dull and dreary hours. Excuse the length of this.

Very truly,
W. L. Hyde
Chaplain of the 112th (Newspaper[37])

Saturday, January 31st

Mr. Sweet and Patterson from Chautauqua. (Diary)

Sunday, February 1st

Lieutenant Dunham recommended for captain.[38] (Chronicle)
Visited hospitals. Preached on "I will guide thee with mine eye."[39] Blessed be God and Father of our Lord Jesus Christ who hath begotten us again to lively hope, etc. (Diary)

Monday, February 2nd

Body of Watson sent home in charge of Doctor Ayres. Rode with Chaplain Hanson. (Diary)

Tuesday, February 3rd

Wrote Dunkirk Union.[40] (Diary)

Sunday, February 8th

Major Smith appointed provost marshal.[41] (Chronicle)
Preached "I will guide thee with mine eyes." (Diary)

Monday, February 9th
    Rode to Magnolia Springs morning. I rode with Whitaker. (Diary)

Tuesday, February 10th
    Went to Drummond Lake. (Diary)

Wednesday, February 11th
    Returned from Drummond Lake 4 pm. (Diary)

Friday, February 13th
    Strict orders respecting drill. (Chronicle)
    Moved Adjutant Marvin's building over from other camp.[42] (Diary)

Saturday, February 14th
    Put up Adjutant Marvin's building. Distributed tract papers. (Diary)

Sunday, February 15th
    Preached on "Ye knows not what ye ask."[43] (Diary)

Monday, February 16th
    Very rainy. Sent my resignation of my pastorate in Dunkirk. (Diary)

Tuesday, February 17th
    Received letter from wife wishing to come to Suffolk. Drizzle day. (Diary)

Wednesday, February 18th
    Spent most of day in the hospital. (Diary)

Thursday, February 19th
    Boys finished log house. (Diary)

Headquarters, 112th Regiment New York Volunteers
Camp Suffolk, Va
February 19th 1863

Colonel D. T. Van Buren[44]
Assistant Adjutant General

Colonel,

    Leave of absence for three days from the 24th inst is respectfully asked to go to Baltimore for the transaction of important business.

                                    William L. Hyde
                                    Chaplain
                                    112th Regiment New York Volunteers

Friday, February 20th

Funeral of John Taylor.[45] Sent home. Mr. Sweet and Patterson went home with their sons. Meeting in evening. Cut logs for walling my tent. (Diary)

Saturday, February 21st

Mr. Ames began on my log house. Was taken sick. (Diary)

Monday, March 2nd

One officer, 3 noncommissioned and 57 men fatigue on Redoubt Hill. (Chronicle)

Sunday, March 8th

Hospital $653.00 (Diary)

Monday, March 9th

From Oliver Nichols[46]
To Arthur P. Nichols
Check----$30.00
Chautauqua County Bank (Diary)

Tuesday, March 10th

Hiram Dickson to Harvey Dickson[47]
$50.00
Chautauqua Bank Jamestown (Diary)

Wednesday, March 11th

To William Pelton, Westfield
From W. R. Pelton $40.00[48]
To Westfield Bank (Diary)

Thursday, March 12th

Check to be mailed to Justin Scott Olto
Cattaraugus County, NY
$36.00 (Diary)

Saturday, March 14th

Hulit, Company E, says send me $5.00 by mail and keep the rest until I need it.[49]
Boys want their descriptive papers. (Diary)

Selden D. Marvin enrolled at Jamestown, New York, as adjutant with the 112th New York Volunteers. He was transferred to the United States Army for promotion to major and paymaster.

William R. Pelton enlisted at Mina, New York, as a private in Company D, 112th New York Volunteers, and transferred to the United States Signal Corps on July 20, 1863.

Sunday, March 15th

Dr. Boyd wants the colonel to have papers mailed so he can get his money. (Diary)

Sunday, March 22nd

Sergeant Brazee sent to Folly Island for baggage, etc. of regiment.[50] (Chronicle)

Sunday, March 29th

Communion. 3 preachers of different denominations participated. Miller Baptist, Cummings Methodist, Hyde Presbyterian.[51] 329 communed. (Diary)

Wednesday, April 1st

Wife left for Baltimore. (Diary)

B. Frank Brazee enlisted at Jamestown, New York, as a private in Company A, 112th New York Volunteers. He mustered out of service on June 13, 1865, at Raleigh.

Saturday, April 4th

Mr. Hart came to see me. He has been a professor but has lost hope. Feels that he ought to be better. Gave him counsel and book to read. Very stormy. (Diary)

Sunday, April 5th

Preached on prayer. (Diary)

Friday, April 10th

Wife rode with me to provost marshals. Great excitement in view of probable attack. Draw bridge over Deep Creek broken through. Captain Bowdish killed.[52] (Diary)

Saturday, April 11th

Enemy attacked and captured our pickets Blackhawk Road. (Chronicle)
All ladies ordered to leave camp. Wife packed her trunks. At night rails torn up by our folks on Portsmouth Road and thus disabled. (Diary)

Sunday, April 12th

Ladies all leave the place. (Chronicle)
Some skirmishing. Great excitement. Wife and children went after dinner on cars. (Diary)

Monday, April 13th

Firing upon Fort McLellan from Summerton Road. Our pickets on Summerton Road driven. Sergeant Tucker killed.[53] (Chronicle)
Skirmishing on Somerset Road. (Diary)

Tuesday, April 14th

Evening open fire on Summerton Road. (Chronicle)

Wednesday, April 15th

All sick sent to Fortress Monroe. (Chronicle)

Thursday, April 16th

Sharp skirmishing on Summerton Road. (Chronicle)

Friday, April 17th

Pickets driven in on Summerton Road. Corporal Baker, Company E, killed.[54] (Chronicle)

Colonel secured for me a permit to go to Norfolk and Fort Monroe, with money for regiment. (Diary)

Saturday, April 18th

Started with near $21,000 for friends of regiment. (Diary)

Sunday, April 19th

8th Connecticut, 89th New York cross river and capture battery and 132 prisoners. (Chronicle)

Tuesday, April 21st

General Halleck visits Suffolk.[55] (Chronicle)

Wednesday, April 22nd

18,000 troops and 30 pieces of artillery have arrived with a wail. (Chronicle)

Friday, April 24th

Reconnaissance on Edenton Road. (Chronicle)

Tuesday, April 28th

Eddy Munson, Company E, and G. W. Heath, Company H, captured on Summerton Road in morning while scouting.[56] (Chronicle)

Sunday, May 3rd

Heavy skirmishing on Petersburg Road. Regiment in line of battle in reserve all day. Night slept on trains armed. (Chronicle)

Monday, May 4th

Regiment started at 3 am in pursuit of Rebs. (Chronicle)

Wednesday, May 6th

260 prisoners sent to Fort Monroe. Company A, Captain Dunham went as guard. (Chronicle)

Friday, May 8th

Received library for regiment gift of Charles Comer. (Chronicle)

Wednesday, May 13th

Regiment start 1 pm for Carrsville on expedition for purpose of turning and receiving rails from the railroad. (Chronicle)

Thursday, May 14th

Moved back to Beaver Dam Church. Dark, half regiment go out to gather tools the contraband had left.[57] (Chronicle)

Saturday, May 16th

J. Davis, Company H, killed by shot.[58] Body brought to Suffolk, embalmed and sent home. Dr. Hand, medical director, captured.[59] (Chronicle)

Tuesday, May 19th

Ordered at night to fall back to near Deserted House. Left about 12 pm. (Chronicle)

6 bottles German wine
3 bottles extract ginger
3 papers farina
3 papers cornstarch (Diary)

Wednesday, May 20th

Camped in corn field 2 miles from Deserted Farm. (Chronicle)

Thursday, May 21st

Left for Windsor on the Petersburg Railroad. (Chronicle)

Friday, May 22nd

Received from Mr. Olmstead to Captain Chaddock.[60]
20 New York Observers
5 Harpers Magazines
6 Petersen Magazines
1 lot Sailor Magazines
8 Reports Hospitals (Diary)

Tuesday, May 26th

6th Massachusetts left for Boston and Lowell. Evening, regiment returned from Windsor. (Chronicle)

An envelope containing $40 to Miss A. M. Davis, Jamestown, care of Mr. Burlin. (Diary)

Thursday, May 28th

Quartermaster. (Diary)

Sunday, May 31st

Walrod came in very sick, dysentery, better not eat ice.[61] Lord scurvy.[62] Better. Richardson afflicted with scurvy. Green wants captain [to] send letters. Wants pay sent. (Diary)

Monday, June 1st

Barhite, Van Vliet, Smith, Kinphenger, Baldwin, Thayer, Mertz went north.[63] Have Smith's descriptive list sent to him. Dr. Applegate surgeon, No. 7.[64] (Diary)

Wednesday, June 3rd

James Walrod lost knapsack, haversack, canteen. Noted on descriptive list.
David Mills, [Company] C, $3.70[65]
Wigtman, [Company] B, $1.00[66] (Diary)

Thursday, June 4th

Delos D. Richardson[67]
Fredonia
Leroy Lord [Company] C payee (Diary)

Friday, June 5th

Augustus Green, Company D[68]
Charles W. Mount, Company C[69]
Pheteplace went north[70]
A. W. Smith[71] (Diary)

Thursday, June 11th

We were ordered to start with three days rations and report at the signal station at 2 o'clock. Order was countermanded. (Diary)

Friday, June 12th

Left on reconnaissance to Franklin. (Chronicle)
We were ordered to report at the signal station at eleven o'clock am. Corcoran in command of a force, 3 brigades with 2 batteries and cavalry. Colonel Drake commanding 2nd brigade. 169. 112. 166 Pa. 13 Ind. Acted as aide. Spent night 6 miles South Quay. Slept on the ground. (Diary)

Saturday, June 13th

Opposite South Quay. Moved to Carrsville. (Chronicle)

Up soon after daylight, breakfasted and pushed on toward South Quay. The country exceedingly beautiful. About 8, halted and deployed columns. House women and five little ones. About 10, advanced. Shelled the works at South Quay from this side of the river. After a vigorous shelling of half an hour, column moved towards Franklin. One man in our regiment wounded by explosions of shell. We spent the night at Carrsville. (Diary)

Sunday, June 14th

Marched to opposite Franklin. Spent night Edwardsburg. (Chronicle)
Sunday morning at 6 moved toward Franklin. About 10, put in line of battle a mile from Franklin Bridge. The 112th in rifle pits in rear of open field. Shelled Franklin for an hour and then moved on toward Windsor. The conduct of many in the command both Saturday and Sunday bad. Stealing, robbing, burning and insulting women and children. We stopped for the night soon after sundown near Windsor. (Diary)

Monday, June 15th

Opposite Lewis. Shelled the place. (Chronicle)
Up at 4 for breakfast. Waited and waited. At 10 o'clock orders to move to Martha River. Shelled the other side of the river. Headquarters at house of an old farm. After shelling, returned to supper where we had our breakfast. I went to a creek in the swamp, bathed, was much refreshed. After supper, marched on to Carrsville. Reached camping ground after tedious delays about 2 o'clock am. (Diary)

Tuesday, June 16th

Marched back to Franklin. (Chronicle)
Slept till 7. Ate breakfast then waited. We then were moved to where we were Sunday. We have been here since. Bathed with colonel Tuesday evening. (Diary)

Wednesday, June 17th

At Franklin. Night near Beaver Dam Church. (Chronicle)
Wednesday morning finished letters to wife. Wednesday spent day about two miles back from Black River. Evening bathed with Captain Scott. Marched from 6 to 9. Bivouacked at Carrsville. Beaver Dam Church. (Diary)

Thursday, June 18th

March to Suffolk by way of Carrsville, Kinsale Swamp and Deserted House. (Chronicle)
Morning up at 3. Breakfast of hard bread and coffee and started at 4 for Suffolk. Terrible march for the men. Had a violent toothache and when 4 miles from Suffolk, had tooth extracted. (Diary)

Friday, June 19th

Regiment received pay. (Chronicle)
Kept very quiet. Visit from my friend Morris who spent the night with me. Troops leaving fast. (Diary)

Saturday, June 20th

Troops still leaving. Very weary. Major box from Christian Commission and gave a part to Chaplain Lee and also to 1st Delaware Battery.[72] (Diary)

Sunday, June 21st

Had service in the log chapel. Very good attendance. After the morning service we had a Bible class and a very interesting examination of the scene at the Sanhedrin when Jesus was examined. Afternoon went to see Chaplain Whitaker whose regiment was under orders to leave immediately. Evening had prayer meeting in chapel. (Diary)

Monday, June 22nd

Monday wrote letters. Had a long and pleasant call from the chaplain of the 169th.[73] (Diary)

Tuesday, June 23rd

Married George L. Nichols of the 7th Massachusetts Battery to Nancy Ann Harris of Suffolk. (Diary)

Wednesday, June 24th

Rumors of immediate changes begin to be ripe. We are expecting marching orders before many days. Suffolk seems like a city deserted. Our brigade and Corcoran's the only left with one regiment of cavalry and 4 batteries. (Diary)

Thursday, June 25th

Orders to pack everything. (Chronicle)
Rode about the lines. Felt very unwell. Canker and piles. Orders came this pm to get ready to move leaving tents and private property. (Diary)

Friday, June 26th

Orders came to be ready to move at 5 o'clock tomorrow morning. Spent the day in packing and making ready. At night had all things in line for early start. 3 boxes, 1 trunk with Christian Commission stores left in Norfolk. (Diary)

Friday Evening
June 26th 1863

My dear Wife,

This is probably the last letter from Suffolk, as we are all packed and ready for a start tomorrow morning. We are ordered to deliver over our tents and camp equipage and all private property except one valise to the quartermaster to be stored at Norfolk. One valise we are allowed transportation for. The adjutant has just called and informed me that we are to be in readiness to move at 5 am by cars, so goodbye to Suffolk. I began yesterday pm to tear up, expecting that we were to leave everything even knapsacks and start at midnight. I am glad we did not have to do so. It was a very rainy night and tonight is not any better in that respect.

It has rained now 3 days almost incessantly, the first rain of any consequence (except very light and infrequent showers) for two months. I feel sort of like leaving home to leave this camp, take down everything I have, throw away all the little conveniences I had gathered about me and go into active field service. The life I shall live henceforth will be a sort of pig's life is until we get back somewhere to garrison. But I thank God for health and strength adequate, as I believe, to bear all the exposure and a determination to do every duty to the best of my ability. I do pity our poor boys. They will now begin to know something of military life.

We have been fairly situated here in camp. Now hard marching and perhaps fighting. We don't know where we are to go but I suspect up the James River. Of course I shall let you know at the earliest practicable moment and keep this letter open until we start. How sudden and uncertain everything is in the military. Three days ago I heard we were to be the last regiment to leave Suffolk because the general was afraid to trust the place in the care of any other. Now we are the first of the two brigades to evacuate it. I have packed everything I could. Three boxes-to be stored in Norfolk.

I take all my regimental library to Norfolk. I have a little map chest made out of the box my coat and pants came in from Dunkirk. Then I take in my panniers all my little fixings. Brush, comb, towels, cup box and hard bread. Then I strap my blanket and overcoat and rubber on my saddle and if necessary put a bag of oats on behind my horse. I shall write you just as often as possible. Good night. I will leave this letter open till tomorrow.

Saturday half past 8

I got up this morning at 3 o'clock and finished up packing, nailed up the last box. Jule came and we pulled up my tents and rolled them up and tied them. Then had breakfast and was all ready. It was a busy scene in camp I assure you. At last 5 o'clock came and the colonel had the regiment in line, knapsacks on back and the drum sounded and we moved off to the cars. It took 3 hours to get started and now we are off. Jule took Frank into the car in front and the boys are piled all over the top of the cars and inside the boxcars.[74] The officers are in the passenger car. When we started the boys gave a score of hearty shouts for deliverance from Suffolk. The day is a fine one for riding, the rain has ceased and it is overcast giving warning of showers before night. Colonel Drake says as I am writing, "give my respects to Mrs. Hyde. Tell her to keep up good courage. There will be an end to it all by and by." Mrs. Palmeter is onboard having spent one night at Suffolk, thinks she will remain in Norfolk a few days.

Adieu, your affectionate husband,
W. L. Hyde

Saturday, June 27th

Load on cars 30 mule team loads of freight and brigade. Leave 8 o'clock, 15 minutes. 644 officers and men. 6 pm reach White House on the Pamunkey. (Chronicle)

Got up at 3 o'clock. Finished up packing and nailing. Took down my tents and rolled them up. Started on cars with the 166th at 7 am.[75] At Norfolk took boat at 11 and reached White House, Pamunkey River at half past 7 evening. (Diary)

York River
[June 27th 1863]
Saturday pm

Well my dear, here we are steaming up York River onboard the *John Brooks*. We got into Norfolk about 11 o'clock. There we left all tents, camp equipage, etc. and have only our valises with us.

Our afternoon destination is the White House on the Pamunkey. You have read of it as the place where General Washington courted his wife. I made a good dinner of a piece of bread and butter and twice roast meat and hope to get supper on board. We were hurried off from Norfolk so that several men and Captain Palmeter with them were left, but they can come on the next boat that comes up. Captain P's little boy is onboard though his pa is left in Norfolk. I had time to run up town and bought some cherries which relished well. The market at Norfolk is filled with all things good and tempting even to new apples.

The sail up the York River is beautiful. The day is overcast just enough to make the sail delightful. We expect to reach White House by dark. I should have sent my letter from Norfolk but did not think of our starting so very soon. I shall finish this and send it back by the captain of the boat and trust you will get it as soon as the regular day for my Suffolk letter. I don't expect to hear from you for several days, perhaps a week, but keep writing and direct WLH-Chaplain 112th Regt N.Y.S.V., 7th Army Corps, Foster's Brigade, Washington, D.C. We have just passed West Point and entered the Pamunkey. I shall wait before closing till we get to our place of destination.

Sunday Morning, 9 am

We got to the White House last evening at 8 o'clock. Had a good supper onboard then remained for the night. This morning landed and all well.

Yours W.

Sunday, June 28th

Land and pitch tents. (Chronicle)

Regiment debarked and marched 4 miles from the landing. Spent the day there waiting for the remainder of the force to come up. No service. The rest of the brigade reached White House by evening. (Diary)

Monday, June 29th

Go into camp ½ mile from landing. Heavy rain. (Chronicle)

In the morning changed camp two miles down the river. Wrote Jennie. Afternoon Morris called to see me. (Diary)

Tuesday, June 30th

Regiment mustered for pay. Rainy. (Chronicle)
Staff Mess accounts from June 30, 1863
Colonel J. C. Drake, Lieutenant Colonel Carpenter, Chaplain Hyde

June 30

Cookies	1.00
Butter	1.00
Sugar	.50
Hard Bread	.50
Cheese	.50
	$3.50

Received and distributed mail. It rained hard part of the day. Afternoon received orders to be ready for 5 days march. Men piled knapsacks in a large pile. (Diary)

Elial F. Carpenter enrolled as a major with the 112th New York Volunteers. He died from wounds received at Drury's Bluff, Virginia. He had previously served with the 49th New York Volunteers.

Wednesday, July 1st

Ordered to be ready to move 3 ½ am. Move at 4. Delayed at railroad an hour, march two miles and halt till 9 o'clock. Move 12 miles. Very hot. (Chronicle)

Were roused up at 3 o'clock and at 4 started on move to Hanover Court House. Men greatly fatigued by 12 miles march. Stopped for night at King William Court House. (Diary)

Wednesday Morning, July 1st 1863
On the march from White House

Dear Wife,

While the regiment is making a halt I will begin a letter to you. Before it reaches you I perceive we shall not be back again or at least some distance from the place of its date. Monday we moved from where we were during Sunday-White House Landing-three miles down the river into a beautiful field, part of the plantation of W. H. Fitzhugh Lee.[76] The clover was up to our knees when we marched into it and considerably diminished in height this morning when we came out of it. It is a beautiful field. Just imagine that field behind R.H. Gardiner's House in Gardiner, lengthened on the riverfront two miles and about the same depth from the river to the woods and you have a picture of this beautiful location.

The boys have enjoyed it highly. Swimming in the water and washing their clothes in it. The bank of the river, like off Mr. Gardiner's, is fringed with trees and right off our camp the bluff is somewhat steep. We had our headquarters directly under the shadow of a big oak tree. A large fly stretched over a pole and pinned down like a shelter tent served as a house to dwell in, or rather as a roof to keep off the rain. One night when it rained we pinned a blanket on one side and last night and night before we slept under it without any front or end. Spread a rubber on the ground, unroll your blankets on it, then for a pillow, take saddlebags and put an overcoat doubled up on it to make it soft. Pull off shoes and coat, pull on smoking cap, roll your woolen blanket all around you and go to sleep. When a wood tick bites, wake up and kill him but never mind black ants. Last night made a sumptuous supper out of fried salt pork and hardtack with coffee to drink. Got up this morning at two and after shaking my eyes open, I went out and Brown, the colonel's cook, poured water out of a dipper on my hands for me to wash. Then sat down to hardtack, fried pork and coffee. Finished breakfast and waited and waited.

We were to have started at 4 o'clock, but of course somebody didn't get up, so several thousand men had to wait through the best part of the day for marching. At length 5 o'clock and the summons came to prepare to march. In half an hour we were ready and forward marched 3 miles to a bridge across the Pamunkey River. There we had to halt an hour for Spear's Cavalry, who came to the bridge by another road to pass us and cross.[77] Then we advanced a mile and were brought up by a baggage train in the road which started out last night. Here we halted 2 hours in the muddy road for it rained all yesterday and part of the day before. During this halt our mail came up. I got your letter of the 21st yesterday and today got the bible sacrament for July and a letter from DeLong with bill of butter.

I am glad if you were able to pay Dunham, but I hope you have saved enough to last you till next payday. I don't know when that will come. You must not spend all your money before you get credit, but get credit for things you need and keep a little money for emergencies that may arise. I only say this because I thought from the way you spoke that you would not have much of the $100 left after paying your debts.

We were mustered in yesterday for two months pay to the 1st of July but when we shall get it, is a question I cannot answer. This great drain for new troops will make it somewhat hard for the old ones. But I believe Uncle Sam is good yet. I was ashamed of Juli Williams and Jim Van Buren. They are as destitute of pluck as I always believed them to be. Am glad to hear that Freddy is better again. I hope he is not going to have a repetition of those fever turns.

I am now sitting in Zion Church, King William County near King William Court House, Va. It is a building that looks very much as the Dutch Methodist church in Dunkirk without any steeple and paint pretty well faded. It is a Millerite church. I got in and am sitting in it to keep the boys from coming in for plunder.

I hope you will get this in good time. I shall hand it to Adjutant Marvin to send in to White House as soon as possible. I will keep you informed as to our progress from time to time. Hoping that you and the children are well and with love to all who inquire.

I am as ever affectionately,
William

I began a letter a few hours ago for the Dunkirk Union and contrary to expectation the regiment has halted long enough for me to finish it. Please send it to them through William Bookstaver.[78]

Samuel P. Spear commanded the 11th Pennsylvania Cavalry. He was promoted to brigadier general and commanded a brigade cavalry during the Peninsula and Petersburg campaigns.

Thursday, July 2nd

Ordered to move at daylight. Move at 6. Very hot. Spend night near Rumford College.[79] (Chronicle)

Up at 4. Breakfasted and marched to Rumford College. Spent day with lieutenant colonel, assisting stragglers and battery. Horses caught. Mischief claims Mr. Rowan. (Diary)

Friday, July 3rd

Ordered to move at 4. Move at 7. Excessively hot. We marched with one hour rest at noon and short halts every hour till 12 at night. More than two thirds of the brigade fell out by the way. (Chronicle)

Slept very sound last night. Did not get up till breakfast was ready. After breakfast we were delayed till 9 before starting. Then were marched with brief intervals the entire day. Seen the Fontaine House, which was barbarously abused. Stopped at Mrs. Hunter's, a beautiful place. Marched till midnight. Cruel and inhumane to the boys. As soon as I got off horse, got some straw, fell down on it, pulled over my covers and slept sound till about sunrise. (Diary)

Saturday, July 4th

Start at 10 from Taylor's, march rapidly past Hanover Court House. Reached point 2 miles from South Anna Bridge, Richmond and Fredericksburg Railroad. 12 [mid] night. (Chronicle)

Marched after breakfast 2 miles both sides of a creek and rested. Then halted till afternoon. Marched on to Hanover Court House 3 miles and to railroad bridge. Reached about 10. At 2 am ordered back. (Diary)

> Court House, July 4th 1863
> Bivouac on the road to Hanover

My dear Wife,

I sent a letter written the first of the week to you by mail yesterday from Rumford College near by which celebrated institution we encamped Thursday night. Our Wednesday's march was quite easy, and we spent the night, where I wrote you the letter near Zion Church and in the vicinity of King William Court House. As we passed by the court house in the morning, we saw two ladies sitting on the stoop of a house with pencil and paper and an officer told us that they were engaged all day, yesterday, taking down the number and description of the forces. They had snapping black eyes and were cut out for Rebels of the purest type. They were very acute in their way of questioning our officers, and it required some avoidance not to give information, which would have incriminated us.

That day our regiment was rear guard of the column and Company H was made provost guard to pick up all stragglers along the route. When the houses were at some little distance from the road, Colonel Carpenter and I would ride up to them and send the men down to the guard. Being there at the rear we had plenty of time to sit down and chat with the people which we imprisoned. We found some very cultivated ladies whose conversation was easy and elegant and who was very grateful for our care in sending the soldiers away from their houses.

I am sorry to say there was some wanton mischief done especially near evening. Men went into a house which the people had left and tore up clothing, took furniture and took away everything eatable and even pillaged a fine library of books. They stole $10,000 in Confederate bonds and other things. Colonel Drake has a $2,000 bond in his pocket. It is of course worth nothing to him, but it is worth having as a curiosity.

As soon as we got to our place of halting, Lieutenant Colonel Carpenter and I went down to the Mattaponi River a mile from camp for a wash. Not 100 rods from us-as we afterwards found-were a few Reb cavalry trying to drive over the same river, two horses and some mules. The horses had been sold to Reb officers a few days before for $300 each. They were magnificent animals. One of our 112th boys and a 13th Indiana were at the place and saw the cavalry men and charged upon them just as though they had revolvers, though they had not a weapon about them. The cavalrymen ran and our boys grabbed on a mule and the other a horse and made for camp. A small company soon went down and got the rest of the livestock.

Our cook got us up a splendid supper that night. We had fricasseed chicken, new potatoes, boiled onions and hard bread with poor coffee. But that of course was a rare opportunity. The fare hard enough as a rock.

Friday morning. I slept very sound last night. I was completely jaded with the march. The bath I took refreshed my system so that after a good supper, having a clear conscience, I slept soundly and the sun was shining when I woke up. I thanked God for his care, read my testament and washed. Carpenter pouring water on my hands from a canteen. I did the same for him. Refreshed, I eat heartily and found mail going in, I sent my letter to you.

The men had been got up at 3 o'clock expecting to move but it was 9 o'clock before we got away. It was cruel. I never knew a harder day for marching and the men were cruelly marched. Old Frank walking slow was covered with sweat. I felt so bad for the boys that I let them ride most of the day and I walked. We were halted twice before eleven o'clock and marched from 11 to 12. Men fell out by dozens. It was [a] cruel thing to march men. That hours march unfitted 70 men of our regiment for duty. I walked it on foot and part of the time carried a musket. At 12 we had an hour for dinner. Then marched at 3 another hour and then marched with brief halts till midnight. Men fell out of every regiment so that for 6 miles before we finally halted, the road on either side looked like a continuous encampment. If the enemy had been near to attack us then, they would have captured our whole force.

The colonel was mad as fury with the general who marched us so. When we were marched into the wheat field the colonel got the men on the line and called out, "Front order arms, fix bayonets, stack arms, now boys there's wheat straw. Grab it, and camp down and go to sleep." I tell you, every man got his arm full of straw scattered it and lay right down without even spreading their shelter tent over them. Our mess each got an armful and lay down. I got my saddlebags and poncho, lay down on the straw, drew my rubber over me and was asleep in 5 minutes. Not a thing had I eaten since 5 o'clock in the morning save one hardtack at noon and after a sound sleep, woke in the morning the sun shining full in my face.

I marched most of the night with the regiment on foot but about half past 10, I took my horse and before we stopped, it was all I could do to sit on him. The adjutant came near falling off his horse half a dozen times. The colonel was so stiff in the morning he could hardly stir. All the regimental commanders protested through General Foster to General Getty against such marching.[80] Will you believe it? After our march the day before, General Getty sent word to Foster to start his brigade at daylight. Foster replied it would be impossible. We had breakfast about 8 o'clock and at 10 moved 3 miles very slow and waited till 3 o'clock before starting again.

I omitted to say that we bivouacked in the wheat field attached to the mansion of a Mr. Taylor, Uncle of Old Zack.[81] He owns thousands of acres and when this war broke out had 300 slaves. Most of those slaves have left him and the man is wild with rage that our forces have quartered on his property, though we have placed a guard about his house and out houses. He has 280 acres in corn and 60 acres in wheat. Owns 3000 acres. The house and garden is beautiful. The house is on the top of a hill, and the garden terraced; the most beautiful weeping willows, flowing azaleas and birches and maples, flowering shrubs, and flowers adorn the grounds; a fountain plays; artificial canals and drains conduct water down through his land, making a nice mill pond about a mile from his house where he has a mill to grind his corn and wheat. Every appurtenance of farming on a grand scale was apparent. All kinds of agricultural implements in his tool house, and ponies and horses and mules. The whole residence was worthy of the F. F. V.'s in their parliament days.[82] I never saw such an expanse of corn in my life. And if anybody dreams of starving the Rebels out, they had better follow the army through the route we have travelled. That dream would be dispelled at once. The only way to conquer the Rebels is to fight them and whip them.

We have marched through the most charming country I ever saw. Such farms, such fertile land, such varied landscape, I never saw before. Well we bivouacked in Taylor's plantation Friday night and Saturday morning. We moved down to a mill stream 3 miles where we washed and under the shade of wide spreading birch trees on the hillside lay down and rested and got a good dinner of coffee, and hardtack and cheese. About 3 we marched again; reached Hanover Court House about 5 and at 9 were near South Anna Bridge, which we intended to burn. Alas, we were not in sufficient force. When we reached Hanover Court House, Colonel Drake was placed in command of Foster's Brigade and he asked me to act as his aide, which I did most cheerfully.

When we got down near the front we were deployed on each side of a road under trees and waited as a reserve, while Colonel Wardrop and Colonel Spear with a battery went down to the point.[83] From scouts, we ascertain that the Rebs had strong earthworks to defend the bridge and that through some means they had learned of our coming and had got heavy reinforcements from Richmond. We were not strong enough to do what we wanted and also were in a bad position, as they might easily get in our rear. Colonel Wardrop however sent 2 companies over who after a brisk fight captured 10 prisoners, with some loss.[84] We don't know how many the Rebs lost. While we lay in our position the Rebs commenced shelling. They did not, however, get our range, as we made no reply. The shells came, few as near as I ever wanted to have them. But I saw so little fall. I was so tired that I actually went to sleep about midnight and slept till 2 o'clock, when we were ordered to retire, as Wardrop had found the position too strong for our force.

So we moved back to Taylor's plantation, which we reached about 9 am, having marched 24 miles in 24 hours. O how I pitied our poor boys. Some of them had their feet so blistered that they could not step without agony. Some of them were overcome by heat and all faded out. We had our breakfast soon after getting back to Taylor's and then I went to sleep.

Tuesday 7th

Just arrived at White House, am well though tired. It rained yesterday during half our march so that I was soaked. My haversack soaked, my saddlebags soaked, my shoes so full of water that I would turn them up and let it run out. I will write you all particulars tomorrow.

Affectionately your husband

How is it about there?

Sunday, July 5th

At 2 am ordered to fall back. No halt until across the Pamunkey. Halt at Taylor's. (Chronicle)

Reached Taylor's at 10. No breakfast till got there. Rested at Taylor's all day and night Sunday. Mr. B. Taylor owns 3000 acres, had 300 negroes. Many left, secesh to the backbone. House elegant, garden fine, 80 acres in wheat. 200 acres in corn. Got in, had a good bath at evening in his garden brook. (Diary)

Monday, July 6th

3 am. Moved in direction of White House. Encamped near King William Court House. (Chronicle)

Up at 2. Breakfast. Started at 3. Hard march, reached Aylett at noon. Heavy rain all pm. Evening bivouacked 1 mile from King William Court House. The boys tore down fences, captured hogs. We got straw mats to keep us off the wet ground. Colonel Drake acted as brigadier. I acted as his aide-de-camp. (Diary)

Tuesday, July 7th

March to White House. (Chronicle)

Up at 2 o'clock. Started soon after three. A very severe march for the length. Reached bivouac ground near railroad bridge about eleven. White House about one. Found that young Peck had died and was buried.[85] Received orders to start at daylight for Fort Monroe. (Diary)

Wednesday, July 8th

At daylight in line, prepared to move towards Yorktown and Fortress Monroe. (Chronicle)

Up all night. Started out at 3. Moved a mile by 5, there [we] were delayed by trains till 12. Moved in drenching rain and heavy mud till 7. Roads awful. Wagons upset. Knapsacks and blankets thrown away. Wagons forward, no supper. (Diary)

Thursday, July 9th

March to within two miles of Williamsburg. (Chronicle)

Up at daylight. Moved officers without breakfast. Noon at Booneville. Eat with ambulance driver. Walked most of day to help foot sore men. Scores of men with blistered feet. Supper at-teams then after supper moved 3 miles and encamped within 3 miles of Williamsburg. Regiment dreadfully fully used up. (Diary)

Friday, July 10th

Marched three miles beyond Yorktown. (Chronicle)

Up at daylight. Moved on. 7 at Williamsburg. Road over battleground. Very sultry. Men fall out badly. Some coming down sick. Reached Yorktown about noon. Camped about 2, a mile beyond. Captain Curtis very sick. (Diary)

Saturday, July 11th

Remained in camp. (Chronicle)

We rested all day. A great mercy to the boys. Many have very sore feet. Some fallen sick yesterday, taken to hospital. Got mail and letter. Sent letter to wife. Horse so galled.

Enoch A. Curtis enrolled at Harmony, New York, as a captain in Company D, 112th New York Volunteers. He was wounded at Cold Harbor, Virginia, and discharged for disability on September 15, 1864.

I did not use him to ride about the place as I wished. Bathed at noon and slept sound. (Diary)

Bivouac near Yorktown
July 11th [1863]

Dear Wife,

I have but a few moments and am poorly prepared to give you a detailed account. We have got thus far from a terrible march. I am glad to say that our regiment has had no man drop down dead, but to see the feet of one of the boys and to have seen them on the march would make your heart ache. I hear that 16 men dropped dead during the march. Yesterday two ambulance horses dropped dead. Wednesday we marched 11 miles in a drenching rain, all the way and lay down in an open field without supper except one hard cracker and a little coffee which we borrowed off one of the boys. Our team containing our food and blankets had been sent on so that officers had nothing to eat, nor their horses.

Thursday morning eat another hardtack between 2 and 3 am, had a small cup of weak coffee then we marched eleven miles and then rested 2 hours for dinner. No baggage train yet and an ambulance driver invited me to dinner. I turned old Frank into a cornfield. I dined on fried hardtack and pork out of the dirty tin dish in which it was cooked and we drank out of the same cup some army coffee and I never relished a dinner better in my life. Then we marched. I had walked almost all the morning letting boys whose feet were blistered so that they bled, ride my horse. I walked all the pm and at 5 o'clock we were halted 2 hours for supper having marched 10 miles, then we were marched 3 miles through the worst swamp I most ever saw. Having walked most of the afternoon, I rode half the evening. It was mud water logs in the track and oh dear, when we got into the cornfield where we stayed, we found it was an old camp ground and horrid unclean. We lit a candle, poked about, found a clean place, threw down our rubbers and rolled our blankets about us and lay down and went to sleep in five minutes and slept like a log.

In the morning my blanket was wet through with the dew. It was near 3 when Brown called me and I got up; rolled up my blanket, eat breakfast. Jule had the horse all ready and we started on. We were soon at Williamsburg, where we found all the forces of Generals Keyes and Getty.[86] It was a magnificent spectacle. I rode over the ground of the battle where Hooker fought and where Barrett fell.[87] I picked two flowers which I enclose. Please send them to Mr. Coleman's bank for Mrs. Barrett. Then we marched on to 3 miles beyond Yorktown, where we have been since 4 o'clock yesterday.

The weather yesterday was intensely hot and men and animals suffered terribly. Men dropped by scores. When we got into camp, I was, I guess, about the strongest man around. Captain Curtis had had neuralgia all day in the face and when he got it in his head it was throbbing and he was crying like a child, a hysterical cry. No doctor was near. I went and got water, bathed his head and gave him chloroform to inhale and whisky to drink and soon he felt better. Colonel Drake was so exhausted that he sank down on his blanket as soon as he got into camp and lay without speaking or stirring for an hour. It is strange to me that I am so strong and hearty.

Where we go from here I know not. I am expecting every moment orders. It is now Saturday about noon.

> With tender love to you and the boys. As ever,
> William

Sunday, July 12th

Marched to Great Bethel. (Chronicle)

Up at 2. Moved at 3 and in at camp at Big Bethel at 10. There we spent a quiet Sabbath. All too tired for worship. Had a bath and a rest. Slept directly. Wrote my father and mother. (Diary)

Monday, July 13th

Marched to Hampton. (Chronicle)

Up at half past 3. Moved half past 4 to just outside the village of Hampton. Arrived there about eleven. The marching was excellent. My poor horse [is] very sore. He has done hard work for the weary boys. Went over to Hampton at evening. We left Hampton suddenly. Embarked onboard steamer *Monitor* about 7. At 9 were in Portsmouth, Va. Dined with Major Smith. Went over to Norfolk. Returned and about 2 started for Bower's Hill. Night without supper; rain, mosquitos made great discomfort. (Diary)

Tuesday, July 14th

Embarked on transports for Portsmouth. Evening marched to Bower's Hill. (Chronicle)

Wednesday, July 15th

Go into camp at Bower's Hill. (Chronicle)

Last night a rain storm. This morning sultry. We have no orders yet about camp. Afternoon ordered to move camp tonight. Riot in New York.[88] Rumors of good news. Moved our camp. Hope to go to Portsmouth. (Diary)

Thursday, July 16th

Changed camp. (Chronicle)

Again ordered to change camp. I think no hope of doing provost duty in Portsmouth. Have sent in for camp equipage. (Diary)

Bower's Hill near Portsmouth
July 16th 1863

My dear Wife,

Lieutenant Barber tells me that his wife who lives on the same street on which J. B. Williams used to live and probably lives now, is to send him immediately a package or box by express and will gladly put in that package of vests.[89] I wish you would immediately call and see her and get her to take your package if she has not already sent. If she has sent it, Mr. Higgins of Fredonia, who helped me last fall, has a box ready to send his son. But Lieutenant Barber just now tells me that he has written his wife to hold open her box until you see her, so you will have no trouble.

I am feeling decidedly better this afternoon and like myself. I have stood the march as well as any of the officers and better than the colonel. When we got to Portsmouth we found Company B, Captain Chaddock doing provost guard duty there and there was held out to us the expectation that General Peck would detail our regiment to do provost duty in Norfolk and Portsmouth. But alas at eventide General Getty, who, since Corcoran has left, is in chief command, sent word to Major Smith that his services were no longer needed and ordered Company B to rejoin the regiment. Major Smith does not relish very well the loss of his honors and evolvements and thinks that Saturday when General Peck returns that there will be an overturn. I do not believe it and I am not anxious for the regiment to go into either Norfolk or Portsmouth, as their temptations in either place would be very great. I should have liked on my own accord to have been in one of the other places, as I should have hoped that we might soon be together again. I do not however wish you in this latitude before October and great changes may occur between now and then.

They had a great excitement in Norfolk the other day. A secesh doctor shot a Union lieutenant who was marching a squad of colored soldiers through the city.[90] He will be tried by court martial next week and probably hung. When he was examined before the marshal he was very violent and his daughter, a gay lady of 20, said to him as they were leading him to jail "keep up good heart Pa, the cowardly Yankees dare not injure you." We are all in good spirits over our glorious successes in the southwest and west and not at all troubled by the riotous demonstrations in New York City. A few doses of grape and canister will settle the question for those rascals. New York needs such a lesson to show her what civil war at the north would be, as well as to stimulate her patriotism. I was glad to see in the last Dunkirk Union that J. L. Williams' case is not so bad as was reported. If he was only an honorary member of the company they could not justly demand his services and his furnishing a substitute was highly commendable, and a good able-bodied Dutchman is far to be preferred. Why one day's march such as our boys took would use him up just out of the storm.

I hope you got my letters I wrote you from the White House, one from Rumford College, one at Taylor's Plantation, one at Yorktown and one from here. I have received yours quite regularly. You can now direct to Portsmouth.

I wish I could step in and talk with you and comfort you this evening. I hope you have looked upon the trial you have suffered from my correspondence and having as a means of God's appointment to incite you to greater watchfulness and self control and to lead you more constantly to lean upon God. I think Mother will soon write me a very different letter if Paw will let her write at all. Did I send Nancy's last letter? I have looked all mine over and over and cannot find it. I fear it is lost. The letter I sent you day before yesterday I had to hurry off as I was almost too late for the mail.

We have a very rustic location here on Bower's Hill. It is eight miles in to Portsmouth, but a good road and I rather enjoy summering out here among the pines. You would laugh at our headquarters. It is the large tent fly that we had on our tramp. We have to stoop to enter the middle of it. Spread on the ground are the rubber blankets and on these woolen blankets, which make our beds. They lie along in a row. Mine's one side, Colonel Drake next, Quartermaster Waters next, and then Colonel Carpenter. I call it the rabbit's nest. It will however be broken up tonight as we are to have our camp equipage all brought up from Norfolk. I assure you the least amount of baggage a man carries with him on a march the better off he is. My saddlebags and roll of blankets and rubber are all I shall ever carry. I now mess with the rest of the rabbits having given up Charley Price and the Steven's mess. We have a cow now, which is to me a great item.

I hope to have service next Sunday with the regiment. How I shall miss my little log building where I held my prayer meetings. But if we settle down here it will take but a short time to supply many of such things.

Spear's Cavalry and Davis' Battery are very near us.[91] Also the 13th Indiana and the 169th New York. The hill is about as much of a hill as where Dr. Roger's house stands compared with Water Street. How do the boys behave? Can you manage them? I wrote Jane. Have you heard from her lately? Love to all friends.

Your ever affectionate husband.

Friday, July 17th

Provost guard returns to regiment. (Chronicle)
I felt miserably all day. (Diary)

Saturday, July 18th

Camp equipage came. I felt very sick but worked in the rain all the afternoon putting up my tent. Got into it and my boxes. (Diary)

Sunday, July 19th

I was very much prostrated by fever. Had the doctor. Had my meals brought to me. No service in camp. (Diary)

Monday, July 20th

Major General Foster reviews the forces. (Chronicle)
A violent rain. Was very much prostrated. Been taking medicine. (Diary)

Tuesday, July 21st

Regiment inspected. (Chronicle)
Spent the day in Colonel Carpenter's tent. Had my tent changed. (Diary)

Bower's Hill
July 21st 1863

My dear Wife,

You will be sadly disappointed at not receiving your letter on the usual day. But I could not write Sunday or yesterday. Friday last I began to have premonitory symptoms of fever, extreme languor and prostration, a heavy feeling about my head, so I kept very quiet through the day and Saturday, I worked a little putting up my large tent. The symptoms would not leave me and at night I called in Dr. Washburn who took hold of it vigorously and arrested it.[92]

The next day, Sunday, I did not sit up and for the first time in years, had my food brought to me. I did however go over to supper. Yesterday I was improving but in the afternoon General J. G. Foster, our new department commander, inspected the regiments of our brigade. I was so anxious to see that I milled about as far as from Mr. Buddington to Dr. Rogers' and it was too much. I was quite sick but the Dr. gave me some more medicine which has worked well and I am going to escape by God's blessing the run of fever with which I was threatened. I have no appetite, ate nothing for supper last night and this morning I got Brown to make me a pint of water gruel, which tasted well relished.

I shall keep perfectly quiet now until I recover my strength. You must not worry about me. I have every kindness shown me and the fever is checked, all I need is building up. I think part of my troubles arise from the fact that I gave up when I came into camp and did not exercise. If I had ridden 6 miles everyday I don't believe I should have been sick. I received a letter from Jane yesterday, which pleased me much. Jane is true blue, no copper about her.

I shall write Abby McCann as soon as I am able. I got all your letters. There is no sort of difficulties when letters are sent to Washington.

If I had an idea that we were to stay here long, I should have letters directed to Portsmouth. Just in case of a move the other is the more certain way. I have lots of things to write you about.

This $20 is for Dr. Long. I will send it tomorrow.

Your affectionate Husband

Wednesday, July 22nd

Bower's Hill
Wednesday Morning
July 22nd 1863

My dear Wife,

I have already been over and eaten my sumptuous breakfast of water gruel, which since I instructed him, Brown makes very nicely. It is the only nourishment I can get here that I do not loathe. Anything sweet creates nausea. I am getting along—shall have to keep quiet this week out and probably the day you get this letter, I shall be at all my accustomed duties. My fever has not been camp fever or anything like typhoid but a mild bilious intermittent coming on after dinner.

The Dr. has been exceedingly attentive. In fact we are fellow sufferers. He has had dysentery in a mild form. Lieutenant Colonel Carpenter has been a little weak and quartermaster. Colonel Drake has been persecuted with cataracts in a very distressing form but I guess if there was any work to be done for Uncle Samuel in whipping his naughty boys who have tried to kill the old man, we should all be able to do our part.

General Peck has returned and I think the prospect now is good for the regiment and I think we shall go into garrison near Portsmouth this winter.

The boy has come, can't write, thought you would be anxious.

Affectionately,
William

Will send them Monday next.

Thursday, July 23rd

Bower's Hill
July 23rd 1863

My dear Wife,

You will be glad to see by this that I am getting well fast. I am still very weak but I feel a little better and grow a little stronger every day. We have a very pleasant and inviting camp now. The tents are all up and much more regular than our camp in Suffolk. Indeed the camping ground is the best between here and Portsmouth.

Camp is a poor place to be sick. I never so realized it before. Everything you get goes against your stomach. Water gruel is the only thing I could eat. And then you can have no conveniences of any sort. But I am thankful that I am so much better off than many others.

Day before yesterday we had a tremendous thunderstorm. I was lying flat on my back with wet cloths on my head and the wind began to drive the rain into my leen tent, soon it came down in torrents and wet everything I had. I pulled my rubber up over my face and kept myself dry and had with one hand to hold the tent leaf. Pretty soon the gale increased and the tent shook and swayed, the pieces that curtains the fly were drawn up and the fly was flapping over the tent. I thought for a time the poles would break but they fortunately held out. The lightening was terrible, it seemed to strike just outside the tent and the thunder was of the loudest. Soon I thought we were going to be submerged, for the water stood an inch inside and outside so far as I could see.

After half an hour it abated and I sent for Jule to come and open the tent while I went over to the colonel's. After tea, Colonel Carpenter insisted on my spending the night in his tent which was all floored. So he took my cot over and I found it much more comfortable than my wet tent. The colonel told me yesterday that he was going to get some floorboards for my tent. I fear we shall not remain long enough to make it pay.

Friday morning

I missed sending to you yesterday, the boy was too quick. I am still continuing to improve. If I could only have you fix me something nice for my breakfast, something that I could relish. I have almost absolutely to fast. Way out here there is nothing to be got. And though I can ordinarily eat any cooking, yet now the coffee tastes of the swamp water and the meat has no taste and the bread looks as though it had the jaundice and I sit down and get up again in disgust. This morning, however, my appetite begins to be a little more natural. I eat my breakfast about half as much as I wanted to and I think it means to sit well. I shall try a little horseback riding by and by I guess.

I cannot write more. When I get stronger I will write you long letters as usual. Don't be anxious for me, I am under favorable circumstances for rapid recovery and have all kind friends around me.

Very truly and affectionately,
William

I got darling Freddie's letter. Tell him that if he would have Pa love him he must keep away from wicked boys and not use any bad language. Tell Harry to try and improve his time and so make his father happy in his good conduct and good reputation.[93]

Saturday, July 25th

Colonel Drake gave me boards and I had my tent floored and moved my cot back to it. Spear's Cavalry and Dodge's Rifles left on a raid.[94] (Diary)

Sunday, July 26th

Captain Stevens took Sunday Mass.[95] Corporal Harter, Company F, pneumonia, was very weak and feeble all day.[96] (Diary)

Monday, July 27th

Regiment paid. (Chronicle)
We hear rumors of a change. We got our pay for May and June. (Diary)

Tuesday, July 28th

Colonel Carpenter went to Norfolk this afternoon. Carried my money to the express office. At midnight orders came for the brigade to move. (Diary)

Wednesday, July 29th

Move with camp and garrison equipage, take cars for Portsmouth. (Chronicle)

The brigade started to march to Norfolk leaving camp equipage. Received orders just as we started to return and pull up and take everything in cars. We left about 11 o'clock. Slept in boxcar at night. (Diary)

Thursday, July 30th

We are waiting transport car train at Norfolk. Eat supper at eating house. Slept in boxcar. 13th Indiana went at night. (Diary)

Friday, July 31st

We are still here. The regiment lying round on their haversacks. It is bad for the reckless. They are getting intoxicated and behaving badly. I have gone to the American House to board. Got letter from wife written Sunday. (Diary)

Saturday, August 1st

Second Lieutenant George S. Talcott assigned command Company I until further notice.[97] (Chronicle)

Rode out 5 miles. Did me good. Still waiting transports. I have kept quite still most of the day. (Diary)

Sunday, August 2nd

Early this morning the 169th left. Our regiment the last of the brigade behind. I went to church in the morning. Very warm. (Diary)

Monday, August 3rd

Captains Palmeter and Oley leave on sick furlough.[98] 6 companies embark onboard *Escort*. (Chronicle)

A very warm day. 6 companies of our regiment left onboard the steamer under charge of Lieutenant Colonel Carpenter. The other 4 and regimental baggage to follow. (Diary)

Tuesday, August 4th

4 companies embark onboard *Convoy*. (Chronicle)

The steamer *Convoy* came over to take onboard the 4 companies of our regiment. We loaded the regimental baggage and the men and at 4 o'clock pm were passing Fort Monroe. (Diary)

Wednesday, August 5th

Convoy put back to Norfolk in distress. (Chronicle)

A heavy gale last night off the capes. Strained our boat so that she put about and returned to Fort Monroe. Reached about 2. At 6 ordered to Norfolk for repairs. I was very sick all day with diarrhea. (Diary)

Thursday, August 6th

Went this morning to Mr. Saunders and got my breakfast and then White House and spent day. Was sent for at 4 o'clock as the regiment was to leave onboard the *Maple Leaf*. (Diary)

Friday, August 7th

Left Norfolk onboard *Maple Leaf*. (Chronicle)

We left Norfolk so as to get to Fort Monroe about noon and left Fort Monroe about 6 pm. Had a boisterous night and the boat was somewhat strained but kept on her course. (Diary)

Saturday, August 8th

I spent the day mostly in my berth. My diarrhea exceedingly troublesome. Took nitric acid, with benefit. I think. (Diary)

Sunday, August 9th

A poor Sunday. Read 18 chapters of the gospel of Matthew. Had a copy of the *Christian Mirror* from which I gleamed much profit.[99] The men, I fear, thought little of the day. (Diary)

Monday, August 10th

Reached Hilton Head evening. (Chronicle)

My trouble decidedly improved. I think in 3 days I shall be well. We are approaching our destination. Reached Hilton Head at 6 o'clock. At 8 received orders to transfer all regimental equipage to steamer *Saxon*. (Diary)

Tuesday, August 11th

Reship on propeller *Saxon* for Folly Island. (Chronicle)

We left Hilton Head near noon and arrived off Morris Island evening. Too late to land. Stayed all night onboard. In morning went to Folly Island and landed. Marched to east shore. (Diary)

Wednesday, August 12th

Spent the day in the colonel's tent. (Diary)

Thursday, August 13th

Land at Pawnee Landing, Folly Island. (Chronicle)

Had my tent put up on a sand bank. (Diary)

Friday, August 14th

9½ pm ordered to proceed at once to Morris Island. (Chronicle)

Am feeling a little better though still very weak. (Diary)

Saturday, August 15th

Regiment returns from Morris Island, reached camp at 9. (Chronicle)
A very poor day. My diarrhea has weakened me sadly. (Diary)

Sunday, August 16th

10 pm: 100 men and officers for fatigue duty. (Chronicle)
Am still weak and not able to sit up much. (Diary)

Monday, August 17th

2½ am ordered to Morris Island immediately. Bombardment of forts. Return 10 pm. (Chronicle)
The regiments were ordered to the front at an early hour. I left with Lieutenant Colonel Carpenter about 6 o'clock. Returned late. (Diary)

Tuesday, August 18th

Rode up to the landing after writing home. Aplin of Company F, called, a backslider.[100] I gave him good advice. Furman of Company F, quite a reader and a scholar.[101] (Diary)

Wednesday, August 19th

Very warm day. Inspection by brigade inspector. Finished reading *Captain Bates' Life*. He was a good man and an example. (Diary)

Friday, August 21st

Received this day 2 letters from wife. Dates 6th and 10th. Visited hospital this morning. Bullock failing, most of the others appear to be doing fairly. (Diary)

Saturday, August 22nd

Evening ordered to Morris Island. (Chronicle)

Sunday, August 23rd

I preached to the regiment from Proverbs 16:25.[102] There is a way which seemeth right, etc. The attendance was very good. We have not had service before in the regiment since the last Sabbath of June. (Diary)

Monday, August 24th

Ordered to occupy earthworks at head of island. One of the darkest stormiest nights of the season. Men thoroughly drenched. (Chronicle)

Wednesday, August 26th

Last evening regiment went out and were in the trenches all night. It was very stormy and unpleasant and many were wet through and contracted colds. (Diary)

Thursday, August 27th

270 men sent to Morris Island. (Chronicle)

Alex Lowry received his papers for discharge.[103] He was a very valuable officer and is a loss to the regiment. Lieutenant Pierce returned to regiment, book and paper with list of drafted men.[104] There is a great eagerness to get hold of it. (Diary)

Friday, August 28th

Adjutant Lowry resigned on account of ill health. Left for Jamestown. Lieutenant G. L. Pierce returned from sick leave. (Chronicle)

Rode up to the head of the island with Colonel Carpenter. Had a fair view of Fort Sumter which looks rather rugged. We then rode to the landing. Found a sutler who had butter, codfish, cheese and some other luxuries. Very rainy night. (Diary)

Saturday, August 29th

Wrote for Captain Stevens who is somewhat sick. Visited the hospital. Found Corporal Neil very sick.[105] Talked and prayed with him. He was fully conscious till near the close of life. Corporal Neil died half past 5. I was asked by Captain [Ferguson] 169th, to attend funeral of man who was shot in the trenches.[106] Did so. (Diary)

Sunday, August 30th

Received letters from wife dates 12, 16, 20. Visited the hospital. Sermon brief Sunday. Preached to regiment at half past 10. Pm visited with Captain Ludwick. Evening attended funeral of Corporal Neil. Talked to the men at the grave. There was a large attendance from the regiments. Sermon in morning from 90 Psalms: 12th verse.[107] (Diary)

Monday, August 31st

This day regiment was mustered in for pay. Wrote letters to wife, J. A. Milhouse, Mrs. Neil, Mr. Heywood, Dunkirk Union and express company, Hilton Head. Captain Stevens sick. Firing not as heavy as yesterday. Heard of new batteries erected by enemy. (Diary)

> Camp of the 112th Regiment New York State Volunteers
> Folly Island near Charleston
> August 31, 1863

Rufus Heywood, Esq.
Dear Sir,

I write to inform you of the death of Corporal Frank Bullock of Company G of the regiment.[108] He had not been very well since the very severe march we had from White House to Hanover Junction and back to Hampton early in July. He however came on with the regiment and did not entirely give up till about 2 weeks ago when a diarrhea which had been troubling him some days began to assume an alarming form. He was taken to the hospital at this time and every care bestowed upon him, which is possible in such a place as this. His diarrhea assumed daily a more aggravated form until a week last Friday we thought he could not live 24 hours. Saturday morning however he was better and continued to improve for 2 days. Then there set in a swelling of the carotid glands—glands of the neck—which is usually regarded as fatal when it occurs under such circumstances. But last Saturday, this too seemed to be yielding to treatment so that we began to be encouraged again. But soon his dysentery reappeared and he lingered along until about [blank] this afternoon when he died without a struggle, nature being completely exhausted. For ten days past he has had but few moments of rational consciousness. I have seen him daily and up to last Thursday, he knew me for a few moments at a time. But from this trouble of the throat we could make out but very little of what he said and much of the time when he conversed, he was very wild and talked about everything in a very incoherent manner. He was always very glad to see me when he knew me, would hold my hand as if to keep me by him even after he had dropped into his unconscious state.

I prayed with him and directed his attention to Him who came to save and bless us. He always bowed assent and after I had gone would sometimes tell the nurses what I had said or that I had prayed with him.

Poor fellow, we all feel a gloom over us in consequence of his death. He was much liked in the company and was an excellent soldier. He would do his duty and would report for duty when he was not really able. He never shirked as many do. Before we left Suffolk, he told me one day that marching used him up and he thought he should try and get transferred into the cavalry and I noticed that he came in from our marches which were very severe, some of them at least, used up completely. But the next day he would report for duty and go to it cheerfully whether well or not.

He ought not to have come down here, but he hated to stay behind and especially as many did so, who if they had had half his pluck would have come with their comrades.

He told me sometime ago that he considered your house his home and sent his money to you. I have therefore written you about him being myself ignorant as to his family connections.

All business matters will be fixed up by Captain P. Stevens in due time. The captain would write you but he is himself very sick with diarrhea, not however as yet alarmingly so. All of the regiments have suffered somewhat from the change of climate and particularly from the diet. We need vegetables and I hear they are coming to us.

The siege progresses slowly. People north must not be too sanguine. Charleston, I fear, will be full as hard to take as Vicksburg was. The Monitors do not come up to popular expectations.

The weight of the work, thus far, has been done by the army and it is the army that must take the forts successfully and reduce Charleston. I ought to have mentioned that we shall bury Frank tomorrow on a beautiful knoll about ¼ of a mile in the rear of our camp where we have already buried Corporal Neil of Company D, who died Saturday of the same disease. Bodies cannot be sent home from here without enormous trouble and expense, as there is no embalmer nearer than Hilton Head, 60 miles distant.[109]

Very truly, etc.
William L. Hyde
Chaplain of the Regiment

Tuesday, September 1st

Regiment goes into trenches on Morris Island. (Chronicle)

Cleaned a barrel to get pure water. Called on Brother Vanscoy, and Captain Stevens.[110] Afternoon—rode round the picket lines with Colonel Drake. The feeling on the other island not at all sanguine as to the speedy reduction of Charleston. (Diary)

Phineas Stevens enrolled at Dunkirk, New York, as a captain in Company G, 112th New York Volunteers. Discharged for disability on February 11, 1864, he had previously served with the 49th New York Infantry.

Saturday, September 5th

Regiment goes into trenches on Morris Island as grand guard. (Chronicle)

Monday, September 7th

Wagner evacuated, occupied by our troops. (Chronicle)

Friday, September 11th

Regiment ordered to Morris Island. (Chronicle)

This is the anniversary of the departure of the regiment from Jamestown, Chautauqua County, New York for the seat of war immediately subsequent to its original organization. I was not elected to my position as chaplain of the regiment until some weeks after. But having within a few weeks lost all my memoranda of events connected with the regiment during the year from January 1, 1863 to the present date. I thought it a good time to commence a more extended journal.

Folly Island near Charleston. Today after a bath and breakfast rode with lieutenant colonel to Stono Landing to satisfy the question "What shall we eat" having heard that there was a sutler's schooner there selling goods at a reasonable rate. My principal reason for going however was the exercise, which I need to take regularly and daily for my health. We did not succeed in finding what we wanted.

This afternoon, I went into the hospital. There were about [number left blank] of our boys lying there, some of them very sick and some of them improving in health. One poor boy, Gage, Company [K], whose father is a minister, seemed to be dying or nearly so.[111] I spoke to him of Christ as a precious Savior. He responded to what I said but I fear had but very feeble consciousness.

Another man, Van Vliet of Company C, Forestville, said he was a member of the church Methodist. His wife and mother Baptist. He had found it not easy to lead a life of active piety in the army. But had endeavored to read his Bible and pray every day. He said with a great deal of feeling to me, "one thing I know I have a wife and mother who pray every night for me." To which I replied, "The fervent effectual prayer of the righteous availeth much."[112]

Another lad, Green of Company D, told me that he hoped he was a Christian. He had professed Christianity though his hope was not as bright as he could wish. He has had a long experience in sickness having been sick while we were in Suffolk, several months in hospital.[113] I endeavored to point McGee and [name left blank] to Christ.[114] I thought both seemed glad to hear the word of Christian admonition. Allen, Company H, said that he felt in the army more than ever the preciousness of religion.[115] "If I had not that to encourage me I should be wretched in dread."[116]

Oviatt ought to be a Christian.[117] He has a pious father, a preacher of the gospel but I fear is quite careless.

[Name left blank], Company A, seems inclined to universalism but is not easy in it. He was very candid and seemed anxious to be taught. I promised to call again. Graham, the sutler's clerk, a Pennsylvania boy, asked me to pray for him. He said he had a pious father, mother, brother, and sister. He promises if he lives to get well to serve God and lead a Christian life. This morning Reed Cummings, Company I, a mule boy, died leaving no evidence of acceptance with God.[118] He was delirious some hours before he died. This makes 5 deaths since the regiment came to Folly Island. The first was Corporal Neil, Company D, Harmony, a Swede, much beloved, a humble man and we trust a Christian.

His last words, "My will is nothing, let the will of the Lord be done" in answer to question are you very anxious to get well.¹¹⁹ The 5th was Frank C. Bullock, Company G, Brockton, a careless boy. But wanted in his delirium to hear of Christ and to have me pray with him. The 3rd was [Company] D, Tezepher, a Hollander by birth, Clymer, a plain humble Christian, and died with a bright hope of a happy existence hereafter.¹²⁰

The 4th was [Sumner] Boss, Forestville, who died giving no evidence of acceptance with God.¹²¹ Poor man he was deranged several days before he died. (Journal)

Saturday, September 12th

This morning we buried Cummings and immediately after, I went up to the post hospital to attend the funeral of a young man in the 117th [New York] Regiment. This over I rode to the head of the island armed with General Gillmore's permit to cross over to Morris Island to see the chaplain of the Christian Commission.¹²² Unfortunately for me he was on this side and so I sat for a while in conversation with the clerk then went to the camp of the 2nd South Carolina Colored Regiment and had a good talk with Chaplain Moore.¹²³ Dined with the lieutenant colonel and other officers. My visit was very pleasant. Learned from their surgeon that they considered the recuperative powers of the negro far less, in sickness, than that of the white. Casualties in the trenches are few. They are now making a new face to Fort Wagner and altering Gregg. Military operations have come to a stand almost.

Quincy A. Gillmore was commissioned from West Point as an engineer. He commanded the Department of the South and the 10th Army Corps and participated in the recapture of Fort Sumter.

There is very little firing. It is thought the Navy are unwilling to do their part. I called on Chaplain Crabbs of the 67th Ohio—an old Suffolk acquaintance.¹²⁴ He finds that as a chaplain he can only do good in little ways as he has opportunity. The great occasions are few. Walked back to the Sanitary Commission building.¹²⁵ I sat there some time witnessing the industry and zeal with which the agents were dispensing the benevolence of the good people north to our suffering soldiers. The good done by this agency is incalculable. I did not see Mr. Emmons, the chaplain of the Christian Commission. He was on this island. About 5, I started to return and reached home about 7. I found letters, one from my dear wife and one from my aged and venerable father. He is now 73 years of age. The letter affected me very deeply, as he spoke of his age and feebleness and of his hastening to the grave. And the tenderness with which he breathed his desires for his children that they might be prepared to follow him. May God still continue him many years to illustrate the beauty of a severely pious old age and give him the desire of his heart and an everlasting home in Heaven. (Journal)

Monday, September 14th

The regiment returned a little before midnight last night. I slept soundly and before breakfast took a bath in the surf. After breakfast I got ready for the funeral service of

Lieutenant Strong of the 13th Indiana.[126] This with the marching occupied the forenoon. Dined with Colonel Wilson and after dinner rested, read several chapters of the 1st of Corinthians which seems to me most admirably common sense.[127] Common sense in the method of dealing with some moral questions.

The corruptions of the church in Corinth must have been excessive and the rapid delusion from the plain Christian simplicity of character amazing. Perhaps only an illustration of the truth that with all its spiritual power Christianity makes slow progress against the habits and customs which are part of the national life. The leaven in the lump works but it only partially and with painful slowness, transfers the mass. Had prayers in the hospital at 4 o'clock. The boys very still and solemn.

This morning I rode up to Light House Inlet, to inquire in regards to transportation and make arrangements to send home some sick men who have furloughs. This with a call upon Captain Ludwick at Pawnee Landing occupied all the morning.[128] After dinner rode up again and at 4 o'clock Captain Mathews went with the men up and by direction of much industry got them on to the steamer. Poor fellows they looked as though a good stiff breeze would sweep them away like straws. Borrowed $15 and lent Ploss.[129] (Journal)

Tuesday, September 15th

Captain Chaddock left on sick leave. (Chronicle)

Spent the forenoon in riding to the inlet to get transportation for Captain Chaddock and Privates Apthorp and Elliott.[130] Borrowed and lent Apthorp $15. The ambulance which was to call for them was late. My horse which I let Elliott have was not brought back and I had to send Jules after him about 8 pm who found him tied to a tree. I suppose they left on the boat for Hilton Head. Evening, we buried Benjamin.[131] The regiment was ordered out with only two hours notice to go up to Morris Island as grand guard. Colonel Carpenter went up. Colonel Drake and Quartermaster Waters are on the sick list.[132] (Journal)

Wednesday, September 16th

Regiment on picket duty at Fort Wagner. (Chronicle)

I was in camp all day. The day was very dull as the boys were on the other side of the inlet. I did not feel much like doing anything. Read most of the day. Regiment returned about midnight. (Journal)

Thursday, September 17th

That night was very tempestuous. The rain fell in torrents, and the wind blowing furiously drove the rain in through the canvas. I got somewhat wet. Many of my good books got wet, and on the whole I passed a most uncomfortable night. The day has been quite as uncomfortable as was the night, cold and wet, with frequent heavy squalls. The poor boys, in the hospital, got dreadfully wet, those of them that lay under the part covered by a fly. Richardson, in consequence, has a relapse of fever and others have had their various complaints aggravated. I have employed myself during the day in beginning a work which I mean shall develop into a history of the regiment from the first formation to the present time to be continued until it is disbanded. I copied one or two rolls during the day. (Journal)

Friday, September 18th

Regiment on duty head of island. (Chronicle)

The morning I spent in overhauling my tent and drying the clothing, etc., which had been wet. It was a great job. The day is as beautiful as yesterday was stormy. After working about my tent, I rode with Colonel Drake to Pawnee Landing for exercise. Afternoon I wrote. I wrote part of a letter to my wife and wrote several muster rolls. Evening wrote and read till quite late. (Journal)

Saturday, September 19th

I visited some sick boys in the hospital. The most are doing well. Our young man, Mount, Company I, told me that he knew he had a praying mother praying for him.[133] I urged him to seek religion. He seemed to feel quite deeply. Had an interesting conversation with Rhodes of Company F.[134] He is inclined to be uncharitable to take gloomy views of the life we had here and to believe the stories that are told about officers true. He recognizes his obligations to be a Christian but is not decided. I fear he lacks stability of character.

Just at evening I attended the funeral of 2 men in the 169th Regiment who died of disease. One of them, his captain said, was one of the worst of men and was so wicked while sick that he would swear fearfully and make those around him shudder as he gritted his teeth with demoniac rage and snapped his eyes like a fiend. (Journal)

Sunday, September 20th

Whole regiment ordered to Black Island. Sick left. (Chronicle)

Had made ready to preach, the drum had sounded the meeting call when I heard that the regiment was ordered away to Black Island with ten days rations. This broke up my plans and completely unsettled the day for the men for after being formed in line 3 times, they were after all sent to quarters to start Monday morning. Had prayers in hospital near evening. (Journal)

Monday, September 21st

Colonel Drake and I went up to the island with 9 companies of the regiment who are under command of Lieutenant Colonel Carpenter. The day was fine, the sail pleasant. From Folly Island we winded about through a kind of marsh intersected by sea channels and go three miles to get a mile and three fourths. General Vogdes has withheld the furloughs granted by General Gillmore for good conduct in the field until further orders. It is alleged that our pickets were found asleep on their post, which officers and men deny. (Journal)

Thursday, September 24th

The new batteries on Forts Gregg and Wagner open on Sumter. (Chronicle)

Rode up early after breakfast to Light House Inlet to make arrangements for the transportation of 6 sick men to Hilton Head. Then to take the *Arago*. After dinner I accompanied the ambulance which took them. They were Tracy and Cook of Company B, Sweet and Gossett of Company I. Hunt and McElroy of Company A. I borrowed $20 and lent $10 to Sweet and $10 to Gossett.[135] They being entirely destitute. Letter sent to Mrs. Waters. (Journal)

Friday, September 25th

First casualty at Black Island, Thompson, Company H, mortally wounded by shell.[136] (Chronicle)

Poor George Thompson. Killed in the trenches. (Diary)

Colonel Drake and I rode up to Light House Inlet and from thence were moved in a launch to Black Island where we were saluted as we landed by a Rebel shell which exploded over our camp and one piece fell with a sound that went all through me about six to 12 feet distant. The other past alas did sad mischief. George Thompson of Company H, was sitting by the fire when that piece of shell struck him, shattering his left arm from the elbow and deeply cutting into his left leg then passing across and tearing his right leg below the knee breaking the bone in pieces. I went to him, assisted the surgeon, then had him put on board a launch and conveyed to Morris Island to the post hospital where the limbs were amputated. He survived the operation half an hour. I then went back to the island and got an escort of men to bury him which we did. It was evening when we got through. The lower part of the island was covered with water which a very high tide had driven on to the beach. I rode back to camp, neither myself or my horse having had food since morning. Reached camp at 8 pm. (Journal)

Saturday, September 26th

Wrote letter to Mrs. Thompson and S. H. Hungsford, Esq. (Diary)

I wrote one or two letters. Colonel Carpenter came down from the island. In the afternoon, I rode over with him to Captain Ludwick's quarters at Pawnee Landing and with Captain L. rode up to the camp of the 2nd North Carolina Colored Regiment when I heard some darkey had found my diary, lost a month ago. I was glad indeed to get it again. It was like an old friend to me. In it a little memoranda of all that the regiment had been through since January last. There was a dollar greenback in it, which I sent to the man who found the book. (Journal)

Sunday, September 27th

Preached at Black Island to regiment from Psalms 84:4.[137] Edward Hewes died heart disease very suddenly.[138] William H. Graham, sutler clerk, died of dysentery. Had been sick since landing. (Diary)

Went up to the regiment. Colonel Drake, Captain Ludwick and myself. We rode up to the inlet, left our horses, and found a boat waiting for us. We had the mail along with us. After a tedious delay—dinner in the meantime—we got the regiment together and I preached to them from Psalms 84:4.[139] It did some good to see the boys once more and speak to them the word of the gospel. We returned, reaching camp about 4 pm. I went into the hospital. Graham is still alive though so low that he can't live long. He told me yesterday to tell his parents he died happy. (Journal)

Monday, September 28th

Review by General Gillmore of General Vogdes' Division. Attended funeral in 169th New York Volunteers. Wrote letter to wife, Mr. Benjamin Graham, Hewes, Captain Chaddock. (Diary)

That evening about 8, Dr. Washburn's servant William came up breathless to my tent, over his wooly head through the fly saying "Chaplain, Mister Jules' brother is dead." "We can't find the doctor." It was Edward Hewes of whom he spoke, brother of my quartermaster. (Journal)

Tuesday, September 29th

Medical inspector sends 13 men including quartermaster to general hospital. Buried

Hewes and Graham. Visited hospital with Captain Ludwick. Visited Lieutenant Fox.[140] Not feeling well. Prepared to send quartermaster. (Diary)

Wednesday, September 30th

Quartermaster and 12 others went onboard hospital boat. Quartermaster very low. Called on Colonel Wilson, 13th Indiana. (Diary)

Thursday, October 1st

Visited hospital. Made application for leave to go to Hilton Head. Rode up to head of island. (Diary)

Friday, October 2nd

Left after breakfast for head of island and later boat for Hilton Head. Lieutenant Alden of 55th Massachusetts onboard.[141] Very low. (Diary)

Saturday, October 3rd

Quartermaster Waters died at Beaufort hospital. (Chronicle)
Started at 1 o'clock for the Head. Reached the Head about 6 o'clock. Went to hospital to get pills for Lieutenant Alden. (Diary)

Sunday, October 4th

Found that Huber and others who left in hospital boat had gone to Beaufort.[142] Got pass and left for Beaufort at 4 o'clock. Reached Beaufort and heard quartermaster died at noon Saturday. (Diary)

Monday, October 5th

Started early for the hospital. Found the few boys left. Inquired of surgeon and nurse about quartermaster. Visited Chaplain Harris who gave me a bundle of papers for the regiments.[143] (Diary)

Tuesday, October 6th

Captain Palmeter returned from sick leave. (Chronicle)
Visited graveyard before breakfast. Left for camp at 9 o'clock. Pleasant day today. After reaching Hilton Head with Chaplain Wells, 11th Maine, slept onboard *Canonicus*.[144] (Diary)

Wednesday, October 7th

At breakfast time started in *Canonicus*. Passed *Arago*. Pleasant day. Pleasant trip reached Inlet 2. Walked home. (Diary)

Thursday, October 8th

Went up to the regiment and returned. (Diary)

Sunday, October 11th

Chris Russ died last evening.[145] Went up to Black Island with Colonel Drake. Carried up papers. Had services and preached from Psalms 84:4.[146] Blessed are they that dwell in thy House. 1 Timothy 2:5, One God and one mediator etc.[147] Hospital 4. Resolutions on death of Quartermaster Waters. (Diary)

Monday, October 12th

Forenoon wrote some. Noon got ready. Pm went up to Black Island. Spent the night there. (Diary)

Tuesday, October 13th

Went over to Morris Island. Met Mr. [Everson] of Christian Commission. Old friend. Called at Sanitary Commission. Got ice for regiment. Returned. Colonel Drake there. Heard that Ellis, Company H, died last night.[148] Returned with Colonel Carpenter. Funeral of Ellis sunset. (Diary)

Wednesday, October 14th

Morning wrote letters. Afternoon I went up to the island by Pawnee Landing took up the mail. Got large number of shells. Spent evening with Captain Palmeter. Read and went to bed midnight. Order to regiment to return to Folly Island. (Diary)

Thursday, October 15th

Regiment relieved from duty on Black Island. (Chronicle)
Morning I came down early with gout. Ordered team to take home baggage of regiment. Spent day in camp. Received mail. Letter from wife. Regiment reached camp about 3. (Diary)

Friday, October 16th

Had visit from Dr. Crane, sanitary inspector. Letter from wife. Wrote wife. Went to port hospital to see the sick boys. Captain Stevens told me his plans, Invalid Corps. Fixed some library pamphlets. Long call from Dr. Washburn. Letter from wife. Wrote Dr. Rogers and wife. (Diary)

Saturday, October 17th

Stayed in tent forenoon. Mended some good books. Went up to port hospital. Carried papers. (Diary)

Sunday, October 18th

Distributed papers to every company. Just as I was ready for service the paymaster came and the regiment, of course, diverted from worship. I spent the forenoon in the hospital conversing personally with the boys. Afternoon in tent. Evening, funeral of Heath.[149] (Diary)

Monday, October 19th

Regiment paid for July and August. (Chronicle)
Forenoon paymaster. Paid up little debts, etc. Regimental inspection. Visit of Colonel Wilson. (Diary)

Tuesday, October 20th

Eight boys detailed to build chapel in conjunction with 13th Indiana. The following boys were sent onboard hospital boat, probably for St. Augustine, Florida. (Diary)

| Parker | Company I | Frank | Company C |
| Scott | Company E | Holt | Company I |

Tarbell	Company I	Combs	Company H
Edwards	Company E	Rolph	Company B
Case	Company A	Tuttle	Company C
Rouse	Company D	Blanding	Company K
Miles	Company H		

Wednesday, October 21st

General Foster reviewed brigade. (Chronicle)

This day Colonel Drake and myself visited Forts Wagner and Gregg. Rode on our horses to Fort Wagner, then walked through. Lieutenant for guide. Forts remodeled and very much strengthened. Stood on the spot from which first gun of the rebellion fired. Wednesday evening very tired. Retired early. (Diary)

Thursday, October 22nd

Morning read. Went round about the camp. Boys have been very busy remodeling their camp. Wright of Company G came.[150] He wants to be more decidedly a Christian. Many boys are thoughtful. Sent in a letter to Mrs. Hyde, October 22, 1863, by hand of George H. Dixon, Sergeant, Company G, 112th New York Volunteers, a note described thus[151]:

No. 4
Hilton Head, South Carolina
October 14, 1863
Captain Lucas of the U.S.[152]
Pay to Francis E. Hyde on order One Hundred and Fifty Dollars.

Edmund J. Porter[153]
Paymaster, U.S.A. (Diary)

Friday, October 23rd

Morning finished letter to wife. Sent it by George Dixon. Sent by ferry for a package containing two conch shells. 10 boys received furlough to go home. Old Mr. Harmon received discharge and died while getting ready to go.[154] (Diary)

Sunday, October 25th

Thanksgiving service in camp, regiment in hollow square. (Chronicle)

I preached this morning in the new chapel from 2nd Corinthians 5:20 "Ambassador of Christ."[155] The attendance was good. This chapel is the joint labor of our regiment and the 13th Indiana. Evening had a full prayer meeting. Blanding went in the boat to St. Augustine.[156] (Diary)

Monday, October 26th

Heard of the death of Scott of Company C.[157] Died onboard the boat going to Beaufort. Heavy casualties at the front.[158] (Diary)

George H. Dixon enlisted at Westfield, New York, as a private in Company G, 112th New York Volunteers. He was promoted from the ranks to captain. He transferred to the 3rd New York Infantry on June 13, 1865 (courtesy U.S. Army Heritage and Education Center [USAHEC]).

Tuesday, October 27th

Gillmore opens new batteries on Sumter. 9 men leave on furlough. (Chronicle)
Evening had a good prayer meeting. (Diary)

Friday, October 30th

Mister Kimball spent the evening with me. Stayed all night. We went into the prayer meeting. 2 got up and requested prayers. (Diary)

Saturday, October 31st

Called with Mr. Kimball on Chaplain Hudson of the engineer's regiment. He spoke of the interest of some of his boys in their prayer meeting building. (Diary)

Sunday, November 1st

I preached on Naaman the Syrian, 2nd Kings 5.[159] Afternoon Bible class at one the lesson from John 14.[160] Evening good prayer meeting though very chilly weather. (Diary)

Tuesday, November 3rd

Schools established for commissioned and non-commissioned officers. Commenced school on tactics for officers. (Chronicle)

Wednesday, November 4th

Lieutenant Fox resigned on account of sickness. Left. (Chronicle)
Lieutenant Fox got his papers and was put onboard the N.Y. steamer at Stono Inlet. (Diary)

Friday, November 6th

Had meeting of chaplains in tent of Connecticut Battery.
4 present: Seymour, Crippen, Kabus, Hyde (Johnson of Christian Commission).[161]
Good prayer meeting evening. (Diary)

Saturday, November 7th

Went to Morris Island. Called on Captain Appleton, Massachusetts 54th.[162] Got sanitary stores. Returned in afternoon. Met Chaplain Hill.[163] (Diary)

Sunday, November 8th

I preached from Mark 6:16.[164] Very attentive audience. Afternoon held a Bible class 1½ hours. Evening a very excellent prayer meeting. Colonel Carpenter went with me into the hospital. (Diary)

Monday, November 9th

Colonel Drake assigned to command brigade. (Chronicle)
I rode to Pawnee. Bought some apples. Captain Stevens weak. Went with horse to Engineer Corps. (Diary)

Tuesday, November 10th

Captain Stevens' papers came and I helped him get off. Also 2 boys, Cramer (I) and Bliss (F).[165] Moved the tent Captain Stevens occupied on to my ground. (Diary)

Wednesday, November 11th

We got the discharge papers and sent north. Gilbert (B), Hogges (K), Wantshouse [Wanshis] (H), Fowler (F), Lowell (I), Kirk (B). Went to General Hospital, Beaufort. Onley (E), Abbott (G), Eslor (E), Pierce (I), Pierce (C).[166] (Diary)

Thursday, November 12th

In camp. Very dull. Went over to engineers. Evening at home. Read Virgil. Funeral of Barber who died at port hospital of paralysis after dysentery.[167] (Diary)

Friday, November 13th

Went over to see the chapel of the drummer boys of Engineer Corps. (Diary)

Saturday, November 14th

This evening I attended Bible class in the little chapel of the drummer boys near the engineer regiment. 13 present. Had a good time. (Diary)

Sunday, November 15th

Heavy firing from new Rebel batteries. (Chronicle)

I preached at 11 on text Acts. Almost thou persuadest me to be Christian.[168] 1 hospital service. Half past our Bible class. Three preached in Engineer's Chapel on Blind Bartimaeus.[169] Evening. Had a good prayer meeting. (Diary)

Monday, November 16th

Early in the forenoon rode to Pawnee then to camp 1st Brigade. (Diary)

Tuesday, November 17th

Spent the morning arranging shells to send home. (Diary)

Thursday, November 19th

General Sprague meets officers of regiment at General Gillmore's headquarters on recruits.[170] (Chronicle)

Friday, November 20th

Meeting of chaplains in my tent. Had a good meeting. Evening a prayer meeting. Colonel present. We heard yesterday plan of going home to recruit. May go. (Diary)

Saturday, November 21st

General Foster reviews brigade. (Chronicle)

Review of the brigade in morning by General Foster. Colonel Drake commanded the review. Evening. Attended class meeting in the Engineer Corps. (Diary)

Sunday, November 22nd

Preached at eleven pm. Bible class at ½ past one. Evening. Prayer meeting at engineers. Crowded. (Diary)

Monday, November 23rd

Morning. Rode and called on Mr. Chapman lately came to 169th.
Met Mr. Taylor, Christian Commission. He dined with us. Funeral of Shaffer, 4 o'clock.[171] Wrote Christian Commission and others in evening. (Diary)

Camp of the 112th Regiment New York State Volunteers
Folly Island, S.C.
November 23rd 1863

Mrs. D. J. Pratt[172]
Dear Madam,

Yours of the 26th all came to camp by the last mail, and as the kind gifts of the ladies of Fredonia to our dear boys had not reached the regiment in order for us to answer by return of boat, I have waited until I could assure you of their safe arrival.

Last Saturday they came up on a boat from Hilton Head. Eleven barrels and kegs and 10 boxes. Unfortunately the two companies in which all the Fredonia boys, with two or three exceptions are found, were sent the day before, by orders from headquarters, to do picket duty on Long Island, which lies west of us and between us and James Island. We would have had a jubilee in camp had they all been here. As it was Dr. Washburn, Lieutenant Russ and myself examined the boxes, found in each box a stamped envelope put in by the Buffalo Ladies, and enclosed an invoice of what the box contained, which proved to be correct.

We then got the names of all the Pomfret boys as Lieutenant Russ said the Fredonia boys could not be distinguished from Pomfret, and found that there were 68. To each one of these a can of peaches was sent. The other articles in the boxes have not yet been distributed except those marked to individuals.

I had the opportunity today to send to Cornelius Parker the wrapper and another little package by the hand of a delegate of the Christian Commission.[173] He is in Beaufort and it is very seldom we have any communication with Beaufort. He was very sick when sent there, and in a very interesting state of mind. I hear he has not gained since he went there. I dislike to have our sick boys sent where I cannot visit them, but they are in most respects better off there, than here. The can for Pollard, I think, was sent yesterday, if not I will take it to him tomorrow.[174] I appropriated one of the cans according to your request; the others are handed to the hospital steward for the use of the convalescent sick. Dr. Washburn will write you as to the disposition of the articles which came in the boxes directed to him. The most of the cans were uninjured; in one or two instances the cans were cut through by nails, yet their contents were uninjured. I believe all the things came through in good order—indeed in excellent order considering the length of distance they were brought.

I know the boys who are in camp are grateful, and those away will be when they receive your magnificent gifts. These tokens of remembrance from those at home assume those toiling in the field that amid their privations, loneliness and sufferings they are not forgotten. It makes them feel that multitudes of sisters and mothers are feeling for them and sympathizing with them amid their hardships. The articles will all of them be exceedingly acceptable.

It is very difficult to get vegetables enough for the men of the regiment, and I think when we first came here the want of potatoes, was one cause of the serious sickness which prevailed. Today a boy belonging to Fredonia, member of Company G, was buried. His name was Shaffer. He had been sick a long time and was wasted to a shadow. In general the health of the regiment is improving. May God bless abundantly your association for the good of our soldiers.

> Very truly, etc.
> W. L. Hyde
> Chaplain of the Regiment (Newspaper)[175]

Tuesday, November 24th

Morning. I sent letters to Christian Commission Inspector General, Buffalo; Mrs. Pratt, Fredonia. Then spent some time in hospital. Lay down till dinner. After dinner, funeral of Bowers and Allen.[176] Evening wrote letters to Mr. Bowers to Mrs. Allen and finished letter to my wife. (Diary)

> Camp 112th Regiment New York State Volunteers
> Folly Island
> November 24th 1863

Mrs. M. A. Allen[177]
Dear Madam,

Your husband, Loyal Allen, of Company H, who has been so long sick, departed this life very early this morning. He has been sick since September last, and when he went into the hospital, he had a very violent bloody dysentery which the doctor found would hurry him rapidly to the grave, but he rallied from it and was better. Soon it was apparent that the form of the disease was only changed. He did not gain any. Some days he was better and others not so well. But all the time his disease was gaining in its power, and he was growing weaker. He thought some days he was decidedly better; then at other times he felt somewhat discouraged. We did all we could to keep his spirits up and most of the time he was very hopeful. His mind was open to religious truth and he always received very kindly what I said to him. He seemed in my last conversation with him to be resigned to the will of God.

It is very painful that I cannot tell you anything about his last thoughts for his family, but it is necessary in the shape in which the disease takes, to keep the mind of the patient from dwelling on themes that would depress him. There is a strong tendency to depression in the disease, and to talk to a man as though he were going to die would be almost sure to abridge what little chance he has of living. For this reason, I always point those who are sick to the cheering and consoling truths of the gospel, the love of God, the mercy of Christ, the freeness and fullness of salvation and urge them to rest upon Jesus. Mr. Allen was very nervous and it required a very calm and hopeful discourse to do him good. I hope the quiet submission of his spirit was a token of the gracious and softening power of God's Holy Spirit leading him to rest upon the rock of ages. May God comfort your bereaved hearts and the hearts of your dear children in your sad affliction, and may you find that light and consolation in your sorrow which God only can impart.

Mr. Allen had every care and attention which a man can have here in the hospital and his remains repose in our regimental burying grounds.

> Very truly and with deep sympathy,
> W. L. Hyde
> Chaplain of the Regiment (Newspaper)[178]

Wednesday, November 25th

About camp. Evening, I prepared for Thanksgiving. (Diary)

Thursday, November 26th

Thanksgiving day. We had a Thanksgiving service at dress parade. Singing, prayers, giving address. Singing. The men formed in hollow square. (Diary)

Friday, November 27th

Thanksgiving. (Chronicle)
We had only two chaplains present at chaplain's meeting this afternoon. (Diary)

Saturday, November 28th

We had a very interesting prayer meeting at the chapel called the Palmetto Chapel or rather Bible class. (Diary)

Sunday, November 29th

Cold froze water ⅛ inch. Division drills on beach. (Chronicle)
Held service in chapel. Preached from who so drinketh this water shall thirst again.[179] Afternoon no Bible class. Evening preached at Palmetto Chapel. Men ought always to pray. The day was very raw. (Diary)

Saturday, December 5th

Mr. Taylor, Christian Commission, came in to tarry with me. He will have his headquarters here during the winter. (Diary)

Sunday, December 6th

Mr. Taylor preached in the morning. Oh praise the Lord for his goodness.[180] Afternoon one Bible class. Evening, Mr. Taylor preached in the Palmetto Chapel. (Diary)

Saturday, December 12th

12 men leave on furlough for good behavior. (Chronicle)

Sunday, December 13th

Preached in morning from "Why halt ye between two opinions."[181] Afternoon Bible class. Evening prayer meeting. I heard that I was to be disappointed about going home. (Diary)

Monday, December 14th

Taylor returned Hilton Head. (Diary)

Saturday, December 19th

Walked down to camp 169th. Order came for 10 men and six officers to go home on recruiting service. (Diary)

Sunday, December 20th

No preaching at our chapel. Brigade review in the morning. Afternoon went down to Cole's Island. Assisted at the dedication of a chapel of the 127th New York. Evening prayer meeting at the Palmetto. (Diary)

Monday, December 21st

Lieutenant Colonel Carpenter, Captains Curtis, Ludwick, Dunham and party started for New York recruiting. Lieutenant Hedges assigned to command Company C.[182] (Chronicle)

Lieutenant Colonel Carpenter, Captains Ludwick, Curtis and Dunham, Lieutenants Talcott and Kimberly and 10 privates and noncommissioned officers went down to Stono to take boat for Hilton Head thence to New York.[183] I accompanied them to Stono. (Diary)

Tuesday, December 22nd

Spent the day in repairing library books. In the evening read the papers. Colonel Drake left for Hilton Head. (Diary)

Wednesday, December 23rd

Was in hospital. All doing well. (Diary)

Thursday, December 24th

This evening attended the Christmas Eve celebration and dedication of chapel of the 169th New York Volunteers. Made sermon remarks myself. (Diary)

Friday, December 25th

General Gillmore opened upon Charleston. Rebs reply from all their batteries. (Chronicle)

Christmas Day. Went down to communion at the chapel of the 169th. Afterwards invited the chaplains here to dine. Colonel Drake had returned. We had Captain Oley and Chaplain Chapman in addition to our usual mess.[184] (Diary)

Saturday, December 26th

Major Smith reported back to regiment. (Chronicle)
Spent at home writing. Rode up to see Brother Crippen. (Diary)

Sunday, December 27th

Preached in morning on Matthew 2:2 and 3.[185] Star of the Wise Men. Very interesting Bible class in the afternoon and in the evening good prayer meeting at the Palmetto Tent. (Diary)

Monday, December 28th

Busy with letters. Major Smith returned yesterday from Norfolk. Will take command in 2 to 3 days. (Diary)

Tuesday, December 29th

Rode to camp 169th. Met Taylor who had returned from Hilton Head. We dined together. Then rode about our lines. Came up through camp of 1st New York. Attended prayer meeting in the evening. (Diary)

Charles H. Oley enrolled at Pomfret, New York, as a captain in Company I, 112th New York Volunteers. He was discharged for disability on November 28, 1864.

Wednesday, December 30th

18 men have lately been sent to hospital at Beaufort. All cases of chronic diarrhea were ordered there. (Diary)

Thursday, December 31st

This is the closing day of the year. I have not done much. This evening we were to have a watch meeting but after the sermon the storm was so violent we adjourned.

The year has been an eventful one to me. Would to God it could carry into eternity a better report. (Diary)

> By the end of 1863, the 112th Regiment had received their baptism by fire. Disease took a devastating toll on the 112th during their service at Suffolk, VA and Folly Island, SC. As with the majority of Union regiments, the 112th suffered more casualties from disease than they did from hostile action with the enemy. Sickness and death became a common theme in Chaplain Hyde's correspondence throughout 1863. However, the real bloodletting of 1864 still awaited Hyde and the men of the Chautauqua Regiment.
>
> The events of 1863 gave promise to the Union, Lee's advance into Pennsylvania was thwarted, Vicksburg fell to Grant and the Mississippi River was now safe to transport Union forces deeper into the Confederacy. However, Union optimism would rapidly turn into despair. Their resolve would soon be challenged, as the armies on both sides of the Mason-Dixon Line face each other in some of the bloodiest fighting of the war.

3

1864

In the early months of 1864, the Chautauqua Regiment received orders ending their stay in South Carolina. Relieved from supporting operations against Charleston, they moved further into the heart of the Confederacy. Between February and April 1864, the regiment would operate in the vicinity of Jacksonville, Florida before returning to the killing fields of Virginia. Death was no stranger to the regiment. Places such as Cold Harbor, Chaffin's Farm and Petersburg would cost the regiment its greatest number of battle casualties. Of the regiment's twelve officers who died during the war, eight would die as a result of combat in 1864. Weary of war, homesick and saddened with the loss of his horse and close friends, Hyde would find 1864 to be a true test of his mettle and faith.

Friday, January 1st

Promotions and commissioning officers hereafter to be regimental. (Chronicle)

Thursday, January 7th

Captain Chaddock returned from sick leave. General Gillmore moves headquarters to Hilton Head. (Chronicle)

Wednesday, January 20th

Grand review of all troops on island. (Chronicle)

Saturday, February 6th

Lieutenant Corbett leaves on sick leave.[1] Drew supplies from Sanitary Commission for hospital. (Chronicle)

Sunday, February 7th

Regiment ordered with 3 days cooked rations to join expedition to Johns Island. (Chronicle)

Wednesday, February 17th

Weather intensely cold. (Chronicle)

Monday, February 22nd

Regiment ordered to Florida. (Chronicle)

Tuesday, February 23rd

Leave Folly Island. Four companies on *Hellen Getty*. Balance of regiment on *Ben DeFord*. (Chronicle)

Thursday, February 25th

Reach Jacksonville 2 pm. Peach trees and roses in bloom. Trumpet Creeper. Oranges on trees. 100 men work all night digging. (Chronicle)

Monday, February 29th

Colonel Drake in command of brigade. Lieutenant Edmonds assigned to command Company C.[2] (Chronicle)

Monday morning
February 29th [1864]

[My dear Wife,]

This morning I am sitting in a large high posted room of a very good story and half house just about ¾ of mile outside of Jacksonville. My window faces the St. Johns River. Just in front of me is a regular down east saw mill built by a man from Cherryfield, Maine, who was driven away by the Rebs 2 years ago on account of his being a Union man. About 40 rods to the left is a large two story house occupied by some citizen, probably the boarding house for the mill in days past. Close by the house in which I am is a very sharp roofed cottage which some down east Yankee formerly built and over the floors of it are scattered any quantity of letters, showing that the family left in the greatest haste.

We have occupied this house just 15 hours and this morning part of us are to vacate it. There is no rest in the army especially in active campaign. Yesterday was Sunday. We were occupying the camp into which we first arrived. It was only a few steps from that Methodist church, and as I had no way to cover them from the hot sun outside, I accepted the invitation of Reverend Mr. Lewis of the Methodist church to take my regiment in there and worship with them. He had just come down the past week from Beaufort, and taken possession of the church as Methodist property, by order of Secretary of War. The church was spacious and we were nicely accommodated. Mr. Lewis preached a regular rambling Methodist sermon to soldiers. I sat in the pulpit with him and took part. In the afternoon, we were ordered to move to our present location. It is quite a pleasant one in the open field, about ¾ of a mile from the old camp. We-colonel, major, Captain Chaddock and myself, have a house near the water, and are as comfortable as possible while destitute of furniture. Last evening we were speculating on the probability of our remaining here or going to Beaufort or back to Folly Island.

We all agreed that we preferred Beaufort to Jacksonville, and either place to Folly Island. Indeed, I had rather go to Texas or to the Army of the Potomac than to go back to that miserable sand heap.

While discussing these various probabilities the news came that General Vogdes had been relieved of his command, General Foster had been put in command of the division and Colonel Drake had command of Foster's Brigade.

So we are to have a complete overturn in mess matters. The colonel is to take a new house nearer the town. He wants me to go with him and have Brown cook for himself and staff and myself.

Major Smith is appointed judge advocate and provost marshal of the division but he has chosen his house and office next to that of Colonel Drake, so that he will still continue in the mess. The colonel got highly indignant last night with the men. He ordered them, in coming onto their new grounds, not to interfere in any way with private property and not to destroy fences. They had hardly got their accoutrements off before they tore down a fence long enough to reach from Mr. Carpenter's to the Baptist church. The colonel was so mad he had to make everybody about him uncomfortable. He called several officers in and hatcheted them well and threatened them with severe punishment to the delinquents. They were also made to work to replace the fence. In order to calm down his perturbed spirit, I read from the *North American Review* to him an hour or so and then we spread blankets on the floor and went to sleep.[3]

This morning the major told me he had an order to make the dire arrangements for shooting a negro, who had been guilty of mutinous conduct, and asked me to accompany him. I went accordingly, and found the man had a chaplain with him, and was engaged with him. The chaplain had been with him during the evening previous and the man had softened down. At first he was very hard but when he found he was to die and no reprieve, he confessed his sins and this morning appeared to be ready to die. As there was a chaplain with him I said nothing to him, but rode side of the marshal to the field of execution. The brigade was drawn upon two sides of a square. The coffin placed on the ground, the prisoner had his hands tied behind him, his eyes blindfolded, his coat taken off. He kneeled on his coffin, the detail stood 10 paces, fired and he fell. Not dead, the major called the other detail and he did not give even a gasp after the fire. It was a solemn sight but I have seen death in so many forms it did not affect me as it would have done once. And then I felt that the fellow was justly condemned and ought to die. He had excited mutiny in the regiment and no doubt his death will be an impressive warning example to the regiments. He belonged to the 3rd United States Colored Brigade and was shot in the presence of his colored brethren.

Tomorrow I hope we shall get a mail from home, and then I shall again hear from you. Oh how much I long to see you once more, and talk over the various experiences of the year. It was about a year ago that you came down to visit me at Suffolk. I hope to hear by your next that you are wholly recovered. I believe I told you in my last, that I have sent some shells and sea greens to you in a box which Captain Chaddock sent to Fredonia. The most precious things I sent were your letters. Keep them safe for me. I want you also to keep mine as I shall depend much on my letters to you for material to make up the history of the regiment, which I intend in due time to write.

Give my love to all friends. I did not write Harry the last time but will try to do so this mail.

Very affectionately as ever,
Wm. L. Hyde

Tuesday, March 1st

Grand review of all the troops. Pm regiment ordered out in haste. Enemy reported advancing. 10 pm again in camp. All quiet. (Chronicle)

Friday, March 4th

Changed camp to near the sawmills. (Chronicle)

Sunday, March 6th

29 recruits came to regiment. (Chronicle)

Tuesday, March 8th

Barton's Brigade ordered to Palatka, Florida.[4] (Chronicle)

Friday, March 11th

General Foster detailed to court martial. Colonel Drake commands division. Colonel Dobbs, 13th Indiana, [commands] brigade. (Chronicle)

Sunday, March 13th

200 men sent out as scouting party. Return night. (Chronicle)

Friday, March 18th

>Camp 112th Regiment New York Volunteers
>Jacksonville, Florida
>March 18th 1864

Lieutenant Colonel Edward W. Smith[5]
Colonel,

I respectfully ask leave of absence for thirty days to visit my family in Dunkirk, Chautauqua County, New York.

Letters received, since coming to Jacksonville, inform me that my wife is in a very precarious condition by reason of sickness and that my presence both on her account and that of my children is an urgent necessity.

I have been constantly with the regiment and on duty the past eighteen months, and until now, have not asked for a leave of absence.

>Very respectfully your obedient servant,
>William L. Hyde
>Chaplain
>112th Regiment New York Volunteers

Sunday, March 27th

General Hatch relieves General Seymour in command of forces in Florida.[6] (Chronicle)

Thursday, March 31st

Convalescents and camp equipage, tents, etc., come from Folly Island. (Chronicle)

Friday, April 1st

Maple Leaf steamer blown up by a torpedo. All camp equipage lost.[7] (Chronicle)

Sunday, April 17th

13th Indiana left for Fort Monroe. Regiment complimented for soldierly appearance on inspection. (Chronicle)

Wednesday, April 20th

Orders came today to strike tents and break up camp, take baggage onboard steamer for Hilton Head. (Journal)

Cyrus J. Dobbs commanded the 13th Indiana Infantry and commanded a brigade within the Department of the South.

Thursday, April 21st

The regiment with all garrison and camp equipage this day embarked onboard steamer *Cossack* for Hilton Head. (Journal)

Friday, April 22nd

We reached Hilton Head, did not land. The steamer *Ericsson* came alongside while in the bay and everything transferred to here. (Journal)

Saturday, April 23rd

Went up to the wharf at Hilton Head, took onboard some horses. General R. S. Foster and staff here came onboard and the boat left for Fortress Monroe about 3 o'clock pm. (Journal)

Tuesday, April 26th

After a very unpleasant sea voyage, during which a large proportion of the officers and men were very sick, we reached Hampton Roads about 5 o'clock am. Orders came for the regiment to proceed to Yorktown on the York River. Sailed at 9 and reached Gloucester Point 3 pm. Debarked immediately and went into bivouac. (Journal)

Wednesday, April 27th

In camp at Gloucester Point. (Journal)

Friday, April 29th

This day in compliance with orders, officers' baggage and camp equipage reduced to the minimum for a march and all extra baggage sent to Norfolk to be stored. (Journal)

Saturday, April 30th

The regiment was this day mustered for pay and also all the forces at Gloucester Point, were inspected by Major General Butler.[8] About this time in the reorganization of the corps, Foster's Brigade was enlarged by the addition of the 8th Maine, which would place a senior colonel to Colonel Drake in the brigade. General Vogdes, who came from Hilton Head expecting to have a division, was ordered to report to General Shepley at Norfolk and then assigned to the defenses of Norfolk and Portsmouth.[9] General Foster objected to being simply a brigade commander while his juniors were at the head of divisions. The consequence was that the 9th Maine was substituted for the 8th in our brigade which left Colonel Drake

Benjamin F. Butler, perhaps the Yankee most hated by the South, was relieved by General Grant after his disastrous attempt to capture Fort Fisher in December 1864.

the ranking colonel. General Gillmore, arriving and taking command of the corps at the time of starting for James River assigned General Foster as chief of staff. General Ames retaining command of the 3rd Division.[10] (Journal)

Monday, May 2nd

Colonel Drake assumed command of the 5th Brigade by general order. (Journal)

Wednesday, May 4th–Thursday, May 5th

Colonel Carpenter, Captains Dunham, Ludwick and Curtis, Lieutenants Talcott and Kimberly and the enlisted men who have been absent on recruiting service since December 1863, returned to the regiment. Colonel Carpenter was received with the highest demonstrations of joy on the part of the men. Regiment was already under orders for embarkation and were placed onboard the steamer *T. Powell*, proceeded to Hampton Roads whence they were transported up the James River and on the evening of the 5th landed at Bermuda Hundred. (Journal)

Friday, May 6th

On the sixth advanced inland to within 2 miles of the Petersburg and Richmond Railroad. (Journal)

Saturday, May 7th

Morning of the 7th the regiment advanced with the other force, encountered the enemy about a mile from the railroad, a lively engagement ensued and the enemy were driven back to the railroad, where they were found to hold a very strong position protected by artillery. Were ordered in the evening to fall back to our entrenchments. (Journal)

Thursday, May 12th

On the morning of the 12th, we again approached the railroad. The track was gained without opposition. We destroyed a mile of the track towards Richmond, burning the rails so as to render them completely useless. On this night, ordered to Walthall Junction with the other regiments of the brigade. Walthall Junction is 14 miles from Richmond, 8 from Petersburg. The object of the move of the brigade was to protect the left flank of the army operating against the fortifications on the James River. (Journal)

Friday, May 13th

On the evening of the 13th, the brigade was divided [into] 2 regiments: 13th Indiana and 169th New York were left at Walthall Junction and the 112th New York and 9th Maine, under Colonel Drake, were moved towards the right wing of the army to act as reserved force. (Journal)

Sunday, May 15th–Monday, May 16th

This day (Sunday) passed in comparative quiet. But it was only the lull that preceded the terrific storm. It seems that General Butler had determined to assault Fort Johnson that night, but the enemy had been moving all their available forces down from Richmond in order to deal Butler a crushing blow. A reconnaissance convinced our general of the folly of attempting an assault upon a position so strong as Fort Johnson and early in the morning, in one of the densest fogs ever known, the enemy precipitated a force upon Heckman's Brigade of the 18th Army Corps forming the left of their line, with such force and fury as soon to throw it into utter confusion.[11] In the melee, Heckman, with a large number, was taken prisoner.

When this attack was made, Colonel Drake received an order to move one regiment immediately to the support of Heckman and ordered Lieutenant Colonel Carpenter immediately to report to General Heckman or whoever might be in command. He then prepared to move his remaining regiment, which he was soon ordered to do. Lieutenant Colonel Carpenter on receiving the order, moved his regiment forward reaching General Heckman's quarters and finding no one, he sent Lieutenant Hedges, assistant adjutant, forward to find someone to whom to report, not returning. (He probably rode into the enemy's lines and was taken prisoner). Colonel Carpenter himself rode forward and about 15 rods in advance of the regiment he heard the summons "surrender." Wheeling about and giving his horse the spur, he shouted "men fall back." The enemy called "shoot him" and the volley followed. One shot struck the colonel as he was bending forward on his horse just below the right lung, which traversing it, struck the shoulder with such violence as to break it. Another shot knocked his hat from off his head, and another penetrated his horse inflicting only a flesh wound. The furious animal tore through the ranks of the 112th and beyond to where Colonel Drake was bringing up the 9th Maine, when he was arrested, and the colonel was assisted to the ground. The regiment hearing the lieutenant colonel's order, thinking he said "fall down," fell on their faces, the volley passed over them, when the colonel came tearing through, not knowing what it meant, they scattered in some confusion into the edge of the woods. Captain Chaddock was acting major, his horse was struck by a spent ball, became unmanageable and rushing under the trees unhorsed him. He, however, at once recovered himself and in a few minutes reformed the regiment in line of battle directly across the road, throwing out a strong party of skirmishers in front. Colonel Drake was near the 9th Maine when Colonel Carpenter was taken from his horse. He gave orders for some men to assist him to the rear and immediately rode forward to see what had become of the 112th. Meeting 2 or 3 men, he asked them where the regiment was. They replied they did not know and gave the impression that it was badly scattered, if not captured. What was the colonel's relief on riding forward to find this noble regiment firmly planted across the road in good position and in good order.

He now placed both regiments in position and kept up such a fierce fire as to create the

William Foy enlisted at Poland, New York, as a private in Company A, 112th New York Volunteers. He mustered out on June 7, 1865, at Fortress Monroe, Virginia.

impression of a much larger force and thus prevent any vigorous movement of the Rebs in this direction. By this sagacious action of the colonel, the right was no doubt saved from an overwhelming defeat. Later in the day, in conjunction with other parts of the force, the enemy were driven back to the rifle pits they had taken in the morning, and opportunity given to bring off our wounded and our artillery from the field. The falling back was accomplished in good order, and before 6 o'clock pm the regiment was in its encampment within the line of defenses. Among the praiseworthy incidents of the day, Foy, Company A, was taken prisoner in the confusion of the morning's fight.[12] After being deprived of his gun, he was entrusted to the care of a single man to take him to the enemy's rear. Watching his opportunity, he seized the gun off his guard and telling him that he was himself a prisoner, he conducted him back within our lines and delivered him over to the provost guard. Edward Shelters of Company A, was shot in the arm and taken prisoner.[13] He watched his opportunity and ran but was fired upon and wounded in the leg. But was soon after rescued by some of his companions and brought within our lines. Both wounds are very severe. The arm having been badly broken and the leg shot, passing directly under the knee and fracturing the bone badly. (Journal)

The losses of the regiment during the day were: (Journal)

Adjutant	S. P. Hedges	Missing
Lieutenant Colonel Carpenter		Mortally wounded, died May 18th
Abram Danford	Company A	Killed, left on field
John Jones	Company A	Wounded hand, accidental
Harvey Davis	Company A	Wounded shoulder
Edward Shelters	Company A	Wounded arm and leg, died
Fred L. Redington	Company A	Wounded arm
Samuel P. Hedges	Company B	Taken prisoner
Walter Strong	Company B	Wounded leg, slight
Benjamin S. Haight	Company B	Wounded foot
Jacob Vader	Company B	Wounded finger
Franklin Harrington	Company C	Wounded bowels, accidental, died before reaching hospital
William Carpenter	Company D	Wounded

Monday, May 16th

The following letter was originally sent to the editor of the Dunkirk Journal *by Chaplain Hyde. It was later reprinted in the* Fredonia Censor.

The 112th—We observe in the Dunkirk Journal a letter from Chaplain Hyde, detailing the incidents of the fight on the 16th, in which the 112th participated losing their gallant Lieutenant Colonel Carpenter of Jamestown. Chaplain H. details the circumstances attending the death of the former as follows:

While at the head of the regiment early in the morning, the fog so dense you could not see 20 feet ahead, he was ordered to report to General Heckman on the right immediately. Moving forward to comply with the order he sent his adjutant ahead to where the fighting was already very heavy to see where to report, and after five minutes he not returning, the lieutenant colonel rode forward himself. He went about fifteen rods ahead of the regiment where the Rebs yelled out, surrender, and he quicker than lightning wheeled his horse, "shoot him," was the command, and the Rebs fired a volley. The colonel said to the men "fall back," the whole regiment fell on their faces and the whole volley passed over them. But the lieutenant colonel was hit in the back. The ball passed through the back of the lung, and struck the shoulder breaking it, and it is still inside. His furious horse was hit and tore through the ranks, the colonel only having strength to cling to the saddle. For a moment the confusion was great; the horse knocked over several men in his passage, and the terrific volley came near stampeding [us]. But the boys behaved splendidly, and in ten minutes Captain Chaddock had them formed in line of battle and in good order. When the volley came, the captain who was acting as major, was riding in the rear and his horse became unmanageable, sprang into the woods and under a tree, a limb of which unhorsed him, but he got up instantly and readied the regiment and had them in line of battle. During the two hours succeeding, they were under heavy fire, and fog lifting up, they made a splendid charge, sweeping the Rebs from the field, way over the breastworks. We lost one man killed and eight wounded.

Lieutenant Colonel Carpenter	[Field & Staff]	Wounded in back
Abraham Danforth	Company A	Killed
Harvey R. Davis	Company A	Wounded
Fred Redington	Company A	Leg
Edward Shelters	Company A	Leg and arm
John Jones	Company A	Hand
Lieutenant Samuel P. Hedges	Company B	Missing
Corporal Walter Strong	Company B	Wounded in leg
Benjamin Haight	Company B	Wound in foot
Jacob Vader	Company B	Wounded in finger
William Carpenter	Company B	Wounded in hand

Colonel Drake commanded the brigade yesterday, and at the close of the day, General Weitzel came and thanked him primarily for his assistance.[14] His praise is in all mouths. Had it not been for his coolness and persistency in repelling the charges of the enemy, our right wing would have been all cut to pieces. The battle raged all day in different parts of the line, and was very disastrous to us, though the Rebs were terribly punished. They poured down reinforcements from Richmond, and calculated to crush us. But they were entirely foiled in this. Company K, Captain Ludwick, was last on the field, and about 5 o'clock made the last charge and drove a regiment of Rebels half a mile, and came in without the loss of a man. They charged through a perfect storm of bullets. After being rallied, Captain Chaddock called for a report, and every man but two were accounted for. What regiment could do better? I was at the hospital and worked all day. (Newspaper)[15]

Tuesday, May 17th

Move camp. Raise tents. No man allowed to sleep on ground in camp. (Chronicle)

The regiment employed in perfecting the defenses. (Journal)

Wednesday, May 18th

The regiment employed on fatigue work and

William H. Chaddock enrolled at Pomfret, New York, as a captain in Company B, 112th New York Volunteers. He was discharged for disability on November 25, 1864 (courtesy U.S. Army Heritage and Education Center [USAHEC]).

held behind entrenchments. Severe firing along the picket line this morning. (Journal)

Thursday, May 19th

Last night heavy firing along the picket line, enemy made several assaults. (Journal)

Friday, May 20th

Last night three desperate assaults along the picket line. About noon today the assault renewed with terrific violence and our rifle pits forced. Hard fighting, about 180 wounded taken to our corps hospital this morning. Corporal M. O'Brien, Company F, shot in the breast while looking over the entrenchments.[16] Lieutenant C. A. Kimberly, Company E, while on duty, struck with small piece of shell, grazed the scalp inflicting only slight wound. Yesterday morning, Bowen of Company F, had his arm bruised by a piece of shell and Sherman Brownell of Company G, was wounded in the knee by a very small fragment of shell while at work as cook preparing company rations.[17] (Journal)

Charles A. Kimberly enlisted at Westfield, New York, as a corporal in Company E, 112th New York Volunteers and was wounded in action at Chaffin's Farm, Virginia. He was discharged for disability on March 23, 1865 (courtesy U.S. Army Heritage and Education Center [USAHEC]).

Saturday, May 21st

Regiment engaged in fatigue work raising the embankment in front. John Nelson, Company A, shot in foot, supposed that he shot himself. Twice attacked at night upon our picket lines. (Journal)

Sunday, May 22nd

Regiment busy on defenses. Heavy detail for picket duty. (Journal)

Monday, May 23rd

Regiment worked on abattis in front of our defenses. (Journal)

> Field Encampment
> 112th Regt N.Y. Vols.
> Near Bermuda Hundred
> May 23rd 1864

Mr. Editors:

I make use of the first leisure since the sad occurrence to give your readers the full particulars of the death of our much lamented Lieutenant Colonel Carpenter. The event has left a deep gloom upon us all. Few men, in the position which he held, were ever more thoroughly loved and trusted by a regiment than he was. His course of life with us from the first has been eminently praiseworthy. He was one of the few men in whom military life develops the nobler traits of manhood. Neither that small pitiful selfishness, nor those coarse and degrading vices which grow so luxuriantly in the army, deformed his career. He came to the regiment with only the limited military experience of a single year, was placed in the responsible position of major and after about four months promoted to lieutenant colonel and grew constantly in favor with both officers and men to the last hour of his life.

Colonel Carpenter reached the regiment at Gloucester Point, after an absence of four months on recruiting service, just as they were about embarking for the present expedition. His reception by the men was most enthusiastic, they cheered with loud cheers, threw their caps into the air and greeted him with demonstrations of extreme delight.

Colonel Drake having been appointed to the command of the brigade, the command of the regiment now devolved on Lieutenant Colonel Carpenter, and no regimental commander could desire the more perfect confidence of both officers and men.

The regiment arrived at Bermuda Hundred the evening of the 5th May and from the morning of the 7th was constantly engaged either in skirmishes with the enemy or in destroying part of the Richmond and Petersburg Railroad. On Sunday Colonel Drake's Brigade was divided, two regiments: 13th Indiana and 169th New York, being left at a point facing Petersburg to hold in check any demonstration from that quarter upon our rear, and the other two regiments: 112th New York and 9th Maine, were marched towards Richmond on the turnpike road to a point one half mile distant from Fort Johnson, where our forces were entrenched as a reserve supporting Heckman's Brigade.

About 4 o'clock Monday morning, the enemy attacked Heckman's Brigade of the 18th Corps with such fury and force, in one of the densest fogs as completely to crush it. Colonel Drake was ordered, soon after the fight commenced, to send a regiment to the support of Heckman's; knowing that his, 112th with Colonel Carpenter at its head, to be ever ready and reliable, he ordered them to advance as speedily as possible and prepare to follow immediately with the 9th Maine. Colonel Carpenter soon reached the headquarters of General Heckman, under a terrible artillery fire from Fort Johnson without loss. Finding no one there to whom to report, he sent Adjutant Hedges forward to find some of the general's staff. It is probable that Hedges rode directly into the enemy's lines, for the fog was so dense that nothing could be seen a few feet in advance and nothing has since been heard from our dear young friend. Colonel Carpenter becoming anxious in regard to the situation, rode forward himself, to reconnoiter, when some 15 rods in advance of the regiment, he heard a summons to surrender and could just see the outlines of men through the fog. He told me afterwards his first thought was "I've led my men into a trap." Wheeling his horse he called at the top of his voice, "men fall back." At the same time the enemy shouted, "Shoot him," and a volley followed. One shot struck the colonel (who was bending forward on his horse which was rushing back at full speed) just below the right lung, which it traversed and striking his shoulder, broke the bone but did not pass through. Another shot struck his hat knocking it from his head. This shot would have been fatal had he not been leaning forward, in which case his body would have fallen into the hands of the enemy. Another shot struck his horse, inflicting only a flesh wound. The furious creature tore through the regiment, knocking down several men in his passage and passing on beyond to where the 9th Maine had advanced was arrested.

Colonel Drake was at hand and seeing the lieutenant colonel was wounded, ordered some men at once to help him from his horse. He swooned at once when laid upon the ground, and a detail of men was sent with him to the rear.

About 7 o'clock I reached the place where he was lying, on my way to find the regiment, having just returned from my leave of absence. I was able to be with him most of the time until his death.

Our surgeon procured the ablest medical counsel on the field to aid him in his efforts to save his life. About 4 o'clock he was taken to the corps hospital. A comfortable place was prepared for him and all that kindness could do was done for him. He suffered but little pain except when moved, was grateful for every favor, conversed clearly and freely with his friends, and on Tuesday morning hopes were entertained that the wound might not prove fatal.

During the afternoon unfavorable symptoms began to develop, and towards evening Dr. Craven, Chief Medical Officer of the 18th Army Corps, came in to see him and frankly told him that he could not long survive.[18]

After the doctor left, he called me to him and said to me, "Chaplain, I must die." He asked me to pray for him, and in strains of great simplicity committed his own cause to his Maker. He sent a brief message to his family, then said, "I am content, let God's will be done," and composed himself like a Christian hero, to meet the inevitable result. Through the long hours of the night and till the morning's dawn, he looked death in the face without dismay; his faculties unclouded, and his soul in peace. About 4 o'clock the angel came and gently unloosed the bonds of mortality, and gave the spirit of our noble chief to his God.

It is sad to think of him as no longer with us, to feel that on the march and in the battle he will no longer lead, and at the bivouac he will no longer rest. In the pleasant intimacies of the camp we shall never more greet him for he had finished a patriot's course and died a soldier's death.

But if he must die, how fit such a death to such a military life. His course had ever been one of self-sacrificing devotion to duty and at last he sacrificed himself to save his command.

Had he surrendered when ordered to do so he would have been taken prisoner, his life probably spared, but the regiment would have moved forward to terrible carnage. He thought only of saving them. He succeeded, but his own life was the cost.

Such a life was not in vain. Such a death has an intricate beauty that gilds with glory even the horrid blow of war. Grateful communities will honor the memory of such men, and many a tear will moisten the grave of the fallen hero.

I send you herewith the action of the officers of the regiment on the occasion of his death.

W. L. Hyde
Chaplain of the Regiment (Newspaper)[19]

Encampment 112th Regt N.Y. Vols.
Near Warrenton Church, Va
May 23rd 1864

For the Dunkirk Journal:

The most eventful week in the history of our regiment has just passed. It has been a week of incessant toil, excitement and sad loss, and yet a week in which the regiment has won for itself the highest praise. I reached Bermuda Hundred on my return from home, Sunday the 15th, and walked out to the entrenchments where we had established a temporary camp. I found there only the sick and convalescents, the regiment having been at the front since Wednesday. Part of the time skirmishing with the enemy and part of the time employed in tearing up the Petersburg and Richmond Railroad for the distance of one half mile each way from Walthall Junction. Colonel Drake's brigade was at this time watching the back door while General Butler was operating against the enemy's defenses on the James River.

On Saturday Colonel Drake was ordered to move up with two regiments on the pike road towards Drury's Bluff leaving only two to watch the approaches from Petersburg. The 112th and 9th Maine accordingly were moved up to a point about one and a half miles from Fort Darling and rested there over Sunday. Heckman's Brigade of the 18th Army

Corps was on our right a little in advance. It was supposed that General Gillmore was to assault Fort Johnson, an outlying fort of the enemy, on Sunday night, but a reconnaissance showed that it could only be taken at too great a sacrifice of life. Thus affairs stood, we not knowing what kind of a surprise the enemy were preparing for us. But it appeared afterwards that all day Sunday, Beauregard was concentrating all the force he could draw from Richmond with troops drawn from North Carolina for a desperate effort to crush Butler's army and sweep away everything from the rear.

The weather was admirably favorable. Sunday was a heavy wet day, the night closed dark and in the morning one of the densest of fogs wrapped everything in obscurity. About 4 o'clock the war cloud burst upon our front, massing his divisions, the enemy charged through our picket line and hurled his columns upon Heckman's Brigade with such suddenness and fury, in the fog, as to completely crush it. Heckman did what he could, but was captured while attempting to gather up his scattered forces. I was at the time five miles distant was waked from a sound sleep by the most awful volleys of musketry I ever heard, which seemed for half an hour almost incessant. At this period Colonel Drake was ordered to send a regiment to the support of Heckman which he did ordering the 112th under Lieutenant Colonel Carpenter to move immediately. In three minutes from the receipt of the order, Colonel Carpenter was moving with his whole column under a terrific fire from Fort Johnson. On the devoted band pressed its way, ignorant of the disaster to the other column and uncertain of the way. The colonel with his only regiment was soon ordered to follow.

When Colonel Carpenter reached the front where he supposed he should find someone to whom to report; he sent Adjutant Hedges forward to reconnoiter and he not returning, the adjutant was taken prisoner, immediately rode forward himself, when about 15 rods in advance of the regiment he heard a loud summons "surrender," and could first see indistinctly the forms of men moving. His first thought as he afterwards told me was "I have led my men into a trap," and wheeling his horse about he called out "men fall back." At the same moment the enemy shouted "shoot him" and a volley followed, one shot striking the colonel just below the lung as he was leaning forward on his horse, traversing the lung it struck and broke his shoulder blade and remained inside. Another shot knocked off his hat, another struck his spirited horse rendering him frantic with fright. The furious animal tore through the regiment knocking several men down and did not stop until he had reached the 9th Maine which Colonel Drake was bringing up. There he was stopped, the colonel lifted from him and a detail of men carried the colonel to the nearest field hospital some two miles. When the boys heard their colonel's voice, and immediately his horse came tearing through them, they were for a moment confused and sought shelter in the woods that skirted the road. But in a few moments, Captain W. H. Chaddock assuming the command, they were formed in good order and fell back some fifteen rods, forming a line of battle across the road in a good position, and ready to give the enemy a warm reception should they advance. So rapidly was this executed that by the time Colonel Drake had reached the regiment he found it in line of battle with skirmishers deployed in front.

Captain Chaddock deserves and has received the highest encomiums for the promptness, coolness and excellent judgment displayed on this trying occasion and with credit of officers and men be it said, there were but three stragglers from the regiment at this time or during the day.

General Weitzel now rode up and entrusted to Colonel Drake the difficult job of holding at bay with only his two regiments the whole force of the enemy while he drew on the right of our army and brought off our dead and wounded. All day long these brave regiments maneuvered from one position to another in connection with Follett's Artillery under the cool, sagacious management of Colonel Drake, and so rapid and terrible a fire did they keep up that they held the enemy till all was brought off in good order and then, charging drove them one half a mile through the woods to the cover of Heckman's rifle pits and then retired in good order, the last to enter the entrenchments. Everyone speaks with highest terms of Colonel Drake and his command. General Weitzel who this day commanded a division sent to Colonel Drake the following complimentary circular:

> Headquarters Department of Virginia and North Carolina
> United States Engineers Office in the Field
> May 25th 1864
>
> Colonel J. C. Drake, Commanding, 2nd Brigade, 3rd Division, 10th Army Corps
>
> Colonel: I desire to return to you, and the officers and men of your brigade my sincere thanks for their excellent conduct, while under my command on the 16th instant. They performed a service in holding that road which was of vital importance not only to my division but to the whole army.
>
> Respectfully Yours,
> G. Weitzel, Brigadier General, United States Volunteers
> And Chief Engineer of the Department

Our loss in numbers was comparatively small, but Colonel Carpenter was mortally wounded. It was my sad privilege to be with him from soon after he was borne to the rear until his death. He was a noble man, a true patriot, and met his fate with a hero's fortitude and a Christian's trust. His death has cast a deep gloom over our camp; every officer and man of the command loved and trusted him. He might have saved his life by a surrender but he chose to save his regiment from terrible carnage. Colonel Carpenter was a man whose manhood developed in symmetry and excellence while in the army; we love to think of him as we knew him, while our tears drop warm over his untimely loss.

We have since coming within our entrenchments repulsed two attempts of the enemy to carry our position. The last was an attack made at the still hour of midnight on Saturday and must have been fearfully damaging to the enemy as he has not repeated it since.

Sherman Brownell, Company G, was wounded on Friday by a small fragment of shell in the knee, and Orrin S. Camp was shot by a sharpshooter the 24th while working on a redoubt. He lived only half an hour.[20]

I should mention as worthy of special notice in the engagement of Monday the 16th, Second Lieutenant H. Allen, Company A, who had command of the whole line of skirmishers when the column first began to fall back and maneuvered them with great coolness and skill.[21] Also Captain E. Ludwick, Company K, who had command of the skirmishers from 2 o'clock pm and with his single company, actually drove back a regiment of Rebels to the rifle pits and brought off his command without loss.

I hope no one will think that because I speak only of the 112th I claim for them all the credit of the day. By no means. I have only attempted to depict the part our regiment took in the great fight. Your readers will have to read the fuller and more general accounts in the New York dailies.

Yours truly,
W. L. H. (Newspaper)[22]

Tuesday, May 24th

Work on defenses. Hiram Dickson, Company D, was shot through arm, slight wound. Orrin S. Camp, Company G, while at work on new redoubt in front was shot by concealed sharpshooters in two places through the chest. He lived but half an hour. (Journal)

Wednesday, May 25th

Regiment had rest through day. Very heavy detail for picket taking almost the whole regiment. About 10 o'clock very heavy firing along the picket line. One of our men Henry Evens, Company I, had his finger shot off.[23] (Journal)

Thursday, May 26th

Circular sent to the regiment today complimenting Colonel Drake and officers and men of his command for gallant conduct on Monday the 16th. This afternoon had orders to be in readiness to move as soon as dark, leaving tents standing. The order was afterwards changed to striking tents and moving out with great quiet. If our pickets had been properly relieved at the hour of evening, the move would have been made strictly in accordance with orders. But unfortunately the pickets were not relieved until late and a portion of them not until 3 am. The result was the regiment were cross and tired and considerable confusion occurred in getting out from the entrenchments. We moved about ¼ of a mile under cover of a hill and then bivouacked for the night. Captain Chaddock and myself spread a confiscated bed under the regiment wagon and were soon in sound sleep. (Journal)

Thursday Evening
26th May 1864

Dear Wife,

We are now under marching orders, I presume to find General Grant's army. I will endeavor to keep you informed. Continue to write to me. We expect to move out of camp tonight. Where we may be tomorrow I cannot tell.

But I hope we are moving on to the final victory over our desperate foe. This little lull of a week has been a good thing for me. I came pretty near getting used up last week.

So much labor and excitement and exposure right on the heel of my laborious though most delightful visit home.

I now feel ripe for work. My poor horse was dreadfully seasick coming from Hilton Head and did not get over it for 2 weeks. He now begins to look and to feel like himself.

I must go to work now to prepare for a move.

Affectionately as ever,
William

26th—We are squat down this morning in the dirt, no news. I have just received your letter of the 20th. It seems strange that you do not mention having received any from me. I wrote I think from Baltimore and from Fort Monroe and have written 3 from this point. May God keep your mind in peace.

Send me some stamps.

Friday, May 27th

We were allowed to remain quiet in our position until 2 pm when we were moved the few miles from our late camp on the road to Bermuda Hundred where we were posted in brigade lines. We expect to remain here a day or two in quiet. The sick and convalescents remain in camp. Those who will be in all circumstances unfit for duty will be sent to general hospital; those who in an emergency can go into the entrenchments remain, under command of Lieutenant Sherwin, Company A. The convalescents of the brigade under command of Captain H. A. Johnson of the 13th Indiana.[24] (Journal)

Saturday, May 28th

Remained in the encampment till 3 o'clock pm, at which time the regiment was inspected by the division inspector then broke camp and moved down to the landing. At dusk, prepared to camp for the night. At 8 pm, orders came to be ready to move immediately, broke camp and moved to the pier where we embarked onboard the transport *Pawtuxet*, and proceeding down the river three miles, cast anchor for the night. It was about eleven o'clock when we left the pier. (Journal)

Sunday, May 29th

The transport weighed anchor at daylight and proceeded down the James River. About six o'clock pm, reached Yorktown the place of rendezvous, then ordered to proceed to West Point. Reached West Point about 10 o'clock pm. Although, thence the holy Sabbath, there has been no religious service on account of the sickness of the chaplain. (Journal)

Monday, May 30th

Early this morning our transport was ordered to proceed to White House on the Pamunkey River, where we arrived about 12 noon but were not landed till about 3 pm when we moved to within about 2 miles of our camping ground last June. After supper we moved camp again half mile and in the evening once more. No incidents worthy of notice occurred. We left 4 sick and convalescents at the camp Bermuda Hundred under Lieutenants Sherwin and Potter.[25] Several cases of slight fevers and diarrheas have occurred since the regiment left the banks of the James. Weather Friday and Saturday showery. Sunday and Monday very beautiful. (Journal)

Tuesday, May 31st

The other regiments of the brigade which had marched up the right bank of the York and Pamunkey from West Point crossed during the forenoon. About 4 pm, the brigade moved on the New Castle Road. The marching was very slow in consequence of artillery and baggage wagons getting mired. It was about midnight when we halted after a march of 9 miles. (Journal)

Wednesday, June 1st

A beautiful morning with the promise of a hot day, we were first moved about 7 o'clock two miles to the banks of a beautiful stream where we were allowed to rest 2 hours. The men had time to wash themselves and get refreshed. The column then moved forward to near Cold Harbor. At noon halted at Old Church Tavern, the men made coffee. At this point some of the 49th New York from our county met their friends in our regiment. The march this

William H. Potter enlisted at Kiantone, New York, as a private in Company D, 112th New York Volunteers. He was discharged for disability on September 28, 1864.

afternoon though short about 4 miles, was very distressing. The air was hot, the roads very dusty. The effluvia of dead animals tainted the air on every side. About 4 we passed the headquarters of General Wright, and moved on to connect our line of battle with that of the Sixth Corps.[26] Our brigade found the first line of our division. As soon as the line was formed the order came to move forward. The battle had already opened. Passing out of a skirt of woods we were to cross an open field 600 yards to another belt of woods in which the enemy had a heavy skirmish line, this they successfully accomplished. Our regiment was so located as to have to traverse this field at its widest point and lost a few men in passing. But after reaching the woods and driving the enemy back to their first line of works, which were run across a little opening in the woods, they charged towards these. After some ineffective firing from behind trees, Colonel Drake commanding the brigade gave the order to cease firing and fix bayonets. The order was instantly obeyed and the men rushed onward, their officers cheering and encouraging them. Colonel Drake was everywhere when his presence was needed inciting his men, both with his voice and by his example, to press on to victory. Soon the works were carried on our part. But beyond our lines on the right, the nature of the ground was such that we were subjected to a galling cross fire from a position of the works yet in the hands of the enemy.

Left: Jeremiah C. Drake mustered in as colonel of the 112th New York Volunteers after prior service with the 49th New York Infantry. He died of wounds received at Cold Harbor, Virginia. *Right:* John G. Palmeter enrolled at Chautauqua, New York, as a captain in Company H, 112th New York Volunteers. He died from wounds received at Cold Harbor, Virginia (courtesy U.S. Army Heritage and Education Center [USAHEC]).

It was from this fire that Colonel Drake who had mounted the parapet and was cheering his men, waving his sword, fell shot in the side by a bullet which passed through the intestines, and came out just below the pit of the stomach. Captain Palmeter had just reached the ditch, his men were pressing forward when he fell shot in the arm, by a bullet which did not break the bone though striking with such force as to flatten out the ball. The great loss in the regiment occurred after gaining these works both from the cross fire of the enemy before mentioned. Also from a second line of works still in advance. These works were attempted but not carried at this time. We held possession of the works we had taken until drawn off by command and our places supplied by others. The losses of the regiment were at this time very heavy, 153 killed, wounded and missing. (Journal)

Casualties at Cold Harbor (Journal)

Jeremiah C. Drake	Colonel	Field & Staff	Wounded in the bowels, died at night
Enoch A. Curtis	Captain	Company D	Wounded shoulder and leg
John G. Palmeter	Captain	Company H	Wounded arm
Robert A. Corbett	1st Lieutenant	Company D	Wounded thigh
Henry Hull	2nd Lieutenant	Company K	Wounded shoulder through body
G. L. Pierce	1st Lieutenant	Company C	Missing
Marvin Arthur	Private	Company A	Wounded hip and foot, died June 16th
Horace W. Barber	Corporal	Company A	Wounded leg amputated, died June 11th
John S. Gardner	Private	Company A	Wounded arm
William Peterson	Corporal	Company A	Wounded arm
De Loss Sweet	Private	Company A	Wounded side and arm
Samuel S. Staples	Private	Company A	Missing
William W. Seeley	Private	Company A	Wounded neck, slight
Thomas Brown	Private	Company A	Wounded head, slight
Albert C. Bond	Private	Company B	Wounded thigh, slight
Harvey B. Grover	Private	Company B	Wounded thumb, slight
John K. Post	Private	Company B	Wounded leg amputated, died June 21st
John W. Palmeter	Private	Company B	Wounded thigh, died
Squire H. Shaw	Corporal	Company B	Wounded breast, died June 3rd
Mason C. Thompson	Private	Company B	Wounded arm
Simeon L. Allen	Corporal	Company C	Killed
Joseph Barna	Private	Company C	Missing
David S. Crowell	Private	Company C	Killed
Robert Erath	Private	Company C	Missing
Warren J. Kingsland	Private	Company C	Wounded in breast
William McLaughlin	Private	Company C	Wounded in thigh, slight
Perry W. Nevins	Private	Company C	Wounded in leg
James M. Potter	Corporal	Company C	Wounded in bowels
John G. Paschke	Private	Company C	Wounded in arm
Newell B. Richardson	Private	Company C	Wounded in finger
Almon Sloan	Private	Company C	Wounded in face and arm
Gideon W. Smith	Private	Company C	Wounded in thigh
Warren Smith	Private	Company C	Wounded in foot, slight
Lewis Scofield	Private	Company C	Wounded in thigh
Charles O. Warner	Private	Company C	Wounded in thigh
Homer Austin	Private	Company D	Killed
Irvin E. Braley	Private	Company D	Wounded, died June 12th
Stillman Brooks	Private	Company D	Missing
Sylvester E. Chapin	Private	Company D	Wounded in arm
James A. Doig	Private	Company D	Killed
Martin Eddy	Private	Company D	Wounded leg & arm amputated, died
Henry Findley	Private	Company D	Killed, he died 2nd in hospital
Benjamin Fritts	Private	Company D	Wounded in arm
B. F. Hurlburt	Corporal	Company D	Killed
James B. Hosier	Private	Company D	Wounded in face and arm
John Huytink	Private	Company D	Wounded in thigh
George Heath	Private	Company D	Wounded in cheek, slight
Lyman B. Keyes	Private	Company D	Wounded in thighs
James G. Kean	Private	Company D	Killed
Ezekiel King	Private	Company D	Missing
Isaac P. Miracle	Private	Company D	Killed
Charles Munger	Corporal	Company D	Wounded side and arm
Lucius Markham	Private	Company D	Killed
Philip Mark	Private	Company D	Killed
David Ploss	Private	Company D	Wounded in thigh
John Springer	Corporal	Company D	Wounded in side
John A. Slotboom	Private	Company D	Wounded in arm

Ezra Slayton	Private	Company D	Wounded in shoulder
Charles B. Traver	Private	Company D	Wounded in foot
Solomon W. Whitford	Private	Company D	Wounded in ankle
George L. Carey	Sergeant	Company E	Wounded in hip
John A. Carey	Private	Company E	Wounded in arm
Chas Edmonds	Corporal	Company E	Wounded in neck and arm
John C. Eddy	Private	Company E	Missing
Marlow Fitch	Corporal	Company E	Wounded in knee
John Fink	Private	Company E	Wounded in leg
John Galloway	Private	Company E	Killed
Levi J. Knapp	Private	Company E	Wounded in arm, bullet extracted
Myron Kesler	Private	Company E	Wounded in head
Hamilton Lenox	Private	Company E	Killed
John Loucks	Private	Company E	Wounded in arm
Charles Lawson	Private	Company E	Missing
John J. Munson	Private	Company E	Wounded in face
Thomas J. Newell	Sergeant	Company E	Wounded in arm
Peter J. Peterson	Private	Company E	Wounded in arm
F. J. W. Rhuling	Sergeant	Company E	Wounded in leg, amputated, died June 18th
John Stowell	Private	Company E	Killed
Charles Slayton	Private	Company E	Wounded in arm
William H. Skinner	Private	Company E	Wounded in leg
William Stowell	Private	Company E	Wounded in thigh
John Tewinkle	Private	Company E	Killed
John Wineman	Private	Company E	Killed
Charles. H. Baker	1st Sergeant	Company F	Killed
Willard Bucklin	1st Sergeant	Company F	Wounded in arm
Woodley W. Booty	Private	Company F	Wounded hip, died June 13th
Judson F. Geer	Private	Company F	Wounded in ankle
Algernon D. Hazard	Corporal	Company F	Wounded in leg, amputated, died June 7th
Sylvester M. Hart	Private	Company F	Killed
Harvey D. Harter	Corporal	Company F	Wounded in shoulder
Joseph Hobart	Private	Company F	Wounded in arm
Augustus Jones	Private	Company F	Wounded in arm
Joseph C. Smith	Sergeant	Company F	Wounded in thigh
William Swanson	Private	Company F	Wounded in arm
Thomas Burns	Private	Company G	Killed
Henry Baldwin	Private	Company G	Wounded hip, died June 18th
Fred Bartmann	Private	Company G	Wounded bowels, died June 2nd
Joseph W. Buffman	Private	Company G	Wounded in hip
James Cohall	Private	Company G	Wounded in hip
Charles Gantcher	Private	Company G	Wounded in arm
John Kelley	Private	Company G	Wounded in arm and hip
William R. Laine	Private	Company G	Killed
Andrew Link	Private	Company G	Wounded in hand
Daniel Mulvihill	Private	Company G	Wounded in shoulder
Charles Pecor	Private	Company G	Killed
Almond Ploss	Private	Company G	Killed
William Pease	Private	Company G	Missing
Thomas S. Rolph	Corporal	Company G	Wounded in hip
Gilman Shirley	Private	Company G	Killed
Wilson P. Tenny	Private	Company G	Wounded in arm and breast
Dewitt C. Tew	Private	Company G	Missing
John Wright	Corporal	Company G	Wounded in arm
Francis Wilson	Private	Company G	Wounded in head
Frank Whalon	Private	Company G	Wounded in arm
Eli C. Beecher	Corporal	Company H	Wounded in arm
Robert L. Coe	Corporal	Company H	Killed
Henry B. Cushing	Private	Company H	Wounded in hand

Edward A. Dutcher	Sergeant	Company H	Wounded in leg
J. E. Freeman	Corporal	Company H	Killed
Chester S. Hannum	Sergeant	Company H	Killed
Albert C. Jones	Private	Company H	Wounded in neck
William C. Keyes	Sergeant	Company H	Killed
Frank McCoul	Corporal	Company H	Wounded in hand
Wait J. Stevens	Sergeant	Company H	Wounded in hand
William F. Smith	Private	Company H	Wounded in leg
Jared N. Tillotson	Private	Company H	Wounded in leg
Nelson L. Wallace	Private	Company H	Killed
Noble Doty	Private	Company I	Killed
Ferdinand W. Dennison	Private	Company I	Killed
Edwin Davis	Private	Company I	Wounded in arm and neck
Charles Mercer	Private	Company I	Wounded in arm
Fred A. Pierce	Private	Company I	Wounded in head and arm, died June 7th
Theodore Burr	Private	Company K	Wounded in leg, amputated, died June 19th
Herbert Christy	Corporal	Company K	Wounded in head and wrist, amputated
Alonzo Carr	Corporal	Company K	Wounded in thigh
Edwin T. Goodwin	Sergeant	Company K	Killed
Avery R. Gould	Corporal	Company K	Killed
John F. Oakes	Private	Company K	Wounded in hand and arm
Alonzo H. Powers	Private	Company K	Wounded in hand
Frank L. Scribner	Private	Company K	Wounded in arm
Loren White	Sergeant	Company K	Killed

Above: Marlow Fitch enlisted at Westfield, New York, as a private in Company E, 112th New York Volunteers. Wounded at Cold Harbor, Virginia, he was discharged for disability on February 17, 1865 (courtesy U.S. Army Heritage and Education Center [USAHEC]). *Right:* Dewitt C. Tew enlisted at Westfield, New York, as a private in Company G, 112th New York Volunteers. He was killed at Cold Harbor, Virginia.

Top, left: Edward A. Dutcher enlisted at Chautauqua, New York, as a corporal in Company H, 112th New York Volunteers. He was wounded at Cold Harbor, Virginia, and discharged for disability on May 19, 1865. *Above:* Hebert Christy enlisted at Hanover, New York, as a private in Company K, 112th New York Volunteers. He was wounded at Cold Harbor, Virginia, and discharged for disability on November 9, 1864. *Left:* John F. Oakes enlisted at Cherry Creek, New York, as a private in Company K, 112th New York Volunteers. He was wounded at Cold Harbor, Virginia (courtesy U.S. Army Heritage and Education Center [USAHEC]).

Thursday, June 2nd–Saturday, June 4th

Colonel Drake died this morning about 6 o'clock. His body was conveyed to White House where it was embalmed and sent home. The regiment remained during the day in the advanced rifle pits. At night moved out and camped on a side hill behind our first line of breastworks. In the engagement of the fourth we were held in reserve. One man was wounded in the hand by a bullet which was the only casualty. Captain Chaddock, who had been in command of the regiment, is seriously sick. On the march from Bermuda Landing he had his horse fall upon him, and though his leg was not broken, it was badly strained and his back injured, a slight fever, Chickahominy diarrhea and kidney trouble, all combine to reduce him. Captain Mathews is in command. (Journal)

Casualties at Cold Harbor (Journal)

Henry K. Gawn	Private	Company B	Wounded in leg
Robert Kilburn	Private	Company B	Wounded in arm
Manhattan Pickett	Sergeant	Company B	Wounded in leg
Palmer Austin	Private	Company D	Wounded in arm
Augustus Neil	Private	Company D	Wounded in arm
Addison P. Green	Private	Company E	Wounded in leg
Harry Crandall	Corporal	Company H	Wounded in groin
Henry Hull	2nd Lieutenant	Company K	Wounded in body
Thomas Coffee	Private	Company K	Wounded in arm
Moses Eells	Private	Company K	Wounded in hand
Levi Darby	Private	Company I	Wounded in leg

White House Landing, Va
June 3rd 1864

My dear Wife,

I have just time this morning to write you a hasty line.

The telegram has already informed you that we have been in a desperate battle and that Colonel Drake is killed. We marched day before yesterday from New Castle 12 miles. Out 8 miles and were then immediately thrown forward to the front and the brigade was ordered to carry the enemy's works which they did with fearful loss. I was, at the beginning of the fight, near the regiment and immediately went to the field hospital with our doctors to make ready for the wounded. They soon began to come in. The fight began about 4 o'clock pm and continued till near dark, indeed there was skirmishing all night. They kept coming in all night and I had with others all we could do in taking care of our own dear boys. Colonel Drake was brought in about 6 o'clock. He had shown the most desperate valor. At every part of the line when there was the least wavering in this charge he was present waving his sword and cheering his men on. While doing this the fatal bullet hit him and he fell. The wound was through the abdomen and of course mortal. He felt it so from the first. "Chaplain," he said as I met him, "I am going to die. Take these things," giving me his watch and field glass. "I want my body sent home. Give my love to my wife, tell my friends and tell the world that I died a brave man. I die at peace with all men, and at peace I trust with my God." He said no more. We placed him in the most comfortable position possible, gave him some stimulants and nourishment, and detailed 2 men to stay constantly with him.

I had all I could do through the night and lopped on the ground with Surgeon Washburn at 2 am. At 20 minutes past 4, I was up again and at work. One of our hospital nurses gave me something to eat, and about 5 am told me the colonel, he thought, was dying. I went to him. Called "Colonel do you know me?" He was just sinking. Looking up I said "Chaplain." He said "wait a minute," and collected himself as if making a great effort. I then said again "Hyde" wait he says be patient, and again seemed to be trying to rouse himself but in vain. As he shut his eyes, I said, "thanks be to God who giveth us the victory through our Lord Jesus Christ."[27] He replied in his clear loud voice, "Amen. Amen."

He lived about an hour and as he was just about going I kneeled by his side. His friends among men standing around and committed in few words his spirit to our Father. He soon passed away. We then tenderly arranged his form and dress and finding I could get no ambulance, I determined to take him to White House on the same mule cart which bore Lieutenant Colonel Carpenter. It was rather a hazardous journey but the risk must not be thought of, for him who have perished and lost his life for his country. Colonel McConihe, 169th New York, was killed at the same time and his chaplain took his remains along with me, we had 2 armed men with us as escort and 4 others as attendants.[28]

But no guerrillas troubled us and the cavalry were in another direction. We did not get to White House till 8 o'clock. On the way 10 miles from here we deliberately unsaddled, fed our horses and got supper. Then after an hour's rest moved on.

I can't begin to tell you the trouble we had. But suffice it to say that after a toil of 2 hours we found an embalmer, got the bodies over a path thought impossible and before I slept Colonel Drake looked as natural as you ever saw him in life. We found some 169th men, at the landing, left to guard baggage. We pressed them into our service. We found an old tent belonging to the 169th filled with officer's effects. We piled them about and had a good night's rest. I thank God for all his merciful goodness to me through all this scene.

Captain Curtis is wounded, shoulder broken. Captain Palmeter wounded in arm. Rolph for whom I carried 2 shirts is wounded in the hip severely. Joseph Buffman has a broken shoulder. John Wright, Company G, will I fear, lose his arm. Charles Gantcher has a bad flesh wound of arm. Andrew Link is shot through his hand, Tenny is in the breast—dangerous, Fred Bartmann bowels—fatal I fear. John Kelley in the hip, Cohall, arm and hip. Billy Laine was killed outright, and the body probably buried on the ground. Ploss, Burns and Miracle were killed, these are from the Dunkirk Company. Adjutant Pierce is missing, probably killed or wounded and in the hands of the enemy.

John McConihe was the colonel commanding the 169th New York Infantry. He was killed at Cold Harbor, Virginia (courtesy Library of Congress).

But of this horrible tale I can tell no more now. I don't know yet what I can do with the colonel's body. I shall send it at once if possible. If not, it is embalmed and will keep for 2 years.

Dearest don't worry, trust in God. I believe he will take care of me and that I am in the way of duty. The colonel died surrounded with the wreath of his own splendid command.

Affectionately,
William L. Hyde

Saturday, June 4th

Casualties at Cold Harbor (Journal)

| Nicholas Sour | Private | Company H | Wounded in head |

White House Landing
Pamunkey River, Va
June 4th 1864

My dear Wife,

I wrote you yesterday the reason of my being at this place. I came here with the body of Colonel Drake which I had embalmed and waited all day yesterday to ascertain what could be done to forward it to his friends.

I had about concluded to send word by telegram that it was at White House and could be obtained by his friends, when Chaplain Chapman, 169th New York, whose Colonel

McConihe was killed the same day—told me that by permission of his lieutenant colonel, who was wounded and had come out from the front to go to general hospital, the surgeon in charge had detailed him to accompany the wounded to Fort Monroe or wherever the boat should be sent. So my anxiety was most over. I could place the remains of the colonel in his care and all would be well. I concluded, however, to wait until I saw them fairly off, and had the gratification of seeing Captain Palmeter come in to take the same boat and saw a number of our slightly wounded boys start on the same boat.

They left about 12 noon today—Saturday. There is a supply train going out tomorrow morning to the front and I expect to start with that train. It is raining hard tonight and I fear it will take all day and into night to ride out. God forbid that I should ever pass through again the horrors of the memorable night of the 1st of June.

Captain Palmeter is not seriously wounded. He is weak from loss of blood but his wound is doing well. The bone was not broken only cracked a little. I long to be back to do what good I can for the men. I shall have a large number of letters to send to friends of soldiers. How sad to think of the carnage and slaughter of that evening, but it was inevitable. The capture of those works was essential to the movements made since which have been eminently successful. You see that Richmond must be taken and if it costs every man in the army, now others must rush in to fill their places. The great cause is what should shine above life or any pleasure of personal ambition.

My dear wife I know your anxiety for me, but remember I am not rash and I trust God will preserve me.

I must now retire to rest. May God bless you abundantly. I feel truly grateful for his aid to me in all that I have thus far attempted.

            Affectionately your husband,
            William L. Hyde

            White House Landing
            [Pamunkey] River, Va
            June 4th 1864

To Honorable George W. Patterson[29]

Dear Sir:

Knowing the great interest you have felt in our brave Colonel Drake and his regiment, I take the liberty to write you briefly and have ordered a telegram sent to you announcing his decease and where his body can be obtained. It may seem strange that an officer so gallant and of such high rank should not have been sent by myself or some officer of his staff to his friends, but in the case of Colonel Carpenter we tried to obtain permission and were told that all such applications for an escort of an officer or private were refused on account of the exigencies of the service. It was hazardous to delay transmitting the body for even an hour. Such is the nature of this climate, so hot is the weather, that he must be sent on at once to White House or we should be obliged to bury him in the out of the way place where we were. Then too, if I could get to White House before night and find an embalmer, the body might be so preserved as to be satisfactory to his friends. We could not, where we were, get board, even for a coffin. Neither could we get an ambulance. So wrapping the body in a soldier's blanket, I took it through on a common mule cart, riding 22 miles between 12 noon and 9 pm with only the escort of 3 unarmed men. The body of Colonel McConihe, 169th New York, was brought on by his chaplain at the same time and in the same style, with the exception, that having started earlier, he made out to get a rude coffin, on the way 5 miles from the front, made for a citizen, and some ice. We had his body in the only suit of clothes he had with him. Throwing away the pants in which he was brought out, as they were so saturated with blood. His sword scabbard was indented by one bullet and broken by another. I send it in his valise. His sword was lost. His wound was just above the hipbone, passing through the bowels and coming out near the pit of the stomach. He was evidently half turned when struck.

I have written Mrs. Drake all the particulars of his death. The colonel has been gaining favor with military men, the more he became known, for a long time past. His military ability was very uncommon, and the excitement of the field always brought out his highest qualities of coolness, courage and judgment. At the unfortunate Battle of Proctor's Creek on the 15th, he displayed such energy and such single good judgment in maneuvering his troops, that with only two regiments, he held the enemy at bay for 8 hours and kept open the only road for drawing in the right wing of Butler's army.[30] The enemy was deceived by the rapidity of his fire and his changing positions into supposing large reinforcements were being brought up. General Weitzel wrote him a handsome note, thanking him for the service he did. It was this that put him in command of the brigade over several colonels who had been in the service longer and over some brigadiers, at the time. The 18th Army Corps was reorganized and two divisions of the 10th Corps added to it only a week since.

We went into action at this time overworked. He had for days had but little sleep. He was harrowed with anxiety and care. The night before, his brigade was marched till after midnight, and then during the day, the hottest and dustiest I ever travelled, 10 miles, and then immediately put into action. His finest qualities as a military man came out when the brigade was ordered to charge. He put himself at the head, his adjutant general on one wing and an aide on the other, and with his clear ringing voice which was heard distinctly above the roar of battle, he cheered the boys urging them to press on, and waving his sword above his head, he passed along wherever the column wavered until the fatal bullet quenched his voice and gave his manly form to the embrace of death.

He has done all for his country that man can do. He has given his life, mourning on our regiment. We are badly cut up. I have all the names I could get to one of our county papers.

> Very truly,
> William L. Hyde
> Chaplain of the Regiment

I now hope to be able to send the body in care of Chaplain Chapman, 169th New York, on the hospital boat to Washington to be expressed from there. The box containing it is rough but the best we could get here, where are no tools. Our loss is over 100 killed, wounded and injured. The expense of embalming and sending home the remains will be paid by the regiment. I shall write to the public through the Westfield paper at once.[31]

Sunday, June 5th–Monday, June 6th

Sunday. I returned from White House, many of our wounded, who were able to take care of themselves, had already left for general hospital, others were doing well. Met friends from the 72nd, it was very pleasant thus to come in contact with those whose course had been so divergent from ours though leaving the same section of our county about the same time. (Journal)

Tuesday, June 7th

Went to White House with a train of the wounded. They were conveyed in army wagons. Poor fellows. It was terrible. Three died before reaching White House. All the men of the 112th New York got there comfortably. Barber who seemed nearest sinking bore the journey remarkably well.[32] Palmeter suffered much. Lieutenant Hull was quite exhausted but was not any worse.[33] (Journal)

Wednesday, June 8th

Casualties at Cold Harbor (Journal)

H. E. Rice	Private	Company E	Wounded in back

White House, Va
June 8th 1864

My dear Wife,

I am here again having been sent in yesterday afternoon in care of a train of wagons laden with wounded men. They have now sent away the last remnants of those wounded in the battle of the 1st June. Mrs. Hunt's husband was not exposed. Frank Wheeler was left out because blind as a bat in the night.[34] That Mrs. Gantcher's husband is lightly wounded. Sergeant Hawley was severely struck with a musket and is somewhat lucid. William Pease is killed. Gil Shirley probably killed. Charley Pecor is probably killed. He was a Portland boy, a mess mate of Laine.[35] I went back Sunday after my sorrowful mission with the body of Colonel Drake and reached the hospital about 3 pm. I found Captain Chaddock very sick. He has some form of gastric trouble. His bladder is diseased and he is generally out of kilter. I am fearful that he will now be obliged to give up. He has just had notice of his appointment as major of the regiment and Major Smith, lieutenant colonel.

Captain Mathews is now in command. Oh dear, the regiment will never again be to me what it once was. It is torn to pieces and my best friends on the staff are gone.

May God in mercy grant that the necessity of my services may soon be over. We know less of what is going on here than you do at home. We only know that we were on the center Sunday and now hold the extreme right.

The Rebs have assaulted us twice lately and been terribly repulsed with but fifty less to us.

Sunday pm. The "Excelsior's" were in our vicinity and Doctor Irwin and Captain Bailey came to see me. We had I assure you a most hearty greeting and soon after Henry Stillman came.[36] He is looking very angular and pale though he has an easy position. I meant to have visited the regiments and hunted Shelton up Monday but could not be spared from the hospital long enough.[37] Send to the Union the enclosed. [The] Dunkirk [Union] will carry it. And yesterday I was sent down here. If the general positions are not changed I shall endeavor to visit the 2nd Corps tomorrow.

I am thankful to say I am well though worn. With much love to all at the house.

Affectionately your husband,
Wm. L. Hyde

Joseph S. Mathews enrolled at Ellicott, New York, as a captain in Company F, 112th New York Volunteers. He mustered out with regiment on June 13, 1865, at Raleigh (courtesy U.S. Army Heritage and Education Center [USAHEC]).

Thursday, June 9th

The regiment still in the rear of the first line of defenses. (Journal)

In the Field near Cold Harbor, Va
June 9th 1864

Editor
Westfield Republican

More than a week has passed away since that sad event, which has left us all in profound sorrow. When Colonel Drake fell, struck down by the fatal bullet, one of the most accomplished soldiers, one of the truest patriots, one of the noblest of men passed from among us. He was one who carried with him into the trying circumstances of the camp and the field, those great principles of life and character which as a minister of the gospel, he had preached to his fellow men. During the issue of this great struggle in which our country has been plunged, so vital to all the future of this land, as to call for the services of every man who could give them whatever might be his calling, he left that sacred office which is ordinarily considered as exempting a man from the rough conflicts of carnal warfare, to lead one hundred of his fellow men, as their chief in the perilous endeavor to save our glorious country from disintegration. While in this position he displayed such eminent abilities, that when the call for true men waxed louder in the summer of '62 and the flour of Chautauqua were gathered—one noble homogeneous regiment, and a man was wanted to command them, who should represent the high morality and Christian sentiment of the county, Captain Drake was fixed upon as the man. Under his command, the brigade has maintained the high character which it had at its organization, and though always ready and doing every duty laid upon it, so free had it been from those terrible casualties of the battlefield which have fallen upon so many regiments raised at the same time, that we have gone by the name of the lucky regiment.

But with the opening of this spring's campaign, we have been obliged to bear our share of the savage ravages of war. We have from the beginning suffered much from sickness, having marked every place, where we have tarried, with the graves of our comrades, now we have to mourn hundreds fallen, within the brief space of an hour, either "in the sleep of death," or marred with ghastly wounds. We were transferred from the 10th to the 18th Army Corps the last week in May. Colonel Drake at that time supposed that he would be remanded to his regiment. There were many colonels older in the service than he, who had been in the command of brigades, and he thought one of them would be put in his place, especially as we had so recently been deprived of that excellent officer, Lieutenant Colonel Carpenter.

But Colonel Drake had displayed such excellent judgment, such great coolness and bravery in every situation in which he had been placed, that in the reorganization of the division transferred to the 18th Corps, he was retained in command. It was a high compliment to him, for it was understood that the experiences of the service should regulate the appointments to positions of responsibility. He was ordered to place his brigade onboard transports Saturday evening, the 29th and Monday afternoon it reached White House Landing. Tuesday afternoon the whole Corps moved out to New Castle, and about 4 o'clock Wednesday, the 1st of June, the hottest, dustiest day of the year, we had marched 8 miles in the heat of the day, and were at once put into position to engage in battle. Soon the colonel received an order to make a charge with his brigade, and take possession of a line of earthworks. It was a work of great peril, and demanded coolness and great daring—work usually committed to veterans—work in which only one regiment of the brigade had ever taken part. No living man would have sooner shrunk from leading men on to such terrible work on his own responsibility, than Colonel Drake, but when the order came, it must be obeyed, and Colonel Drake was not the man to send his command to any position he would shrink to expose himself. The first work was to get across an open field into a skirt of woods. This was done with slight loss; the enemy's skirmishers were forced to retire behind his works. Then passing through this woods and across an open space in face of a terrible fire, they were to charge over the breastworks and take them. These works were on enemy's ground, and were irregular, so that at certain points the assaulting party were subjected to a flank as well as front fire. Gallantly the brigade advanced to the charge; at times the line was staggered by the terrible fire, but whenever it needed cheering, then was Colonel Drake's splendid voice heard above the roar of the musketry, inciting his men and waving his sword above his head. He seemed to infuse his own dauntless spirit into the whole command.

On they pressed till at length the last desperate push was to be made. "Stop firing and fix bayonets," was the command. "Now boys give it to them," and over they went, carrying the works and holding them, but just as the works were reached, the colonel fell, struck in the side by a bullet, which passed through his bowels, inflicting a mortal wound. His sword was lost and scabbard broken by a bullet, another indented it, and another still glanced across the edge of his watch and the end of his field glass. He was brought back to the hospital, where our surgeon was at hand to examine his wound. He felt at once that his wound was fatal; received the assurance of it with great composure; asked for opiates to soothe his pain; in few brief words he delivered the last messages to his family. "Tell my friends said he, and tell my countrymen that I died a brave man." He then asked to be kept quiet. He said but little; as the night advanced he needed stronger opiates for his pains; towards morning the quiet of approaching death came over him. The young men who had served him in life, watched all night about him, administering to him opiates and cooling drinks, and keeping all about him quiet, as he desired.

His last words were a clear amen in response to those words of Christian confidence in which the Holy Apostle declares the "victory over death through our Lord Jesus Christ."[38] As his end drew nigh, the men who loved him gathered about him, and as the strains of Christian prayer committed his departing soul to our Father and our God, the tears of strong men rained around him, and expressed the sense of desolation and gloom which had settled upon their hearts. We hear on every side, only eulogy. His character, his judgment, his courage and devotion are upon all lips. The country can ill afford to lose such officers, at such a period, as the present. Amid the abounding intemperance in the army he kept his faculties clear and unclouded. He maintained the high example of total abstinence, and used his endeavors both in the regiment and in the brigade, to enforce by example and influence, the high principles of morality and virtue. The brigade trusted in him, and felt safer under his guidance than under that of any other leader. They all mourn his loss.

But to those of us who enjoyed his peculiar intimacy and friendship, who mingled with his daily life for a year and a half, had seen and known him in all the varied experiences of camp and field, who had relied upon his counsels and his help, who knew him not so much as a commanding officer, as a brother and a friend, what words can measure our loss! But then we turn to that lovely home, the spot loved above every other on earth, to those dear hearts, of whom he ever spoke in tones of manly tenderness and anxieties for whom troubled his dying hours. We think of them—the widow and the fatherless, and words of consolation seem but the mockery of woe. We rejoice that beyond this war distracted world there is a peaceful Heaven where the plaint of anguish and the wail of bereavement is known no more.

Would that we could speak in terms of fitting eulogy of the many excellent who have fallen in our regiment.

There are many death sad homes in our country now. May we not hope that the present campaign will be so successful as to stay the constant flow of blood and sorrow.[39]

W. L. Hyde
Chaplain of the Regiment (Newspaper)[40]

Friday, June 10th

Last evening the regiment went into the advance line of rifle pits as picket. 12 sharpshooters in advance in their own pits. Friday, the 47th New York occupied our ground. Colonel Piper, New York Heavy Artillery, who had been in command of the brigade, was this day relieved and Colonel Curtis, 142nd New York assigned to the command.[41] Colonel Curtis makes at the outset a very highly favorable impression. (Journal)

Saturday, June 11th

Regiment in camp a little to the left of yesterday and on the bow of the hill. Rumors of a move begin to be rife. We are to go to James River. Wagons this day moved to Tunstall. (Journal)

Alexander Piper, colonel commanding the 10th New York Heavy Artillery. He survived the war and returned to West Point Military Academy as an instructor of artillery tactics (courtesy U.S. Army Heritage and Education Center [USAHEC]).

> Near Cold Harbor, Va
> June 11th 1864

Dear Wife,

I have been having for two days a kind of breathing spell after the fatigue. Since the 1st of the month, I was very sick with diarrhea. This Sunday we came from the James round to the York River. But a little quinine and opium soon straightened me out and Monday I was pretty well except weak. We landed at White House about 3 o'clock Monday pm and camped for the night about a half mile from the place, where we were camped, about a year ago. It was a beautiful evening, the air soft. We pitched our tent, and Captain Chaddock, Adjutant Crane, Dr. Washburn and myself all stretched out on the ground.[42] I have the cork bed of Lieutenant Colonel Carpenter, a sort of rubber blanket with a filling of cork which keeps the dampness out. Tuesday morning woke in good season, the sun up in all his glory. Had a good wash and breakfasted on the luxuries of hardtack, and pork with coffee. A little tendency still to diarrhea. Am obliged to hold on to the quinine. I wrote my monthly report, and got everything ready for a march. Major Smith gave us a mule and cart at Bermuda for a headquarters team, which enables us to carry our mess chest and our blankets, and a large fly to cover us at night. Colonel Drake had landed with three regiments at West Point at the head of the York River and had to march yesterday 14 miles. He was all tuckered out and those regiments did not cross over to White House until about noon of today. After dinner we received orders to hold ourselves in readiness to move at a moment's notice and we packed up all our loose articles and were soon ready.

About 4 o'clock, the whole brigade was in motion toward Cold Harbor. The roads were very bad in consequence of rains. The artillery got mired and we would move ten paces then halt. So we were till 12 o'clock getting nine miles, and covered with dirt. We poked about and got a place to lie down, but it was full of most unsavory smells, so I covered my head with my blanket and shut out everything but sleep. Captain Chaddock is very lame having had the misfortune to have his horse fall upon him Saturday afternoon. It was a wonder he did not break his leg. It was about 7 o'clock when we woke. Brown had got us a good breakfast of stewed hardtack, ham and pickles, with French mustard for a relish. We eat heartily and had hardly swallowed it when the order came "fall in," and the regiment moved about 2 miles to near a fine run of water. Did not I enjoy a good wash! I had some lemons and made lemonade and we had quite a treat. Then we learned we were to go forward to Cold Harbor, but alas how little did we know what awaited us. It was a very warm day and the dust ground up by a thousand wheels and the tramp of tens of thousands was very fine and suffocating, but we must march through it.

About 12 we reached a place called Old Church Tavern where was a huge well of water. There we halted half an hour and most of the men made themselves coffee. I satisfied my simple wants with biting up some hard bread and drinking a little cold water. You never saw such a looking set of boys. The dust filled everything. Their clothes were of the color of the Rebs, and their faces a sight to behold. We pushed on very slowly, teams crossing us in all directions. And soon met the 6th Corps of the famous Army of the Potomac. The 49th New York was crossing our path and there was many a glad greeting between fathers, sons and brothers. We halted half an hour about 3 o'clock. The men almost utterly exhausted by the fatigue of the march. Then on to the front. We passed the headquarters of the 6th Corps and arrived at those of the 5th. I accidently saw there Thomas Hyde, lieutenant colonel, 7th Maine.[43] Son of Uncle Zina. He was very glad to see me and told me that Mr. Fisk had been laboring for a time in the 5th Corps as agent of Christian Commission. I passed a few brief words with him and rode forward. Soon we reached the right of General Grant's line of advance. General "Baldy" Smith, our Corps Commander, was ordered to put his corps into position.[44] Our brigade touched the right of the 6th Corps. A line of battle was formed on the edge of the woods such as we rode through in Suffolk. The battle just then opened on our left.

Whang, whang went the cannon pouring forth incessant death. Whiz, whiz the bullets all about us though we could see no enemy. Knowing that the engagement had begun and that our boys would soon be in the thickest, I went back to where the hospital was to be established to assist in arrangements for the wounded. I had our horses taken back two miles and left Julius to take care of them and of one or two men who sickened on the way up. I did all that I could to help get ready for the wounded. We were only a mile from the scene of conflict and the roar of artillery and the terrific volleys of musketry filled the air with tumult. Soon the wounded began to come in. Those wounded in the arm or hand or slightly in the legs came in with a little help. Others were brought on stretchers. Everybody soon was busy. I dressed myself quite a number of slight wounds and assisted Surgeon Washburn in others. Soon the number began to increase. The 112th men were coming in thick and fast. Poor Buffman called me to pour some water on his arm all crushed.[45] For every one of the wounded, as I went about, I heard "Chaplain" and found some dear boy who wanted something. Part I could supply, but to many I could only give a drink of water and urge them to be patient and wait their turn.

Clarence A. Crane enrolled at Pomfret, New York, as a 2nd lieutenant in Company I, 112th New York Volunteers. He mustered out with regiment on June 13, 1865, at Raleigh (courtesy U.S. Army Heritage and Education Center [USAHEC]).

The hours sped on. About 9, one said, have you seen the colonel? No, I replied. "Well, he's gone up I guess," and just then I saw men bringing in a stretcher with the man I had known and loved so well. I about reeled with faintness, but recovering myself I went up. His eyes were closed but one of the boys said, "Chaplain this is the colonel." He immediately raised his eyes looked me in the face and groaned. They sat the stretcher down. He looked up again and said in a fine voice, "Chaplain, I must die." Oh I hope not, I replied. "This is a mortal wound," he said and asked me to take his watch, his field glass and send them home. Then again he said, chaplain I must die. Give my love to my wife. Tell my friends and tell the world I died a brave man. I die at peace with all my fellow men and I trust in peace with my God. Then he asked for the surgeon, who having been informed of his case had at that instant come to him. He bore the painful examination of his wound without flinching and then said, "Is it mortal?" I fear it is said the surgeon. "I know it is" he replied. He then complained of faintness. We gave him stimulus. He asked for morphine, which was given. After a while he said it did no good, and asked for chloroform. We gave it freely and it enabled him to pass the night with but little consciousness of pain. I went to visit him every opportunity I could get until about 2 am.

Overcome with exhaustion, I lay down beside Dr. Washburn and fell asleep and slept two hours. I was very much refreshed by it and got up, went to the colonel and went about among the others. Three of ours and 18 in all had died during the night. I asked the colonel if he knew me. He was in the extreme of prostration, but endeavored to rally to speak to me, but could not. I then bending over him repeated the words of Paul, "thanks be to God who giveth us the victory through our Lord Jesus Christ."[46] His response was loud and clear, "Amen." "Amen." Soon the surgeon in charge came to me and requested me to superintend the burying of those who had died. I had a detail of men examine the person of each one as I found them scattered all over the field and by nine o'clock they were all buried. Then, after finding that an ambulance could not be procured to take the body of Colonel Drake to White House, sent for our little mule cart. The boys fixed an awning of shelter tents over it and men of his brigade: orderlies, his ostler and Austin Stafford, with myself started with it.[47] I wrote you about our journey. It was somewhat hazardous but our dear Lord watched over me and prospered me and after great toil and anxiety, the body was started for Washington enroute to Westfield.

In regard to the battle. After the line of our brigade was formed in the edge of the woods, they moved forward through it. The distance was not greater than from Captain Dwight's to Montayer Corner. When they came to an open field and just beyond the field was a belt of woods in which the Rebs had their skirmishers. The field they had to cross under heavy fire about the distance from Dr. Rodgers' up to Dr. Williams'. They did so and drove the Rebs through the woods towards their breastworks, which were across another field not so wide. Then they were to charge those works in the face of a murderous fire, and in doing this we lost most of our men. When issuing from this last belt of woods Colonel Drake ordered the men to "cease firing and fix bayonets" then said he at the boys. The woods were irregular so that as they advanced in some

Austin Stafford enlisted at Ellington, New York, as a private in Company B, 112th New York Volunteers. He mustered out with regiment on June 13, 1865, at Raleigh (courtesy U.S. Army Heritage and Education Center [USAHEC]).

parts they were met by a most galling flank fire. The colonel sent one aide towards the right and another towards the left to keep the line up and press it forward. He was near the center, but he was all along wherever men wavered he was urging them on. At length they gained the works and rushed over them. The colonel waving his sword and cheering. Major Colvin of the 169th said he moved to the parapet and fairly danced with exultation as the brave fellows pressed their way on, but a fatal bullet soon struck him and he fell.[48] Another bullet struck his sword scabbard and broke it, another his field glass case and made a dent in that and also in his watch case.

At this time, Captain Mathews took command of the regiment. Captain Chaddock, being too lame he could not do anything. He behaved nobly and the boys after sweeping the Rebs, took a large number of prisoners. They attempted after taking the first to take a second line of works, but found them very strong. Yet we got a portion of them and would have held them but the reinforcements sent up to our support, lay down on the ground instead of pushing up. Willie Laine had advanced beyond the main line as he saw some men falling back, he called out and said, "that's not the way, there's less danger in going forward than in falling back." Soon he moved to the rear with the others and while moving along helping a wounded man a bullet struck him through the heart and he fell dead. Captain Palmeter was on the left and some men had got behind trees and were firing at the Rebs. The captain came up and said, "Boys, you won't do anything that way. Fix bayonets and charge. I'll lead you." They did so and just as he was going over the captain fell heavily having been shot in the arm. The bullet was all flattened out on the bone but did not break it.

That night the regiment all lay in the rifle pits, and have been in the dirt ever since. I went back after seeing Colonel Drake's body off and was too tired to go to the regiment, so I went to the wagon train two miles back and got a good rest. I was intending Tuesday to go and see Dr. Irwin and Mr. Shelton, but was sent down to White House in charge of a train of wounded when I wrote you. I returned Wednesday but could not go to the 2nd Corps Thursday, as they had moved further to the left. I wrote all day Friday after visiting the hospital. Saturday, I was engaged in making arrangements for moving. We supposed we were to be sent around to the James River by land.

Saturday, Captain Ludwick came in to command of the regiment. Captain Chaddock had to give up Sunday and was very sick. Thursday his friend, Dr. Goodrich, surgeon of the engineers, took him and had him put in an ambulance and sent to While House, where I found him.[49] His troubles are complicated kidney and bowels so that he suffered very intense pains. I began this letter Saturday evening but did not write much. I had almost constant interruptions. Sunday morning we expected to have a quiet morning and religious worship. It was calm and cool and the bullets did not fly very thick. We held a meeting of officers to make provision for the expense of sending Colonel Drake's body home and pass some resolutions. It was about half an hour before the time we were to hold worship when the orders came to prepare to march in half an hour. Of course our worship had to be dispensed with, and all was bustle and preparation.

Our new brigade commander is Colonel Curtis of the 142nd New York. He is a very fine officer and has made a most favorable impression upon our officers. Saturday he invited me into his quarters, and asked me all about the regiment, the sick and wounded, asked me where I stayed, if I visited the hospital and etc. And requested me to have a general oversight of the sick of the brigade in the hospital and report to him. I met him Sunday morning. He told me he thought we were going back to Bermuda Hundred. We were to march to White House and take transports. We started about eleven o'clock and marched very easily. It was quite comfortable except the dust, which was awful. About 4 we stopped and dined then pressed on quietly reaching White House about 7 o'clock. I went immediately to the hospital about a mile to see our men and Captain Chaddock. I found the captain very feeble. About 9 we moved to the wharf and are now onboard a transport steamer moving down the Pamunkey River.

It is quite cold. I think my diarrhea will be improved by the change of weather. It is not yet so bad as to trouble me. Julius and the horses are onboard another transport. So is our noble commander Captain Ludwick. I wish that man could be our colonel. Every officer and man dreads the return of Major Smith, now Lieutenant Colonel Smith. I think it a shame that a man of no military knowledge, who never was with the regiment on but one march, and who has kept aloof from it in all its perilous experiences, should seek to be put in the place of highest honor and involvement in preference to the officers who have toiled and suffered with it and who know infinitely more than he does. I think "Lud's" friends might put him in colonel if they chose to do so.

I received your good letter Saturday. You had not heard of Colonel Drake's death. Do write and send regularly twice a week. It seems an age before I get a letter from you. I send you a blank note for $50 dollars which you can get discounted at Mr. Colman's Bank. The paymaster will not pay the troops until after the present campaign is over. But at the end of June I shall have 4 months pay due or rather 3½ as I received ½ pay for the month I was at home. I enclose a dollar for you to send Harry for 4th of July. He wrote me a letter complaining that some of the money that was in his purse had been taken out by me and he wanted some to get his shoes mended with. I wrote him that I found a dollar and some postage currency in his purse, which I left there putting in his trunk key and that if he had spent a dollar since being in Stamford he had spent too much. I am not going to indulge him and Fred with too free use of money. I suppose you will have to send him money to get home with, if he is to return and spend his vacation at home. I am sorry I did not know that he could not be kept there through the summer and don't know now that he cannot. I don't care about the matter of expenses, that is a trifle but you ought not to have the bother of him through the hot months. Do as you judge best. Perhaps you had better write to Mr. Wilde about it.

John F. Smith enrolled at Jamestown, New York, as a captain in Company A, 112th New York Volunteers. He was promoted to colonel and commanded the 112th at Fort Fisher, North Carolina, and died of wounds received at Fort Fisher (courtesy U.S. Army Heritage and Education Center [USAHEC]).

Give my warm regards to Mrs. Cobb. May the Lord lead her through her sorrows to a better hope. Have I had not a good long talk with you? I miss Colonel Drake greatly. It makes all around strange. So great is the change here. But blessed be God for his goodness. I believe the men love me more than ever. As I went through the hospital last evening they fairly clapped their hands when they saw me coming. Poor fellows my heart aches over the sorrowing households that war has left desolate.

With ever kind and loving affection,
Your husband

Sunday, June 12th

This day is the Sabbath. Yesterday Captain J. S. Mathews having received notice that his muster was defective and was to date from May 4th was accordingly relieved of the command of the regiment. Captain E. A. Ludwick, Company K, being the senior officer, assumed command.

Captain Ludwick had notice given of divine service to be held in camp at eleven o'clock. We were all pleased to be able again to join as a regiment in sacred worship of him who holds us all in his constant care. Before the time arrived, orders came to strike tents, break camp and be prepared for a move in half hour. All was bustle and toil. In the course of half an hour, we had moved out in good order. It is understood that we go to White House, embark on transports for the south side of the James. Colonel Curtis issued excellent orders in regard to marching the column. We marched quite leisurely and about half an hour before sundown we were again bivouacked only a few rods from the spot where we spent two nights, less than a fortnight since on our way to the Army of the Potomac. I took occasion to go over while it was yet light to the 18th Corps Hospital to visit Captain Chaddock who had been conveyed there the Friday previous. I found him suffering acute pain in the region of the kidneys with other somewhat alarm....[50] (Journal)

Thursday, June 16th

Casualties at Cold Harbor (Journal)

Elisha A. Herrick   Private   Company I   Wounded in arm near Petersburg

Near Petersburg
June 16th [1864]
18th Army Corps, 3rd Division
112th Regiment in the Dirt

My dear Wife,

I think I wrote you last onboard the steamer *Mary Washington* bound from White House to Bermuda Hundred. We passed Fort Monroe about 5 o'clock Monday eve. Our adjutant went ashore and I sent by him all letters to be mailed.

After his return we moved up the river a little distance and then anchored for the night. About nine o'clock the next morning we landed at the very point we had left only about a fortnight before. It was a cool day and I was not feeling well so I put on woolen drawers and stockings and was not at all too warm.

We did not tarry at the Hundred but passed on towards Point of Rocks on the Appomattox and in about an hour, Captain Ludwick with 4 companies that had embarked on another boat joined us. Captain Ludwick makes a fine regimental commander, much better than Captain Chaddock. Captain Chaddock is too hasty and nervous. I think the whole regiment would be perfectly satisfied to have Ludwick put in command of the regiment.

We pitched our tent at night and made rather close stowage. Captain Ludwick, Surgeons Washburn and Mead, Quartermaster, Adjutant Crane and myself we lay on the ground.[51] I felt better rather than I had been feeling for some days. Before we went to sleep we received orders to be up at one o'clock, let the men make coffee, and be ready to move precisely at two. We were roused up in season but as usual did not move precisely at two. The whole corps moved and it took a longer time than was anticipated.

We left about 4 am and toiled on marching and halting, and did not get to this point until about 9. We crossed the Appomattox on a pontoon bridge. We found that part of the 2nd Corps men already before us having crossed the James near City Point and marched across. Just before we crossed the Appomattox we heard some heavy firing and when we marched [to] the outer line of the defenses of Petersburg about 5 miles from the city, we came across an earthwork and line of rifle pits which the colored troops had just taken by assault. These troops had never before done any storming of fortifications and they were tickled enough.

After we got in front of the 2nd line of defenses we were met by a pretty rough artillery fire and quite a number of casualties occurred in driving back their skirmish line.

I remained at the hospital till afternoon then went and lay down to get some rest if possible. About 4, I went up to where the regiment was lying. The shot and shell came over us once in a while though we were in reserve. After being there about half an hour, the musketry began to rattle and the cannon poured in an awful fire. The Rebs replied, and shell and shot came whizzing over our men engaged and fell into our camp but fortunately no one was hit. It was a terrible strife but brief for soon the cannon ceased. We heard a yell, then a volley and so on for ten minutes, when a tumultuous shout arose, we had taken a redoubt and the earthworks.

Soon the order came for the regiment to advance, as the whole line was now being pushed forward, to take possession of the new works. I fell back to where my horse was and unrolled my cork bed under the shade of some pines and lay down. Meanwhile Julius and Austin made me a cup of coffee and with a hardtack for luxury I fared sumptuously and went soon to bed and to sleep. Our casualties during the day were very small.

The whole Army of the Potomac is here today and we are, I hear, to enter Petersburg tonight. This morning our forces carried the main line of the evening's work by assault and we can now shell Petersburg out if necessary.

But Burnside and Wright are getting round so that in a few hours we will have the city invested. Perhaps I may date my next at Petersburg.

>Very truly and
>Your husband

Monday, June 20th

>Near Hatcher's House
>In front of the entrenchments
>June 20th 1864

My dear Wife,

I get your letters quite regularly now, and wonder that you have not got all of mine. It may be that one week I did not write you but once. I was very busy when able to do anything. I am not very strong this summer thus far. While with the Potomac Army I took the Chickahominy fever, and had with it a virulent diarrhea. Since that I have had an influenza which prevails in the army. It begins with inflammation of the throat and then affects the head, causing a great flow of mucus. But by the blessing of our kind Heavenly Father, I have thus far got along and feel a little stronger today than any day the past week. Notwithstanding sickness, I have kept on working and kept with the regiment.

We have been constantly on the move and are now not far from where the regiment was when I first joined it after my furlough. The country around Petersburg is very beautiful. The wheat was just ready for the sickle, oats look all fiery. Corn in abundance growing. Two days tramp of the Army of the Potomac left not a vestige of a fence and horses and mules noted in the abundant crops of oats and wheat. I was surprised at the strength of the fortifications which we took Wednesday morning. I wish I could describe them to you. General Grant said they were stronger than Missionary Ridge. Wednesday evening our brigade was advanced from where it had rested during the day, down into a field preparatory, as was thought, to a general charge. For though we had the heights commanding Fredericksburg on one side yet there was a space of a mile and a half which the enemy had cut into rifle pits, etc. But on the other side southwest, the 2nd Corps were engaged taking possession of some works, and they did not get through so that we escaped. The next day we lay quiet and Thursday night very quietly drew back to this place and as I hear go again into our old corps, the 10th.

We were able to have worship yesterday, the first for weeks. I spoke of Colonel Drake. Colonel Curtis, our new brigade commander, was present and the brigade band discoursed their sweetest music at the opening of the service.

We have again had a change in the composition of the brigade. Yesterday about 200 of the 13th Indiana, whose time was out, went home. The others are to form 2 companies of sharpshooters. The 169th New York and the 9th Maine go into Colonel Bell's brigade and we are brigaded with the 142nd, 117th and 3rd New York.[52] This makes a very pleasant arrangement for us. The 117th were neighbors to us at Folly Island. The 3rd New York was a little further off at the same place and the 142nd is Colonel Curtis' old regiment. We all admire the colonel.

Major Smith, I mean Lieutenant Colonel Smith, returned to the regiment last evening. His little son, who was wounded, is in very feeble health. The wound is not healed but doing well. Yesterday afternoon we moved 2 miles and I don't know what awaits us. There was no firing yesterday, has been but little today and we know nothing of the whereabouts of the different parts of Grant's army. They are only about 6 miles from us but I could not get permission to go over and I have no strength to spare to run about. I never could feel right if I should get wounded when looking about out of mere curiosity. You will have to be patient in regard to the fall of Richmond. It will take some time yet. But at present everything looks well.

I have full confidence in the final assault. I hope you have gotten my letters before this. Love to all.

Very affectionately,
Wm. L. Hyde

Thursday, June 23rd

Lieutenant Sherwin appointed assistant adjutant. (Chronicle)

Friday, June 24th

Casualties at Cold Harbor (Journal)

| John B. Hosier | Private | Company D | Wounded in hand, accidental |

In the night the regiment was moved into our advanced line of rifle pits on the right of the late action. There were no other casualties at this time. (Journal)

Sunday, June 26th

Near Petersburg
June 26th 1864

Dear Wife,

I am not very well and cannot write you much of a letter. I have had a relapse of my fever and Saturday I feared I was going to be very sick, but by a merciful providence I have been kept thus far and am now convalescing. The symptoms of the fever here are quite peculiar, headache, loss of appetite, nausea, generally constipation but sometimes diarrhea. The fever sometimes follows by chills. I have not had a severe attack but enough to make me very weak. I have eat nothing for about 4 days except a little corn starch cracker and have to drink my tea and coffee clear.

I crave fruit. This diet of ours is very hard for me in the summer. I was determined I would not be laid aside from duty. So last Sunday our corps having been back in camp on the hill, I asked Colonel Smith to have service hours appointed. He appointed pm 3 o'clock but protested against my officiating as feeble as I was. Colonel Curtis, commanding brigade, sent me word to preach at brigade headquarters at 5 o'clock. I sent word I would [be] glad to have the opportunity to do additional good. About 2, Colonel Curtis called to see me and finding I was sick, he remonstrated with me but I insisted and preached twice that afternoon in the open air. At 5 o'clock I had the brigade band out to make the music and as auditory. Major General Ord, commanding 18th Army Corps, Brigadier General Ames, commanding division, 18th Army Corps and Brigadier General Turner, commanding division, 10th Army Corps and Colonel Curtis, commanding brigade.[53] I got through without any difficulty and no harm. Sunday night was the coldest stormiest night of the season. It rained torrents. Yesterday I was not as well, but today am better.

I will write again tomorrow.

Your affectionate husband,
Wm L. Hyde

In the field near Petersburg
June 26th 1864

My dear Wife,

We have again moved from the earthworks near Bermuda Hundred to the earthworks in front of Petersburg. Last Thursday night we were ordered to be ready to move in half an hour and we learned that we were to go into the trenches in front of Petersburg. Captain Ludwick was field officer and in command of 400 men who were on picket and could not go until he and they were relieved. I stayed with him at his request and lay down expecting every hour the order would come relieving us. But the night wore away. The day also wore away and we heard that General Butler would not have any more men leave the front where we then were. So towards evening I started off alone to find the regiment. The weather had been intolerably hot all day and there was not much of a let up when I started. I jogged on very slowly. It was only about 7 miles and I let old Frank walk most of the way. After finding the location of the 18th Army Corps, I endeavored in vain to find the 112th Regiment. After wandering about till after dark, I went back and found in the edge of a skirt of woods a quartermaster whom I knew and got him to find me lodging and my horse forage for the night. In the morning, I started off refreshed by sleep for the front, and soon found the regiment way to the front. Not 40 rods back of the Rebel rifle pits, and near one of their strong redoubts.

It was expected that they would have stormed the enemy works that night but the order was countermanded. I believe Colonel Curtis hopes to take the works by a slower process which will involve less loss of life. Last night our brigade attempted to advance their line of defenses and in so doing were met by a murderous fire from the Rebs, and the troops behind us opened fire too so that for a time we were between two fires. Several men were killed and wounded, 3 out of our regiment. One man, J. D. Findley of Company K, lost his arm.[54] A [Robert] Henry—a Canadian, Company G, and Asa Sweet, Company I, was killed.[55] We got off well considering. I was a mile and a half back of the regiment at the time, having had one of my poor days. Today I am feeling better and think I am really much better. It is the lingering remains of the Chickahominy fever. I think if we had not come over to this side of the James, I would have been obliged to go to general hospital. You speak of the report that Colonel Drake was killed by his own men. Nothing could be more false. He was killed by Rebels who were in an angle of works which gave them a flank fire while we were occupying their works in front of our brigade. And as to Captain Ludwick, he was very sick, so sick that he could not move. The surgeons both wanted him to stay back at White House but he refused and at last when he could no longer walk was put into the wagon on top of the baggage. No cooler or braver man in the regiment than Ludwick. Colonel Smith has done well since with the regiment this time. I have no reason to complain of him.

He feels quite worked at the action of the officers a week ago. It won't hurt him. I miss Captain Chaddock not a little. If you hear of him in Fredonia, I beg of you ride up and see him. He was a good friend of mine. We have chummed together months at Jacksonville and since my return. I certainly think him one of the pleasantest most accommodating men of my acquaintance.

I am just now with J. M. Shaw occupying a part of his big fly.[56] It is I think a little, the hottest day of the hot days we have had in June. There has not been 15 minutes rain since the 2nd of the month. Everything is suffering for want of it, men and animals. My poor old horse looks very gaunt and so do most all the others. They get about half rations to eat. Billy Shaw lost his $125 horse not long ago.[57] I received last night a very kind letter from Mrs. Drake. How tenderly I do pity her. May God who is all merciful comfort her heart. Go when you can and see her. In a few days we shall again be mustered for pay. The government owes me four months' pay now at the close of this month. The money will come in time and you will be all straight again. I approve your decision with regards to Harry. I get your letters now quite regularly.

I will see Benjamin Vandewark tomorrow and in my next tell you how to dispose of that note.[58] I am much obliged to Mrs. Bellows for the good opinion she has of me. So you see poor Mrs. Cobb often, I am glad. Does that vixen come there often now? I am sorry Willard is not more popular. I don't think that he is at all disloyal. But perhaps he is somewhat faint hearted and desponding. This is an awful war and the desperation of the Rebels increases as the war is prolonged. I still have faith in Grant, but my chief trust is in God.

Your affectionate husband

Tuesday, June 28th

Corbett absent 30 days, January 13. Received June 28.[59] (Chronicle)

Wednesday, June 29th

Bermuda Hundred
June 29th 1864

My dear wife,

You see by this letter's date that I am at this present moment at some distance in the rear of Petersburg.

Another sorrowful event has brought me here. Lieutenant Samuel Sherwin, Company A, and acting adjutant was shot dead yesterday in the forenoon by a sharpshooter concealed in a clump of trees half a mile distant from our breastworks. He had been very careful about exposing himself and had faithfully warned his men against doing so, but in the way of his duty he was giving some regimental orders when the eye of the sharpshooter marked him and the fatal bullet quenched his life. He only groaned once. We have lost some very valuable men by chance shots within a few days. Sunday a Mr. Bush was instantly killed.[60] Tuesday, Phillip McEvoy, Company C, Samuel Sherwin and Hiram Vorce, Company E, were shot. McEvoy had not died when I left yesterday.[61]

Vorce was son of the late sheriff of Chautauqua County. His father and wife live in Westfield. Sherwin's wife lives in Jamestown. Thus we are constantly in the midst of death. Vorce had just eaten his supper and was in what he considered a safe place but he raised his head above the breastwork for a single moment and the work was done.

We have had both bodies embalmed to be sent home to their friends. I received Sunday an excellent letter from Charles Larrabee, also one from Mother. Henry has been very sick and they had purposely kept the knowledge of it from me, fearing it would alarm me too much. I must say I do now feel great anxiety. I fear that Henry is not long for this life. Nannie will outlive him. Mother writes in her beautiful Christian manner concerning him. I sat down and wrote Henry immediately.

I do pray God to spare the dear boy's life for my parent's sake and for Nannie's as well as for my own. I wrote Harry and sent him a dollar for the 4th of July. I hope it will reach

Left: Hiram Vorce enlisted at Westfield, New York, as a private in Company E, 112th New York Volunteers. He was killed in action at Petersburg, Virginia (courtesy U.S. Army Heritage and Education Center [USAHEC]). *Above:* Phillip McEvoy enlisted at Hanover, New York, as a private in Company C, 112th New York Volunteers. He was killed in action at Petersburg, Virginia.

him. I would send Fred some money but am rather short. The paymaster has not yet made his appearance.

There are a large number in the regiment sick with slight diseases such as diarrhea. I am gaining strength slowly. I cannot say that I have a super abundance of fat.

We are all anxious to have this present campaign close. But I fear it is to be a long one and the great test will be the test of endurance.

Mrs. Drake wrote me a very pleasant letter, very sad but submissive to God's will. May God comfort her afflicted heart.

I think of you daily. Be cheerful and trust in God who is all our help.

> Affectionately,
> William

Thursday, June 30th

> Near Petersburg
> June 30th 1864

My dear Wife,

Last evening I returned from Bermuda Hundred. It is about four hours slow ride from the landing to our present position in the field. The afternoon was not as warm as it had been and by choosing shady paths I got along without discomfort. My escort was Lieutenant Sixby, Company E, and a boy who drove the mule cart in with the body of Sergeant Hiram Vorce was conveyed to the landing.[62] We left the landing about 12, having purchased some few articles at the sutler, such as a blackberry pie and cheese. We rode out two and a half miles to a nice spring and a clump of trees which must have been in other days a splendid place for a picnic. Lieutenant Sixby had bought a new coffee pot and we consecrated it by boiling water in it and then put in a strong pinch of nice tea. The boy fried three pieces of pork in his little fry pan. I spread an old newspaper on the ground, put on it the blackberry pie and cheese. Sixby had some soft crackers and sugar in his haversack. And with the fried salt pork and tea we had all the material for a luxurious dinner. Hunger seasoned it. One plate sufficed for the pork and we alternated in drinking tea from the same tin dipper. The tea was extra nice and the pie made by some intelligent contraband was an illustration in pie crust of the doctrine of miscegenation. One half the crust being black as coal the other half white as a soldier's face. I did not forget old Frank but letting the venerable rascal run in the tall clover while we eat, I gave him a luxury, which he seemed highly to appreciate.

We ate and chatted an hour, then started on. About five o'clock we reached the front. Oh what a lively road it must have been before the war for miles on each side was a row of the red cedar trees under the shade of which the slight breeze made a delicious coolness. And I thought of you and wished that there was no war but that under the banner of peace we were journeying side by side; you on a nice little pony and I on a good horse. When I got to where Brown dispenses his luxuries, I tarried, drank a quarter more of tea, and then went back to the wagons. Remember my rations are three pints of coffee for breakfast and dinner and one quarter of tea for supper. I believe I shall soon like both coffee and tea best without either sugar or milk. All is quiet today, no more casualties.

Herman Sixby enlisted at Westfield, New York, as a sergeant in Company E, 112th New York Volunteers. He was wounded at Petersburg and discharged for disability on February 3, 1865 (courtesy U.S. Army Heritage and Education Center [USAHEC]).

Send that draft to:
Alexander M. Lervry
Chautauqua County Bank
Jamestown, NY
Enclosing this within.

Monday, July 4th

Near Petersburg
July 4th 1864

Dear Wife,

This morning I received and have just finished reading your dear letter mailed the 30th of this month. It really seems like old times to get your letters so regularly. Yesterday I received yours of the 26th. One reason I get them so regularly is the direction is so plain that they do not get tossed about here and there.

I got one yesterday also from Harry. He writes very affectionately. I had written him about the death of Colonel Drake. He said when he read that in the letter, he let it drop out of his hands he was so astonished.

I am not quite satisfied with his explanation of the money. He says he found his dollar afterwards in another pocket. I think he is rather artful. But his father was so before him.

Yesterday morning after reading your letter I determined I would see Shelton if it cost me a day's ride.[63] So I had Frank saddled and took Julius along on the doctor's pony and started to find the 2nd Corps. I was lucky enough to stumble upon the camp where they are now located, what remains of them. It is the 120th New York. I found Shelton. He was looking very thin but otherwise well. He thinks that the noncommissioned staff of the 3rd Excelsior will get their discharge within a few days. I had a very pleasant chat with him. An hour fairly flew and I was obliged to bid him goodbye and come back after extorting the promise of a visit from him should he [be] remaining long enough in the camp.

I was so feeble before the regiment left for home that I did not get over to see them. I am now daily gaining strength, though I cannot yet get along without my quinine every day. I saw also Batty Myers, who formerly lived with Hanson Risley.[64] He has grown and is looking finely. In the afternoon, I had just settled myself to take a nap when an order came from brigade headquarters to have brigade services in the woods near the front. Our regiment and the 142nd New York being in the advanced line of rifle pits, only a very few of them were permitted to leave but I had quite a good congregation from the reserved 117th and 3rd New York and some from the 47th and 48th.

The brigade band was out and gave us excellent music. The enemy also assisted and shot and shell were briskly flying off to left of where I stood. And directly before me was a solid 12 pound shot and also a three inch unexploded shell and some fragments of iron showing that the locality, where I was there preaching the peaceful gospel, had been rather hot at some short period before.

I must say I enjoyed the service exceedingly, and full as much the coming up of the men at the close to shake hands with me.

On my return to my quarters (which I presume you are aware are quite in the rear, a mile from the regiment where the quartermaster and the wagons are). I stopped at the request of Colonel Curtis to have a talk with him. He was suffering from fever and a virulent diarrhea and had been obliged to keep quiet all day. The colonel was very kind. I think him a delightfully pleasant man. He wanted to know all about our Lieutenant Colonel Smith, etc. I was very cautious as to what I said to him. Hought Allen wants to be discharged [from] the service.[65] He says that his father's business and health require him to return and he has tendered his resignation.

I fear that his family have written him such letters that he is almost distracted. It is too bad. Hought is a plucky boy and is now an aide on Colonel Curtis' staff. The colonel speaks of him in terms of the warmest eulogy. It is very unwise in his friends to make him unhappy and drive him to desperation. If he leaves now while in presence of the enemy it will injure him for life.

This 4th of July is wonderfully quiet. I have scarcely heard a shot since I got up this morning. Not even the big gun, that every 15 minutes of the day for sometime past has sent its compliments into Petersburg, does ought to disturb the universal silence.

It is much more of Sunday than yesterday was. You told me sometime since that Mr. Willard had given General Grant till the 4th of July to take Richmond. I guess he will need some longer time. But I have faith to believe it will come. We have not this year so much to discourage us as we had a year ago this time. We must recollect that it is for the Rebs a death struggle and they will hold out as long as they can. And they are commanded by the very ablest of military generals.

I hope Dunham will procure a valid substitute. If he were to come out himself he would not live six months. You must keep up good heart concerning me. I have been wonderfully preserved and am in excellent health and spirits just now.

It always makes me sad to hear of the extravagance of people at home. I fear more from the wickedness at home than I do from the power of the enemy. I fear God's judgments may fall upon us because of abounding wickedness. When will the people learn to humble themselves before God?

I am glad you can luxuriate in strawberries and cream. I wish that I could get a delicious taste now and then. But if God will only give success to our endeavors, I will gladly live in the dirt and eat hardtack and pork till the war is ended.

I think you did well at your festival. There will never be much enthusiasm in that society in Dunkirk.[66] They are so divided. Everything religious in Dunkirk dwindles. You speak of warm weather. You ought to be here. The weather was so warm last week that a canteen of water lying out in the sun got so hot that it was about as much as you could bear to pour it on your hands. We merely laid down and sweltered. This morning it is very cool and comfortable. It is also overcast but no present prospect of rain. I knew that the story about Mr. Willard being disloyal was all gammon. It is very easy for a set of slicks there in Dunkirk to accuse others of being copperheads.[67] I think they had better boast a little less of their patriotism and go to war themselves.

Very affectionately,
William

Saturday, July 9th

Near Petersburg
July 9th 1864

My dear Wife,

Had it not been for the intense heat and prolonged drought, the last week would have been the pleasantest of any since we came out. I have been gaining strength and feel more like work than I have for a month. The truth is I was sick when the regiment went to join the Army of the Potomac and at the Battle of Cold Harbor and after. I overworked and then being much exposed I took the malaria of these swamps and so I ran clear down.

I assure you it has been very hot. The sun in the middle of the day seems fairly to burn and the wind, when there is, breathes hot upon your cheeks like the blast of a furnace.

And how dry and dusty! The breeze sweeps up the dust like snow and when men or horses move it is almost suffocating. But we have been very quiet this week, very little firing. The only change our regiment has is from the advanced rifle pits in front to those in the rear and this change only enables them to get a little more rest. No one can conceive how terrible it is to spend 2 or 3 days in succession in those rifle pits. A man sweats as he lies down, like rain, no breath of air visits him, and he must keep in about the same position. If he raises his head above the breastwork he drops. If he is not careful how he goes out or comes in, he finds a bullet or a shell crossing his path. He has to lie and sweat and ache all night long, the whistling of shot or the crashing of shell keep him feverish and excited and deprive him of sleep. As a consequence we have moved 27 sick men back here by the wagon train and some 20 have been sent away to Fortress Monroe. When I am with the quartermaster and the wagons, the air is comparatively salubrious and the distance so great that shell seldom comes very near us.

I go over to the regiment almost every day and go down to the hospital. I am midway between the two. I think there is something brewing on military matters but just what I can't say. We are not at all disturbed by the Rebels making a raid into Pennsylvania. And I think that Grant will not be persuaded to change his plans on that account. I think he is now giving his faded troops the rest they so much need.

The whole of the 2nd Corps is now lying between the front and City Point and have been for 8 days. If we could have some gentle showers it would greatly refresh us besides cooling the air.

This morning I received yours mailed the fourth. I am sorry and anxious on account of your illness. I hope it is nothing serious. If you think that a journey east would do you good, by all means pack up and start for Warren, Bristol and all along shore. I expect the paymaster every day. Parts of the troops are being paid this week. As soon as the paymaster comes I will send you some money. If you need any before, ask Drs. Rogers or Smith or Mr. Bellows.

Dr. Rogers, I know will lend you small amounts such as $50 or $75 anytime. I am not surprised at what you say of Mrs. S. and am glad you are able to rise superior to it. What a pity a young and sickly woman should contrive to make everybody hate her. Thursday I went to City Point after sanitary stores for the regiment. I wish there was some way to provide those things in quantities that would benefit the whole regiment more. I got enough to give each company half bushel of crackers (soft), 4 cans of meat, 1 can of tomatoes, 1 of apple pulp, 8 plugs tobacco, and 13 lemons. I got also some wine for the sick boys here on the hill and canned milk and corn starch enough to do them much good.

It was a ten mile ride and if you imagine the dust thicker than any snow in winter, the clouds rolling up covering you all over, filling your eyes, mouth, nose, hair, eyebrows, covering your coat so that you looked like a walking brickyard and you may know something of the discomforts of the ride.

Yesterday I had a boy called "Shorty," a Dutchman who is a good washer. Washes everything I had on me the day before. I manage to keep clean. Have had all my clothes washed and they are now in prime order. I have lost, in our various marches, all my towels save one, 2 handkerchiefs, spur, necktie and the white shirt I wore when starting from Dunkirk. But have enough left for the campaign if it doesn't last too long. I hope Fred had "fun" the 4th, also Harry. Harry really surprises me. I thought he would be really homesick before this, and I expected a stout rebellion against being kept there all summer.

I am thankful you find the consolations of the gospel sufficient for you in all your tribulations. If we will only accept it God's grace is always sufficient for our every need. I wrote up the biography of Colonel Drake a few days since from the period of his going to Charleston till his death. Ex-Governor Patterson of Westfield wrote it up to that period and I completed it.[68] Mrs. Drake appears in her letters like a true Christian woman. I believe nothing but grace could enable her so to triumph over the bitterness of her situation. I think with you about the study. When it is sold, I want the parish to have it, and it is worth more than the interest of $50 to store your things in. I hope this will find you in better health and feeling cheerful and happy under the sense of God's goodness. Remember be kindly to Mrs. Cobb.

> Yours most affectionately,
> William

Tuesday, July 12th

> Near Petersburg
> July 12th 1864

Dear Wife,

Hot Hot Hot. Dry Dry Dry. Dusty Dusty Dusty. No news. The same old story as for 2 weeks past. Pretty quiet on the lines during the day. Every night they get up a little excitement on the picket lines. First you will hear 2 or 3 guns, then 3 or 4 more, then half a dozen or a dozen in succession, then a volley and then the big guns open and for a half an hour there is a general hubbub. Then it cools off. The man in some picket thought he saw a Reb coming, fired. Then somebody next to him fired, and then they fired from the other side, then the pickets fired, then the line in the rear fired and so on it went. We have these serenades every night. Sometimes it is crack, crack all along the line the live long night.

It sounds very clear and plain at the distance from the line to my tent. Sometimes my slumbers are disturbed. Sometimes I sleep well all through. Now and then we have a perfectly quiet night, and so it goes. Grant is working at something he has not told us what and he no doubt thinks he can wait if Lee can. I suppose everybody north is troubled about the raid into Maryland. We had just as soon the Rebs would walk into a lot of those stingy old copperhead Pennsylvania farmers as not. I hope the president will not be so unwise as to disturb General Grant in his plans and draw away troops from here. I suppose people wonder that we are not pushing on faster here. Perhaps they think men can fight the year through. I can assure our friends that if the army had not had this rest one half of it would by this time be utterly useless through sickness. If we were on the old route to Richmond by the Chickahominy swamps, we would be decimated by fevers.

Here, we are on quite high ground. It is rolling land much like the land about Gardiner. And what a breeze there is stirring we have. Our men when they can get out of the steaming hot trenches back upon the hills recuperate fast.

Since I began to write I heard that this raid of Lee's assumes somewhat vast proportions and that troops are being drawn off from this point. I must say I am glad the 18th and 10th Corps were not the ones to be marched over that long tedious route. Still we may have worse than that.

I don't care what way is taken by either side if it only helps us in the work of putting down the rebellion and ending the war.

Oh how long must this terrible business of butchery go on. Well my dearest, I must close this poor letter. I will write a better one next time.

With much love as ever. No casualties of late in the regiment.

Your husband,
Wm. L. Hyde

Sunday, July 17th

Near Petersburg
July 17th 1864

My dear Wife,

We are still enjoying comparative quiet, a quiet which the first good rain or even the lapse of a week without it will undoubtedly break up.

People at home I know are very uneasy at the delays here. But if they had a little more self-sacrificing patriotism themselves. If they would only send on the recruits rapidly to replenish the ranks of our already decimated armies, they might then complain.

General Grant could have taken Petersburg with a sacrifice of 20,000 men at any time since we came here, but by delay he will accomplish that object with slight loss. I expect to hear a tremendous explosion one of these mornings or evenings. Then there will be a fight and I hope an occupation of this beleaguered city. Our brigade has had a long tedious time of it in their rifle pits and I am not certain that they would not rather run the risk of a charge than endure the confinement of so long a season. Frank Wheeler has been quite sick. I have helped him to some delicacies from the soldier's fund I have. I am glad to believe that these have been of essential service to him. Newell Toles is still quite miserable.[69] He has had an infection of the throat. I have helped him also as well as others. He is now gradually improving.

Monday 18th, I received your letter of the 14th this morning. How good it seems to be so few days distant from you.

The 3rd Division of our corps are receiving their pay. I hope our turn will come very soon as we all sorely need it. I have enough for present use but you need yours.

Colonel Carpenter's horse is doing finely. I ride him frequently and he will soon I think, be in condition to offer for sale. I may trade him with Dr. Mead who has a small Florida pony. I would if I could get the little animal home.

The government now allows me forage for two horses. Old Frank is beginning to look like old times. Poor old fellow he hates the water. It always makes him sick.

I rode with Colonel Smith last evening 3 or 4 miles along our line of defenses. There was no firing. The Rebs were out in hundreds and thousands upon their works and all seemed to enjoy the pleasing truce. It was a magnificent sight on the left of the 5th Corps where the ground is open to see them lining the parapet of their front and also our men on top of their slight earthworks. The advance of our pickets and those of the Rebs could talk to each other.

If our officers would let them, the whole line would be in earnest conversation, but it would not do. Some of our well meaning men would let out the very things we desire to keep the Rebs ignorant of. I preached yesterday at the convalescent camp. Our regiment being far to the front. On our front there is a good deal of mortar firing which renders it dangerous to hold religious services in the pits. It would not do either to gather many men together in one place. You must act your pleasure in respect of visiting Harry. You would find it indeed a tedious journey. The only way to endure it would be to rest at Hancock or Delhi. It is a days ride from Hancock to Delhi and the question would be could you as well endure that ride after riding all night from Dunkirk, as by resting there before going further on. You would be obliged to rest at Delhi from 5 pm until 2 am. If you were to ride directly through from Hancock it would be best for you to rest in Delhi till after breakfast and then hire a private conveyance to take you on.

I want you to go on to see Harry but I am not prepared to advise it because I know the journey will be very fatiguing to you. It might bring on fever. If you cannot go on you must send him some acceptable present. You ought to go somewhere. To squat down there in Dunkirk and feel blue, give way to your melancholy is a poor way. Go somewhere and see your friends. But oh you say where is the money? Just as I ought to have thought of that and I will. If we are not paid this week I will take some measures to have your pecuniary wants supplied.

I am glad that everybody has not such a silly little wife as Mary Shelton. Shelton is a good fellow, and though I doubt not he feels blue now, yet he will do no mean or unpatriotic deed. I hope he may be released from his position and sent home. If not, I think he will be placed in such a one as he can fill with honor. I said nothing to Shelton that I have not freely said to you. I am very thankful for Mr. Peets' good opinion and especially for that of his wife. If you chance to ride up to Fredonia, call on Captain Chaddock without any ceremony. He wrote me a letter received 2 days since. He is I fear a cripple for some months. I shall write him today.

Tuesday morning.

I did not get this letter off yesterday and it is raining so bountifully this morning. I intended to ride out to see Henry Stillman and Shelton but the rain comes in my way.

I am tormented to death with the flies. They are like the plague of Egypt. At night the wall of my tent is covered with them, and this rainy day they bite sharp. I have just seen poor Fisk.[70] He wants sadly to get home. I don't see how he can. I don't know how anybody not sick can get out of the army. Except an officer does some mean thing and get dishonorably discharged. It is a hard case. But the public welfare should be placed above all private interests.

How sad Mr. Stiles' case is. That is as bad almost as a wound from a shell. I hope that before I write you again we shall have accomplished something in a military way so that I have something about which to write. The great scare at Washington is over. Had we been as resolute and bold when we first came down we could have been in Petersburg 3 weeks ago. Oh these timid counsels, and these generals afraid of doing something which may lose them their past success. Well, give my love to Fred and all friends. If that little scamp had pouted about his packet to me, probably he would have got up with a spark.

Good morning to you—as ever,
William

We are 1st Brigade, 2nd Division, 10th Army Corps. General Gillmore was the commander but General A. H. Terry is now for a few days in command.[71]

Monday, July 18th

Alfred Terry commanded the second and successful expedition against Fort Fisher and commanded the Wilmington Campaign. Post–Civil War, he negotiated the surrender of Chief Sitting Bull.

Near Petersburg
July 18th 1864

My dear Wife,

It is like old times to get your letters as regularly as I do now. The last dated July 11th I received this morning.

How rapidly the days of July are leaving us. We have heard of the paymaster but have not yet seen him. I will write Mr. Fullager about your having some money. It is too bad for the government to keep the soldiers without their pay as they do. I am truly sorry that Harry is separated from you and if there was some good place where you could all be together and Jane with you, I should feel more comfortable about all of you.

I think Harry is well off where he is. He will learn much outside of the school house that will be valuable to him. He is getting towards that age when we may expect him to be more and more away from us. I think the last letter must have left you in a little better health. I truly hope so.

When I know you and the children are well, I can much better bear my own exile. It is very quiet here today as it was yesterday.

Yet there is activity. Grant is shortening his line and making sure his present position preparatory to some move. They say he is not at all alarmed by the invasion of Shadbellydom by a handful of boys. If they could only be put into New York City and let them gut the houses of the gold gamblers, I should not cry. We have not lost a mail by this raid. We do not get New York papers quite as soon as we should otherwise. We get every evening the *New York Daily* of the previous morning, is the paper that the intelligent Dunkirker reads while sipping his morning coffee out of white china. I read in the evening of the same day after drinking my quart of tea out of a rusty tin dipper. Now however our papers are two days old. We get the Washington papers of the day before as usual. I had the pleasure of a visit from Otis Shelton day before yesterday pm. It was very pleasant. We talked over old times. He seemed rather sober. I think he feels anxious about his position. The old 72nd [New York] have been transferred to the 120th New York and he and the other non-commissioned staff are in no position at all. I hardly think they will be put into the ranks but will be transferred to other positions. He took supper with me and I walked out a short distance with him on his return. The Second Corps are now drawn back from the front and are resting in a fine skirt of woods in the rear of the 9th [Maine Infantry] and 5th [Battery, New Jersey Light Artillery] and night before last they were ordered out to level the Reb earthworks in the rear of our position.

Grant has been anticipating an attack from Lee. I think he is very anxious to have Lee attack him. But probably Lee has ascertained that we have not sent off any amount of force and is not anxious for a field engagement on equal terms. It is not pitiable that there should have been no more energy displayed at the north to repel that invasion of Maryland and Pennsylvania. I hope it will lead the people to feel that they must furnish men if they would soon break the rebellion. You are all no doubt impatient at the slow progress of things here. But we are hard at work. Grant cannot afford to lose men as he did at first. He is working away at the Rebel works and will soon make a move that will give him a decided advantage. The weather has been delightful the past few days. Cool and bracing air. It is still very dry. Were it not for our splendid position, men and beasts would suffer exceedingly for want of water.

When you hear by the papers that the Sanitary Commission are sending boat loads of fresh vegetables every day, don't for pity sake imagine that our boys get any. Our division has had cabbage once 2 weeks ago and our regiment got some. They also sent at one time one lemon to a company and 2 or 3 onions. I won't blame the Sanitary. But this matter of supplying regiments in their way is impracticable. I have made good use of the sanitary funds put into my hands, and have begged of the commission for our sick boys. The convalescent camp is close by now and I have really turned doctor. The boys were telling me this morning that what I have got for them has done more to cure them than all the doctor's work. I am very glad that I can do for them. It pays for all trouble and long rides to see the gratitude the poor fellows display. I hope we are not going to lose any of these men now sick. Most they need is rest and change of duty.

Very truly affectionately,
William

Thursday, July 21st

Near Petersburg
July 21st 1864

Dear Wife,

I have nothing new to report, indeed I should imagine nothing doing in this region had I not rode down to the left of our position. When General Grant moves, he does not mean to leave a large gap through which the Rebels can come in upon his rear. His connection with the river must be made secure, then he will be at liberty to move. I must say I wish he would hurry up.

This hanging along as we are now doing is very unpleasant. I find enough for a lazy man to do every day in the care of the sick and convalescents, but I want movements made for the sake of the cause.

I was very glad to hear that Mrs. Hunt had become a Christian. I don't want you to tell her, but her husband was overpowered by temptation and got too much liquor in his skin and thereby fell into disgrace. I hope he will be kept in the future, but where a man has such a terrible thirst it is almost like an Ethiopian changing his skin.

I am anxiously waiting a letter from Harry. The last one he wrote me amused me highly by the aged style in which it was written. When he read about Colonel Drake's death he let the letter fall and sat struck dumb with "amazement."

I have had two letters from Captain Chaddock and have answered them. I have had one from Captain Scott and have begun an answer. You know he

Naham S. Scott enrolled at Jamestown, New York, as a captain in Company C, 112th New York Volunteers. He was discharged for disability on May 24, 1864 (courtesy U.S. Army Heritage and Education Center [USAHEC]).

has an insane wife. She is so much better that he has been to see her and she was allowed by the Superintendent of the Insane Asylum to accompany him to a relative's in the country for a visit. He himself is very poorly.

How much of sorrow there is in this world. There are many wives whose husbands are not in the army who have many more sources of unhappiness than you. I rejoice that there is a world where there is no war, no sorrow. I suppose you may see some of the returned soldiers who are wounded. Captain Ludwick opened a box sent about the time of the battle of Cold Harbor to a sergeant of his regiment who was killed there. It had nice dried cherries, quantities of nuts, cans of fruit, a pail of butter of her own make and etc. A neat little housewife also filled with needles, thread, buttons. I thought how many smiles were shed over the packing of that box, how much love was unburdened in these gifts and how many fond wishes, hopes and prayers went with them. Alas, the noble man to whom they were sent fell in the thick woods and was buried by strangers at night.

The paymaster has not yet arrived. I am sorry but you must try some of my friends. Captain Ludwick's is just now in very poor health. I believe I am about as tough as any officer we have. Lieutenant Colonel Smith has been back here since Sunday morning and has just left for the regiment. He is not over vigorous.

Yours affectionately as ever,
William

Tuesday, July 26th

Near Petersburg
July 26th (Tuesday) 1864

Dear Wife,

I put in the day of the week but I might be mistaken in the day of the month. I am much better today and have great reason to be very grateful to God. Many of our officers have been affected in the same way. It is called Appomattox fever. Some have had its worst form. Captain Oley is now very sick at Chesapeake General Hospital. Lieutenant Hought Allen, Lieutenant Crane, Captain Russ, Captain Ludwick and Colonel Smith, Surgeon Mead have all been quite as sick as myself. So that I am not the only one. Quite a large number of chaplains and Christian Commission agents are also sick. Chaplain Taylor is very sick at Washington.[72]

A fine little boy from Fredonia who came out with the brigade guard was walking with a friend towards the rifle pits where our regiment are again, and was hit in the elbow by a stray bullet and the wound is really quite serious. He is a dear sweet boy and we feel great solicitation.

I can write no more for the mail is nearly made up. The solicitude I feel for all gunshot wounds is the danger of fever setting in.

The wound of Lewis is not dangerous of itself.[73]

Love to all. A long letter the middle of the week.

Affectionately your husband.

Wednesday, July 27th

Field Encampment 112th N.Y. Vols.
Near Petersburg
July 27th 1864

My dear Wife,

I always mean when I am sick, to keep you informed precisely as to my condition. I have written you twice this week and now I am seated for the third time.

I am glad to be able to say in this as in my letter yesterday that I am again on the uphill grade. I hope also that care and as good diet as can be obtained will keep me in this condition. The climate along this region I am told is a bad one for fevers.

Someone told Colonel Smith that City Point would have been made a large commercial mart before this, were it not for the unhealthiness of the locality. I did not believe a week ago that we should have been here at this time. I supposed then that movements were in progress which would give us possession of Petersburg. But it seems that Grant meets with obstacles which it tasks all his energy to meet.

He has tried to draw out Lee to fight him on open ground but thus far without success. Evening before last the 2nd Corps was moved round across the James and had a pretty smart little fight yesterday morning. We took a four gun redoubt and about 100 prisoners with but small loss on our side. I don't know the meaning of it, but I think Grant means to get between Petersburg and Richmond.

We are hoping to hear of the fall of Atlanta tonight. We have heard rumors of it and are sure that we are in possession of part of the city, but we believe only what comes well confirmed. There are so many unreliable stories in the papers we are getting very skeptical.

I don't see as the prospect of a speedy termination of the war is very flattering. But one thing is certain. The three years of your humble servant are getting narrowed down to one year and 2 months and then if God spares my life, I will let younger men take my place and find some little nook of earth by the banks of a babbling stream, with "a cot in the valley I love" sending forth from its two embowered chimneys the smoke that speaks of domestic comfort. Then with my wife and children, old horse, cows and pigs, I hope to enjoy that "calm repose" which the old warrior needs, and live the little rest of life's brief day in peace. Give love to all friends. Tell Freddy I don't forget him if I don't write him.

> *Author's note: It appears that Hyde intended to end this letter at this point. For whatever reason, he continued and added two additional pages before closing the letter.*

I am pleased with the idea of presenting Mr. Bookstaver with an engraving either that or some valuable recent publication such as Kirk's History of Charles of Burgundy 2 volumes.[74] I thought Cobb was very cool when I was at home. He did not come and sit down in the cart and make conversation as formerly but still he did not act the hog as he did to you.

I bought my ticket which I need not have done but thought best as I did not wish to be under obligation to him.

I wish I knew if Willie Carpenter is in this region.[75] If he is, I will try and see him. We are trying to get Uncle Abe a furlough. I signed a certificate for him which I think will materially help him and his letter went with it. Lieutenant Talcott has no doubt talked of resigning. He thinks he ought to be captain, and has not been used just right. I think he won't resign in a hurry just now. Five officers in the 3rd New York resigned the other day because they thought the colonel commanding the brigade had given them too much to do. And Butler has ordered them dishonorably dismissed [from] the service with loss of all pay and then to be sent to the trenches as laborers to dig with spade and pickaxe. I kept hoping that soon some time will be given to affairs which will close up this sad war. We lost 15 men the other day, prisoners when the picket line was assailed.

Love to Freddy and kind remembrances to the Carpenters and friends.

Most truly,
Wm. L. Hyde

Monday, August 1st

Camp 112th N.Y. Vols.
August 1st 1864

My dear Wife,

Here we are this Monday morning having made another change of base. Saturday morning about five o'clock our brigade with the Ninth Corps were drawn up in successive lines preparatory to a charge upon a redoubt, which had been mined. The first operation was to blow up the fort. This was done in fine style, a complete success. The mine was lighted at precisely 5 o'clock and the huge mass of earth with men and guns were lifted up into the air. Some men were blown over into our advance pits. One man who came over unharmed said he thought it was rather unceremonious to send a man kiting through the air in that shape before he had eaten his breakfast. After the redoubt was blown up we opened a terrible artillery fire along our whole line. Then the troops made a charge. The negro regiments first. We got possession of the redoubt without the loss of a man.

With a very slight loss we got possession of the main works of the enemy. We held two lines and were preparing to make our position secure when the negros and some white troops in front were seized with panic and broke and ran and pressed the troops in the rear by sheer force of numbers. Some officers stood well and tried to stay the rush but it was in vain and in a few minutes the work of weeks was lost. Our brigade was just getting into position when the stampede took place. They did what they could to arrest it but were too feeble. One man told me that a huge nigger came tumbling over him and almost broke his back! In our endeavoring to hold the position till the line could be reformed, our regiment suffered some casualties. We had one man killed and eleven wounded. Two men mortally wounded. I do not know of any with whom you are acquainted. We remained in the front of our works until about five o'clock pm when the regiment was marched back into the trenches where they had been so long.

We had heard that we were to go to Washington. At any rate that we were to leave the position in which we then were. So about 2 am yesterday morning we were woke up and told to prepare for Washington. I assure you I did not feel very well pleased with the proposed change. For to go to Washington I knew would be equivalent to marching all over Northern Virginia and Maryland. When we got started we knew that we were not going to City Point as we supposed, but were to cross the Appomattox for Bermuda Hundred. We had an awful march. Six men were sun struck in our regiment and in every regiment in the brigade there were large numbers. It seems to me that it was the hottest day of the season.

About noon we went into a field this side of the river and collected the sick together. There was no medicine for the sun struck men. So I jumped on my horse and rode off to the Sanitary Commission, got a bottle of Jamaica ginger and a bottle of spirits and went around and administered it myself. We had very good success with most of the cases and when we left for our bivouac, we put them into the hospital. I was very tired at night. Slept under the open canopy of heaven and slept well. Here I am this Monday morning writing to you. I hope this will find you in good health. I feel quite cheerful since we have not to go to Washington. We understand here that Terry's Division went. I must say that I think affairs in the country look somewhat gloomy. I am astonished at some things the government is doing. This recruiting new regiments and enlisting almost solely negro soldiers will prove in the long run very disastrous.[76] I shall hope to hear from you tomorrow. I get your letters quite regularly. I have not heard from Harry for sometime past. I shall write to him this week.[77]

With love as ever,
William L. Hyde

Thursday, August 4th

Near Bermuda
August 4th 1864

My dear Wife,

We are still here quiet in camp. It is a safer place then opposite Petersburg and seems absolutely lonesome after the excitement at Petersburg. There every day and especially every night the cannonading was incessant. The musketry firing also was continuous and I could never visit the regiment at the front without having the unpleasant sensation of a bullet humming side of my head or knocking the dirt off the parapet into my face to say nothing of a shell now and then bursting and raising the dust generally.

But here the quiet is almost like that of home. Our pickets go out in broad light and take their places within musket shot of the Rebs who look on without firing and there has scarcely been the discharge of a gun for three weeks. How long this will continue I know not. I am glad for our men that we can have a season of repose. The work we did in front of Petersburg was the severest. Run-ins were constant, exposure in the marches boiled with heat by day and no sleep at night. In peril going in and coming out. The sickness began to increase very fast.

I am much better since coming here. Though it is hard to keep well an army face in the summer time. Lieutenant Parker has just returned and it seems almost like getting home to talk with him.[78] He has not got his baggage yet but expects it every moment and when he gets it he says I have a little package. I shall be glad to get it. As soon as I get pay which I am expecting every day, I think I shall have to send for some clothes. I shall not, however, get a thing that I can decently do without as I want you to have all the money I can send home.

We have got our camp fixed quite neatly here for a shelter tent camp. Today is the day of fast and I hope that the country feels the importance of the day. Oh if the night's spirit of prayer and humiliation pervades the land, the Lord I believe will turn the tide of prosperity in our favor. I don't think there is any observance of it in this part of the army. We are to have here a sword presentation to General Foster. The money was raised last winter. 13th Indiana, 112th New York and 6th Massachusetts and General Foster's staff participated. The sword is a magnificent affair. Colonel Smith is to make the presentation speech. I will write you all about it. I must now close as it is about mail time.

> Very affectionately,
> William

Sunday, August 7th

> Camp 112th N.Y. Vols.
> Near Hatcher's Va
> August 7th 1864

Dear Wife,

It is again the evening of the Holy Sabbath. I cannot realize that about three months have passed away since I left you. I am surprised at those who don't care to have furloughs. That furlough is a bright spot in the horizon of the last two years, I live on the memories associated with it. They come up before me almost constantly and I verily believe that the preservation of my health if not of my life is greatly owing to the quickening impacts of that brief visit home.

This has been a pleasant day to me. I have had regimental service and also prayer meeting. I've had a most excellent prayer meeting this evening. Several men of the 117th New York were over and it was good to be there. Monday is never a blue day to me in the army when I have been able to hold my wonted services.

We are for the present resting in camp. I rather think we may be here now three or four weeks. A large detail for some important work is called for and it is to be filled by volunteers. I [am] inclined to think quite a number, some 2 or 300, will volunteer from our division and if so the probabilities are that the remainder of the division will be kept here on this part of the line to do picket duty.

We now send for our regiment 190 men every other day for picket. So I hope that we can look with some degree of certainty to a period of rest during this hot weather.

It is rather lonesome here compared with what it was [on] the other side of the Appomattox. There you had a full view of the vastness of the Army of the Potomac. All of the apparatus of war on a scale of giganticness rarely equaled in the history of war. Then too every step beyond certain limits were fraught with peril. Death lay in wait for you in every side. Now you can ride out onto the picket line in full view of the Johnny's without being molested. Then almost every night your slumbers were disturbed by the sound of hostile cannon and though a mile or two from the line of fire, the crack of the rifles were heard all night long and if you were a little nervous, it would be sure to keep you awake all night. But here you want to hear a cannon once in a while for the sake of the music of it. I was at Bermuda Landing Saturday morning and a gunboat was firing into the woods opposite. I stood a long time and watched it. It really quite thrilled and inspired me to hear a cannon near enough to make a respectable noise. They had a man wounded on the picket line last night. He was so careless as to shoot himself. He did it accidentally. I felt sorry for him for he is a fine young man. In our present quiet camp, we pair off two by two. Dr. Washburn and I have a tent together. The colonel and Captain Ludwick tent together and mess together and Quartermaster Shaw and I and the surgeon. But Shaw says he will not mess with Dr. Washburn and I suppose the mess will soon be broken up. If so, I shall try to get some captain to board me.

The doctor is one of those unpractical beings that you cannot change and his peculiarities are such that most cannot get along with him. But I have no trouble with him whatsoever. He seems to me a very inoffensive man. He is old maidish and asks questions very much as John Merrill used to and about as much to the purpose.

The colonel I don't like and never can. Yet he is very kind to me and willing to do anything I want for the religious welfare of the regiment. I shall be heartily glad when the time comes for me to retire from the service. I don't know when that will be.

We are having today, Monday, the hottest day yet. I have been keeping quiet in my tent all day. Your letter reached me this morning. I hope you will be able to stay at Mr. Carpenter's but if you cannot you must do the next best thing. I am sorry in many accounts that I did not try and get another small house [to] buy one when I sold mine. I am almost sorry that I sold at all. Well there is no use in sighing. You must do the best you can. I hear they are beginning to pay the troops. If so, I shall be able to send you some money very soon and then if you can go nowhere else you care to go to a hotel. I think perhaps you had better offer a little now for board. Perhaps there is where the shoe pinches. I am indignant at Mary Shelton's treatment of you and Fred. I would go to Fredonia or Westfield and board rather than be treated in that way. I wish you were keeping house in that little house opposite Mrs. Bellows. I am much obliged to Charlie Cander for his good wishes for me but I think it would be wretched poor policy both for the church as well as for myself to settle again in Dunkirk. I feel utterly afflicted as to all the future of my ministry but truly God will assign me some place.

The offering of the country looks very dark to me, darker than they ever have dear. I almost despair at times but in God is our trust. He will use us best to subserve his great purpose.

I am glad you hear so often from Harry. I must write the boy this week. May the Lord keep and bless you and make all your path clear.

Very affectionately,
William L. Hyde

Wednesday, August 10th

This camp is in excellent order. Colonel Smith deserves great credit for the manner in which he keeps everything up connected with the regiment. (Journal)

Thursday, August 11th

The commanding officer of the brigade is piling on orders thick [and] fast. The commands are very restrained under them. There are 6 roll calls a day. Drills, recitations and all arrangements as if we were in a camp of reserve or at a post rather than in the field and in open campaign. (Journal)

> Camp 112th N.Y. Vols.
> Near Hatcher's Va
> August 11th 1864

My dear Wife,

I have just finished a letter to Harry and now I must put this one through to you. I am pleased to get your letters with such regularity as I have for sometime past. I almost always get one Sunday or Monday morning. Generally Monday and then again Thursday or Friday. It will be Friday this week as Thursday's mail has already been received and there was nothing from you. I presume that a letter is here about the fifth day after leaving home. I saw a Rebel paper of last Tuesday, last evening. It contained the very brief dispatch from Mobile that every Reb vessel had been either captured, sunk or beached by Farragut excepting the *Morgan*, which got away over Mobile Bar.[79]

I take it from the accounts that Farragut has gained a splendid victory. To that with the steady progress at Atlanta, Farragut's success and Averell's good fortune in western Virginia, the horizon looks lighter than it did.[80]

We are still suffering from excessive heat. Mercifully the nights are cool. If the nights were as hot as the days, I don't know what would become of us. But we can sleep nights. Yesterday the heat was overpowering. It seemed as though it was a labor to breathe.

I went down Tuesday to the hospital at Point of Rocks and it seemed on my return as though the sun would scorch through me. But there is one consolation, the days are growing shorter and even if the dry weather continues the weather must become cooler. We had an alarm last night. It was feared that the Rebs were about to make a dash and at 3 this am the regiment marched up to the breastworks and took positions. But no Rebs came and at breakfast time the regiment all came in. We now get all the news from Petersburg by way of the New York papers. It is almost impossible to learn anything here.

I forgot to tell you in my last that Lieutenant Barber had been here and had gone again. He brought me some towels, handkerchiefs, which were very acceptable. As soon as we get pay, I shall send for a box of goodies, etc. We can get things here by express when properly directed without difficulty.

John A. Dix commanded the Department of Virginia and Department of the South during the war and was responsible for establishing a prisoner exchange between the North and South.

Tomorrow Quartermaster Shaw goes to Norfolk to get some things for officers. We have all our extra baggage stored there. I shall send for some things by him. I have two boxes of camp conveniences there.

I want to tell you more about Lieutenant Barber. He came back here very lame with rheumatism and unfit for duty. He had on his way here reported to Washington and the doctors there told him that if he went to Annapolis as he expected, he would be mustered out of the service. So he thought he would not report there but to the regiment. Three days after he got here came an order for him to report for duty to General Dix at New York City.[81] This will probably allow him to go to Elmira on recruiting service. I am glad, for Barber is a sick man. His joints swell to nearly twice their natural size and he does not take a step without pain.

He finished up all his business with the regiment and left last Sunday night for Bermuda Landing to take Monday's boat for New York. He did not know whether he would get to Dunkirk or not at present. Indeed he does not know what he will have to do.

Newell Toles, Mrs. Peek's brother, is now very sick. He has had diarrhea so long that he looks like those pictures of men out of Libby Prison which were in Harpers. I fear he will not live long unless he goes north. I am afraid he has squandered his health. He is a very reckless boy and when he has anything good to eat he feeds like a hog. I fear he has fatally abused himself. It is almost impossible to do anything with such a boy.

If you grant them furloughs or discharges, it only encourages other boys to make themselves sick for the sake of getting home. Now there are men in this and every regiment who would risk the severest sickness for the sake of getting home three months. There are men who came into the service with bodily infirmities such as breaches (hernia) which they knew would in the course of a few months present for them their discharge. They thus get a high bounty, serve a few months, do nothing and get through. Now, I have not much pity for such men. I think that since few ought to die as a warning to others. Surgeon Washburn has made out an application for furlough for Toles and I hope the boy will be permitted to go home if he lives to get there. I wish you could have seen Mrs. Drake and Mrs. Carpenter. I wrote Mrs. Drake the other day. I expect Captain Chaddock will pay you $8.00 or $8.50 for me. If so use it. The money was what was due onboard and what was due on a subscription when he left. He was robbed while sick of $150 in money and a nice field telescope. There are some men who ought to be hung.

Well dearest, I hope this will find you in good health and that you will be provided with house at present and home. Bye bye.

Very affectionately,
William

Friday, August 12th

The numerous roll calls provoke a spirit of sedition among the men of the regiment. Today at every beat of the drum, shouts and outcries were pushed from one regiment to another through the brigade. The consequence was the colonel commanding ordered roll call every hour, day and night, and every man and officer to be present. He soon, however, rescinded the order. (Journal)

Saturday, August 13th

Two of our men who were at Hospital Point of Rocks returned to the regiment. Goodrich (I) [and] Vanscoy (E).[82] The most of the others have been sent north. Today orders have been received to send all the sick and those not able to go on with the regiment to general hospital. There is a movement of troops. The Second Corps embarked on transports. We are to be ready to march any moment after dusk. The men have the idea that we are going north. (6) Six sent to hospital. 59 sick in quarters. For week. (Journal)

Sunday, August 14th

Last night troops and artillery were moving all night. We had, early in the evening, an extra team sent to us. But later were ordered to remain. All the brigades were sent to the front either as picket or in the breastworks. Today the men are all lying in the works. The other brigades of our division have gone; the 1st and 3rd Divisions are gone. They are now known to have gone to the vicinity of Deep Bottom and that the Second Corps moved farther down the river to land at some place for a move on the flank of the Rebels. It was reported this morning that we had an engagement which resulted favorably for us giving us the picket line of the enemy. (Journal)

> Camp 112th Regt N.Y. Vols
> Near Hatcher's Va
> August 14th 1864

My dear Wife,

This is the afternoon of the holy Sabbath and I was just getting ready to go up to the regiment in order to hold regimental service when a short shower came up and while it is pouring out its grateful drops to cool this fevered atmosphere and lay the excessive dust, I will begin my letter to you. I wrote you last Thursday. All was quiet then and there were not even any rumors of any present change in our position. But yesterday in the forenoon we began to hear rumors of a move which towards the latter part of the day assumed fear. One was that we were to leave at night for Bermuda Landing then to take transports probably for Baltimore or Washington. Another was that we were going to North Carolina, etc.

We knew that the 2nd Corps have been moving from the front of Petersburg and had taken transports but from what point we did not know. We also knew that there were some more active movements near Deep Bottom that is across the James River and farther towards Richmond than we are. So far we knew and the rest we could not even guess. But last night all the troops of our division and in fact all the 10th Corps except our brigade moved from this point leaving our brigade here to picket this whole front some five miles in length. We do not however feel any alarm for our position is a very strong one and one hundred men with the cannon we have, are equal to a thousand outside the fortifications.

We know that there has been a very sharp fight this morning across the river. We drove the enemy and have guarded some important points. But we are anxiously awaiting the operations of the 2nd Corps. We received orders in the evening to be in readiness to move at a moment's notice and then we heard that we were not to be moved. So after preparing to go and making all ready, we are again so lucky as to be permitted to remain quiet in our present position. The shower did not last long and it's cleared off. More sultry than before but I started out to hold service.

The regiments are today in the breastworks. I went into there about as far as from the post office to Dr. Williams' and had the regiment called together and had worship. Some were present from the 142nd New York. I was quite overcome with the heat but it has been cloudy since and of course not so uncomfortable. I always feel thankful when the regiments are exempt from marching and fighting. I think a fight must be going on this evening for I now hear the roar of the cannon in the distance. I hope Grant will accomplish now some little success that shall take us nearer Richmond and such as will encourage the northern heart. Unless Harry writes me and if he does I wish you would enclose his letters to you. I want to hear from him more directly than I do.

Monday. Julius has been out with a little cart and tray. There is a lot of lumber to fix up my tent so I have been trying to work just as though we were to stay 3 months and my tent is floored with hardtack boxes. I have a table and Dr. Washburn and I each of us a bunk. We are now ready to move for just as soon as a soldier gets fixed up comfortably, then he must be ready for a move. I have made what I think quite an ingenious chair out of some boards and Jules found a chair for me. So I am well provided for. We expected an attack last night and every man who could lift a musket was sent out to the front. But the night passed off as quietly as ever. A corporal of the 117th Regiment either deserted or was caught while out for an exchange of papers. This made us all very nervous for if the Rebs had known how small a force we have they might think they could force our lines hard. We have heard nothing yet of the force that went out Saturday night.

I got your letter of Thursday this morning. It was brought to me before I got up. So you have had a slight taste of warm weather. You can appreciate our situation.

Very Affectionately,
William

I hope to get my stamps soon. I have plenty of paper.

Monday, August 15th

The sickness in the regiment is increasing. Fever and diarrhea the principal complaints. We report 72 sick in camp today. Held division service yesterday at the breastworks. The day was excessively hot. A shower in the afternoon only served to leave the air more stifling. A shower in the evening was more grateful. Today the heat has not seemed to abate. Towards evening constant thunder showers. Last night, all the cooks, ostlers and every man capable of carrying a gun was sent to the front. It having been reported that a corporal of the 117th either deserted or was forced into the Rebel lines while out for an exchange of newspapers. If he chose, he could give such a statement of our weakness as would induce an attack upon us. But the night passed off quietly. (Journal)

Tuesday, August 16th

Last night heavy firing in the direction of Petersburg. All quiet on our front. (Journal)

Friday, August 19th

There has been no change in the position here. We heard very heavy firing yesterday near Petersburg. The Tenth Corps is reported to have done themselves honor in the actions near Deep Bottom on the north of the James. They took three lines of the enemy's works and yielded the last for want of reinforcements after holding it one hour and twenty minutes. The four pieces of artillery and the battle flags captured and sent to General Meade by command of General Hancock were taken by the 10th Corps.[83] The loss of our corps was severe. One thousand at least in Terry's Division, 50 officers. 15 officers in Colonel Hawley's Brigade.[84] The Second Corps is already back again in front of Petersburg. (Journal)

Near Hatchers
Camp 112th Vols.
August 19th 1864

My dear Wife,

This is Friday morning. It should be Thursday so far as writing to you is concerned. I meant to have written you yesterday but in the morning Captain Ludwick came to me saying that he was going to Bermuda Hundred and would like my company. I was very glad of an opportunity to get a little relief from the monotony of camp life here so I cheerfully accepted the proposal not thinking of being gone longer than until noon. But I did not get back until night and our mail leaves here about noon. The result is you will not get your usual letter from me so soon by a day. But before I tell you about my journey, I must tell you that this morning early I got your precious letter of the 14th containing the photograph of my darling Freddie. It is I think a very good likeness, but subject to the same discount in a degree that applies to yours. His face in repose is not natural so that those who do not see him except when lighted up with enthusiasm, do not recognize the portrait. But I am very much delighted with it and shall put it with my choice things.

You speak of my answering your questions that is the same old complaint I used to make. I suppose it occurs in this way. I receive your Monday letter Friday morning, just the day after I have written, and I get your Thursday letter either Monday or Tuesday morning, generally Tuesday. And I always send one Monday. And though I have read them over and over yet I most always sit down and write rapidly and in consequence. I fail to write what I would wish so far as questions and concerns. I am sorry that I did not answer your inquiries in regard to Mr. Shirley. There is no positive certainty that he is dead. He was not seen after the first charge at Cold Harbor. He may have died as did others and have been buried by the prisoners of some other corps. Or he may have fallen inside the works and when the enemy charged may have been taken prisoner. We do not know anything about him and cannot learn. The probability is that he was killed. What a terrible suspense it is thus to be uncertain as to the fate of one's friends; not to know whether they are dead or are lingering in hospitals in the Rebel dominion, or whether they died outright or suffered all that human nature can bear of pain.

Winfield S. Hancock was wounded at Gettysburg while commanding the 2nd Army Corps. He was a Democratic candidate in the 1880 presidential election.

Mr. Hunt wrote his wife about Shirley and I think wrote Mrs. Shirley. Mr. Shirley became a much better man after he came with the army than he had ever been before. He was a great drunkard at home. It did Mr. Hunt a vast deal of good having Mrs. Hunt join the church. He says he hopes when he gets out of the army that they will have a much better home than ever before. I can't think the Williams ever wanted Erasmus to be minister at Dunkirk. What they want is a sensation preacher, a Henry Ward Beecher man, and they want to introduce such a man themselves so that they may keep their influence prominent. They were once "the Presbyterian Church" and they can't endure that newer people should throw them into the shade.

By all means send Freddie up to Kate Hegunbourg if she keeps a good school. I am rather pleased that Mr. Wright has concluded to remain in Fredonia. It seems good to have a man planted in a parish, and so good a man. Yet I think his personal interests would have been promoted at Cincinnati. So the Mr. Scott who is to preach at Silver Creek, Mr. Scott whose wedding we attended. If so, when you go to Silver Creek call on them. He is an excellent man. I have not seen that communication from Reverend Mr. Judd and hardly think I know him. He may have come to know me through the commission. I am there often. I wrote Mother a few days since but have not heard from them since I was at Petersburg.

I hope to hear that Henry has entirely recovered his health. Penn Magorin is going to Europe. All broken down by the loss of Annie in poor health. I am truly sorry for him. I hope that he has done wisely in accepting the president of Ierva College, but I fear not.[85] The salary is too uncertain.

I had a letter from Colonel Redington from Nashville, Tennessee. He will find it hard to fill up the quota of Pomfret with northern negros. It is very unjust to the army in the field to fill these thinned ranks with undisciplined negros. It is degrading to them. The negro is not the equal of the white men at present and the country has as much claim as the thousands who stay at home as upon the noble men in the field. I am not certain that I shall vote for Lincoln. I am disgusted with the administration. Yet I shall vote for no copperhead, unless the soldiers are soon paid. Lincoln will not get a corporals guard to vote for him. It is outrageous to send men to fight while at home their families are starving. Grant has money enough for speculators but none for the poor soldiers. I declare I won't vote for Lincoln unless the administration shows more vigor between now and next November. This is between us. You need not tell Dunham. I think that our cause stands better here than people at home realize.

Our army holds its own in numbers while the Rebs are wasting away. Shelling and bullets are slowly wearing away the vigor of this army. Grant too is fertile in places. He does not give up because one fails. He is now near Richmond on the north of the James and is compelling Lee to do what he does not wish to do—fight him. Thus he is making breaches in Lee's forces continually. True we lose men but when they lose men the loss cannot be repaired.

I am most concerned for affairs at home. The currency and the conscription. I fear that people at home will not make the sacrifices necessary to give us present advantages. I fear that the war will be prolonged through the weak pusillanimity that shrinks from a draft. Indeed I know not what will become of us unless the administration puts things right though. Fill up the army and force the Rebs now right to the wall. Farragut's victory is cheering. I am glad you went to Buffalo. I hope you will to Niagara and if the man that hired that money wants to pay it let him do so and use it up for your own advantage. I have nearly six month's pay due. It will be six months at the end of this month. I have had Fred's picture before me all the while I have been writing this. How I would like to have him with me. I hope to hear from Harry soon. I sent the 2 dollars for stamps. Got 8 this morning.

Your affectionate husband,
William L. Hyde

We are having a nice rainfall now and I think the drought is over.

Saturday, August 20th

We learn that while the operations over the river were going on, the Fifth Corps Warren's was held in reserve near City Point.[86] When the object aimed at by General Grant of drawing a large part of the Petersburg force away to resist an advance towards Richmond, had been accomplished, the Fifth Corps moved (18th) towards the Weldon Road striking it at Ream's Station. There advancing towards the city, they drove the enemy's pickets on to his reserves and drove them back to the fortifications of the city and commenced tearing up track. They had torn up a mile of the track when Hill's Division, which had been moved to the other side of Petersburg and held in reserve in consequence of operations north of the James, was reported advancing. A sharp fight ensued and the enemy made desperate efforts to recover possession of the road. The assaults were successively repulsed with severe loss to the enemy. This evening our regiment, which were temporarily occupying positions of the 1st Division at the earthworks, were relieved by their return from the north of the James and returned to camp. Frequent and heavy showers have occurred during the week. The weather debilitating though not the excessive heat of the first of the month. Sickness still rather increasing.

There were 5 sent to general hospital and 65 are sick in quarters. Assistant Surgeon Mead, Captain Dunham, Lieutenants Potter and Crane and Sergeant Major Ticknor among those sick.[87] Colonel Smith also, though not reported.

The whole number of the regiment present and absent sick and well is 733. The number of officers and men for duty 335. (Journal)

Sunday, August 21st

Sunday. Service held at 11 o'clock in the rear of our camp. Evening our regiment with rest of brigade ordered to be in readiness to move at a moment's notice. Light marching order [with] twenty-four hours rations. (Journal)

Monday, August 22nd

Yesterday in the morning there was a terrific cannonading near Petersburg. We learned that several assaults were made by the enemy to get possession of the Weldon Railroad. All of which were repulsed. The regiment left about midnight last night. Moved to the left of Butler's defenses passed out and along to an old mill near our picket line. Then halted and soon the whole force returned to camp which reached about 5. It seems that General Birney had proposed to seize the railroad between Petersburg and Richmond but ascertained that the enemy had strongly reinforced this line.[88] The attempt was therefore abandoned. 5 taken sick near Petersburg returned this evening from the 18th Corps Hospital. Three of them utterly unfit for duty. (Journal)

Near Hatcher's Va
August 22nd 1864

Dear Wife,

I was glad to get your letter this morning which brought your personal and family history down to within five days. It always pleases me to hear of your going about whether to Buffalo, Silver Creek or Fredonia or anywhere also. I would like to see that wonderful picture at Buffalo, also to sit in Dr. Rogers' buggy and let you drive me around town.

Dr. Smith wrote me last week that you and his wife had been riding somewhere with Dr. Rogers' horse making some sort of a joke out of it. I am glad Nan wrote you so newsy a letter. I suppose you remember Mr. Clark Hyde, Pa's youngest brother, who was so kind to us at Jersey City when we were traveling with Harry and Wallie from Bath to Dunkirk.[89] I hope by writing frequently and ignoring all the past that then may be brought about a better state of things in the feelings which have existed.

I sometimes think that I have not been sufficiently generous and charitable towards Nannie. It must be awful to be shut up so long to one little confined room and nothing but thirst, think, plot, scheme, etc. Nan had a great deal of energy and power about her and a disposition to rule and having been pitied almost to death since her sickness, was naturally inclined to feel that she must have her own way in everything and everybody about her under her thumb. But it is not best to harbor grudges or unkind feelings. I think the family has suffered much, especially Father and Mother, for we never have had any family jars of any kind.

I hope you will continue to write and just as far as possible as though nothing had ever happened, never alluding to or mentioning it if they do not. I imagine Nannie feels worse towards me than she does towards you. I never speak of her in my letters to brother and she never sends any messages to me. I guess my last letter to her was rather severe. I don't feel as hard as I used to and hope I shall outgrow all evil feelings.

It would not be pleasant to me to visit Bath with just my present feelings towards her though if I had the opportunity I should probably go. I am glad to hear that Henry is better. I fear however he will not outlive Nannie. I think his symptoms are rather alarming. How sad it would be if Nannie should outlive both Henry and Mother. Sister would take care of her as Mother has done.

I suppose by this time the doctor here returned from his visit and that you and Carrie have had a long talk about matters last.

I keep thinking of you all, all the time, and begin to count the months, which must elapse before the regiment's term of service expires. I laughed well at the idea you had that Captain Chaddock had $850 for you. I wish it had been that little smug. I am glad you have got $8.50 to spend, part of it was mess money and part subscription. You can spend it and I will make all right here. I expect we have this week inflicted a terrible blow upon Lee's Army. Grant made a rapid move a week last Saturday to the north of the James as you have read. So large did it seem that Lee really expected an attempt upon Richmond, a thing which Grant did not hope to accomplish, but it drew away so much of Lee's forces from Petersburg, that Warren was able to seize the Weldon Railroad. At first the Rebels succeeded in pushing Warren back, but with frightful loss to themselves, still he held the road. Yesterday beginning about 2 am they made seven distinct assaults upon Warren and were repulsed each time with fearful slaughter. This is just as it should be. If they will not give up, they must be crushed and as it is impossible to do it in our overwhelming battle. For Lee will not risk a general engagement it must be done by a series of smaller ones. Grant by his strategy has forced them to fight, to dash upon our earthworks and the result is just such as ever attends their or our hurling men against earthworks. With the Weldon Railroad in our hands, Petersburg must soon fall. Deserters say, thus it has for a long time been common talk in their army, that when the Weldon Railroad is in our hands they must give up. Last night our regiment was ordered to be prepared with 24 hours rations, leave knapsacks and start about 12 o'clock. The rest of the brigade was also ordered out. We supposed that the object was to advance about 4 miles and take up the railroad between Petersburg and Richmond and I guess it was. But after getting out in that direction that Lee, fearing such a result, had been pouring men in upon that part of the line as fast as cars could take them, we therefore concluded that the loss of life would be too great and turned about. The whole expedition occupied the time between 12 midnight and breakfast time.

David B. Birney served as colonel of the 23rd Pennsylvania Infantry and commanded the 10th Army Corps in the Army of the James in the early stages of the Petersburg campaign.

Let our friends north keep up heart. Grant will come out right in time. He has the greatest military man of the age, Robert E. Lee, to contend against, a matter which materially interferes with all well laid plans but Grant is fertile in resources and by small blows delivered in succession, he will break up the army of Lee. When this is done, the worst is over. And be assured, dark as things look, it is being done faster than we have any idea of. Grant has positive knowledge that Lee is losing men very fast by sickness, overwork and the bullet, and when this army is gone there is nothing to take its place. Grant is not a genius and I am glad of it. But he is a great commander and his men believe in him. Our government ought to sustain him better and ought to pay the army. Tell Dr. Rogers to say to Mrs. Toles that Newell left for Fort Monroe the 19th or 20th and that he is in a very critical condition. I urged his care upon Dr. Washburn and he did his best to have him sent north on furlough. I hope he may get it at Norfolk. As to Charlie Koepke, the only way for him to go is to get a doctor to make an affidavit that he is very sick, unable to travel and will not be able for so many days and send one copy to the regiment and if his furlough requires him to go to the hospital, to send a copy there.[90]

I hope you are still well. We have hot weather but nothing like the weather we had in July and first of August. We have now an overabundance of showers.

With love to my Freddie.

Your affectionate Husband,
William L. Hyde

Tuesday, August 23rd

Tuesday. Rumors of a change begin to be rife. We have just got our camp in excellent order, good quarters, good walls, ovens for baking for officer's mess. We are too well established to stay. (Journal)

Camp 112th N.Y. Vols.
Near Hatchers Va
August 23rd 1864

My dear Wife,

This is a day earlier than my usual day of writing to you. But we have had the premonitions of a move tonight, so I will write you this afternoon and then if I should be so situated tomorrow that I could not write, you will get your letter a day earlier rather than later.

I hear that our corps, having been spending the month of August in this woodland retreat, are to be sent over to Petersburg to exchange places with the 18th Corps who are coming over to take their turn. I must say the prospect is anything but pleasing. The locality in front of Petersburg is far from being healthy. The shot and shell are apt to be thrown about in a very careless manner and it is often that our men get hurt. But I suppose it is only fair that we stand our chances with others.

Since I wrote you, military matters have not changed. We have had frequent showers and the weather is not quite so intolerable but it is hot. Too hot for comfort and I am glad to be able to keep quiet during the middle of the day. I can't imagine why that little two-headed flibbertigibbet at Stamford does not write to me. I want to hear from him "more than tongue can tell." Will you visit him this fall? I wrote H.C. Wright today to inform Newell Toles' mother that Newell is away at some hospital sent last week and yesterday, a furlough application for which was filed three weeks ago, came for him. If they know where he is, I will try and get it to him. We are trying to get a furlough for poor Fisk. He had a letter from his mother this morning saying she was very low and the poor man is almost distracted. I wish he could go on to see her once more. But it is almost impossible to get one through unless it is to save life. Two men went home this morning on leave. The doctor certifying it was necessary to save life.

I was glad to hear from Dr. Smith last week that the feeling towards Mr. Willard had greatly improved. I hope the people will have the good sense to secure him and support and sustain him. I wish you would say to Dr. S. Carrie that I would be glad to step into their house and welcome them home, but as I cannot I send them a hearty one from this little out of the way place. I want to hear all they have to tell about Bath. Tell Carrie that Zina H. Robinson is colonel of a regiment in the 2nd Brigade of our division.[91] I am sorry to say he is not considered over smart.

I am inclined to think it will be much more lively where we are going then it is where we now are. O how I long for this war to cease! It seems as though it would never end sometimes. I am constantly making plans for the time which shall succeed the close of this sad strife. I received a letter the other day from a young lady in the country who has a sick brother in the regiment. Among other pathetic strokes she says urging me to help him to a furlough. "O friend of the 'weary and heavy laden!' can you not aid this poor sick worn out young patriot to visit again the green house of his youth." I had to read that of course to the officers. It was about all that I could stand I assure you. Some of my letters are rich [and] others are deeply affectionate. I am ever glad to hear in your last that you had received my Bible sources for July. Please be kind enough to tell me if the numbers for January and April are also in the study or are where you know about them. I am very anxious not to have them lost. O what would I not give to be in my study once again and spend a week with my books. Please inquire of Dunham what will be the price of a suit of clothes, black frock and vest and dark blue pants. I don't care for the finest cloth but want that which will wear. As soon as payday I shall send for you to make me up a box.

Very truly and affectionately,
William L. Hyde

Direct the same as usual.

Wednesday, August 24th

This evening regiment under marching orders for Petersburg where we are to relieve the 18th Corps. Moved out of camp at evening and were located along the breastworks. (Journal)

Thursday, August 25th

This morning early the Rebs dashed upon our picket line and captured 15 of our regiment in the brigade. They were bravely repulsed along the line occupied by us and driven back. 1st Lieutenant G. F. Mount took command of the pickets along our lines after Captain Ewing, 117th New York, was shot and wounded.[92] He had just given the order to advance and was urging his men on when a bullet struck him just below the left shoulder and passed through his body coming out near the spine. He was brought off the field, complained of numbness in his limbs, was disinclined to talk and about eleven o'clock died. His remains were taken down to Bermuda Hundred to be embalmed and sent home. (Journal)

Camp 112th N.Y. Vols.
Near Hatchers Va
August 25, 1864

Editor, Dunkirk Journal:

This morning near daylight the enemy attacked the pickets on General Butler's line, in front of Bermuda Hundred. It was unexpected, from the fact that there had been no firing between the opposing forces on this line for more than two months. But though unexpected, we were not unprepared.

The sudden onset of the enemy on a portion of our line, where the nature of the ground was favorable to them, enabled them to gain temporary possession of that portion held by the 2nd Division (Turner's). They held it, however, but a short time, and were driven back with considerable loss in prisoners as well as in killed and wounded. We lost some men taken prisoners, and a few killed and wounded. Of the detail of the 112th New York Volunteers, occupying this line, there was one killed and two, perhaps four, taken prisoners. Lieutenant G. F. Mount, Company K, while bravely rallying his men to charge and drive back the enemy, was shot through the body, the ball entering first below the left shoulder. August Neil, Company D, and Thomas Brown, Company A, were taken prisoners.[93] Tenny, of Company G, and one other man were not accounted for before noon.[94]

Lieutenant Mount was a young man of fine intellect, and a brave, faithful soldier. A recommendation had been sent on for his commission as captain. The regiment was under marching orders for Petersburg where the 10th were to relieve the 18th Corps. They struck tents last evening, and were marched to the fortifications on Butler's front, expecting at daylight to be marched to Petersburg. The attack of the enemy detains all our division, at least today. Our new Major Ludwick, has already been mustered in, and wins esteem and confidence from his own commander, as well as the military powers superior to him.

Yours & C.,
Hyde (Newspaper)[95]

Friday, August 26th

The regiment has been detained until noon and it is uncertain how soon we shall be relieved. At eve orders came for the wagons to report at the brigade train at 7 o'clock. (Journal)

Saturday, August 27th

Orders last evening to march at midnight, were countermanded, and the brigade did not move till about 7 o'clock. They moved very slow and did not cross the Appomattox till about 9. At evening they were moved into the rifle pits at the left of the railroad and having the fort so familiar in the past, just on our left, its front in full view. (Journal)

Near Bermuda
August 27th 1864

Dear Wife,

I have a few moments leisure this Saturday morning and I thought I could not make better use of it than by writing you a few lines.

The regiment left for Petersburg early this morning. It was expected that they would move last evening. They had been packed up and under marching orders since Wednesday last, but the order came in the afternoon yesterday to move at 6 o'clock. Then it was countermanded to 11 and then they were ordered to wait until morning. I have been in the army long enough to know that it is wise policy to take care of yourself while you can. So I remained quietly in the old camp last night under a fly and got a tolerably good night's sleep. The regiment must have had a hard time at the breastworks for there were two violent thunder showers.

I start very soon for Petersburg and have not much doubt I shall get there as soon as the regiment, or soon after. We had got a nice camp here and hated to leave it. I received yesterday a very excellent letter from Mother, which I send to you. I received one also from Mrs. Drake.[96] Poor woman, she is very lonely. I will write you your usual letter to go Monday.

Very truly your husband,
William L. Hyde

Sunday, August 28th

Train which left for Bermuda to get material to furnish tents returned today with flooring, etc. All is unsettled yet but headquarters of regiment are tented, established in rear of regiment toward the ravine. (Journal)

Near Petersburg
Sunday August 28th [1864]

Dear Wife,

I found in my coat pocket this morning the letter written to you last Wednesday. In the confusion of packing, I put it there instead of into the mail bag. I am sorry for your disappointment. I started for the regiment yesterday noon. Spent part of the afternoon at Point of Rocks Hospital, then rode over and found the regiment lying in a field on the grass about a mile from where they are to be encamped. After dark they moved into the rifle pits. We are in about such a place as before. I will write you my usual letter tomorrow.

Affectionately,
William L. Hyde

Monday, August 29th

The names of the men captured last Thursday in the dash upon our picket line were:

Corporal	L. H. Stoddard	Company A
Private	Thomas Brown	Company A
Private	James Williams	Company A
Private	John Myers	Company C
Private	Oliver C. Myers	Company C
Private	Patrick Hodge	Company C
Private	William McLaughlin	Company C
Private	Augustus Neil	Company D
Private	Andrew Bennett	Company E
Private	John P. McDonald	Company E
Private	Simon Beyer	Company E
Private	William H. Hewitt	Company E
Private	George Apthorp	Company I
Private	Samuel F. Apthorp	Company I
Private	George Clute	Company I

The whole number reported present on the morning of the 27th was 361. Absent sick 259. The 22nd then were 398 present, 238 absent sick. Sent to hospital during the week: 27. Sick in regiment 8. The regiment still in the trenches on the left of the railroad. Three men joined the regiment from the general hospital on David's Island. Weaver, Company C, Richardson, Company C and [blank].[97]

Richardson was one of the slightly wounded in the action of June 1st and one of the first to return. Very few of those wounded at that time have as yet returned. And as will be seen above, of the available strength of the regiment, nearly one half are reported absent sick. (Journal)

Tuesday, August 30th

The regiment was relieved from the trenches last evening. They are today located in a pleasant ravine where they can rest. Last evening, the artillery from our whole line, cannon and mortars, opened upon the city which was at first sharply responded to. The scene from the rear of our headquarters was magnificent. (Journal)

Camp 112th N.Y. Vols.
Near Petersburg
August 30th 1864

My dear Wife,

I did not get yours of the 22nd until yesterday, it having been put in some desk. It was received while the regiment was moving. I have read Harry's letter with much amusement. I think he spells very well and is quite careful about beginning his sentences with capital letters. I was quite amused at his telling Fred he was glad to hear that he was well and "his hair is growing fast."

I am a little uncertain as to what it is best to do in regard to his education. I want him to study grammar either Latin or English very soon. I see he is going over geography again. I am afraid this is permitted because he wants to. My idea is that it is useless to go on with the same kind of studies year after year in the hope of being more perfect.

I think that change quickens the mind and helps to acquire a better education. I often worry as to what Harry will be best fitted for. But I will give him as good an education as possible and then he must go into life's battle to do the best he can.

I am indignant at what you tell me in regard to Mary Shelton's treatment of Fred. If I were home I should let Fred settle accounts with him in his own way. I should let him give him a good thrashing when he insults him. I am inclined to think the English way of letting boys settle these quarrels by their fists is the best in a world like this. I don't believe it best to buy back the house for we shall not live in Dunkirk after I get home from the war. But I wish you were in a little house by yourself or else at a boarding house or hotel where the people are really gentlemen and ladies. Had you not rather go to Fredonia and board than to stay there and be insulted? When you feel unreconciled to my continued absence, just think what you would do should I be taken away. Just think of Mrs. Drake with their children, and she is in poorer circumstances today than you would be, to be left alone. I had a very pleasant letter from her the other day which I will enclose in this. I sold Mrs. Carpenter's horse the other day for $125.00. By keeping him three months I saved $75.00 for her, as I could not have sold him for $50 when the colonel was shot.

I spent a poor Sunday, day before yesterday. We were so that I could not preach and all the morning I was riding about to see about a place to pitch camp. But we have to do such things in [the] military. I hear there is a probability of our being paid this week. I hope it is true for your sake as well as my own.

Very truly affectionately,
William

Wednesday, August 31st

The regiment was today mustered for pay. Six months' pay is now due the men and I see no signs of any paymaster at present. The result of this neglecting to pay the men is unfortunate. (Journal)

Thursday, September 1st

Rode over to the base hospital. Our men there are improving with few exceptions. General Grant has commenced a railroad track from the City Point to the Weldon Railroad. Our regiment was moved last evening into the trenches and now occupy the extreme right of the line resting on the river. The situation is peculiarly exposed to random shots from riflemen and, were not the works very strong, would be a very hot place from the fort opposite. The 117th Regiment lost 5 men while in these works. Nine men came back from general hospital last evening. (Journal)

Chaplain's Monthly Report[98]
112th Regiment New York Volunteers
For the month of August 1864

Camp of the 112th Regiment New York Volunteers
In the Field near Petersburg

September 1st 1864

Brigadier General L. Thomas[99]
Adjutant General

General,

I have the honor to submit the following as the chaplain's report of this regiment for the month of August 1864.

The first day of August found the regiment retired from the front of Petersburg in camp near the defenses of Bermuda Hundred.

The duties devolving upon them were now light, being simply picketing a portion of this front, and only about one third (⅓) of the effective force of the regiment was called upon daily for this work.

A regular camp for the whole brigade was established about five hundred yards in the rear of the entrenchments and nearly opposite Battery No. 6. Here, the command was enabled to rest and recruit after the severe and prolonged exposures in front of Petersburg. There was no firing between the pickets on either side.

Nothing worthy of note transpired until the evening of the 13th when, in conjunction with the other regiments of the brigade, we were moved from camp forward to the earthworks and stretched in a very attenuated line along this position; in consequence of the absence of Major General Birney, with the bulk of his corps, to cooperate in the movements then in progress on the north of the James.

On the 20th, Major General Birney having returned with his command, the regiment was relieved and returned to camp.

On the evening of the 22nd, in conjunction with the remainder of the brigade under Colonel Curtis, moved out on the road towards Port Walthall on a reconnaissance, and returned to camp early the next morning.

On the evening of the 24th under marching orders, we broke camp and moved forward to the entrenchments where we lay all night waiting further orders.

Early the next morning the enemy broke the long quiet on our front, dashed upon our picket line, capturing some prisoners and gaining temporary possession. We lost fifteen (15) men taken prisoners. The foe was however soon dislodged. In moving forward to expel the enemy from this line, 1st Lieutenant George F. Mount, Company K, was mortally wounded by a bullet, and died in a

Lorenzo Thomas served as Adjutant General at the beginning of the war and was responsible for organizing the first black soldier regiments in the Union army.

few hours. On the morning of the 27th took up line of march reaching the heights of Petersburg about 2 pm; where, remaining till evening, were moved into our position in the approaches to the city. The brigade occupies the extreme right resting on the Appomattox River.

During the month, the sick list in the regiment has been somewhat increased, as the following figures from the morning reports of successive weeks will testify.

	Sick in quarters	Sent to hospital
August 6	40	5
13	59	6
20	65	5
27	38	27*

*This large number on account of regiment being under marching orders

The sickness, however, has been in general less virulent then a year ago. It has consisted principally of light cases of fever and diarrhea.

Six (6) enlisted men died of wounds or sickness in hospitals during this month. Captain J. G. Palmeter, Company H, wounded in the arm at Cold Harbor died the first of the month at his home Jamestown, New York. 1st Lieutenant G. W. Barber who had been sick in hospital was on the first of the month detached and ordered to report to Major General Dix for duty. Captain E. A. Ludwick was on the 13th commissioned and on the 17th mustered as major of the regiment.

There are no other changes in the regiment worthy of note.

Religious services have been regularly held on the Sabbaths of the month with the exception of the last Sabbath when the situation of the regiment precluded it. A healthful moral tone has pervaded the regiment generally. During the days of the week the attention of the chaplain has been much devoted to visiting the general hospital and aiding in the care of those sick in quarters.

    Very respectfully submitted
    Your Obedient Servant
       W^m. L. Hyde
          Chaplain 112th Regiment New York
          Volunteers

Saturday, September 3rd

No change in the condition of the regiment or the forces contiguous. Last evening there was sharp shelling on the part of the enemy, responded to vigorously by our folks. The news from Atlanta being proclaimed on the left of our lines caused a loud cheering which increased the rapidity of the firing on the part of the Rebs. A shell from a fort across the river struck within our advanced works and exploded in one of the traverses where our regiment is lying. It fell near three of our men who were lying prostrate and bruised them severely but caused no serious wound. The number reported present for duty this morning is 356; extra duty 8, sick 15, equals 379. Number absent in hospital 243. Simmons, Company D, Solomon Whitford, Company D, were bruised so as to be sent to the hospital.[100] (Journal)

George W. Barber enrolled at Dunkirk, New York, as a 1st lieutenant in Company G, 112th New York Volunteers. He was discharged for disability on October 4, 1864.

Monday, September 5th

A most terrific mortar firing near midnight opposite our immediate front. Do not hear of any casualties resulting therefrom. (Journal)

Tuesday, September 6th

Colonel Smith left for Norfolk for the purpose of getting his family north. Last night, our regiment resumed their position in the trenches. The 117th New York were so unfortunate the few days they were there as to lose 5 men wounded, two killed.

The orders at present look to a renewal of the attempt upon our left. In case this happens, our brigade is to cover this corps' front as picket and the other brigades of our division in connection with the corps are to be moved to the scene of action. General Grant has nearly completed his railroad connection between the City Point and Weldon Road. (Journal)

Wednesday, September 7th

A temporary convalescent camp has just been established for the brigade at a large frame house near the banks of the Appomattox. The object is to take incipient cases of fever there and treat them endeavoring to heal them at once. Men sent to hospitals are lost to the regiment for months. (Journal)

Heman S. Fox enlisted at Ellicott, New York, as a sergeant in Company F, 112th New York Volunteers. Wounded in action at Petersburg, Virginia, he mustered out with regiment on June 13, 1865, at Raleigh (courtesy U.S. Army Heritage and Education Center [USAHEC]).

Saturday, September 10th

The morning report of this morning shows [the remainder of this entry left blank]. (Journal)

Wednesday, September 14th

There was heavy artillery firing about noon of today. Our regiment in the pits. Lieutenant H. S. Fox, Company F, was severely wounded by a piece of shell which struck the arm just below the shoulder and tore the flesh in a ragged manner, inflicting however, no ostensible injury to cord or bone.[101] He went to base hospital.

Private William Ward, Company C, was about noon struck by the bullet of a rifleman while at work upon a new redoubt now building. The ball entered the back between the ribs and passing just under the skin, was cut out on the other side. No injury to the spine.

Corporal J. J. Munson received, as was supposed, a severe contusion of the leg on the 13th. It has, however, proved comparatively trivial. After four days he was on duty.

The number of extra daily duty men is being diminished. All men in camp are ordered to be armed except one cook allowed to each company and 2 or three others. We learned that Captain E. A. Curtis has been honorably discharged September 13th, because of disability arising from wounds. Private M. Dolan died at Hampton Hospital August 26th. Private Smith Peacock, Company K, died at base hospital, 18th Corps. Private John Peters Jr. died of typhoid fever at sea enroute for Hilton Head and was buried off Wilmington.[102]

Recruits for the regiment have been coming since the 4th instance. Enoch Russell and Isaiah Gilvin joined Company H, on the 3rd. Thomas Robbins, Deloss Robbins, Charles W. West and Martin B. Stone joined Company A, on the 4th.[103] (Journal)

Sunday, September 18th

Sunday. Chaplain Palmer 142nd preached in camp.[104] The attendance of the regiment was good. (Journal)

Monday, September 19th

The news of Sheridan's victory was announced this evening by telegrams sent to all the brigades and regiments of both armies, Potomac and James. There was vociferous cheering all along the line. The news has electrified the whole command. There is considerable political discussion but not much excitement thus far in the army. Men read and canvas all matters fully. (Journal)

Wednesday, September 21st

This forenoon about eleven commenced a salute of shotted guns from all our batteries. The enemy replied with spirit. Nehemiah Davis, Company H, was struck in the hip and a piece of shell, after passing 6 inches down the limb, lodged and was cut out by the surgeon.[105] No bones were injured. (Journal)

Thursday, September 22nd

Camp 112th N.Y. Vols.
September 22nd 1864

Dear Wife,

How fast these days of September are whisking away. We are now only 8 days distant from the first of October. Today is one of those sombre days, clouded and cool which remind one so forcibly that the summer is past and winter with its frost is coming on. It is a thoughtful and sober day and three or four weeks ago I should have been very much depicted during the day. But the glorious success of Sheridan coming as it does along the same track with Atlanta and Mobile makes me feel exultant as to the prospects of the war for the future.

Grant is biding his time. When all is prepared for him you may be sure he will strike and that vigorously. We of the Army of the James will not probably move with the column. We are now acting temporarily with the Army of the Potomac but are not of it.

I have yet hopes that we shall spend the winter either in Petersburg or some village between Petersburg and Richmond. I do not doubt that both Petersburg and Richmond will be in our possession before the year closes.

The army is now in fine spirits. September has not done a tithe of the injury that the Rebs expected of it. We have about as many sick men coming back to the regiment from the hospital as are taken sick. The sick list is for the season small and the type of disease much milder than usual. You know how many men we lost a year ago. We have from sickness had only two men die this two months. You may be sure there is no mistake about the desire of the Rebs to desert. The other day one came inside of our lines and our boys gave him some coffee and soft bread. He took his bread and cup of coffee, got up on the parapet and hollered over to the rest of the Johnnies, "here boys if you want some of this come over and get it."

Since the cattle raid a few days since, when our boys call out "What's the news from Early?" the Reb screams out "If you want fresh beef come over here."[106]

Friend Taylor of the 48th New York has returned from Washington where he has been sick several weeks. He is looking well and is in good spirits. He is a gay bird. I hope you try and keep up good spirits. Will you call and see Mrs. John Hunt and see if she is well. He says he has heard nothing for three weeks.

Fisk, Company I, has not yet returned. I wonder what has become of him. He is behind time.

I wonder if Captain Chaddock is going to return to camp. Perhaps Colonel Smith has called to see you.

How often I sit and think of you and wish I had just a little snug country parish away from the noise of the big town where I had a little farm and my wife and children with me there. I believe with them and my books I could be happy. I would be perfectly contented to live on a meager salary if promptly paid if I could be with you. If we are in post anywhere this winter where we shall be likely to stay, you and Fred shall come on.

But cheer up, cheer up. The morning light is breaking. We may move slower than we hope but we move with power. This republic will stand and copperheads will go down. There are lots of copperheads in the army but they are not the mass of the soldiers. They are pledged second lieutenants, gambling sutlers, captains who were brother politicians at home and came with a way to make a living, also a few ambitious higher officers who would like the war to remain a military despotism.

Goodbye.
Affectionately as ever,
William

Friday, September 23rd

Several of our wounded men have returned from the hospital. We have also received eleven new recruits. (Journal)

Daniel E. Bullock	Company C
William E. Martin	Company A
James Ward	Company C
Henry Markham	Company C
Henry Eveleth	Company E
E. Bushnell	Company H
Chalmers Hammond	Company F
William Kenniston	Company H
Samuel Kenniston	Company H
James Pangborn	Company H
Roland D. Abbey	Company H

Saturday, September 24th

A week since on the 17th Colonel Smith left for Chautauqua County on duty to direct recruits raised there to this regiment. His leave of absence is for 15 days. Last evening three men deserted from the 49th New York Volunteers. An alarm was

James Pangborn enlisted at Carroll, New York, as a private in Company H, 112th New York Volunteers. He was wounded in action at Chaffin's Farm, Virginia.

raised and our picket line reinforced. The night before three men from the enemy in a boat floated down the Appomattox River and came in through our picket line near the river and gave themselves up to the commandant of a battery. A week last Friday, Bronson, Company D, was tried by court martial for sleeping on picket post. The man was found guilty, sentence not known.[107]

The whiskey and quinine ration is very obnoxious to the men. Many throw it away. Those who would use the whiskey refuse it with quinine.

There appear to be symptoms of a change again. Last evening a telegram came from Washington announcing Sheridan's victory at Fishers Hill, south of Strasburg. This forenoon a terrific cannonade was opened on Petersburg in commemoration of victory. This afternoon, we received orders to be in readiness to move at dark. We are to break camp and for the night bivouac in the rear of General Birney's headquarters. (Journal)

Sunday, September 25th

The command busy in making themselves comfortable. Corporal [Addison] Hollenbeck, Company E, and 1st Sergeant Amenzo Miller, Company I, have both been discharged [from] the service for disability. I took their discharge papers to them this morning. (Journal)

Monday, September 26th

All quiet with a prospect of remaining in our present position several days. (Journal)

Camp 112th N.Y. Vols.
In the field near Petersburg
September 26th 1864

My dear Wife,

Saturday evening about 9 o'clock our mail came to camp bringing to me your last written upon the eve of starting for Stamford. I was very much pleased. I would willingly deny myself, were it necessary, twice all it will cost to have you enjoy the visit and Harry the pleasure of seeing you. It will, if no more, do you the good of a change, occupying your mind for a season and take your thoughts off the one subject that so incessantly occupies it by day and by night.

I think too you will be able to judge as to Harry's way of spending his time whether he is making suitable improvement and whether his manners are attended to as well as his studies. I want him to cultivate good habits and learn to be polite and pretty mannered. I wrote him in one of my last letters about his conduct, etc. I want him to write me soon after you get these. He is not very punctual in writing me.

I hope this letter will reach you this week. It takes about a week for a letter to get to Stamford from here. When I last wrote you we were located in the fortifications around Petersburg. Since then we have been relieved and drawn back about two miles to the rear. So you see there is nothing more uncertain than military life. I confidently thought that our corps was to remain in the entrenchments whatever was to be done with the rest of the army. It is said that there is some disagreements between Generals Meade and Butler and that this is the cause of the withdrawal of our corps. I don't know where we are to go. I am inclined to think that we are to be here on the high ground until the corps is reorganized and until we are paid and then I should not be surprised if we had some action, part of the fall campaign.

That campaign will of necessity be a short one. It may be somewhat severe for the troops. The weather will no doubt be cold part of the time, but if we can only make an end of Lee's army this fall we won't care for the weather.

Saturday morning we celebrated the late victory of Sheridan. I think about 200 cannons and mortars opened at once from the Appomattox way round to the Weldon Road. I am glad you were not as near as I was. I am afraid you would have gone crazy. You never heard such a noise. It shook the ground and at times over about a mile from where I stood the air appeared to be full of bursting shells and then the Rebs opened. And roar and whiz and blaze and smoke and when a volley of cannon went off together, the air fairly serviced by crack with the sounds. I stood about fifteen minutes on the parapet just back of our tents and witnessed it, when the peculiar hum of some minnie bullets from the enemy came humming by and I thought that as I was not ambitious to have a small hole made in me I had better get under the bunk.

But I saw enough to satisfy me as to the cruelty of war. Only think what a savage way of reinforcing it is to open all the terrific artillery of an army like ours upon a city and upon the army opposed to it.

Such an amount of iron never falls without leaving some mangled limbs and crushed forms in its course. The evening seems to entertain a peculiar spirit against General Grant's new railroad. Only think of building a road ten miles to take supplies to the army. And that road is one of the greatest of blessings to poor mules and horses as well as to hungry men. With it all the supplies for every part of this vast army are delivered with the regularity of a well managed hotel. Without it, hundreds of mules or horses would be worn out on these bad roads and scores of men used up in long drives and exposed day and night.

My poor old horse Frank is about used up. He has taken the horse distemper which has proved very fatal this summer and he is a mere skeleton, skin and bones and lame withal. I fear he will soon be numbered among the things that were. He has not stood army life well since coming from Florida. And on our marches we sometimes have full and sometimes only one half food enough for the horses. Sometimes the oats are good and sometimes musty. Poor old fellow. I shall be sorry to lose him but if he goes, I can't help it. I shall not buy another. I hope I can get along without one while in the army. Only eleven months at the utmost. The 112th won't reenlist if called upon. The boys all say, "we have given three years of the best of our lives to the government, now let them who ought to be interested as much as we are take our places." But I hope there will be no necessity of any re-enlisting after the present campaign is over.

We are daily expecting the man who carries the greenbacks along to pay us off. It sounds very natural to hear as I now do the cars rolling along a few roads distant from our camp. I wrote Dr. Rogers last week and told him not to enter the service on any account unless he should come as a surgeon in which case he would have a chance to take care of himself. Dr. Rogers as a private wouldn't live long enough to give the Rebs a chance to shoot him. I told him to pay $1000 rather than come. I think we are not going to lack for men. The prospects just now look bright. The army is in good condition and victory sure I believe to perch upon our banners. I have been improving in health decidedly for two or three days past and the yellow is all gone from under my skin, which has again its natural color. I hope you and Fred and Harry are all having a good time. Write me how I shall send your next letter. I will write Wednesday of this week so that you will get it at Stamford and then I should write to Dunkirk until I hear from you again. Give my love to the boys and may God bless you and them.

If at anytime we should take up lines of march, I will let you know, but I do not anticipate at present anything more than a move to the opposite side of the Appomattox.

But anything to end the rebellion. Colonel Smith wants to stay in Chautauqua fifteen days longer. I fear he won't be gratified.

Truly your ever affectionate husband,
William L. Hyde

Tuesday, September 27th

Orders have been received from division headquarters for daily drills and inspection parades. This pm however, we learn that the field hospital of the 10th Corps has been broken up and that the sick have been sent to the base hospital and the convalescents remanded to camp. Rumors of an immediate move are rife. (Journal)

Camp 112th N.Y. Vols.
In the field near Petersburg
September 27th 1864

My dear Wife,

We are all in confusion. Yesterday we suffered. We were to be quiet here for several days and to have our pay. An order from headquarters told us that we were to be paid before the 30th. But this morning an order has come to send all extra baggage to be stored and to be ready with two days cooked rations for a march. We don't know where we are going but think we are bound for North Carolina. The 10th and 18th Corps. I imagine that Sheridan's great victory over Early has rendered necessary quite a change in the disposition of the military forces of the U.S. Well I don't care if our changes only conspire to end the war. What becomes of us for the next three months?

I commit myself to the care of that same heavenly Father who has been so abundant in mercy hitherto. He has truly preserved my life from destruction and loaded me with his loving kindness and tender mercy.

I am again getting my strength and having had a pretty thorough medication. I hope that my health will be better than it has been for a long time past.

I am now very glad I did not give up and go to the hospital. It would have done no good and I should not have had the satisfaction of pluck and grit in staying by the regiment and getting well in the field.

I am sorry to say Frank is no better. Poor old horse. I fear he will have to be shot for I think he has got the farcy of the worst kind. This is the worst disease a horse can have. He breaks out in sores all over. The puss gets into the blood and he dies as men do that have what is called pyaemia. There is just a bare possibility that I may be able to save him. I am glad that I am well enough to march.

If I was as sick as a fortnight ago I should have to go to the hospital. I am now somewhat uncertain whether we go to City Point or march by land.

I thought I would write you a few lines this morning while I had time as we may be in no position to send letters after we start. I send this to you or Harry. If you have gone back to Dunkirk, I want Harry to send it to you.

Very Affectionately,
William L. Hyde

We hear that the 10th, and the 18th and the 9th Corps are to be sent away from here.

Wednesday, September 28th

Early this morning orders received to reduce baggage to marching order to send all extra clothing to depot for storage and to be ready to move at 3 o'clock. The nature design and course of the movement is all shrouded in mystery. (Journal)

Thursday, September 29th

We moved from our temporary encampment in the rear of General Birney's headquarters and about one and a half miles from the entrenchments line, at 3 o'clock pm after advancing half a mile, our division halted while the First Division, which had moved out on a parallel road, passed by. Their whole division train was between us and them which made our march long and tedious. Various speculations were afloat as to our destination but almost everyone thought we were to take transports. No doubt hope dictated the opinion, for we all have a dread of the conflicts which are inevitable between the armies under Generals Lee and Grant.

We have suffered severely in killed and wounded during the present campaign. Indeed we have previous to this summer known but little of actual hard fighting. So closely had our destination now been kept secret that it was not known until we had crossed the Appomattox and had passed across the road leading to Bermuda Landing and found ourselves moving on the road to Deep Bottom. This was about eleven o'clock at night and we realized then that we were to take part in military operations north of the James River. Our movement was rendered very slow by the train of the 1st Division which was in advance and it was half past 2 am before we were upon the ground of our temporary bivouac inside of the entrenched fort at Deep Bottom. We had just thrown ourselves down upon the ground for a few hours sleep when Lieutenant Baber, aide to Colonel Daggett, temporarily commanding the brigade, rode up and informed us that there would be no time for the men to sleep as they must have their breakfast at half past three o'clock and marched precisely at four.[108] The men were very tired having marched in the most fatiguing manner since three o'clock, nearly 12 hours. They thought nothing of breakfast and the whole command were soon sound asleep.

At half past three all hands were roused up and those that could get something to eat and drink had breakfast. The officers many of them depended on their mess chests which were in the regimental wagons. Supposing that we were to take transports they had neglected to provide for a land march. This was the case with our mess and as we had gone to sleep supperless so we without breakfast prepared to march.

We moved out to the New Market Road and soon the skirmish line of the 18th Corps became engaged with the enemy. From the position occupied by our division of the 10th Corps we could see the colored troops who were in the advance moving forward to the woods in which the enemy's videttes were posted and charging through, they encountered quite formidable works. These they carried with rare gallantry and with severe loss.

After these first works were carried we moved on driving the enemy before us and beyond their 2nd line of works four miles in advance. Our brigade then advanced to a position where the enemy had planted a battery with which they were making great havoc in our ranks. Colonel Daggett ordered Major Ludwick to take this battery. The regiment moved forward with alacrity but the enemy instead of waiting our coming up fell back and took their artillery with them. Major Ludwick, on starting, received a severe contusion of the arm, but led his men gallantly on. After the Rebs had retired we gained a position which screened us from the galling fire of some earthworks, but the line could not be established unless an earthwork commanding a position of it was taken. Our brigade attempted this. The 112th in advance. Gallantly the charge was made but the line recoiled, shattered and disintegrated by the terrible fire they encountered. At this time Major Ludwick received a bullet in the arm which had already been wounded. The bullet shattered the bone so that amputation became necessary just above the elbow. Adjutant Kimberly received a blow on the shoulder while quite in the advance and was knocked over and stammered. On recovering, he found himself alone and near the enemy's works, the storming party having fallen back. He began to crawl back between the windrows. Raising his foot a bullet pierced his boot, fracturing the bone of his leg and crushing it for six inches. The limb was amputated. Both operations were performed by Surgeon Clark, 39th Illinois.[109] The movement was not successful and the force fell back to the entrenchments covering the New Market Road. (Journal)

The casualties in our regiment were: (Journal)

E. A. Ludwick	Major	Field & Staff	Fracture arm, bullet amputation
L. J. Parker	Captain	Company C	Severe contusion, shell below eye
C. A. Kimberly	1st Lieutenant	Company E	Fracture of ankle, amputated
F. E. Pennock	1st Sergeant	Company A	Shoulder, bullet, severe
G. W. Fox	Sergeant	Company A	Slight wound, scrotum
J. B. Clark	Corporal	Company A	Flesh wound, thigh
G. W. Gardner	Private	Company A	Wound of foot
R. Warner	Corporal	Company A	Thigh and foot severe
J. Vanderwark	Private	Company A	Hands, bullet, severe
Theo Sweet	Private	Company A	Head
D. C. Hotchkiss	Private	Company A	Very slight wound
E. L. Harris	Corporal	Company A	Missing, prisoner
Deloss Robbins	Private	Company A	Wounded
M. Sullivan	Private	Company A	Both legs through bullet, flesh
C. West	Private	Company A	Killed
William Henry Sears	Private	Company A	Missing, prisoner

Above: George W. Gardner enlisted at Jamestown, New York, as a private in Company A, 112th New York Volunteers. He was wounded at Petersburg and Chaffin's Farm, Virginia. *Right:* Elbert L. Harris enlisted at Jamestown, New York, as a private in Company A, 112th New York Volunteers. He was captured at Chaffin's Farm, Virginia, and mustered out with regiment on June 13, 1865, at Raleigh.

William Edgar Martin	Private	Company A	Contusion from shell
S. E. Smith	Sergeant	Company B	Breast shoulder
Ira Marsh	Private	Company B	Breast gunshot between ribs, through
E. W. Felton	Private	Company B	Forehead shell, slight
S. P. Stuart	Private	Company B	Head wound, leg
H. B. Grover	Private	Company B	Slight
Simon Bigalow	Private	Company B	Missing, prisoner
D. O. Putnam	Private	Company B	Missing, prisoner
C. E. Fisk	Private	Company B	Missing, prisoner
G. W. Giffin	Private	Company B	Missing, prisoner
S. A. Ferrin	Sergeant	Company C	Through thigh, flesh bullet, severe
N. L. Cooper	Corporal	Company C	Leg
Judson Gage	Corporal	Company C	Leg
W. P. Nevins	Corporal	Company C	Contusion severe hip
F. Phillips	Private	Company C	
W. N. Coonrod	Private	Company C	[Killed, Darbytown Road]
J. Ward	Corporal	Company C	[Wounded]
A. J. Weaver	Corporal	Company C	Dead
John Schmidt [Smith]	Corporal	Company C	Missing, killed
Daniel E. Bullock	Corporal	Company C	Missing, killed
Henry Warner	Private	Company C	Missing, killed
J. A. Powers	Sergeant	Company D	Arm fracture
E. Skellie	Corporal	Company D	Leg amputation, below knee
S. Heath	Corporal	Company D	Killed
S. Hosier	Private	Company D	Fracture, arm amputated
Hiram Dickson	Private	Company D	Fracture ankle, amputated, died
O. Nichols	Private	Company D	Slight wound
G. W. Eddy	Private	Company D	Thigh severe
G. Park	Private	Company D	Wounded
J. Dunnewald	Private	Company D	Prisoner, returned

Companies E, F, G, & K were on skirmish line and suffered hardly any loss.

L. Clark	Corporal	Company E	Severe contusion, thigh
John Warner	Corporal	Company G	Killed
E. Denton	1st Sergeant	Company H	Leg amputated
A. C. Jones	Corporal	Company H	Breast shell fragment, just under the ribs
F. Nichols	Private	Company H	Prisoner, returned to action
J. DeLain	Private	Company H	Prisoner, returned to action
S. D. Taber	Private	Company H	Wound hand and arm
Henry Cushing	Private	Company H	Missing, prisoner
O. S. Allen	Private	Company H	Shell exploded under him, contusion
Robert Adkins	Private	Company H	Killed
R. D. Abbey	Private	Company H	Killed
W. Appleby	Corporal	Company H	Dead
A. B. Cobb	Sergeant	Company I	Finger crushed, severe
James Ball	Sergeant	Company I	Left shoulder flesh
H. Ives	Corporal	Company I	Severe wound leg
F. J. Kazer	Corporal	Company I	Severe contusion under knee
J. K. Hempsted	Private	Company I	Very slight bruise
W. A. Spear	Private	Company I	Wounded and missing
Myron Gould	Private	Company I	Wound neck, slight, did not leave the field
John Mahoney	Private	Company I	Prisoner
Samuel V. Mount	Corporal	Company K	[Wounded]
Daniel Nichols	Private	Company K	[Wounded]

Killed 4, Wounded 47, Missing 16.

Friday, September 30th

Chaplain's Monthly Report[110]
Camp of the 112th Regiment New York Volunteers
In the field north of the James River

September 30th 1864
Brigadier General L. Thomas, Adjutant General
General,

I have the honor to submit the following report of the regiment for the month ending September 30th 1864.

At the commencement of the month our regiment was established along the entrenched lines in front of Petersburg, the right resting upon the right bank of the Appomattox River. The duties were now comparatively light. Attenuating with another detail from the brigade, three days and nights they were employed in the trenches doing general picket duty, and strengthening the position, then for a like space of time relieved and retired in a ravine a few rods at the rear, where they were free from the exposures and toils to which they were subjected at the front.

Thus in the unvarying monotony of picket and fatigue duty, twenty four (24) days of the month passed away.

On the afternoon of the 24th, orders came to be ready to move out from the entrenchments at dark, it being understood that the movement was in connection with the withdrawal of the whole Tenth (10th) Corps to the rear.

Moving at dark to the designated encampment in the rear of General Birney's Headquarters about one and a half miles from the front, we remained until the afternoon of Wednesday the 28th, when General Birney moved his corps across the Appomattox and James to the north side of the James River. Our division arrived at the place of rendezvous near Deep Bottom about ½ past 2 o'clock on the morning of the 29th where we rested an hour and a half, then moved out towards the New Market Road.

After the first line of the enemies' defenses had been carried about 8 o'clock am, we moved forward and became engaged with the enemy near noon. In two of the assaults made during the day, the regiment had a prominent part and our loss, considering the numbers engaged, was very severe.

The only field officers present with the regiment, Major E. A. Ludwick, commanding, and 1st Lieutenant C. A. Kimberly, assistant adjutant, were severely wounded.

The major lost an arm by amputation, the adjutant his left foot above the ankle. One of the three captains present received a severe contusion upon the right cheek. Every man of the color guard was either killed or wounded, yet the colors were borne triumphantly as far as the column was able to advance and when obliged to fall back were brought off safely. The total of the casualties were 4 killed, 47 wounded, 16 missing. The previous casualties during the month while on duty in the trenches were [blank] wounded, one (1) commissioned officer and four (4) privates. Religious services have been held in the regiment but one Sabbath during the month. Chaplain Palmer of the 142nd New York officiating in the sickness of the chaplain.

I have suffered from severe sickness during the month, but remained with the regiment for the sake of the example. But though not able to do full duty, I have been able to do much for the sick of the regiment during this time.

The circumstances under which a body of men are placed in the field, privations, hardships, sickness and suffering incident to it are not calculated to forward moral development.

They are however well calculated to test men and prove the strength or weakness of their moral principle. The vice of intemperance is often stimulated by resorting to this excitement as a refuge from the eminent discomfort of this kind of life, as well as the erroneous idea that the free use of intoxicating drinks enables one better to bear fatigue and hardship. I am glad to be able to say in regard to the general moral condition of this regiment that infliction of discipline has been deemed necessary in the case of but one private soldier during the month, that no officer has been deemed worthy of censure. And that the general good order and discipline in the regiment is owing to the high example afforded by the officers.

    Most respectfully.
      Your Obedient Servant,
        W[m] L. Hyde
          Chaplain, 112th Regiment New York Volunteers
          1st Brigade, 2nd Division, 10th Army Corps

All of our wounded with few exceptions were sent during the last night and early this morning to general hospitals north. The regiment is now feebly officered, 7 commissioned officers being all that are now present for duty. The recent losses have somewhat affected the spirits of the men. Yet most of those on duty are ready for any work and will obey any requisition that may be made upon them. Captain Dunham now commands the regiment and Lieutenant C. A. Crane is assistant adjutant. There has been no important change of position since last night. (Journal)

                                    Camped in the field, near Chapin's Bluff[111]
                                      September 30th 1864

The sudden transitions to which we are subject in military life are proverbial. And our experience of the last week will illustrate it. We had supposed that our position in the entrenchments near Petersburg was fixed until the return of our brigade and regimental commanders. But on Saturday Colonel Daggett, of the 117th New York Volunteers in temporary command of our brigade, received orders to be ready as soon as dark to move his brigade to the rear of General Birney's headquarters, about a mile and a half in rear of the fortifications.

We soon learned that the whole corps in military parlance was to be "retired from the front" and made ready for a move. There came the many rumors as to the nature of the approaching move, all of which were wide to the actual one. We were going to South Carolina or North Carolina or the Shenandoah Valley. The north side of the James was indeed mentioned, but only as improbable. Sunday, Monday and Tuesday, curiosity was eager, speculations rife, but uncertainty everywhere. Even division headquarters were in the same blissful state of ignorance with the rest of the crowd. On Tuesday there were twenty men at work at corps headquarters making them comfortable for a winter sojourn.

Wednesday morning, orders came to be ready with two days rations to move at three o'clock pm. At that time Dame Rumor was almost certain that we were going to Wilmington or New Berne. At three, the various divisions of the corps were moving in their order with their immense trains following. The progress was very slow and tedious and as we passed down the road leading to City Point or Bermuda Hundred, we were quite sure it was to the transports from one or the other place. It was dark before we reached the pontoon bridge across the Appomattox. After crossing the bridge, we began to think we might be moving toward Deep Bottom. Still hope predominated that we were going out of Virginia away from the vicinity of the sanguinary battlefields of the Army of the Potomac. Soon however we came to the forks of the road where we must turn if at all to go to Bermuda Landing. Instead of turning we passed into a gloomy piece of woods, a road leading to Deep Bottom. This settled the matter of our destination.

The 10th and 18th Corps were to make a demonstration toward Richmond. The march was very tedious. The train of the 1st Division was in front of us and it was after two o'clock in the morning before we reached our place of rendezvous on the north side of the James. We had just thrown ourselves down on the grass for a rest when an orderly came to notify us that the men must prepare their breakfast and be ready to move at 4 o'clock. In spite of the warning that there was no time for sleep, the men and officers were soon sound asleep and got at least an hours repose before they were roused to prepare to march. At four o'clock, the whole command was on the move. It was a magnificent spectacle as the three divisions moved out from the side hill of our night's bivouac on different roads leading to the front.

After our division had reached its position, we saw the 3rd United States Colored Troops deployed as skirmishers and moving cautiously toward a piece of woods about a half a mile in advance. Soon firing became lively. With a yell, the colored boys rushed forward. They were lost to sight, the firing was rapid and we heard the cheers, they had carried the first line of the enemy's works but in doing it near one hundred of them bit the dust. After this line was carried the whole command moved rapidly forward four miles, where the Rebs had fallen back behind formidable works.

We were now six miles from the city of Richmond. In front of these works, both the 18th and 10th Corps were formed, the left of the 18th resting near the river and the 10th on the right. Our brigade is the first in the 2nd Division of the 10th Army Corps and when the column was formed for a charge the 112th and 3rd New York were in the first lines of our portion of the front and there were two other lines behind us. The boys, when the order to charge was given, did not waver until they had swept over the enemy's works and had them in their possession. So well and so quickly was this accomplished that we had but comparatively few casualties. Major Ludwick, who commanded the regiment, had his arm grazed by a piece of shell, but he bound it with one handkerchief and slung it with another and though suffering intense pain directed all the movements of the regiment refusing after the charge was over to go to the rear.

There was another and formidable earthwork, however, which must be taken or the line already gained would be untenable. With this in our possession, Lee would be obliged to call off a large part of his forces from Petersburg or lose Richmond. Twice the attempt was made to carry this work and the 112th was in the leading line of one of these charges. Nothing could surpass the desperate gallantry of their charge. They forced their way through sheets of fire and a storm of lead and iron, but it was in vain, when they had reached the parapet there were too few left to pass over it. Had there been equally desperate men in following lines perhaps the line might have been carried at that hour. But we were compelled to fall back.

Our loss has been very severe and the hairbreadth escape almost miraculous. When the charge was made the wound on Major Ludwick's right arm was intensely painful, but drawing his sword with his left hand, he waved the boys on, and in the charge was struck in the same arm with a bullet. The bone of the arm about the elbow was so badly shattered that amputation became necessary. The work was done at Surgeon Washburn's office with great skill, by Surgeon Clark of the 39th Illinois one of the most accomplished operators in the army. Lieutenant Kimberly, acting adjutant, than whom there is no one pluckier, had nearly reached the fort when he was struck upon the shoulder a glancing blow from a shell, which knocked him over and stunned him. When he came to his senses, he saw the force was falling back and immediately began to crawl or drag himself along the ground. It was a cornfield and he was sheltered somewhat by the windrows. In this position, he threw up his left foot, which was then struck by a Reb bullet. After he was hit he crawled a fourth of a mile until he came out where he could be borne away. A most careful examination was made by several surgeons and it was ascertained that the bone was so crushed that his foot could not be saved. His limb was also most skillfully amputated by the same surgeon who had operated upon the major. Corporal Skellie of Company D was operated on by the same skillful hand.[112]

The color guard suffered very severely. Sergeant Ellis fell from sunstroke and every one of the guard was either killed or wounded.[113] As the colors fell from one hand, another was extended to grasp them. Sergeant Frank Brazee caught the state colors after they had repeatedly fallen from the hands of the wounded and planted them upon the enemy's works. The tattered flag pierced by bullets and its staff broken is being prepared to send to Jamestown. Glorious old flag, it has traversed the length of our seacoast from New York to Florida, and the men who have fought beneath its folds have been true to their banner in every contest. After the failure to carry the earthwork, our forces fell back a half mile to the position before carried which at this time writing they still hold.

What the next move is to be, you will know before this letter is published, from the city paper. The sorrow of the boys at Major Ludwick's calamity was intense. As he lay upon the table they would come along suffering many of them from their own wounds and with unfeigned sorrow exclaim "Ah! I'd rather lose my own arm than have that man lose his!" At present the regiment is under the command of Captain A. Dunham who will in the future, as he ever has in the past, prove himself equal to any position he is called to fill. And while the writer feels deep sadness as he thinks of so many of the bravest and best who have fallen or maimed for life by wounds yet cannot help reflecting with honest pride, upon their courage and patriotism, which led them to give even life to save their country from ruin. The 112th has in this conflict as ever before covered herself with honorable fame. I would like to state instances of individual bravery but my sheet is full. Some of those wounded at Cold Harbor as the list will show are more seriously wounded now.

Truly,
Chaplain Hyde (Newspaper)[114]

Saturday, October 1st

Lieutenant Milo Arnold, Company K, was today while on skirmish line hit in the left shoulder. The wound is not considered very severe. The results of the week's battle give us a fine position inside of the outer defenses of Richmond and four miles nearer the city then we were at the time when Hancock and Birney made their demonstration a month since. (Journal)

Saturday, October 1st 1864

My dear Wife,

I suppose before this reaches you that you are at home and will be anxious to hear from me. We left the front of Petersburg Wednesday at 3 pm and were marching until 2 o'clock the next morning. We then rested about an hour. I wrapped myself in a blanket, my saddle for a pillow (I rode Colonel Smith's horse) and sweeter sleep I never enjoyed. We were moving precisely at 4 am in splendid style towards Richmond. Having crossed both the Appomattox and the James since dark, part of our force became engaged about 9 am and the action became general soon after noon. Our regiment was in two charges. The first we carried strong works with little loss; the second charge was terrible and our loss fearful. I shall try and send a list to the Journal tomorrow. We have lost 44 men wounded, 18 missing and four killed. Major Ludwick was shot twice in the same right arm and it is amputated just above the elbow. Lieutenant Kimberly lost his left foot. I held both while they were cut off and was well spattered with their blood. I dressed wounds of 15 out of the first 17 of our boys myself with only one helper.

I then rode in the night seven miles to see Major Ludwick, if possible, before he was carried off. We should have been in Richmond, could our corps have carried the work where we lost so many men. Yesterday the Rebs charged on us but were badly repulsed. We are holding the first line of the immediate defenses of Richmond with our troops. I will write you the particulars today. I am writing this in great haste on my knee while Lieutenant Potter, who leaves for home, discharged for deafness, is packing.

Truly, etc.
William L. Hyde

Near Jones Landing
North of the River
October 1st 1864

My dear Wife,

I received your letter from Stamford this evening only 5 days from mailing. I had not expected to hear from you before last evening. I wrote you a few lines to send by Louis Potter who has resigned and gone home. He has grown so deaf as to be utterly incapacitated for any military use. And he never was cut out for an officer. I wrote to Dunkirk but thinking you may be at Stamford by the time this can get there and I write again.

I know you will feel anxious when you hear that the 10th has moved from Petersburg and especially so if you read in the New York papers of the sanguinary battles of the 29th. We had a terrible fight. I have written a full account for the Jamestown Journal and the Dunkirk too. Our regiment covered itself with honor and our losses are very severe in wounded.

That dear little Kimberly lost his foot, his left foot. He told me and the tears started as he spoke, that he could not bear the idea of losing it. I said to him, my dear young friend, better lose your foot than your life. He then said if after examination Dr. Washburn decides that it ought to come off, I am satisfied. The doctor was not well and got Dr. Clark of the 39th Illinois to operate for him. This Clark is a splendid surgeon. He did the amputation very handsomely. I held the foot until the work was done. I held Major Ludwick's right arm too while they took it off just above the elbow. You may believe I shed some tears after it was over. The major did not lose much blood. He was wounded twice in the same arm. The first thing he tied the handkerchief about the limb, and stayed with the regiment, on the 2nd charge he got a bullet through it which smashed the bone badly.

We lost 4 killed, 14 missing, most supposedly killed and 44 wounded. I dressed 15 of the 17 of our regiment first brought in myself and before we went forward to the front, I dressed the wounds of twelve colored men belonging to the 18th Corps. They fought splendidly and I took great satisfaction in doing for them. At night after all our men had left in the ambulances, I left too and came down to Jones Landing to see Major Ludwick. It was near midnight when I got down. I had had but one hour sleep the night before, and I could not go down to the boat but threw myself on my rubber with my saddle for a pillow and was soon fast asleep.

In the morning the boat had gone. I have been all day writing letters here in the quartermaster's tent and tomorrow early I go again to the front. I am sadly troubled about my horse. I cannot use Frank and have to get along as I can with a loaned horse of the quartermaster's. This much going and coming a very troublesome business for me. I still fear Frank will not get well but the men encourage me to hope that he will. He is very sick now and the weather is bad-cold and wet. It rained all last night and has all day today. It bids fair to be pleasant tomorrow.

There was a terrible cannonading over toward Petersburg last night. The general will have Petersburg or Richmond I think before the dawn of another week. Lee is being pursued on every hand. Yesterday he assaulted our lines twice and was repulsed with savage slaughter. We took 300 prisoners. The army is in fine spirits. I hope we shall have no more charges to make. The wounds of our men are generally not as severe as at Cold Harbor. I think about six will have to undergo amputation. How glad I was that I was well enough to help take care of the men who were wounded. I am improving daily in health and hope to get some flesh on as soon as we take Richmond.[115]

Truly and affectionately,
Wm L. Hyde

Monday, October 3rd

Quartermasters are ordered to be with their regiments, leaving their teams in the rear in care of their sergeants. Officers' baggage has been taken to the front. (Journal)

Thursday, October 6th

Near Chapin's Farm
Five miles from Richmond
October 6th 1864

Dear Wife,

    I suppose that this letter should be sent to Dunkirk in order to reach you. I am sorry that you have not received my letters. I am afraid that the movements of late have been such as to confuse the mails and that is the reason you have not got my letters. I got both yours from Stamford 4 and 5 days after they were written.

    You must not get blue. I am now in excellent spirits and for the reason that I am in excellent health, a fact that has not been true before for several months. Indeed since the 10th day of June until within a week, I have not seen what might be called a well day. Yet most of the time I could do duty and was able to accompany the regiment on all marches. I am sorry to tell you that poor Frank is dead. He had to be killed last Monday to put him out of misery. He had the worst kind of glanders. You may imagine how bad I felt. Indeed I believe I felt worse because you and the boys thought so much of the horse than for my own personal loss. I shall not buy another horse. Just as soon as I can honorably, I shall come home and there is no prospect of any long marches. I can with a pair of army shoes do all the marching necessary and the quartermaster is very kind letting me ride one of the public horses when it is necessary.

    Colonel Smith has returned to the regiment. He got back night before last in good health. He called at Carpenter's house but you were not there. No one at home when he called. If I were you, I would not hesitate about going to Westfield or somewhere else if the Carpenter folks cannot board you. The paymaster of our regiment is actually on the ground and will probably pay our regiment tomorrow. I shall send with others to the bank and your allotment is $4.50, which I will send by mail as it is just as safe. The check being good to no one else. Keep up good heart. We may be together sooner than you expect. You can't think how much I miss Major Ludwick. He was at all times a noble warm hearted friend, and we had planned together a long course of reading when we should get into camp this winter.

    There is nothing of news here. We are strengthening our position, so are the Rebs. On the Petersburg front we have gained something. This is a beautiful region of country much healthier than around Petersburg.

    I hope you will be able to make arrangements for winter satisfactory to you.

    You must excuse a short letter. I have had a great deal of writing lately. My two reports, my journal, letters about the sick and wounded and two long letters to the public papers.

Your ever affectionate husband,
William L. Hyde

Lincoln stock is going up.

Saturday, October 8th

    Yesterday the regiment was started out very early. An attack having been anticipated from reports of deserters. The paymaster was prepared to pay off the command and soon after breakfast two companies were drawn up in line to receive pay when the order came for the brigade to move out towards the right of our line. About 9 o'clock we moved out under a sharp artillery fire, and forming line of battle about ½ a mile down the New Market Road. Moved forward through the woods as reserve to the 1st Division of our corps. We have hardly got into line when the firing was rapid and continuous directly in our front. In less than half an hour it had subsided, the enemy having been repulsed with severe loss. It seems that Kautz's Cavalry men attacked in the morning with fury, and after a feeble resistance fell back in disorder and with loss.[116] The attempt was then made by the Rebs to break through our line of infantry when they in turn were repulsed. Within our lines there was great confusion, wagons, ambulances, cavalry being mixed up. The cavalry following to the rear created a panic and for an hour the scene on the principal road was disgraceful. About 3 o'clock pm, our brigade was thrown forward on the left of the line of advance. After proceeding to an earthwork which enclosed a small house not far from the Darbytown Road they halted in line while skirmishers advanced through the woods in front. At the same time, more than the brigades of the First Division moved around towards the right and swing towards the road. They first saw the enemy fleeing in haste to his entrenchments. After remaining in this place till eleven pm, the force was drawn in our brigade retiring into the woods in rear of our former position. This evening we were paid off 6 months pay. It was near midnight when the paymaster finished his work. (Journal)

Sunday, October 9th

Today in view of a prospective movement it was thought best to give the men an opportunity to send their money home by express. Colonel Curtis had already procured an order sending me to Fortress Monroe with the money and it seemed to be my duty under the circumstances to receive their money. I did so. It took all day and at evening I transferred it to my saddlebags and rode to Jones Landing where I slept with $26,000 for a pillow. (Journal)

Monday, October 10th

This morning left for Fort Monroe, arrived at Bermuda Hundred just in time to take the steamer for the fort. Reached Old Point about 4 pm and transferred my valise with its contents to the express office. Went up to the hospital and spent the night with Major Ludwick. (Journal)

Steamer *Daniel Webster*
Enroute Fort Monroe
October 10th 1864

My dear Wife,

I am now as you see by the heading of this letter, far from the front and moving farther still. The reason you will imagine before I tell you, when you see what this contains.

I send to you allotment checks. One for yourself and two for Mrs. Fanny Hunt, wife of John. One of the checks Mr. Hunt sends her, the other her brother, George Mason. George was intending to sell his check but told John that if he could get thirty dollars of it, he would send it home. George is what they call a hard boy, but I think he has improved somewhat since he came into the army. In order to secure the thirty dollars for Mrs. Hunt, I bought the check, that is I gave him thirty dollars and he gave me an order which I enclose on Mrs. Hunt for it. George can't write and John Hunt wrote his name. You take the check to Mrs. Hunt and tell her about it. She cannot write. You offer to sign her name for her and draw her money then take out the thirty dollars and on the back of the order you find a form of receipt which you sign with your name and give to Mrs. Hunt. You sign Mrs. Hunt's name thus Fanny (her X mark) Hunt. She makes the cross between the "her" and "mark" or it will, if she expresses the wish, only be necessary to sign her name. Perhaps she would rather go to the bank with you.

Hawley has once or twice before paid George Mason half the check in order to get the rest for Mrs. Hunt. I shall send besides the allotment check, one hundred and twenty dollars, which with thirty from Mrs. Hunt will make for you six hundred dollars. What kind thing do you think the enlisted men of the regiment did for me? They felt so much sympathy for me in my loss of old Frank, that they raised a subscription among themselves. They would not allow any commissioned officer to subscribe a mill. The subscription I think will reach two hundred dollars and if a good horse cannot be got for that, they mean to raise fifty more.

When the colonel handed it to me yesterday after I had got ready to start and told me that the men would not allow an officer to put down one cent because they wanted it a gift from the men of the regiment, I had to make a little bit of a fool of myself on the spot. Do you wonder I love those men? Our officer told me the sum could not be raised for any other officer in the regiment.

I shall not be able to send you quite what I hoped and what I have said. I shall have to send seventy-five dollars to C. F. Reed, Buffalo County, a patient in the hospital $75.00 and smaller sums to others. It has cost me a great deal to live this summer, $30 a month. You know I have been sick a great deal and have been obliged to buy fruit at any price, as fruit and vegetables were an indispensable necessity. It will not be so expensive.

Letter No. 2
Same Series

We had had a hard day's work and the night was very cold. I had my overcoat on. I should have suffered exceedingly. The middle of the day was hot but the night very chilly. The next day was Saturday. We did not know which way we were to move but found that we were to be kept in reserve ready at a minute's notice. So our brigade about noon was moved back into the woods, a fine place for us to be ready for use when called upon. Towards evening the paymaster came back. Everything was ready for him and he worked until eleven o'clock and paid up every company and the officers. In anticipation of his coming, Colonel Curtis who like me, at the suggestion of Colonel Smith, had procured at General Butler's headquarters an order sending me to Fort Monroe with the money. This gives me transportation so that my expenses are very small. I have about $22,000 (twenty-two thousand dollars) in my little black valise who not a soul onboard suspects of containing anything but a few clothes and trinkets. I am anxious to get it safe with the officer.

Yesterday was Sunday. We were momentarily expecting orders to move. The families of many of the men were suffering for their money. What was to be done? Why but a thing. Get the money of the men together immediately. "Is it not lawful to do good on the Sabbath day?" Was not the Sabbath made for man? Will not this $22,000 scattered over so many families be a moral power for good. Will it not rejoice many hearts and make a Sabbath of joy to multitudes in distress? Yes and I felt that though a strange work. I was doing a good work in gathering these sheaves and sending them to the poor. I worked hard from five in the morning until five [in the] evening to get ready and then started with the money in my saddlebags for Deep Bottom. Then Quartermaster Shaw and I wrote until 10 o'clock to get things shaped. Then I went to sleep and had a blessed night's sleep, with $22,000 under my head for a pillow and a loaded revolver as my sole guard. This morning I got up with the sun, worked an hour, and changed my clothes, had a good breakfast of chopped liver and potatoes with raised biscuits and coffee and two of the men on horseback accompanied me to the Fort Monroe Bank. I had hardly time to get my transportation ticket and get onboard.

This fall I expect I shall have great difficulty in getting a good horse. I want to buy one that has been in the army as there is too much risk in taking a nice petted horse that has its ways been stabled and blanketed, kept warm and fed high; out here where a horse has to go through with every species of hardship.

I spent yesterday quietly. But I must explain by telling you the preliminaries. Friday morning the paymaster came and two companies of the regiment were marched up to his ambulance to be paid. He was delayed half an hour by the necessity of fixing up the odds and ends of the 142nd, which had been paid the evening previous. Just as he was about to pay us, orders came for Colonel Curtis' Brigade to move. A fight had been going on upon our sights for some time and the cavalry had been driven in and the evening had forced our pickets into the lines. I assure you there was hot haste and the most absurd rumors. We went out with General Terry's Division and were employed as reserve. It was a terrific fight for half an hour at a time twice but the point where the enemy expects to come in was defended by men with the Spencer rifles that fired six times without reloading and it mowed them like grass. They fell back in great haste and we followed them quite a piece. That night, I slept on the ground about three miles from Richmond, but we had not force enough to go in so after midnight we fell back to our old camp ground.

I will write you a second letter so as not to make the envelope too bulky.

Truly, etc., your husband,
William L. Hyde

Tuesday, October 11th

All day in express office. (Journal)

Wednesday, October 12th

All day at Hampton visiting hospital. (Journal)

Thursday, October 13th

All day at Chesapeake Hospital. (Journal)

Chesapeake General Hospital
Fort Monroe
October 13th 1864

My dear Wife,

This is a beautiful bright October forenoon and the chill wind reminds me of our dear northern house.

Two years have passed since we broke up our associations with a quiet household and me scattered to the war, you to New England. We then hoped that the savage part of this war would by this time be ended and that we should in some way be restored again to each other. But we are forced to submit to a little longer separation. When I look upon the two poor married friends, Ludwick and Kimberly, when I think of a chaplain [T. Ambrose] at Petersburg, who died of a wound received there.[117] When I think of a poor dejected chaplain here sick and nigh unto death who can't get his discharge. When I think of the many suffering men better than I am, I feel that I have no cause for complaint. I feel thankful that I can, in the midst of this war, still provide for your wants. I feel some little curiosity to know how you are situated just now. I suppose that you are by this time in Dunkirk and that you are making your arrangements for winter quarters.

I am so glad that you could have a visit to Harry and see how he gets on. I think if they have a good quiet way of managing him with firmness and kindness … (*Editor's note: this sentence ends abruptly. It appears a page is missing that links this paragraph with the rest of Hyde's letter*)

… the clothing department can be left to others care. I want you to send Mr. Wilde a check for $50 (fifty dollars) on account. I left fifty with him when I was at Stamford. Mr. Fullager will fix it for you. I think you will be satisfied with the amount I have sent home. I believe it makes $600, $450 in a check, one hundred and twenty in the express package sent to Dunkirk, Lake Shore Bank and thirty dollars order on the check of Mrs. Hunt. I shall have to draw on you for some small sums of which I will inform you soon. I want as soon as possible a box from home with my woolen undershirts in it. If you think about it you may get me two new men's drawers and I will send the pair I have on home and perhaps you had better send the old ones, and wait events.

Send the package, a small box, by express directed to:

Reverend W. L. Hyde
Fort Monroe, Va

Then I can send and get it at the express office without it coming through all the red tape of corps, etc. It takes an age to get things up the river.

I must now close. I sent today $20 to Mother.

Very affectionately,
William L. Hyde

Friday, October 14th

Went to Norfolk. Returned fort evening. (Journal)

Chesapeake General Hospital
October 14th 1864

My dear Wife,

This is Friday evening and I am still here but expect tomorrow to start for the front again. Today, I have been over to Norfolk. I left very early for this latitude half past 7 and took the Baltimore boat which leaves for Norfolk at 8. By reason of this early start I did not get breakfast until I got to Norfolk. The habits of boarders at this hospital are decidedly easy; breakfast at 8, dinner one to two and supper 7 to half past 8. I was entered as guest to Major Ludwick when I came which entitled me to a seat at the officer's table at the great building. The major insisted upon my taking an empty bed near him in Ward 6 so I have been having a nice little visit of five days and it has done me as they say here "right smart o'good." I would not object to a few days longer provided it was consistent with duty. But a long tarry would be very dull. I had the company of my friend Chaplain Chapman, 169th New York, going over to Norfolk and enjoyed the trip highly. I went to get some things that were put away in a box when I left Jacksonville. I don't want you to send me any stockings. I have now six pairs which are all I can take care of. I want my undershirts and drawers, the best, if Dunham has made it, and what of sanitary stores you can put up for me. I only want a small box. I shall buy some shirts to wear over my undershirts and shall send home some extra clothing that I now have. I have a blue blouse that I think will make Fred a jacket. My shirts that you sent me last winter I send to Harry. I cannot get them on without working as hard as to put on a new glove. When I get my velvet on my dress coat I think I can make it do for the winter unless we get to some civilized place. I found my other coat over at Norfolk as well as many other little matters that I had need of. I find my old overcoat about gone up. I think I shall send it home and use a soldier's blue overcoat this winter. I may make up quite a bundle to forward by someone going or by express. I think it pays to save everything these days. I don't know how I shall replace my horse. It is very hard to find one to suit me.

I wish you to draw twenty (20) dollars from the bank and send it to Mrs. Drake. It is part of the money which I took from the pockets of the colonel to pay for embalming and which I have since collected. I sent $20 by mail but do not like to send the rest in that way. I prefer to send by you. You can write a short note saying I requested you to send $20 to her, which you do, etc. I am glad to find the major and adjutant doing as well as they are.

I must close for I am very tired.

Your affectionate husband
William L. Hyde

Saturday, October 15th

Left for the front. (Journal)

Sunday, October 16th

Reached the regiment about 10 o'clock. The only occurrence during absence worthy of note was the moving of the brigade on the 14th to support a move of the 1st Division. The fight was sharp and bloody. No one of our regiment was killed or wounded. One man, Frank R. Case, Company A, is missing.[118] The regiment has been and is still voting. Will not probably get through with this before tomorrow evening. (Journal)

Tuesday, October 18th

Quartermaster's Department
Deep Bottom
October 18th 1864

My dear Wife,

You will wait one day longer than usual for your letter this week.

I returned from Fort Monroe last Saturday. It was after breakfast when I set out from the hospital and about 9 o'clock before the boat started for up river. The freight and cargo onboard the steamer were quite miscellaneous. We had white troops and colored troops; brigade commanders; regimental commanders; naval men with their gold stripes on their arms; and citizens of every description; Christian Commission delegates, Sanitary delegates, newspaper reporters. State commissioners to take the election vote and suttlers to take the money away from the soldiers. Of all the crowd there were but two or three whom I had ever seen before, and not one with whom I had any sympathy.

I felt somewhat easier than I did going down for the responsibility of conveying $25,000 is one by no means to be coveted. I read some and slept some and about 4 pm we were at City Point. There I took a train for Bermuda Hundred and did not know how I should get to Deep Bottom. I was waiting the return of the post quartermaster who had gone from here to the front when I heard a small train was to be dispatched to Aiken's Landing with the mail. Deep Bottom is on the way and the quartermaster clerk, a perfect gentleman, ordered them to land me where I wished.

It was quite dark when I reached the pontoon bridges for though only about an hours ride by land from Bermuda Hundred to Deep Bottom. It is 18 miles by the crooked course of the river. I found the quartermaster with the trains here. He had a nice tent and I did not think best to try to get to the regiment in the night. So I stayed with Shaw and in the morning we rode up to the regiment. The men and officers were all glad to see me. It was Sunday but a regular army Sunday. A lot of new recruits to be clothed, inspection, etc. I did not enjoy the day much. I could have no service.

This morning, I left again to see the men at the hospital here and at Point of Rocks. The 10th Corps Hospital is about ½ a mile from the quartermaster's tent and the 18th Corps Hospital is at Point of Rocks, about 6 miles distant. I have been busy all day and am now quite tired. I have seen all of our wounded men, carried them their letters, etc. It is pleasant to meet them; they all think a great deal of me and would do anything for me. I have not as yet been able to get me a horse, but I hope to have one within a few days. Horses are very scarce here and a good one will cost $225 at least. I received your letter written the Saturday before you intended to leave Stamford on my return to camp. I shall expect another in a few days. I thought you would not be able to write me before Friday or Saturday. I suppose you found when you got home several letters from me. I am quite anxious to hear where you design boarding and all about your prospects for the winter.

I am satisfied you did well in leaving Stamford before it was any colder, and I fear from the state of the atmosphere in this region last Wednesday, that you found it rather cool for comfort where you were.

Our regiments have not been in any fight since the one in which Major Ludwick was wounded. They are in very good spirits and I think have done themselves credit in sending home as much money as they have. Frank Wheeler, Irishman though, he voted for Abe Lincoln. Our regiment will go Lincoln by a large majority. About ¾ of all the votes. There is a commissioner here to take the votes of the men to the county. The 3rd New York will go largely for McClellan.

I got a long and very interesting letter from Dr. Rogers—three sheets. He gave me the particulars of his visit, etc. I shall expect my box before long. I hope the money will reach you safely and that you won't be so embarrassed hereafter as you have been. Send me the express receipts when you get it. With fond love as ever.

Your husband
William L. Hyde

Wednesday, October 19th

Mr. Forbes, commissioner from the county, to receive the votes of the regiment came down last evening. Captain J. S. Mathews accompanied him. The employees of the Quartermaster Department with the quartermaster and myself voted. Mr. Forbes states the regiment voted unanimously for Fenton for Governor and all but 9 for McClellan. It is probable, however, that the vote for McClellan was 25 or 30. (Journal)

Friday, October 21st

Heavy firing last evening all along the line in honor of Sheridan's victory. (Journal)

Sunday, October 23rd

Held service in front of the surgeon's quarters. Good attendance. (Journal)

Camp 112th N.Y. Vols.
Near Chapin's Farm
October 23rd 1864

My dear Wife,

I came up to the regiment yesterday. It was an exceedingly raw and blistering day. Indeed we had a few flakes of snow fall in the early morning at Jones Landing. The wind seemed to go right through me and at night we built a huge fire of pine logs in front of our tent. We packed four of us into one tent and covered ourselves up well with blankets and I was warm enough. But for some reason I did not sleep very well. I got your letter yesterday announcing the dispatch of my box or bundle but you did not tell me how you directed it nor whether you got any express receipt. It will probably delay my getting the bundle one week till I can hear from you. If the bundle is sent to me as Chaplain, 112th, 10th Army Corps, it will not reach me till the corps' freight is sent up and that may not be this month. If sent as I requested, I can send down for it any week. I wish now I had sent for some other things to come with those. I shall have to order a thick winter sack. I fear if I do, it shall be paid for from my next pay. I think that the government will pay next month the two months which will be due us the last of this month. You must not be frightened that it cost you all you can get to live on; it is so with almost everybody.

If we make all the ends meet, it will be fortunate. But there is, I hope, a good time coming. I wrote Harry a letter yesterday and sent him a 25 cent shinplaster. I think that will pacify him a little. I have just sent to you by lieutenant or rather Captain Corbett who has just resigned and gone out the service, a package consisting of three shirts partly worn neither of which I can wear. I have bought two new shirts for which I gave the trifle of six dollars each. They are very nice over shirts. When I get my woolens which you have sent me, I shall have the mate to one of those shirts already sent, to send. I put in my old portmanteau having had a new one given me, you may get a new elastic and put it on it and keep it to send to Harry by and by. I believe I promised him one. I have thought much of you today. I am really much pleased that you can remain at Mrs. Carpenter's as you seem to be better suited there then you could be elsewhere. If it were not for Mrs. Shelton's treatment, I should be very happy about it. But you know I am of such a temperament that I could not stand anything of the kind.

We had our Sunday service this morning at regimental headquarters. The brigade commander came over and attended with us. If we stay here this week, I intend to hold some prayer meetings. I was staying about on horseback most of the time last week after I got my new horse. I like him better and better. He will make a splendid carriage horse. He can trot very fast and carries his feet high. We have now a new mess. Major Ludwick, Lieutenant Kimberly being away made Colonel Smith quite alone and the quartermaster would not mess with Surgeon Washburn. I was despaired at first to blame Shaw but the doctor is really disagreeable to mess with. If he gets hold of mustard and vinegar, he will go to work and make the nastiest looking mess on his plate and then mix bread or potatoes with it and to see him stir it with his knife and eat it with that idiotic looking mustache he wears is not very agreeable. I found the first of last July that my mustache made me look nearly as hideous as his does him and I shaved it off and have kept a smooth upper lip ever since. Our mess now consists of Colonel Smith, Captain Dunham, Oley, Shaw and myself. I told Captain Corbett to forward three shirts and my used up blouse by express if they were any trouble. We have heard from some of our men wounded and missing after the battle of the 29th. They have got back as far as Annapolis paroled. One of them lay 4 days outside the earthworks, then was captured and taken into their lines, his leg amputated and he [was] sent back to Annapolis. I am truly sorry for Dunham's misfortune. I hope his loss is not large.

I hope you will attend the course of lectures this winter. Don't hesitate to use all opportunities to enjoy yourself. We have glorious news of Sheridan. All these reverses to the Rebels, will tend to hasten the end of the war. We have a grand review here tomorrow. I shall appear on my new horse. I have now quite a number of acquaintances among the chaplains: Wells, 11th Maine; Tiffany, 6th Connecticut; Taylor, 48th New York and Chapman, 169th New York.[119] All very pleasant men. I sent in my bundle two envelopes, one for T. C. Thompson and one to be sent to Fredonia.

Give my regards to all friends. Tell Freddy I was very much pleased with his letter and will write him soon.

Very truly your affectionate husband,
William L. Hyde

Tuesday, October 25th

Rode to Jones Neck and Point of Rocks to visit patients in those hospitals. Found those of our men wounded in the action of the 29th and sent to Point of Rocks doing well. Sergeant Denton, Company H, has a leg off. Judson Gage has a severe wound and is quite feeble. There were at the hospital the following patients: (Journal)

E. W. Felton	Company B	Wound head
H. B. Grover	Company B	Wound hand
S. E. Smith	Company B	Wound shoulder
S. P. Stuart	Company B	Wound left foot
Milton Phillips	Company B	Sick, debility
Nathan L. Cooper	Company C	Wound left leg

Judson Gage	Company C	Wound foot
H. Morse	Company D	Sick, chills and fever
C. H. Robinson	Company D	Sick, debility
A. C. Jones	Company H	Wound side
E. G. Denton	Company H	Wound leg amputated
J. Pangborn	Company H	Sick sun stroke
J. Ball	Company I	Wound shoulder
A. Cobb	Company I	Wound hand

Wednesday, October 26th

All hands busy today and yesterday making camp. Fixing up as for winter quarters. At ten heard we were under marching orders. About midnight regiment ordered to be ready to move at daylight. (Journal)

Hiram P. Morse enlisted at Stockton, New York, as a private in Company I, 112th New York Volunteers, and mustered out with regiment on June 13, 1865, at Raleigh (courtesy U.S. Army Heritage and Education Center [USAHEC]).

> Jones Landing up the James River near Bermuda, Deep Bottom, Chapins Farm, Drewry's Bluff and Rebeldom Generally
>
> October 26th 1864

Dear Wife,

How pleased and glad was I to hear the mail boy cry, "A letter for the chaplain, 2 letters for the chaplain." Both from you. One written from Stamford and the other from Dunkirk. I would advise your going to Stamford since it's not so many degrees of longitude outside of creation. I want you to be where you can have more of variety this winter. As to Harry. He must learn to bear his exile as best he can. It is good for him. Don't for a moment indulge the feeling that the expense is too great. I would rather go ragged and give my children the best of opportunities than to have a magnificent fortune and have them suffer any deprivation of what is best for them. I shall not value the $250 a year it will cost me. Provided Harry improves in his habits and becomes intelligent and fitted for usefulness. I want to keep him at school these years if I possibly can.

I am sure I think you have quite a pile of money left. I preferred to send $600 to you and draw on you for some matters that must be paid than to keep more with me. I shall probably draw on you for some $25 or $30 more and that I think will close up, unless we are left a long time without pay.

The boys raised $211 for my horse and I was told to get a good horse. If it cost $250 the sum would be made up. I have been devoting part of this week to seeking me a horse and I have at last bought one. I feel as though I was providentially aided in the matter. For I had my eye on one last Monday which was a Virginia blooded mare, a fancy animal, held at a fancy price, only $300. I might possibly have bought her at $225.

But the next day as I was riding along, I got into conversation with a soldier of the 11th Pennsylvania Cavalry who told me of a captain in his regiment who had been sick most all summer and had just resigned on account of disability. He said he had a splendid horse, which he would be obliged to sell as he could not take him home. So when I was returning from Bermuda, I just called on the captain. The horse was brought out saddled and I fell in love with him at once. He is just about Frank's size, the same color, the same white mark on the nose, but a much handsomer head and smoother prettier limbs, an eye like a hawk yet as gentle as a lamb. I jumped on to him and found he was not quite as gentle as old Frank. He was much higher mettle, nothing ugly, only for going ahead all the time. His name too very singularly is Frank. This captain has had him three years and he would not have parted with him on any consideration if he could have got him home. I asked the captain to give me till 9 the next day to consider the matter. He said he would. I then rode up with Billy Shaw and had him taken out again. He is a gay bird. Steps high and light and curves his neck and moves as proud as a peacock. I thought a moment and then I told the captain to make out his bill. He asked $200 for him. Everybody is pleased with him.

I should have bought only a very cheap horse if I had bought one with my own money. But as the boys raised $200 for me, I felt authorized to spend it and I am glad I have got a horse that will please them. They would not have been satisfied had I bought some sorry old plug with part of their money and they will all be delighted when they see this one. The only drawback to the pleasure of owning him is that you will not be able to ride him. I bought him yesterday and today I have rode him in company with Dr. Boyd all around the country. I don't want any spurs. All that is needed is just loosen the reins and he will spring with a gallop as quick as lightning. I don't know how fast he can run but he can walk as fast as old Frank used to trot on a light trot. He is all the more valuable for having been seasoned to army life. It is much better to buy such a horse than to get one from home and indeed such a horse at home is worth over $300 at present. The captain thought Frank worth $500 in Pennsylvania if he could have got him home. But it is against the law to take a horse out of the department who was ever bought by the government.

I have had a very pleasant visit from Dr. Boyd, also have voted for Abe Lincoln, also am in tiptop health, also want to see you and Fred.

So be amused of my fond love and constant desire for your happiness.

Truly your husband,
William L. Hyde

George W. Edmonds enlisted at Chautauqua, New York, as a sergeant in Company H, 112th New York Volunteers. He was killed in action at Darbytown Road, Virginia.

Thursday, October 27th

Up at daylight, packed everything moved out of camp about 5 am. Moved through our fortifications toward Charles City Road. Formed in line near the Johnson House. The skirmish line of our brigade moved through the woods and became engaged with the enemy when they drove into their works. While thus occupied, Lieutenant G. W. Edmonds, Company H, in command of a portion of said line, was instantly killed. Also, George Westly, Company B. The 18th Corps were considerably on to the right. All day there was severe fighting. It was a cold drizzly rainy day. About 5 o'clock a charge was ordered and executed by our brigade which resulted in the loss of some 300 men by us without accomplishing anything. Corporal Hart, Company B, and W. W. Story, private, were brought in just after dark both mortally wounded. It was truly a dismal night, cold and frequent showers all night. The men built a large campfire close by the earthwork from which the Rebs had been driven in the morning and rolling themselves up with their rubber blankets completely covering them. They lay down on the wet ground for the night. The division was moved about noon and reached camp about 2 o'clock. Captain Davis, on General Foster's staff, assistant adjutant general, was severely wounded. Lieutenant Baker, aide to Colonel Curtis, was also dangerously wounded. (Journal)

The casualties were in our regiment:

G. W. Edmonds	1st Lieutenant	Company H	Killed
W. Hart	Corporal	Company B	Mortally wounded
G. T. Westley	Private	Company B	Mortally wounded
W. W. Story	Private	Company B	Mortally wounded
Franklin Bullock	Private	Company C	Killed
Samuel Hull	Private	Company H	Shot himself
Frank W. Harris	Private	Company K	Killed
Henry Hubbard	Private	Company H	Mortally wounded
Alfred Dunham	Captain	Company A	Wound neck
Jason Ordaway	Private	Company A	Wound shoulder
Levi E. Woodard	Private	Company A	Wounded

Left: Jacob Ruch enlisted at Chautauqua, New York, as a private in Company H, 112th New York Volunteers. Wounded at Darbytown Road, he mustered out with regiment on June 13, 1865, at Raleigh. *Right:* Israel R. Raymond enlisted at Stockton, New York, as a private in Company I, 112th New York Volunteers. Wounded at Darbytown Road, he mustered out with regiment on June 13, 1865, at Raleigh.

E. A. Haskins	Private	Company A	Wound arm
Chapin H. Martin	Private	Company B	Wound left leg
Amasa Hemenger	Private	Company B	Wound right leg
Willard King	Private	Company C	Wound forehead
James Stafford	Private	Company C	Wound leg
George Whitford	Private	Company D	Wound hand
Robert Jackson	Private	Company D	Wound back
William R. Skellie	Private	Company D	Wound right forearm
John Johnson	Private	Company D	Wound shoulder
Charles Thompson	Private	Company D	Wound right arm
Seth Foster	Private	Company E	Wound face
Samuel C. Pitt	Sergeant	Company E	Wound through shoulder
George D. Wilson	Private	Company E	Wound leg and foot
J. B. Ruch	Private	Company H	Wound back
Israel R. Raymond	Private	Company I	Wound contusion leg
William Bisset	Private	Company I	Wound back
James Renne	Private	Company I	Wound shoulder
James T. Hamilton	Private	Company I	Wound shoulder
Leewellan Lewis	Private	Company K	Wound right axillary
William Wilson	Private	Company K	Wound left arm
Walter A. Coonrod	Private	Company C	Missing
John Carleson	Private	Company E	Missing
Silas Morehouse	Private	Company E	Missing

W. H. Buchanan, Private, a new recruit shot off his finger after skulking back to camp. He managed to get away onboard hospital boat, or he would have been severely punished.

In the field near the Darbytown Road
October 27th 1864

Dear Wife,

Yesterday morning I was very busy preparing my tent for at least a several week sojourn. I have now my quarters with Lieutenant Shaw, the quartermaster. We had our wall tent brought up and I was very busy all the morning making a bunk. Had just completed it and was lying down reading the *Atlantic Monthly*, when Shaw came in. He had been down toward the river and brought up a load of birch. Also, the intelligence that there was a move up. He did not want to believe it for you may be sure old soldiers have no longing to be out in the field at this season of the year and a fight is what a man who has ever been in one like that of the 27 years or Cold Harbor, never hankers after. When you read of men spoiling for a fight, either set it down as a fiction of the imagination or that the men are green. Old soldiers will go where they are sent if to certain death, but they don't because they have any fancy for it.

At suppertime we had orders to be ready to move at dark leaving knapsacks and tents. I asked the colonel if he did not think I could stay in camp and find the regiment in the morning. He said perhaps so, but what if we should have a fight about daylight? I then made up my mind to go when the regiment went, but I lay down to get some sleep before starting. About 9 o'clock, the colonel came in and told me that the orders were changed. We were to break up camp; the wagons to go to Deep Bottom and the men to be in light marching order taking three days rations and their shelter tents and overcoats. So I pulled off my boots and got what sleep I could though waked up several times during the night.

Very early in the morning, all hands were started out. Yorker (our cook) got up a good warm breakfast of beef steak, potatoes and fritters. Then we soon put our houses in order or rather our blankets and valises and soon we were on the move. There was not a soul in the division who knew anything of our destination. But we moved out and soon found that we were "on to Richmond." We marched about 3 miles and then were formed in lines of battle and skirmishers thrown out in advance. We had hardly got formed before Lieutenant Edmonds, Company H, was brought on a stretcher, dead. A bullet had pierced his brain in such a way that he must have died instantly. Soon a poor fellow by name of Westly was brought in.[120] He was a member of Company B, and during the forenoon we have had 7 casualties, 2 killed and 5 wounded. We are yet in the fight not knowing who may come next. I am as usual with the surgeons. (Have just been called to see a wounded man, William Wilson of Silver Creek).[121] He has his left arm broken.

How deeply I feel for Mrs. Edmonds. You recollect her, a sweet little woman who called to see me coming up from Silver Creek. They were a very happy loving couple. It is sad to think how many sweet little homes are broken up, how many hearts are made sad by the casualties of war.

I am quite well and strong. How thankful that I am so recovered from my long sickness at Petersburg. I hardly think we shall reach Richmond this time. I stated I am inclined

William Wilson enlisted at Hanover, New York, as a private in Company K, 112th New York Volunteers. He died of wounds received at Darbytown Road, Virginia.

to think this is a kind of blister on the north side, to make a little irritation while Grant strikes for the Southside Road. It is a very raw disagreeable drizzly day. It has at times rained hard but now though cloudy, it does not rain. Lieutenant Barber, 3rd quartermaster on General Curtis' staff, has his leg broken. Captain Davis on General Foster's staff has a bullet through his. I will write you again when we get through with this scrape, if God spares me.

         Very Affectionately,
         William L. Hyde

Friday, October 28th

In the morning, I rode to hospital, dressed two wounds and in anticipation of the wounded being speedily moved, I immediately returned to camp and made preparations and sent to the men their knapsacks. Evening went to Bermuda with the body of Lieutenant Edmonds and had it embalmed. The expense including expressage home was $89.00. (Journal)

Sunday, October 30th

Preached in front of camp at eleven o'clock. Text: My [thoughts] are [known] even the thoughts of my heart.[122] (Journal)

Monday, October 31st

Muster for pay. The regiment was mustered in the afternoon. (Journal)

Tuesday, November 1st

Camp 112th Regt N.Y. Vols.
November 1st 1864

My dear Wife

You will miss your usual letter sent on Monday and get, I fear, rather a shorter letter than usual. The last days and few first days of muster month are very busy and I shall not be able to write you a full letter today and yesterday and day before. I could not find time to write even a line. Sunday was a cool but beautiful day. We had our worship in front of the colonel's tent and a very attentive audience was present. In the evening we had a good prayer meeting. Our regiment and the 142nd uniting. After service I helped Captain Russ, who is sick, get ready for the muster and yesterday, I worked all day helping the corporal, who now commands Company H, make his company rolls. It was work that Lieutenant Edmonds would have done had he been alive. It made me sad to think I was working in his place.

The colonel invited me to spend part of last evening in his tent. He felt lonesome and sad. Captain Dunham and Ludwick and Chaddock, each of who in succession have tented with him this summer, have been wounded and have left. There is not, now present with the regiment, a single captain and but 3 lieutenants who came out with the regiment as line officers. Captain Russ, Captain Talcott and Captain Crane all came out as 2nd lieutenants and of all the lieutenants we had, they are the only left here with us. Captain Mathews, who was originally a captain, is now provost marshal of the division. I pitied the colonel. He showed more signs of deep feeling than I ever knew him to. And certainly he is doing well for the regiment. He gives more personal attention to all its matters than Colonel Drake ever did. I am willing to give him credit for what there is of good in him.

I got your box Sunday and was rejoiced to get my winter clothing. I guess, however, you did not examine them very carefully. They need a good deal done to them. The edges ought to have been worked over with yarn to prevent fraying out and the undershirts need some little stitching. Still they will answer. I send back by a box that goes to Fredonia, 3 pairs stockings and my old overcoat, my shirt, and old vest. I would not have sent the vest and overcoat but I should have to throw them away and the lining is worth taking out to use over. The vest will do for some poor fellow. I put in also a book I found on the battlefield in front of Petersburg the 18th of June. It has a pen in it spoiled. I would like you to sell the pen and keep the case. Charley Price came and paid me the $5.00 he borrowed of you.[123] He also paid ten due Mr. Carpenter. I wanted the very receipt you sent me but, having got the little box, it was of no use. I sent to Dunham for some clothes. I was getting absolutely ragged. I have had my collar nicely fixed by a soldier.

I sent you by express a $100.00 (one hundred dollar) bill of the 7/40 loan, a compound interest note. I think you might as well keep that but I would not invest the other hundred dollars at present. I may get my pay in November and I may not. I don't want to be left as I have been before without available resources. I think you had better keep that $100 where you can draw on it when you wish. I shall not pay Dunham till next pay day. I think the 112th did well for Lincoln and Fenton. Are not the folks at home astounded by the frauds attempted to be perpetrated by the copperheads upon the freedom of the ballot box? But here are found out, thank God, in season to defeat their schemes.

I am very sorry not to have mentioned Frank Goodrich in my letters. He left the regiment just before we left the front of Petersburg. I tried to get Dr. Washburn to recommend him for some northern hospital or for a furlough, but he was so absorbed in his newspapers and correspondence with Marianne that he did not do it. He was, however, sent away and I have been very anxious to know where, as I have some letters for him. I think he will go to Fredonia at election time. If any of Mr. Carpenter's folks know where he is, I would like to learn. He was a noble man but is too delicate for the service. I hope he will get a detail to do duty in some hospital or else his discharge. I am truly happy that your situation at Mrs. Carpenter's is so much pleasanter than it was. As to Harry, I am confident he is well off. It makes me very happy and more contented to think of you all as so well situated, you and Fred at Dunkirk and Harry at Stamford. May the Lord keep us through the scenes of the coming year and give us before it closes a home together.

We are now resting in our old position previous to the late reconnaissance. Today Shaw is having a fireplace built. We may not use it 3 days but it costs nothing. So we say be comfortable while we can.

Very truly your loving husband,
William L. Hyde

Wednesday, November 2nd

Rode with Captain Russ to Bermuda. It was rainy. Went to post hospital. (Journal)

Thursday, November 3rd

Last night near midnight, had orders to move, with knapsacks, but no superfluous baggage. At 4 o'clock broke camp and left everything not transportable. We did not even take advantage of permission to store extra camp equipage with Captain Lord, so sure was the colonel that we were not to return to this point. As usual when we reached Deep Bottom at 6 o'clock this morning we found no transports and waited in the rain for them till 3 o'clock pm, when we began to load. There were several regiments of oldest and best disciplined troops from the 1st Division, and some from the 18th Corps. From our division, there was only our 112th and the 13th Indiana. The embarkation commenced about 3 pm and was certainly the most bungling performance ever inflicted on a body of men. We were packed closer than hogs and in this condition moved down to Bermuda Hundred where we lay all night at anchor. In the morning moved down the river very slowly and about 5 were off Craney Island where large ocean steamers awaited us. The most of our regiment were onboard the *General Lyon*. Two companies remained on the *Powell* till morning when they were landed at Fort Monroe. (Journal)

Friday, November 4th

Onboard Steamer *Thomas Powell*
James River near Fort Monroe
Friday, 2 pm, November 4th 1864

My dear Wife

Last Wednesday I went from the front to Bermuda Hundred on business for the regiment and came back in a very chilly, uncomfortable rain. I found Shaw had got our tent in complete order, a floor to it, a frame inside and a nice fireplace of the Suffolk pattern with a bright fire upon the hearth. I assure you it was comfortable and as the rain pattered and the wind howled we often congratulated ourselves on the comfort we had secured. But alas for ole comfortable surroundings in the army.

About 12 o'clock I woke hearing someone call for the sergeant major and soon hearing the colonel's voice ordering every officer to report to his tent at once. It was half past 12 and the colonel when we were all together, told us we were to leave that place, and must pack everything, leaving what would interfere with light marching order, and be prepared to move out of camp at 2 o'clock. Soon camp fires were burning bright all around us, and instead of going back to our comfortable bunks, we went to make our parcels of luggage as small as possible. This in my case was speedily accomplished. I had, however, Captain Dunham's and Major Ludwick's bundles of blankets to look after and was very busy till near two. Then with my saddlebag across the saddle and Major Ludwick's blanket shawls strapped on the saddle, with my valise and blanket in the cart and an army overcoat on my shoulders, I was ready and followed the column as it moved slowly out. The rain pouring upon us and darkness almost that could be felt surrounding every object with gloom. As usual, we were kept all day at Deep Bottom, waiting for the transport which was to have been on hand at 6 am to take us on.

It was very tedious but we built good stout fires and gathered round them and made ourselves as comfortable as possible. At 4 we began to embark and after an untold amount of confusion, owing to the folly of a staff quartermaster, we did not get the troops on in any comfortable shape. But we started and after moving 18 miles we anchored. It is 18 miles to Bermuda and there we were all night. Today we have been moving very slowly toward Fort Monroe as our steamer was disabled somewhat by [a] collision with a tug just at dark last evening. The colonel and I were furnished with the nicest bedroom on the boat and had an excellent night's sleep but the men are packed as close as live hogs.

We do not know our destination whether Wilmington or New York City. We have heard that we were to go to New York to cow down any attempts at riot. The composition of the force looks a little like this. The regiments that have the Spencer rifles, and all old seasoned troops some that have been in the field 4 years are all here. They are 112th New York, 10th Indiana, 7th Connecticut, 6th Connecticut, 148th and 118th New York, 7th and 3rd New Hampshire, 11th Maine, etc. But we are not certain where we go. I write you this to mail at Fort Monroe. If we go to New York, we shall get there sometime tomorrow and I will write you immediately. I shall find my way as soon as possible over to my cousin Herring's and if we stay in New York many days, I shall send for you. If however we should go there merely to stay 2 or 3 days and then take a new start for Wilmington, I shall not feel it worthwhile. If you don't hear from me by Tuesday noon dated New York treat this whole thing as one of the thousand camp rumors which float and disappear, and expect next to hear from yours affectionately at or near Wilmington, North Carolina.

My horse is onboard of another boat. Fisk takes care of him now. He is [the] quartermaster's guard and takes care of my horse and the quartermaster's. I hated to have him go onboard another vessel but it could not be helped. He is a very fine animal, and were my time to be out in 3 months, I should not take him back into the army but buy a cheap horse and send him to Chautauqua, provided I got him as far as New York City. I am afraid the democracy of New York are prepared for any, even the most desperate measures to cheat the people out of their rights and I have no doubt that it is in contemplation to make the fraudulent vote of New York City swamp the true vote of both the soldiers and the citizens in all the rest of the state. I think that next Tuesday is the day that is to decide whether we are a nation or a crumbling aggregation of states; whether we a proud body of free men, or the mean lick splitters of Jeff Davis. I fear too if Seymour is elected that he will contrive to array the great state of New York against the general government.[124] I am greatly anxious but I hope the evil designs of wicked men will be most singularly defeated.

I hope we shall be at Fort Monroe soon. I will mail this then if possible. You may not, however, get it sooner than one from New York. I expressed from Bermuda some old clothing to you. It would cost but a trifle to send it and I could not give it away where I was. If I had been near Fort Monroe, I would have given the old coat and vest at least to the Freedmen's Society; but the linings are worth something to you.[125] I wear an army overcoat that belonged to one of our deceased officers. I should not, however, have thought it worthwhile to send such a bundle to you, had it been a matter of much expense. I sent it in a box that goes to Fredonia to Colonel Redington and contains Walter Hart's effects as well as those of some other men who have died.[126] Tell Dunham not to send my clothes till you hear from me.

With true affection your husband
William L. Hyde

Saturday, November 5th

Then we waited the coming of the horses and about 5 pm Saturday left onboard the steamer *Star of the South*, a large propeller, which had the horses of the whole expedition. Two companies, 112th men, detailed in Quartermaster Department to care for the horses. 74 men, surgeon, self, and etc. (Journal)

Sunday, November 6th

Very pleasant. Held service at eleven o'clock am on the deck of the steamer. Arrived off Sandy Hook about 8 pm and at 9 landed at Fort Richmond. All the men who could went into barracks. (Journal)

Monday, November 7th

Was a drizzly chilly day. We were kept closely confined at Fort Richmond and not permitted to go even across the island. About 8 o'clock evening we were packed on the ferry boat *Westfield* and started off. The fog was so thick, lay at Quarantine all night. (Journal)

Fort Richmond, Staten Island
November 7th 1864

Dear Wife

Our regiment arrived at this point yesterday and near evening were landed at Fort Richmond. I came on a steamer which had only two companies of the regiment onboard and had a delightful passage. We are, however, more cribbed, cabined and confined here then near Petersburg. Not a man or officer can get a pass to go to the city. Write me immediately on receipt of this. Tell Dunham not to send my clothes till he hears again. All is uncertain as to our destination. Will write tomorrow.

With much love,
William L. Hyde

Tuesday, November 8th

On the morning of the 8th started early for New York City. Stopped at the Ferry Landing just long enough to get the tanks filled with water then moved along up North River to 42nd Street, where we were moved between two piers, and lay all day long. It was far more quiet than Sundays usually are. The day was cold with drizzling rain now and then varied by a smart shower. Here and there were a few men working on the wharfs. But not a sound of busy life reached us from the city. The family of one of our men came down to the wharf and talked to him from the pier. But no communication with the shore was allowed. Night came and no sound of riot. At one time the fire bell gave an alarm and this was the only bell heard. (Journal)

Onboard Steamer *Westfield*
New York Harbor
November 8th 1864

My dear Wife

We are here close to the ice pier North River, about 47th Street in full view of the city or should be, could we see anything. But the fog covers the whole and it has been a drizzly, dirty day. Fortunately, however, for our comfort, not cold. We were just making ourselves comfortable for the night at Fort Richmond Barracks. I had got my bed made on a bunk under a roof and as it had drizzled and rained all day, hoped for a comfortable night. But alas, for human expectations in [the] military. I had hardly got my bed made before the order came for the regiment to prepare to march immediately with two days cooked rations. We all supposed we were to move somewhere by land, but we moved a few yards down to the pier and went onboard this boat.

The fog was thick enough to cut, and the captain would not venture out so we moved up about 3 miles to the Staten Island ferry and fastened the boat to the pier for the night. I had a pretty good night's sleep on a bench and was up safely in the morning as soon as it was thought we could work our way safely up the North River. We moved up stopping on our way for a few moments at the Staten Island ferry station near Castle Garden. I was the only one permitted to go on shore and I went to buy us something to eat, as we had only raw pork and hardtack, with coffee in our mess kit. I was surprised to be absent only 5 minutes, the length of time the boat was to stop. I could buy nothing but soft bread and apples. Yet that was a variety. Yorker made coffee and cutting a thin slice of raw pork with a biscuit buttered. I made a good breakfast.

So dinner this pm at 3 pm with the exception of hardtack instead of soft bread. Raw pork is certainly not one of the delicacies but hungry as I have been today it is very good. We could purchase nothing at Fort Richmond so in the very vicinity of all that is delicious in the way of food within half an hour's ride of my cousin's where [there] is abundance. I have faced much more poorly than I usually do at the front. We are not allowed to go into the city and are with the 3rd New Hampshire and 11th Maine held for any emergency that may arise. The day has been wonderfully still. We have not heard a sound even from New York. It has been drizzly and disagreeable also, so that the men have felt the influence and there has been none even of their usual playfulness. We think that our service will not be needed and that before tomorrow night, we shall be permitted again to return to Fort Richmond. I shall send you a telegram if we are in any position where it would be practicable and proper for you to visit me.

I saw a sight today that affected me much. Two of our new recruits are from this city and their families came down to the wharf this afternoon to see their husbands. The steamer was made moored between two piers about 20 feet from each and the poor men's wives and children had to talk across this space to them. Colonel Smith said he wished he could give those men permission to visit the city for a while, but he could not. The children look bright and pretty and I could imagine how it would tantalize me to be so near you and the children, as close within 20 feet of the pier at Dunkirk and not permitted to go to you or you come to me.

I would far prefer you to be as you are, 500 miles off.

Surgeon Washburn has sent a telegram to Mrs. Washburn [to] meet him in New York immediately. But I very much fear that he will not have permission to go there at least for anything more than a few hours stay. Colonel Smith wanted to send me to the city yesterday on business for the regiment but the orders from General Butler were imperative. No one was to go to the city unless sent on strict military business.

Surgeon says he would be perfectly satisfied provided his wife could be with him those days. I think for the expense [of] $50.00 it would be only an aggravation. I would like to see you but it would be harder parting.

I have not seen my horse since Sunday. All our regimental horses are with the quartermaster sergeant somewhere near the city. Surgeon Washburn has lost his horse which is the last of the horses which came out from the county with the regiment. Not one of them now living unless it be the horse Colonel Drake brought out, which is now somewhere in Pennsylvania.

What a pity it is the doctor is not more like other men. He is the butt of much ridicule for his perfect childishness and want to practical ability.

I feel sometimes as though I ought to tent with him and mess with him, but if I tented with him every time we moved, I should have everything to do myself and he would have the tent in disorder all the time. I am inclined to think he feels it that I don't. But I am not inclined to tend babies unless they belong to you and I conjointly. Shaw is the very model of neatness and indefatigable in fixing up.

Well dearest, this has been a dreadful dull day and the regiment would nearly unanimously vote to go back to Virginia if the last two are specimens of the kind of days we are to spend here.

I wish you to write me as often as possible. If my clothes are done have them all packed nicely to send at a moment's notice. Lieutenant Talcott will send up a package to go with them.

I will keep you informed of our changes.

My present address is
Chaplain, 112th N.Y. Vols.
2nd Provisional Division
Fort Richmond
Staten Island

Charles E. Washburn enrolled at Jamestown, New York, as surgeon in the 112th New York Volunteers. He died of typhoid fever on April 10, 1865 (courtesy U.S. Army Heritage and Education Center [USAHEC]).

Very affectionately your husband

Wednesday, November 9th

Almost as quiet as yesterday. We had a few visitors come to see us. Some ladies and gents, friends of our officers, came down. We had scant fare [of] hard bread and pork. Some officers had nothing and the men were short. In the evening the base quartermaster was permitted to go on shore to procure rations. I went with Shaw. We were gone till 9 pm. Procured two days supply for officers. (Journal)

Thursday, November 10th

Several visitors. A barrel of apples was sent and distributed to men in the morning. In the afternoon a gentleman, Mr. Manley formerly of Chautauqua, interested himself and sent about $80.00 worth of provisions to the regiment. Colonel Smith relieved me from duty and allowed me to go among my friends. I spent the night at Mr. Manley's. I spent Friday am making purchases for officers and myself and went in the evening with my cousin, Mr. Herring to his residence at Montclair, New Jersey. Upon the boat were relieved from duty and returned to Fort Richmond in the afternoon. (Journal)

>New York City, 2 pm
>November 10th [1864]

Dear Wife

I am ashore for a little time on duty for the regiment. I am in hopes to have time to write you a letter tomorrow but today you must be satisfied with a few lines. I saw Mr. Stillman this morning. He was just from Dunkirk. Mrs. Washburn came to the city with him. I want to see you bad enough but I should feel bad not to see you but a few hours. I am well.

>In haste
>William

Saturday, November 12th

>New York City
>November 12th 1864

My dear Wife

I am now sitting in the office of Mabic, Manley and Company. Mr. Manley is a former resident of Panama in our own county. Being an ardent friend and admirer of the late Colonel Drake, he was quite disposed to like me. Mrs. Manley met you last summer at the funeral of Colonel Drake. She is [the] daughter of Elder Rathburn and is a very lovely woman. I came on shore Thursday by Colonel Smith's permission and have been on shore ever since. I was on business for the regiment during Thursday and at Mr. Manley's invitation, I spent the night at his house. Oh was it not delightful to sit down to a civilized table and sleep in a bed with one's clothes off. I went into the bathroom before going to sleep and had a very refreshing tepid bath which secured to relax my frame and give me one of the most refreshing sleeps I ever enjoyed.

I found that I was not entirely a barbarian from my long absence in the army but could adapt myself to sheets and feathers very well. I was quite busy all day yesterday doing errands and at 4 o'clock I started for Montclair with my cousin, Mr. Herring. I saw Auntie and she begged away my pictures of you and Fred. I want you to send me by and by another pair. She has a very large collection of Hyde photographs. I am going to give her mine and Harry's when I can get them. I am still in hopes we shall stay about here a few days but I hear that we are ordered to be ready to move at a moment's notice.

If we stay, cousin Robert wants me to send for you and Fred and take you directly to his house, which I shall most certainly do, but I do not hope for it. It would be great folly to have you come here for a short three day visit, and then go back. I should feel worse and I think you would and unless we go into winter quarters where I can send for you, I shall try and live through the few months to intervene between the present time and the time when I shall be free to rejoin you.

Are you not elated at the results of the present election and such a large popular majority for Lincoln. There is now no reason why the most vigorous efforts should not be used to suppress the rebellion. Mr. Lincoln's modest speech at the congratulatory visit has raised him immensely in my estimation. He is a good man. No one can gainsay it.

I did not tell you what the good people about here did for our men while at the wharf. They raised a very large subscription, about $100, and sent them up butter and apples and cheese, etc. It was most gratefully devoured.

We had a dull time onboard the boat but am thankful that we had so many mercies. You can't think how tantalizing it is to be so near to you and yet cannot get to you. It is worse than being on the banks of the James. If Dunham has my clothes done, I want them sent Monday to:

Reverend W. L. Hyde
Care A. J. Manley
14 Warren Street
New York City

Please prepay the expressage. Mr. Manley says that if the regiment is gone at that time, he will send the package forward. They can be sent in a strong paper envelope. I would like to write more but there is such an incessant interruption that I forget what I have written.

> Most affectionately,
> William L. Hyde

I saw Mr. Stillman Thursday. Was glad to meet anyone from Dunkirk. He came with Mrs. Washburn.

Saturday, November 12th–Sunday, November 13th

The regiment was in quarters Saturday and Sunday. No passes to the city were granted. Officers who needed winter clothing and wished to procure it in the city, thereby saving for themselves 33 percent, were not allowed to do it. General Hawley is understood to be the cause of these abominably strict rules, and he is execrated by all the subordinate officers. We had during Sunday a number of visitors from Chautauqua County. It was very pleasant to see them and to witness their interest in the regiment. (Journal)

Monday, November 14th

Orders came last evening to be in readiness to embark at any moment. In the morning the hour set was 8 o'clock but it was past noon before any signs of embarking and we finally were all embarked about 5 o'clock. Our regiment onboard the steamer propeller *Thames*. (Journal)

> Monday
> November 14th [1864]

My dear Wife

We had orders late last evening to be ready to sail back this morning. I had just got my few articles of comfort ready and expect soon to be off. We had visits yesterday from J. Forbes, Fredonia; Mr. Post and Mr. and Mrs. Angel of Forestville; Mr. and Mrs. Shaw, Jamestown; George Bunker of Fredonia; etc.

Saturday, Mr. Forbes invited me to dine with him. I got your letter of the tenth Sunday. It was the first and only one received from you since leaving Chapin's Farm. Send in future as of old 112th Regiment, Tenth Army Corps. I have made arrangement for Colonel Smith to bring in my express packages. He is to be ashore for 5 days to get recruits.

All is hurry about me here. I am much disappointed in the way things have taken shape and am glad now I did not send for you. Mrs. Washburn has hardly had any company of her husband except to sleep with him 2 or 3 nights. He has had to be here and there and everywhere.

Where we go I can't tell but I think Wilmington. It may be back again to Deep Bottom.

I am very sorry that our regiment came up here. The officers have had no privileges whatever, not even to go ashore and buy clothes. I have no cause to complain myself, but if I get back all safe without my horse being injured by the sea voyage, I shall be very thankful. I rode him one day in New York City about an hour and he attracted much attention.

Well my dear, every week lessens the time of our enlistment. Keep up good heart.

> Very Affectionately,
> William

Tuesday, November 15th

A smooth sea and fair wind. We are getting on finely. Will be at Fort Monroe before midnight. (Journal)

Wednesday, November 16th

Colonel Smith remained behind in New York City having 5 days leave of absence in which to recruit the regiment from Hart's Island. The quartermaster also remained behind to bring on the horses. We were quite a distance up the James River when I got up this morning. The day was pleasant and at noon we were off City Point and at 2 o'clock were at Deep Bottom. We remained, however, onboard the boat, as the rest of the troops had not arrived. (Journal)

Thursday, November 17th

The remainder of the troops composing the expedition came up this morning and we all disembarked with our regimental baggage. There was an earnest effort made while in New York to have our regiment retained in the state. And many thought it might be accomplished. We were all disappointed at being dumped down again in the same old spot. When we reached brigade headquarters, we were shown a piece of ground from which the underbrush had not yet been cut down and told to make camp there. In some respects it was much better than old grounds because timber was at hand wherewith to build quarters. But we were without any facilities, axes, there were but 3 or 4. And all our chairs, bunks, brick chimneys, floors and other camp conveniences, the result of our foraging through the summer were all gone. We also lost during the voyage 2 large flys. So that we had but little material wherewith to repair our tents and put ourselves again in condition of comfort. (Journal)

Friday, November 18th

With a pass from Major Stevens, provost, I went with team and 5 men outside the lines and procured one load of brick. I also got from the major a few boards with which I have constructed two bunks. (Journal)

Chaplain's Monthly Report[127]
112th Regiment New York Volunteers
1st Brigade, 2nd Division, 10th Army Corps

Headquarters 112th Regiment New York Volunteers
Near Chapin's Farm
November 18th 1864
Brigadier General L. Thomas, Adjutant General U.S.A.
Sir,

I have the honor to submit to you the following report of the One Hundred and Twelfth (112th) Regiment New York Volunteer Infantry for the month of October 1864.

After the action of the 29th inst, this regiment in connection with the other regiments composing the 1st Brigade, 2nd Division occupied a position along the line of works last taken from the enemy; its right resting at a point about one fourth (¼) of a mile from the New Market Road in the direction of the river James.

For several days large details from this command were occupied in changing and improving the works already taken, for our own defensive purposes.

The casualties of the summer are severely felt in the loss of most valuable field and line officers. At the commencement of this month, but seven (7) commissioned officers were present and on duty with the regiment. Lieutenant Colonel Smith who had been absent on recruiting service for 15 days returned to the regiment on the 3rd of the month.

On the 7th, early in the morning, heavy musketry firing was heard on our right, and about 8 o'clock orders came for the regiment to fall into line immediately. Colonel Curtis, commanding the brigade, having been ordered to report to General A. H. Terry, commanding the 1st Division. We moved out to the New Market Road, under a heavy fire of the enemy's artillery, but without suffering any casualties. Moving down the road about one fourth of a mile, this command was put in position in reserve of the force at that time engaged with the enemy. The musketry fire was heavy and continuous for about a half hour. The enemy it seems had charged our infantry lines vigorously endeavoring to break through but were repulsed with heavy loss.

About three (3) o'clock pm, Colonel Curtis' Brigade was thrown forward on the left of the line and an advance made towards the Darbytown Road. On reaching an earthwork from which the enemy had been driven by our artillery, the command was halted in line and skirmishers thrown forward into a piece of woods in front without meeting the enemy. At the same time, the First Division moved on the right and swung round towards the road. As they did so they saw the rear of the enemy's column moving rapidly toward his entrenched works.

After remaining in position until about eleven o'clock pm, the skirmishers were withdrawn and the brigade moved back within lines. The next day the brigade was posted in reserve, in a skirt of woodland in rear of our former position behind the entrenchments.

On the evening of the 9th the regiment received six months back pay, out of which they sent home to their families somewhat over twenty six thousand (26,000) dollars. Which at this season of the year will prove most timely aid to them.

It is unfortunate that the payment of the troops in the field should not be made promptly and at periods not too long separated. When kept out of their pay six and eight months after it is due, the best of soldiers become sour and discontented, grow slack in the performance of duty, become a prey to unpatriotic sentiments and influences and are less efficient in the field.

On the morning of the 14th, Colonel Curtis was sent with his brigade to the assistance of General Terry, who was to make a reconnaissance of the enemy's works, deserters having told us that these works were held by a small force of the enemy. Our brigade was not engaged in the conflict which was short and bloody and with considerable loss to the division engaged.

One man from this regiment, Private Frank R. Case, Company A, was reported missing. It is supposed that he was taken prisoner while straggling, having lost his way.

During this week a commissioner from the 31st District, New York state, visited the regiment for the purpose of receiving and conveying to the state the votes of the soldiers of this command, which were enclosed and transmitted according to the provisions of the state laws.

During the latter part of the month, the officers and men were busily occupied in preparing huts as for winter quarters. On the evening of the 26th received marching orders and at midnight received notice to be ready to move at daylight. About 5 o'clock of the 27th we moved out of camp in light marching order, crossed the New Market Road and passed on to the front of the enemy's position between the New Market and Darbytown roads. A heavy skirmish line was thrown out which soon became engaged with the enemy who were steadily pressed back from their advanced position through a piece of woods to their line of entrenchments. First Lieutenant George W. Edmonds, Company H, while bravely cheering on his men and keeping his portion of the skirmish line steady to its work, was instantly killed by a bullet from the enemy, which passed through his brain. His loss is deeply lamented by the command. Two privates of our regiment, George Westly,

Company B and William Henry Hubbard, Company H, were at this stage of action mortally wounded.

The day was chilly and a drizzling rain made our situation very uncomfortable. About 5 pm a charge was made by the brigade led by Colonel Curtis, upon the enemy's entrenched position. They pressed forward gallantly under a galling fire. Lieutenant Colonel Smith keeping his men close to their works, before reaching the enemy's abattoirs, the order was issued recalling the troops. The brigade lost severely in killed and wounded. Our own regiment suffered as follows: 1st Lieutenant G. W. Edmonds and 3 privates killed. Captain Alfred Dunham, acting major and 26 enlisted men wounded and two privates missing. Of the men wounded, 6 have since died.

The regiment lay all night in the position to which they were recalled, the chilly air and frequent showers rendering their condition dismal and uncomfortable. About noon of the next day, the 28th, the command was ordered back to camp without change of situation for the remainder of the month.

Religious services have been held in camp during but two Sabbaths of the month. Military exigencies seeming, at least, to require their suspension during the other Sabbaths.

The health of the regiment generally has been excellent during this month. A very great improvement in this respect having taken place since our transfer to the north side of the James River. Only six (6) sent to general hospital during the month from sickness, and only an average of 17¼ per week sick in quarters while the average per week of those returned to duty was 29¾.

The whole number of officers and men on the roll at the close of the month is 767. The whole number present for duty 363. The general morale of the regiment continues unimpaired. No officer has been subjected even to censure. No private subjected to military discipline.

> I have the honor, General, to be
> Your Obedient Servant,
> Wm L. Hyde
> Chaplain, 112th Regiment New York Volunteers

Saturday, November 19th–Sunday, November 20th

Quartermaster Shaw returned with the horses. It is fortunate for the officers that I was so successful in foraging. My tent is the almost only refuge for officers from the cold rain which is pouring down. No service today. (Journal)

Sunday, November 20th

> Camp 112th N.Y. Vols.
> Near Chapin's Farm
> November 20th 1864—Sunday

My dear Wife

You did not get the letter from me usually written the middle of the week and I fear you are anxious about me not having heard. Since you heard we had left the vicinity of New York. We waited all day Monday as usual after being ordered to be in readiness at 8 am. About 5 we were all stowed safely upon the steamer *Thomas*, and moving out towards the ocean. We had a very pleasant night and it was not very rough the next day. It was about 11 o'clock at night when we passed Fort Monroe. We were off Newport News when I got up Wednesday morning. It was quite mild and the sail up the James was beautiful. About 2 o'clock we had reached Deep Bottom and found that we were the first boat up; the boat containing the brigade commander had not come up so we remained tied up to the pier till Thursday.

After breakfast when in answer to a telegram, Captain Mathews, who was in command, moved the regiment back to camp. We had when we left here a very large number of little camp conveniences which we had been gathering all summer. But we lost them all. Two hours after the regiment left, everything movable was taken and carried away. So chairs, bunks, fireplaces, floor boards, stoves went to supply, the wants of others. The mischief of the whole is that we can't supply their place. We came back to camp utterly destitute. If Colonel Smith had not been absolutely certain that we were to remain in New York or go from there to Wilmington, I should have consigned my few comforts, chairs, bunk, our little cook stove, which we miss more than all else, to the Chaplain of the 142nd New York. But the colonel thought he was shrewd enough to manage, through Governor Fenton's influence, to get the regiment retained in New York. The result is we were taken in.

Colonel Smith sent me ashore as soon as he could to telegraph to Jamestown for Fenton to come there. But I guess Mr. Fenton thought that General Butler knew better than he what was the proper place for the 112th. And yet I believe he wrote General Dix a letter stating that it would gratify him to have the 112th retained in the state if any veteran troops were needed there. I hear too that Mr. Shaw, William's father, had an interview with General Butler who told him that he was willing to swap with General Dix. If General Dix would give him 500 regular troops, he would send the 112th back to him. But there is not the slightest possibility of it being done in my opinion. General Dix would not strip his forts around New York of his nice clean trim regular soldiers to give place to the 112th. It would cost the government $10,000 to make the exchange now. So it won't be done. So I shall not have the pleasure of showing you round New York this winter, not quite. But never mind. Just count from January to next September.

What do you think I did as soon as we got here? I did not do as Surgeon Washburn did, sit down in my chairless tent and wait for someone to take care of me. I went over and took dinner with General Curtis, our brigade commander, and he very kindly offered to give me a note to the deputy provost marshal asking him to furnish me a pass outside the lines to get brick and boards. The next morning I went to Major Stevens on General Butler's staff and asked him to let me go outside the lines and forage. He was very polite to me and wrote me a pass, and told me if I could not get boards, he would give me enough for a bunk.

I then borrowed General Curtis' horse, as mine had not come, and went out to some old buildings six miles on the New Market Road with a team and five men and got a load of brick, came back and went to Major Stevens who gave me boards for two bunks and I got a man to help me and that night I slept above ground. Yesterday I got a man to build me a fireplace, in spite of the rain. About noon, Shaw got back. He came with the horses and expected to find us emphatically out in the cold. On the contrary, he found I had got the tent up, a fireplace partly built, and bunks for sleeping on. Before evening, it rained hard and today it is raining as it only rains in Virginia.

I can have no service so I should have the privilege of writing you. Mine is the only fireplace in the camp, so you may imagine I have plenty of company. I got however, a permit for the other officers to get brick and boards if boards can be found so that [by] the [end of] week all hands will be supplied. When I got back here, I found 12 letters waiting for me; 3 from you. But you must have missed some of mine. You speak of hearing that Dunham was making me a suit of clothes. I wrote you the same day I did him and told you. I sent for winter coat and pants. I gave Captain Talcott permission to send his coat in the same package and I guess that was what Mrs. Talcott referred to. I supposed Lieutenant Corbett would take that bundle I sent you, to New York City and express it there or I would not have sent it by him. It cost rather too much. I sent another in a box to Colonel Redington which will not cost as much if it does anything. I thought it better than to throw the things away.

You speak of my not taking my horse with me on my return to New York. Never you fear. I will work some cure to get him home. If I had not felt certain of it, I would have sent him from New York City, as Colonel Smith did a little Virginia mare. I could have bought out of the cavalry camp a cheap horse for my use 9 months. But I am not often baffled in what I am determined to do.

As to Morgan Phillips, I hope he is at home by this time and with his family.[128] If at Hampton Hospital, I can do nothing for him. It is too bad he has not been paid. But I think he is himself at fault. I had a letter from Mrs. Drake lamenting the sight of her husband's horse. I have sometimes regretted I did not keep him. But I fear he would have caught the disease Frank had. Cobb is not worth minding. Poor miserable copperhead. He will be marked and found wanting someday. I would not receive everything Dr. Rogers says as laws, gospel. I am not afraid of Dunham's sponging me. All kinds of clothing are excessively high. Pants such as cost $6.00 when I first came into the service, cost $15 in New York now. But I must have good clothes. You certainly would not have associating as I do constantly with well-dressed officers go as Dr. Washburn does with an old threadbare coat, that makes him the laughing stock of the regiment and of all about. It is far more important in the army to be dressed than in civil life. In the field we do not pretend to dress every day, but we want to have clothes for inspections, reviews, visits, etc. I thank God still for good health, and comfort; for cheerful spirits, and hope for better things for us both.

I would like to go to Westfield one of these days. I certainly do not want to live in Dunkirk again in any situation. I was much pleased with Fred's letter. I will write him this week. Number your letters hereafter and I will mine.

Very affectionately,
William

Tuesday, November 22nd

Colonel Smith returned from the north today having been detained through failure to connect at Baltimore. (Journal)

Thursday, November 24th, Thanksgiving

We are having a pleasant day for Thanksgiving. We heard yesterday that the people at home had contributed turkeys enough to give us all a good dinner throughout both armies. I went to Bermuda to inquire and hasten the forwarding of the things if possible. We were assured that the provisions would be forthcoming. Today, however, we cannot hear of it. There is great disappointment. Though in our regiment we have learned not to expect so that we are not as much disappointed as many others. (Journal)

Thanksgiving Eve
November 24th 1864

My dear Wife

Yesterday I received your letter informing me that my clothing was forwarded, and soon after Colonel Smith came saying that he received the box and that the clothing would be up with his baggage. Today, I have tried them. They are very handsome and for the style and quality, very cheap. They offer the same general style at McCormick's at $80.00. McCormick's is the great army clothing dealer. He has establishments running from Baltimore to New Orleans; so you see I am not so extravagant after all. Today I dined with General Curtis, our brigade commander, and there was quite a dinner party. We were to have had a large variety of nice things but the colonel did not receive them from Bermuda. We had however, a very good dinner. Turkey, roast beef, oyster soup, oyster pie, cranberry sauce, cranberry tarts, mince pie. Cold water, sherry wine, nuts, raisins and cigars. Those who like, had whiskey flip to wet their nuts with, but I could not endure that. We had a very social and entertaining party. There was not any but the most moderate drinking from any of the party, and not an offensive word. I was very much pleased. What happened after I left I don't know but I think they were all gentlemen.

Colonel Smith was not present. He is very sick with diarrhea and tendency to inflammation of the bowels. It is a bad time for such complaints. The weather is damp and cold. We had almost incessant rain for 3 days and since, it has been cold enough for New York. Today the weather has been softening. But last night was a bitter cold night. I was very comfortable myself having plenty of clothes, but I fear many a poor fellow on picket had a hard night of it. I had written Mrs. Hart before I got your letter. Johnny Wood of Portland called to see you about a week ago or more.[129] He was in Captain Steven's company and went home on a furlough to see his mother who has consumption and cannot live long. You were away. It was the day Governor Seymour said something in Dunkirk or Fredonia. I am very sorry you did not see Major Ludwick. I want very much to be at home when Fannie Carpenter is married and if I can know 3 or 4 weeks beforehand or perhaps 2, I will make every effort to get a leave of absence. I think with my influence with General Curtis, I can succeed in this. I wish now to tell you of something which must be a secret for the present. Don't even whisper it to anyone.

Colonel Smith sent me ashore in New York City to work for the retaining the regiment in the state. I found in conversing with friends of the regiment that one word from Governor Fenton would do more than all New York City.[130] I then, at his request, telegraphed Governor Fenton to come to New York immediately or send [a] letter to General Dix, the colonel having previously written him. Colonel Fenton could not come but wrote [a] letter and sent it by the hand of Mr. Shaw, William's father, who went to see General Butler, who thought considering the losses in the regiment and the necessity of recruiting it with good men, it might be sent to Elmira to take the place of some regiment there which would be sent to the front. After Mr. Fenton had been to Washington, he came to New York and Colonel Smith saw him. He gave Colonel Smith, so he says, positive assurance that our regiment should be sent to Elmira this winter to recruit and guard prisoners. Colonel Smith says if there is any faith in promises, we shall soon be on our way north again.

If we go to Elmira this winter, we shall probably stay there our unexpired term. Now I don't know whether to feel hopeful on this matter or not. I tell you as it was told me. There are only 2 or 3 of us who know anything about it. I regret that you did not send me Harry's letter. Why can't you send them to me? I have asked the favor twice I think. I approve your plan for a Christmas present for him, and shall try and get something for him myself, or send him some money.

I sent in the package to Colman's Bank, a treasury note $10.40 for $100 and $20 in a bill. I don't care a straw about the note at present it is only worth its face, i.e., $100. But I thought if it had not been credited to your cash book you might keep it. I think however in view of the prospect, that I may yet be in [New] York state that it would not be well to invest any. Let the matter rest as it does now. I suppose Colman used the note as currency. That is all right and fair, as I did not direct him to save it. I have been receiving the letters you wrote me while you were north.

I rode my horse to Bermuda yesterday. I like him better the more I ride him. I never put on spurs at all. I only have to loosen the reins and speak to him and he will do just what I want. I have got him so that he is much more manageable than when I first had him. I wouldn't look at $300 for him. Billy Shaw and I make a gay pair. I went with him after I bought the horse and picked out for him a little Virginia blooded mare. She is a little beauty, not quite 4 years old, and she treads as though the ground may not [be] good enough for her to step on. She would not do my work but she will do all his and improve on it.

I am going tomorrow to build a log shanty. We shall use our present wall tent for a roof to it. Most of our officers and men have good quarters now. Colonel Smith has just completed his log house and is living in it with brick chimney and good bunk.

I hear the Dutch Gap Canal is approaching completion. All that is now wanted is to blow out the seed. I have never been to it as it is a very great exposure and one I have no right to make. The Rebs throw shell into it and casualties occur daily. I don't think it a settled fact as yet that Butler is to be Secretary of War. But think it may be so. I am sure he would make the best possible Governor of Richmond if we get it.

With fond love as ever,
William

Regards to Mrs. Carpenter and family, also to Dr. Rogers and Carrie. Doctor Rogers sent me the *New York Times* containing Cushing's exploits.[131] It was very interesting. Many thanks. Tell dear Freddie, Pa will write him next time. I meant to today but was interrupted.

Friday, November 25th

The Thanksgiving for our brigade came today. Our regiment received some apples. Also one pound turkey per man. The weather is very cold. (Journal)

Saturday, November 26th

Weather cold, cloudy appearances of softening down. (Journal)

Sunday, November 27th

Weather soft. Service at 11. Afternoon frequent showers. (Journal)

Monday, November 28th

Camp 112th N.Y. Vols.
Near Chapin's Farm, Va
November 28th 1864

My dear Wife

I am going to put you off with a short letter and write you a long one the middle of the week.

We have been building a new log house and are all in confusion, so I have no place to sit and write. Yesterday was a cloudy, drizzly Sunday but it was clear long enough in the morning for us to have religious service. As the men on Thanksgiving were so occupied making themselves comfortable, that we could not have services. We had a kind of thanksgiving service yesterday. In the afternoon it rained most of the time and the evening and night were very dark. I spent most of the evening in the colonel's tent. He was in good view and I had a very pleasant visit with him. Before I left the mail boy came in with the *New York Times* of the 26th. We then learned that Sherman was well on his way to Savannah. I presume the future of this army will depend on Sherman's movements.

We are quiescent just now but are not allowed to get anything that looks towards winter quarters. Friday, the thanksgiving turkey came. Our men had a pound each and our mess had one. It was all cooked and was very palatable.

I will close now as the mail goes soon. I am in the most excellent health and good spirits. I don't place any great reliance upon Elmira but think it may be so, provided General Grant has not other plans.

Very truly your husband
William L. Hyde

I have yours of October 31st, November 4th and November 9th, I received at Fort Richmond.

Wednesday, November 30th

No change in military situation. The weather is very mild for the season of the year. In the middle of the day too warm for comfort in the sun. Rumors of making two new Corps de' Armies out of the 10th, consolidating the negros into a Corps de' Afrique to be called the 24th and the white troops into a corps to be called the 22nd. (Journal)

Camp 112th Regt N.Y. Vols.
Near Chapin's Farm, Va
November 30th 1864

My dear Wife

There is a great dearth of news here, and a great deal of work to do before we are fully prepared for all the changes of the seasons.

I am very much surprised that you did not get a letter Thanksgiving day. I wrote one which went out in the mail the Saturday previous which ought to have reached Dunkirk as soon as Thursday, if not one day earlier. It is not always my fault that you do not get your letters regularly. The weather since Monday has been exceedingly warm and delightful. Yesterday, it was like summer. So warm that in the sun, one was uncomfortable. I rode to Bermuda Hundred and my horse sweat just walking. Our situation here is quite uncertain. I hardly know whether to hope to go to New York or not. I am so used to the uncertainty of military life that I shall not feel at all as I did last winter if we do not go.

I suppose it is all over the county, by this time, that we are coming north. I hear that it is much talked about in Jamestown and Shaw's folks write that they fear this letter might not reach him as he was on his way to Elmira, probably. It will be perfectly safe for you to continue writing to me here until you have definite information that we are on our way. If I knew certainly that we would soon be there, I should have you go down and engage a boarding place for us. But General Grant may not have the fear of Governor Fenton before his eyes and may think he can put us to a better use here or further south. Never mind. December to September is how many months?

I want to make you and Harry and Fred a handsome Christmas present. What shall it be? I think I will send Harry $3.00 in money if I cannot think of anything to buy him. I most heartily approve of your present and as to Fred and yourself, I wish you would spend a sum of money not less than $20 for yourself and $2 for Fred. I am going to send him a little postal currency in this. Dear little fellow, how I would like to have him with me this winter. It will be hard for Harry should I come home not to be able to be with us. I think I should take him out of school for a little time.

Two small boxes have just come to the regiment for hospital use from Fredonia. I don't know who sent them. They had some old shirts, some luit, some towels, some blackberry cordial (very nice), and some dried fruits. I have already with the advice of the surgeon, sent the dried fruit to the two Fredonia companies, and the shirts and luit will be sent tomorrow to the division hospital. The towels will be given to some men who need them. And the cordial is in the surgeon's hands to dispense daily to those who need it. There were some magazines also which are to be put in our regimental library.

I am very sorry at Mrs. Bellows' disappointment. Tell her I hope one day to see her and all the kind Dunkirk friends. I have had a letter from Frank Goodrich lately. He is at Grant General Hospital, Willets Point, New York Harbor. I have written him and sent his letters.

Sergeant Hawley, I hear is recommended for promotion to lieutenancy. We had a regimental inspection this forenoon. My new clothes elicit universal commendation.

If I go north, I shall be obliged to have a uniform coat, as my present uniform coat is getting threadbare. I had my last coat made for what is called a fatigue coat or fatigue sack. And if we remain in the field, I have now all the clothing I shall need, except perhaps a uniform coat next spring, until we get out of the service.

Clothes cost something. But my dear, we have enough for our use and am able to make our children comfortable. Let us thank God. What should you say to my starting a school on the plat of Mr. Wilder after this cruel war is over? If I could go to such a place as Westfield, I would accept a parish. But I don't intend to get into such a parish as Fredonia or Dunkirk if the Lord wills.

We have just heard that the 10th Corps is to be composed entirely of smoked Yankees or the [Culled puns], and we are to be in the 24th Corps. Hurrah for the 24th Corps!!

Wouldn't I like to give you a drive with old Frank. I think he would take a sleigh over the route between Dunkirk and Fredonia, a little gayer than you have been accustomed to of late.

Affectionately
William

Thursday, December 1st

Situation unchanged. Weather still warm. (Journal)

Friday, December 2nd

Chaplain's Monthly Report[132]
112th Regiment New York Volunteers
1st Brigade, 2nd Division, 10th Army Corps

Headquarters 112th Regiment New York Volunteers
Near Chapin's Farm Va

December 2nd 1864

Brigadier General L. Thomas
Adjutant General, U.S.A.

Sir,

I have the honor to submit to you the following report of this regiment for the month of November 1864.

On the first day of the month, the command was busily engaged in perfecting camp and doing the ordinary duty required while in camp. About midnight of the 2nd, the officers of the regiment were ordered to report at once to Colonel Smith's quarters, where we were informed that we were to leave early in the morning but were to take no superfluous camp or garrison equipage, that we were to be embarked onboard transports, regimental teams to be turned over to the Quartermaster Department. At 4 o'clock we broke camp and left arriving at Deep Bottom about 6, where we expected to find transports in waiting for us.

On the contrary we waited for them until 3 pm when they arrived and were placed onboard. There were a large number of troops from the 1st Division of our corps and some from the 18th Corps, all of them veterans. Near Craney Island, we were transferred on the afternoon of the following day to ocean steamers and then learned that our destination was New York Harbor. When we arrived on the 6th after a prosperous voyage and on the evening of that day were transferred to the barracks at Fort Richmond, Staten Island.

On the evening of the 7th, our regiment with three others and a section of artillery, all under the immediate command of Lieutenant Colonel Smith of the 112th New York was placed onboard the ferryboat *Westfield*. And after spending the night near Quarantine, were in the morning moved across to New York City and stationed off 42nd Street, to be in readiness to operate, in case of any violent outbreak on election day. No communication with the shore was allowed. The day passed over with a degree of quietness which was surprising. Hardly a sound of any kind was wafted to us from the great city. Some boys and a few grown persons came down during the day to gaze at the visitors, but our presence was evidently unknown to the distant multitude. We were kept onboard the steamer till Friday afternoon, when we were again landed at Fort Richmond and remaining in barracks until the afternoon of Monday the 14th, were then reshipped onboard steamers for the James River. And on the morning of the 17th disembarked at Deep Bottom and rejoined our brigade. Everything we had left upon our former campground having disappeared, we were ordered to lay out camp and commence erecting quarters upon new ground in the vicinity. Since the date of our return, the regiment has been chiefly occupied in making comfortable huts and preparing for the inclement season approaching.

There were seven (7) cases of desertion while in New York Harbor; a small number in comparison with some other regiments. Of these, 5 were men who claim that they originally enlisted in the artillery, were assigned to a specific battery, and afterwards arbitrarily and against their wills assigned to an infantry regiment.

The command was crowded in a most uncomfortable manner during the voyage to New York. This with the exposures, change of climate and of irregularity of diet, caused an increase of sickness during the first half of the month. 4 were reported sick in quarters the week ending the 12th and 27 the week ending the 19th. The average per week for the month is:

Sick in quarters	Sent to Hospital	Returned to duty
17½	2	19

Religious services were held with the regiment two Sabbaths during the month. In regard to the moral condition of the regiment, there is nothing specially to vary the tone of former reports. The command is well cared for, is in comfortable condition, in general good health, and excellent spirits.

I have the honor to be, General,
Your Obedient Servant,
Wm L. Hyde
Chaplain, 112th Regiment New York Volunteers

Sunday, December 4th

Camp 112th N.Y. Vols.
Near Chapin's Farm
December 4th 1864

My dear Wife

This is the afternoon of the Holy Sabbath, and while you are sitting before a fire or are taking a little siesta on your lounge, I am sitting without a fire and with the flap of my tent open. It is certainly one of the most charming days "so calm, so cool, so bright," that we have had this season. We had several warmer however the last week. While I sit writing to you, I hear the rumbling of wheels indicating the moving of artillery. The process of consolidating the troops of the 15th and 18th Corps has already begun, the white troops are to form one corps to be called the 24th instead of 23rd as I told you last, and the negros from the "Corps d'Afrique" under General Weitzel. Our new commander, General E. C. Ord; General Foster goes out of the command of the 2nd Division, and takes the position of chief of staff to General Ord. General Ames comes into the command of the 2nd Division. Our brigade relations remain unchanged. I hope we are not to move camp, but we can't tell what any day may bring forth.

This fine weather would be magnificent for military operations if it would only continue. But weather is as uncertain as military. I was last Thursday at Dutch Gap and should have gone down in but it is a very dirty job. And the Rebs were shelling the works, making it rather too much risk to run. So I contented myself with gazing down into the cavernous depth. It is well pictured in *Harpers*. I am of the opinion that the concern will not amount to much after all.

We had our regimental worship this morning in the open air near the colonel's quarters.

The attendance was not large. I shall have before another Sabbath, a regimental chapel if the weather permits and we do not move camp before that time.

I hear from the boys that our coming north is much talked of in the county. Some who have returned this week had heard from various sources that such is to be the case. But I would give more for one word of "Ulysses The Wise" than for all the governors or subordinate generals.

If that Mrs. Douglas comes to see you again, tell her I would be glad to help Mr. Phillips in any way I can but he is a hundred miles away and under the control of the chief surgeon at Hampton. He ought to have been paid before this but I suppose was away sick when the regiment was paid and had not his descriptive list at the hospital.

We have a chaplain's meeting at the Christian Commission rooms tomorrow morning. You can imagine how pleasant it is to be in the immediate vicinity of such friends as Taylor and Tiffany and Chapman and there are one or two other very fine men. My new clothes are beauties and I believe I look as well as any chaplain when I am dressed and especially on my horse. It is splendid and attracts notice everywhere. Wouldn't I like to give you some sleigh rides behind him this winter! I am glad Mrs. George Shaw got through as well as she did and hope the child will live to be a comfort to them both. I was truly glad to see Mr. Stillman. What an odd stitch he is!

Martin J. Stafford enlisted at Jamestown, New York, as a private in Company A, 112th New York Volunteers. He mustered out July 1, 1865, at David's Island, New York Harbor (courtesy U.S. Army Heritage and Education Center [USAHEC]).

Our colonel is very gracious and pleasant. He is the most singular man I ever knew. Sometimes I can't bear him and then again I think I am uncharitable, and feel ashamed that I have ever thought that of him. He makes an excellent colonel. Everybody is pleasantly disappointed. He does take better care of the regiment and gives it more personal inspection than any man we have ever had at the head of it, except Ludwick. The regiment begins to like him. He is a man who, when he has a purpose, is untiring. Well Johnny Wood wants my letter. He called to see you and Fred when you were away. I told Martin Stafford to call on you.[133] He is Colonel Smith's orderly and a nice fellow.

Yours truly,
William L. Hyde

Tuesday, December 6th

We have been hoping since our return from New York City for an order to take us to Elmira, New York to do guard duty this winter. When Colonel Smith was in the city, an effort was made through Colonel Fenton, governor elect, to procure this change. It is known that Governor Fenton saw General Butler in Washington and the general promised to send him the 112th the first of December. Yesterday rumors having reached us of a move to some distance, the colonel persuaded me to call at General Butler's headquarters and remind the general of our expectations. I brought the subject before General Turner, his chief of staff, who promised to see the matter attended to that day. Today, however, our whole brigade has orders to be provided with 3 days cooked rations. Evening, orders came to be ready to move at 8 o'clock tomorrow morning taking only men able to be as a march. Rumors take us to Savannah and Wilmington. I think Wilmington. We were busy all day reducing baggage to the smallest compass and otherwise preparing for a march. (Journal)

Wednesday, December 7th–Thursday, December 8th

At 4 o'clock pm, the regiment moved out from camp. Each man is in light marching order, having ½ shelter tent, blanket or overcoat and rubber with one change of underclothing. Mounted officers are to take on their horses, their own baggage and rations. We marched until 12 midnight and halted at signal tower near Point of Rocks. Breakfasted very early in the morning and soon after light moved to Bermuda Hundred. Transports were awaiting us. Our regiment embarked onboard the *Charles Thomas* transport propeller and about 5 pm moved down the stream and anchored off City Point. (Journal)

Friday, December 9th

Moved slowly down the river and anchored near Hampton Roads. (Journal)

James River
December 9th 1864

Dear Wife

We are now on the James River, moving along very pleasantly. The day after I sent you my last letter we were kept waiting all day in momentary expectation of orders to start transportation for forage. Was to be ready at 8 am. Having so much time, I prepared all my little effects in good shape to leave. My valise with all my most valuable clothing and papers. A box about as big as a large raisin box with my sundries. My blanket I rolled up snug in a rubber, and had my great coat wadded in soldier style so that it was as compact as a roll of cotton batting. My big saddlebags are stuffed with rations. And about 4 o'clock we were ordered to start expecting to find transports at Deep Bottom. Shaw and I rode there in advance and found not a boat had come. It rained all the morning and at times very hard. The soil was awful. Slip, slip at every step.

It was warm and my horse was very sweaty just traveling down from Chapin's Farm. The boats not coming perplexed us and we rode across the pontoons and about a mile and a half to Lieutenant Morse, the commissary, who said that he had no less than 7 different orders about rations, and that we were at last account to march over to Point of Rocks. We then rode back to Deep Bottom where we had left our wagon with rations and our pack mule, and soon the brigade made their appearance, and we moved on. The night was very mild, the rain had passed away and we marched very slow. It was nearly two o'clock before we reached Point of Rocks and half past two when I climbed into the army wagon with Shaw, rolled our selves up between 2 blankets and soon were fast asleep. About 5 we were roused up and got our breakfast. Yorker had made us a cup of excellent coffee. We had a good nice boiled ham, which relished with biscuit and butter. Yorker makes cream of tartar biscuits in a style which would do credit to Delmonico. And I happened to get hold of some most excellent butter before we started at only 75 cents per pound. So we sat round a campfire on the logs and made a breakfast fit for a major general.

About 7 o'clock we started from Point of Rocks where we had gone as a feint to deceive the enemy and moved back 2 miles and then turned down to Bermuda Landing. When we got there I was well satisfied of one thing, that our destination was south of Cape Hatteras as there were 15 ocean propellers lying there waiting for us. Embarking onboard transports is always a very tedious operation and especially such when there is not a very energetic quartermaster. We were on this occasion all day embarking and did not leave the wharf till half past 3 pm. We then moved down about 20 miles and anchored for the night.

It was a remarkably beautiful night, clear moonlight. We had supper about 7 pm, after which a portion of the officers went to playing whist or euchre, some to read, and others among whom was myself went to bed and to sleep. I was very tired. Indeed I hardly recollect a time when I have been more so. Shaw, Lieutenant Dixon, Dr. Mead and myself had a room together, with 2 bunks and two mattresses. When the rest of them came to bed, I was fast asleep and only woke twice before it was time to get up. I slept so sweetly that I feel this morning like a new man. But you ask, where are you going? I can only say I can't tell. I presume no one onboard knows. General Ames and General Curtis both seem to be in the dark. When we get to Fortress Monroe we shall probably get sealed orders and go where we are ordered.

I think still it is Wilmington and if successful our whole corps will follow. So goodbye New York! Mrs. Shaw wrote William the other day that she had got a Christmas turkey, all ready for his dinner expecting to welcome him home to eat it, and several very pleasant plans were made having reference to his counter plotted advent. Only you can tell nothing about military. We're all blind. Here today and there tomorrow. Ripped up when you least expect it, and sent where you don't care to go. Led to hope for something and get something else. So it goes! Be sure and send Harry some present for me and give Fred one and yourself.

May God keep and bless you. I shall write as soon as possible.

Your affectionate Husband

Sunday, December 11th

Still here. A dull Sabbath. Great confusion onboard the steamer, changing troops. There seems to be a great lack of system in loading these boats. (Journal)

Onboard Steamer
Sunday Noon
December 11th [1864]

Dear Wife

I received yours and Harry's a few minutes ago just after I had dispatched a letter to you. I wish you would send Harry $3.00 for me. I have hardly money enough to last me this expedition and probably will have to send to you for some as soon as we get back, unless we are paid in a few days. Four months' pay will be due the regiment. Had I thought while in New York of our going on this expedition, I should have sent for you to come and see me.

How lonesome I feel this morning and how much I wish to see you. I would like to be transported in a balloon to Dunkirk and dropped in the woods near Dr. Smith's farm. I would then cover my face so no one could see me and come down the railroad and go up into your room and no one should see or talk to me but you and Fred and the family for 2 days.

If you see any of John McCourt's folks, tell them that Fisk is in excellent health. He is detailed on extra daily duty in the Quartermaster Department, and has the care of Shaw's horse and mine. He is at present on another boat. When I see him, I will tell him to write. I think the reason he has not, he has had a swelled hand so that I think it was difficult for him to use a pen. He is one of the kindest hearted, most faithful men I am acquainted with. I guess they did all they could to make a Catholic of him though he does not say he has joined their church. He takes splendid care of my horse. This expedition will not interfere with our prospects of coming to New York, if we are only going to get possession of the forts near Wilmington. For in that case the white troops will probably rejoin their corps and very likely we shall be stopped at Fort Monroe and sent north. Governor Fenton has told Mr. Shaw that we are coming and I am certain he can take us there unless we go below South Carolina. If we go to Savannah or Charleston, it will be difficult for us to get north as the expense to government would be very great and we might be indispensable to the service there. I want you to be sure and purchase something for yourself. Use at least $20 to $25, more if it will better serve you. I am such a poor hand at selecting things for ladies. I don't know what to send. You can judge much better yourself. There is nothing I desire more than your happiness and that of the children.

May God keep us all in his holy care. I trust we shall escape the perils of the sea. You will read the New York papers with interest. I'd get a *Herald* as that has most military correspondence.

Very affectionately,
William

Onboard Steamer *C. Thomas*
Hampton Roads
December 11th 1864

My dearest,

Here we are still onboard this filthy old propeller, waiting the completion of the preparations necessary to a start. And of our destination is as yet a mystery to us outsiders. We have 20 days rations onboard so that I presume we are provisioned for out and return. There is a very large naval fleet accompanying us. I am told 1100 guns. The huge ironsides, 3 or 4 monitors, the *Wabash, Brooklyn*, etc., which comprise the fleet. Admiral Porter's beautiful flag steamer, the *Malvern*, lies within a stone's throw of us.[134]

Our tarry here has been exceedingly tedious. We have been cramped into very close quarters and if we went ashore, had to come back directly for fear of being left. So I have only been twice ashore and no further up than the entrance to the fortress. I am of the opinion that Wilmington is our place of destination. I did think we were going into Hatteras Inlet and thence up the Roanoke and James Rivers, make a dash inland upon the railroad above Weldon, turn up the track, take Weldon and do all the damage possible to the enemy besides cutting off Lee's communications with the south. But the vessels of the expedition are too large and the expedition itself too formidable for any such small raid. The land force is largely colored troops, with about three or four thousand of the best white troops of Butler's army. I presume if successful, we shall winter in South Carolina instead of Virginia. I must say that if we are to winter away from [New] York state, the further south the better. I was perfectly charmed with Florida and all the regiment would prefer to go to Florida of any part of the country below New York.

O' how I hope we of the land force will be so situated as to see the sea fight or rather the bombardment of the batteries if there is one. It will be sublime. I was thinking this morning as I stood looking at the monitors and new ironsides, how I would like to see all the Rebel navies in Richmond, the North Carolina waters and the gulf in a fight with them, those three monitors and the ironsides. I must say however that I would much rather see the day of peace than any more war of any description.

We are having it very mild since Thursday night. Friday night and last night it rained hard and the men on deck were very uncomfortable. I fear there will be many very severe colds unless the weather gets to be very favorable. I do pity enlisted men onboard these transports. They have to live like hogs in the wet straw down under the decks.

I had a letter yesterday from Dr. Smith and was very glad to get it. He speaks of constant rains.

I hope we shall soon be off and our voyage over.

There I must stop, the mail goes ashore instantly. The paper will tell you soon all about us.

Very affectionately,
William

Monday, December 12th

Visited Chesapeake Hospital. Major Ludwick there. (Journal)

Tuesday, December 13th–Thursday, December 22nd

The transport first left Hampton Roads at about 3 am. Instead of moving south as all expected, we moved due north. In the course of the forenoon entered the Potomac River. Saw much ice in the river along the shore. It was a raw chilly day. After proceeding as far as Matthias Point, we turned and anchored for the night about 30 miles from Fort Monroe. In the afternoon passed a boat loaded with returning prisoners of war going to Annapolis. (Journal)

Onboard Steamer C. Thomas
Potomac River, Va
December 13th 1864

My dear Wife

After our long tedious delay at Hampton Roads, we are again afloat. This morning about 3 o'clock, we weighed anchor and all the 17 large transport ships moved, not as I supposed when I wrote, you but in the opposite direction. And today we have been going up the Potomac River as far as Matthias Point. There we all turned round and since dark have been busily making our way seaward. It has been a very fair day, only cold, and on reaching the vicinity of the point, I saw snow for the first time this year. Otherwise the day has been all that could be desired. The gale of Sunday night and Monday morning had entirely subsided and the sea was smooth as a floor. I hope it will continue so throughout our voyage. It is very dull and monotonous here. I have never felt so the tedium of the hours as they pass along. This afternoon, I lay in my berth a long time, thinking of you and Harry and Fred. I felt happy thinking of you, but I longed to see you. What sort of a Christmas will I spend? Will it be amid scenes of suffering and woe? Is our regiment destined to another bloody encounter and must some others fall in this terrific struggle.

I dread campaigning at this season of the year. It will come rather hard to be out upon the cold ground with only a single blanket over me. Well if we are where wood is plenty, we can get along for we will build a big campfire at night and roll up and with feet towards it we shall be tolerably warm. I got a letter from Harry just in time to write him an answer before we left. I told him I had directed you to send him $3.00. It was a very pretty letter, written with more than his usual care though with lead pencil.

When and where shall I get the next letter from you. If the mail could only be distributed at Fort Monroe I think we should get it the day after our arrival but if it has to go up to corps headquarters before it is distributed, it will not get to us for a week. I could better go without half my meals than go without my mail.

I bought an *Atlantic Monthly* while I was at Fort Monroe with which to amuse and wile away the time. But we can't always read.

Wednesday 14th. Last night was a bitter cold night. I pitied men who lay on deck. This morning a high wind. We passed Hatteras about 8 am and about the middle of the afternoon it began to clear up. We were off Wilmington about night.

Thursday. It is a beautiful day. The air as soft as May without this chill. At noon it was uncomfortably warm. We have not yet landed any part of the force. The sea is almost as smooth as a floor and the great fleet lies lazily about floating at will. An easterly storm would soon distract the quiet of our dreams to send us whirling out to sea. Towards evening, appearance of storm and more rain and wind.

Friday. This morning I supposed we would certainly land, but no signs of it at present. If the good weather continues this is all the more favorable, as the enemy will suppose we are gone further south. We have not as yet been within 30 miles of shore.

Saturday. Not ashore yet. It is very tedious. Water is getting scarce. We have been so long confined below decks that several are getting sick. It is hard work to pass the time. I have read 2 magazines and borrowed a novel, *Days of Shoddy*, but the time hangs heavy.[135] Our band have twice discoursed their sweet music. Appearances now indicate that we shall land tomorrow. I hope General Butler will not take Sunday to open his iron hand upon the Rebel fortifications.

Monday 19th. Still afloat. The beautiful weather which accompanied our setting out has continued thus far. I fear that if the expedition is delayed a day or two longer, a storm will drive us off shore and then this will share the fate of so many abortive efforts of the past and life treasured and time all be sacrificed to blundering incompetence or to a guilty want of cooperation between the army and navy. We hear that the present cause of delay is the navy is not ready. It is said General Butler has a ship filled with powder, 200 tons, which is to be run up between Fort Fisher and the land batteries and exploded. It is supposed that in this way the garrison will be so stunned that the fort can be easily carried by assault. Yesterday was one of the most beautiful days of the season, mild and bright. The sunrise was such as can only be witnessed at sea. We had religious worship a little before noon. The band played Old Hundredth at the opening and one of Mendelssohn's sweetest arias at the close.[136] Brother Palmer, Chaplain of the 142nd New York and myself conducted this service. I talked a little. It was a unique scene. I stood on top of the engineer's room and the top of the cabin aloft the main mast was covered with men and men in every posture were clustered round on the deck below. After worship we had singing. The day passed much more pleasantly than I feared. There was no card playing, which is the standing amusement of the officers and some outward respect paid to the day onboard. The card players and wine bibbers went over to the *Baltic* where, I suspect, they had a very noisy time. Some of General Curtis' staff, and the lieutenant colonel of the 142nd New York came back evidently the worse for liquor. I am thankful for the good conduct of the officers of the 112th. Colonel Smith sets a good example and there is no dram drinking among them. The example of the commanding officer is all powerful with those junior. As to cards, I don't discountenance it where it is played merely for amusement. They can't read all the time and must have some kind of amusement to pass away the time. I believe I have now read about everything decent onboard the boat and I don't know what I shall find for amusement today. If I had my valise with me I could write but all my writing material except the little I shall send for letters is up the James River.

If my horse comes out all right and I don't get sick, I shall feel that a special providence has watched over me for good. The poor horses are having a hard time. They are down in the hold of a propeller, where there is little air, where it is stifling hot and 200 of them crowded in together.

I wish I had sent mine home when in New York and bought me a cheap plug here. But is no use borrowing trouble. January is coming and September will follow on. I will close this letter. A merry Christmas to you and Fred. I am pleased that you are happy and shall think of you in Buffalo.

Your affectionate husband,
William L. Hyde

Thursday 22nd. We have just arrived safe at the site of Beaufort, North Carolina. Yesterday we were driven to sea by one of the most terrific of storms. Last night the most awful night I ever experienced. Seven horses were killed and thrown over. By God's mercy we are now all safe. William.

Wednesday, December 14th

Early in the morning the fleet led by the *Baltic* sailed passed Hatteras about 9 am. (Journal)

Thursday, December 15th

Last evening reached the blockading squadron off Wilmington. Floating about all day. Beautiful weather. Why does not the general land his forces? (Journal)

Sunday, December 18th

Sabbath. No change since last entry. General Curtis and staff left today and went onboard steamer *Baltic*. Held religious worship on the deck of the steamer before noon. (Journal)

Monday, December 19th

It is very calm and mild. The captain thinks it foretokens a storm. (Journal)

Tuesday, December 20th

Some wind off shore. It is too late now to land. We are getting short of water and coal and are moving up toward Beaufort, NC. We reached the entrance to Beaufort Harbor about 12 noon. Having no orders, the Colonel (Barney) did not like to assume the responsibility of going in.[137] We put out and worked slowly towards sea. A gale sprung up suddenly and raged with great fury. Pm, had to throw over three horses. Evening gale increased, sea running very high. Wind from the southwest. The vessels headed so that the wind comes over our quarters and we made progress about a mile an hour. All night the violence of the storm continued. Threw over three more horses. (Journal)

Wednesday, December 21st

In the morning, we found ourselves again in the vicinity of the blockading fleet. Being almost out of coal, put about for Beaufort. (Journal)

Thursday, December 22nd

Reached Beaufort or rather Morehead City about 3 pm. Colonel Smith went over to the city to spend the night. (Journal)

Thursday, December 22nd 1864

My dear Wife

I already have told you in a postscript to a letter finished 2 days since, of our being out in the gale of yesterday. It was one of those gales to which, at this season of the year, this coast is subject. Day before yesterday, there began early to be symptoms of an approaching blow. We had been having the most charming of weather and nothing was done to accomplish the object of the expedition. We all felt it was tempting providence thus to waste 5 of the most quiet days of the winter season. The captain of the steamer said that the coast was so peculiar that no force could be landed if the wind blew in shore in any degree nor if there was a high wind blowing off shore. Somebody of course is responsible for the delay of the expedition. It matters not much who it is. In all probability, the result is irreparable misfortune. All this tedious voyage full of such discomforts as we, none of us, have ever endured before for a like space of time. All our pains and willing efforts are wasted by the fault of some blundering booby who is at the head of military power in this region. In the afternoon of Tuesday, the wind began to increase. We were most out of coal and lying in a bad position so that it was necessary to move north. We moved along our division ships following the *Baltic*, the division flagship, until in the morning when off Beaufort, we lost sight of her. Our orders were to follow the *Baltic* and we go out to sea against the advice of the captain of the boat who predicted a heavy blow which would sweep our decks if we were caught in it.

    About the middle of the forenoon, it came with the force of a hurricane. The sea was tossed with heaps and the spray was sent flying like white snow from the top of a drift. We had about 20 horses on deck. They were in pens which were well lashed but whenever our ship was struck by the gale and tossed like a chip from wave to wave, the poor animals grew frantic in their struggles to keep on their feet. The soldiers were all driven below except the guard. And such a scene I never witnessed. When the gale struck us, the officers were sitting with the captain round the table. Some playing cards, others reading. Immediately, one half of the men tumbled over to one end and the next moment the rest were all piled in a heap, with table and stools and spit boxes, in one promiscuous mass. Lieutenant Crane was in his berth, a cup of tea on the washstand beside him, which was unceremoniously emptied with his basin. In the afternoon, the gale increased. Our ship would plunge her nose in and at every turn the waves covered the deck knee deep. Two of the stalls in which the horses were confined were dashed into kindling wood. The horses thrown down trampling and tumbling over each other, kicking and making frantic attempts to rise which were all in vain. At last the guards were obliged to use their pistols, put an end to their misery and threw them overboard. Towards evening the wind veered round to the west and for a time there was a lull when it chopped about to the northeast, and from 10 o'clock to 2 am, the wildest, most awfully sublime scene I ever witnessed was displayed. How we got through with no more of accidents, I can only say God saved us. I felt nearer death than at any time since leaving the Petersburg trenches. But I felt wondrous calm. I moved around trying to assure the faint hearted, but most of the time I sat in my room. After committing you, the children, myself and the boat's company to the care of God, I felt as though all would be right, and as I could do nothing outside, I sat bolstered up in my bunk, holding a lamp in one hand and a book in the other and read until one when my light went out. Then I got up, went on deck, walked about a little, clinging to whatever I could hold on by, but only for a minute. I was glad to get back as soon as I could, for the ship gave two or three of those stupendous lurches. And as she came up, a wave struck her on the quarter which made every timber groan, and sent the horses, which were left jumping and pulling and tumbling, and raised the stalls in which they were blown from the deck. And then came from forward the sound [of] shot then and 2 poor animals were put out of misery. I then went to bed and tried to go to sleep. But as I would get into a doze, some bit wave would strike and roll me almost out of my berth. I tell you it was a long night. In the morning we were heading for Beaufort Harbor or more properly, Morehead Inlet, which is the Port of Beaufort. We reached there about noon. Our men and some officers say they would much prefer risking a charge against Fort Fisher to another such night. I can now say that I have seen a storm at sea. I don't know but I guess Colonel Smith suffered utterable agony. I went into his stateroom in the night. He was shaking and shivering. I threw his great coat over him and left him.

    The boat was admirably handled by her officers and men. God bless and keep you, dearest. Would I not like this lonely evening to sit down by you and talk a long, long talk with you. Would I not like to roll Fred over on the floor and give him a stick of candy. Unpleasant things cannot last long. If God spares our lives, we shall soon be where you can get your letters regularly. You have not had any for more than a week, if for a fortnight. We have had no intercourse with the outer world.

                                           Truly affectionately,
                                           William

Friday, December 23rd

General officers visited Beaufort. General Butler was there. The place is old and out of date. (Journal)

Saturday, December 24th–Sunday, December 25th

Orders to move out at 12 noon. We moved at 3 pm. Reached the blockade fleet at midnight last night. We heard yesterday morning an explosion and during the day yesterday heavy firing which we conjectured and rightly was from the fleet on Fort Fisher.

9 am. Fleet moved towards the shore. We anchored off Half-Moon Battery about 4 miles from Fort Fisher. At once troops began to disembark. Small boats from all the naval vessels came about our vessel which was the first to be unloaded. The men piled into the boats with great enthusiasm, their long stay upon boats having prepared them to greet the land eagerly. The sight of the boats laden with troops moving to shore, was truly brilliant. And the bombardment by the fleet which now was at the height of intensity, exceeded in grandeur anything of the kind ever witnessed.

General Curtis with the 142nd and 2 companies [of the] 112th New York moved up to very near the fort. The 117th New York moved up and captured about 200 prisoners who were in a line of works outside the fort. The other companies of the 112th New York under Colonel Smith, picketed quite across the island and guarded the landing place. It was supposed that the assault would be made about 4. But after waiting till near dusk, the colored troops that had just landed were re-embarked. All the troops were re-embarked except a portion of our brigade. These could not be got off on account of the surf, which the rising winds, was driving high up the beach. General Curtis, Colonel Smith and our regiment, with part of the other regiments of the brigade, were left ashore, about 1500 men. Why the attempt was not made to capture them is a mystery. Probably it was owing to the presence of the gunboats. The troops on shore felt that the fort could at that time be taken with small loss and were anxious to make the attempt. The night was very dark and the rain fell in torrents.

About 12 pm a boat which had been floating about for some hours came alongside and put onboard a part of 3 companies of the 142nd New York. About 2, I heard a loud culling and a crush followed. It proved to be our boat had drifted into the *Baltic* and got her propeller fouled in the great chain of that ship. We came near being crushed but fortunately the *Baltic* clipped her cable and floated clear. It was a terrible night. The boat lay broadside to the waves and was furiously pounded all night. (Journal)

Monday, December 26th

The next day, Monday, we were at work all day freeing our propeller. When done it was found the rudder was so disabled that it would not work. The troops remained on shore all day, no help could be got to them. A few boxes and barrels were floated ashore. (Journal)

Onboard U.S. Steamer Transport *Charles Thomas*
At anchor off Beaufort Harbor
December 26th 1864

To the Editor of the Jamestown Journal,

One of the most expensive, abortive, mortifying military expeditions, and disgraceful to those connected with the managements of it has just terminated. To do justice to it, as illustrating the epithets already used, would task the descriptive power of Charles Dickens. I shall not pretend to attempt it, but while lying here off Beaufort, NC in a wrecked transport ship, waiting the pleasure of the authorities that hold the lives of men in their keeping, whether to suffer us to take shelter inside the bar, or to lie here and be pounded by the waves with large risk of drifting ashore, or to be sent to Fort Monroe without a rudder and the stern crushed in, as is most likely. I thought I would kill a little time, which just now hangs heavy, in giving your readers some slight idea of what their friends had to suffer for the past twenty days. Just think of it, twenty days on a transport steamer. The men crowded down on the lower deck and in the hold so close, that when lying down every inch of space is covered, then remember that the hold is floored with coal for ballast, and that is their bed. But in this crowded space they must lay day and night; they eat there too, so that the difficulty of keeping clean is easily guessed. But all cannot be got below, about fifty men have to be on the upper deck exposed to the wind, rain and cold and sometimes washed by the waves of the sea. In the hold it is so close and hot that the sweat runs off men like rain, while perhaps on the upper deck they are shivering in the northern blast. After being well steamed below they take turns—fifty at a time—with those on deck, a plan admittedly adapted to keep our doctors in practice and furnish new recruits for Uncle Sam's hospitals. Even this could have been endured a few days—and we were told the expedition was to be short when we started—but it has dragged its slow length through twenty days to its melancholy termination.

We left our encampment in front of the defenses of Richmond the afternoon of the 7th and embarked the afternoon of the 8th onboard the steamer propeller *Charles Thomas*, one of our largest class transport ships, with as smart a captain as ever trod a ship's deck. There were onboard the men and officers of the two regiments 142nd and 112th New York. General Curtis and staff, General Ames and staff besides twenty horses. The generals finding themselves rather crowded, left with their staffs, one at Fort Monroe and the other off Wilmington. Four companies of the 112th were transferred at Fort Monroe to the *Baltic* and another steamer, still leaving us very much crowded.

About three o'clock the morning of the 13th, the transport fleet—eighteen vessels—steamed out from Hampton Roads, and instead of going south moved up the Potomac River—"strategy, my boy, strategy." When we had got up as far as Matthias Point, we turned about and anchored for the night about thirty miles from Fort Monroe. There we remained until the next afternoon when we started for the south. The weather which had been very cold at first, was now delightful, the sea smooth, and we reached the blockade squadron at night of the 15th. It was supposed the attack would be made the next morning, but morning came and the day passed. No better weather could have been desired, the sea was as smooth as a floor. It was understood that troops could only be landed near Fort Fisher while the sea was smooth and no surf rolling. If the weather had been made purposely for us we could have had nothing finer than from Friday morning the 16th until the morning of Tuesday the 20th.

Soon after noon of this day, the wind began to rise and we put the head of our steamer north, and the next morning were off Beaufort, NC. The captain of the boat predicted a storm and wanted to make the harbor till it was over. But that could not be done without orders, and orders were to follow the *Baltic*. "If we go to sea after the *Baltic*," said the captain, "the horses will probably all be lost." But there was no *Baltic* to be seen and nobody to order us to shelter, so the ship was pointed out to sea. Soon a squall struck us with the terrible suddenness and fury. The ship jumped as a horse pricked with a spur. And now tables, chairs, men, crockery, lanterns and everything moveable, was tumbling about. The stalls in which the horses were would be lifted from the deck and then dashed down with a violence which threatened destruction to them and the animals. Everything moveable had to be lashed. Fourteen men, once sailors, were detailed from the military, to help work the ship. The storm increased in violence early in the afternoon, the stalls of two of the horses were broken by the waves and the poor animals so maimed, they had to be thrown overboard. At night three more followed and the others were saved only by the greatest exertion.

The night was exceedingly dark, rain at intervals poured down in torrents, and the winds howled and shrieked through the rigging, and none but a practical foot could stand upon deck. The scene was one of the wildest sublimity, the ship lifted one instant upon a huge crest of water, the next would be plunged into a scathing trough of angry foam, and as the wind combed the tops of the waves, the phosphorescent light shed its momentary, fitful glare athwart, the gloomy tumult revealing the staggering masts, the ships full outline and the shadowy forms of the sailors moving or clinging to the shrouds, then all was inky black. So the night wore on. The ship was admirably handled and with the rising sun of the next morning the wind abated and we were again in the vicinity of the blockading fleet. Only one or two of our consorts were visible.

Nothing was now left to us but to get back to Beaufort speedily for our coal would not last twelve hours longer. We reached the bar soon after noon and were piloted inside arriving in the harbor about three o'clock. There we remained until Saturday afternoon taking in wood and water and replenishing our haversacks—those that had any money. The transport fleet had suffered severely. In the propeller containing the ambulances, most of the horses and ambulances were ruined and thrown overboard. Another propeller had to throw over twenty-seven horses. Having recruited and gathered up the scattered vessels, the fleet steamed out of Beaufort Harbor on Saturday afternoon and early the next morning were off to the scene of hostilities. The original plan was understood to be that a vessel loaded with two hundred tons of gunpowder was to be run up very early in the morning within half a mile of Fort Fisher, exploded, then the navy was to move up and open a furious fire. At the same time the army, having landed on the point, was to charge the fort, and the work to be done in a brief time and without loss.

It was supposed that the explosion of so much powder so near the fort would destroy or utterly paralyze the garrison. It seems that the powder ship was exploded early Saturday morning, while the army was at Beaufort. The navy then opened upon the fort, firing at long range all day. Sunday morning opened beautifully. It was Christmas day and ought to have been kept sacred, but orders were received to be in readiness to land and soon after noon all the small boats from the naval and transport vessels began to cluster around our vessels. Curtis' Brigade was to be landed first. The swearing and intoxication among the officers of these small boats was altogether in excess of the usual amount and the consequent confusion so great that an operation which should have occupied one hour occupied two. And it was quite late in the afternoon before our brigade was landed. General Curtis was the first on shore. He formed his command rapidly and they moved up the beach in line of battle, with skirmishers deployed in fine style. Having been left onboard the ship, I had a fine opportunity to see the bombardment and the landing of the troops. More than fifty of these small boats manned by sailors took the troops onboard, and as they moved towards the shore, the band on the ships played the national airs, and when they landed there was a shout that might have been heard ten miles. The view was grand, and about three miles distant Fort Fisher glowering and gloomy frowned upon the scene and upon the cluster of huge naval vessels that lay offshore within short range, pouring into it an incessant stream of what the darkeys call "rotten iron."

Those who witnessed this naval bombardment can hardly expect ever again to witness anything so terribly sublime. It was estimated that the ships could deliver a broadside from 210 guns of the heaviest caliber. The ships were most of the time wrestled in smoke, but the bursting of the shell over the fort could be distinctly seen. Beginning about ten o'clock in the forenoon the firing was kept up till after dark. Now and then the fort replied, but seldom, the troops within were only safe under the shelter of their bombproofs. As the troops were landed, gunboats moved slowly along the coast throwing shell into the woods beyond the beach. The fire upon the fort too increased in intensity, and part of Curtis' Brigade moved up under the parapet of the fort. A soldier from the

142nd New York crept up and brought off the flag, which had been shot down by a cannon ball.

The whole command was in a state of enthusiasm which promised the best results. They longed for the word "charge," believing that they could carry the fort with very small loss and thus gain some glory to compensate them for their sufferings on the voyage. Already a portion of the brigade had taken over 250 prisoners, all of them boys of 18 years of age and under, mixed with a few over 60. They were called the "North Carolina Junior Reserves." Captain Jones of the 142nd had deployed his skirmish line quite across the point and had cut the telegraph wire, thus completely isolating the fort from all communication with Wilmington.[138] The troops were two thirds of them landed, and a bold move must have occurred. It was one of those critical moments when a man of military genius would have thrown forward his forces and grasped a victory that would have stamped his name on one of the brightest pages of the annals of this war. What was the astonishment of those of us who from shipboard were watching anxiously, to see the colored troops which were landing, tumbling back into their boats, and heard that the force was to take ship again without doing anything. As our brigade had the post of honor in landing, so now it was to retain it in protecting the embarkation. Most of the other brigades had got back safely to their transports before 8 o'clock. Then to our horror the wind increased and the surf began to roll violently and there was no possibility of our comrades getting back. What a situation! There were not over 1,500 men on shore and we could neither get to them, nor they to us. What if a force of 6,000 men were on their way from Wilmington. Nothing but a miracle could save them from capture. Four or five gunboats moved up along shore for their protection.

Soon the rain began to pour down in torrents. Thank God it was a rain from the southwest and the weather mild. About 12 o'clock a detachment of the 142nd New York reached our ship, having been floating about the harbor in boats three hours, the men and officers wet through. They were picked up by a tug and brought onboard. The storm had now reached the proportions of a gale, and we were near a treacherous coast. While lying sleepless in my bunk, I heard a loud call for our ship, three times repeated. Hoping it might be our friends, I jumped up and was hurrying outside when there was a tremendous crash and I was thrown quite across the cabin. I was soon on deck, and then crash again and directly overhead the bow of that huge ocean monster, the "*Baltic*." It seemed inevitable that we must be crushed and our ship sunk. The propeller of our vessel had got fouled in the chain of the *Baltic*, and could not be disentangled. Again, crash! And our captain called out: "slip your chain, or the next time you'll go through us." The chain was slipped, and the *Baltic* backed away from us, leaving us held fast by two anchors, one where an anchor was wanted, and one around our rudder post and propeller; but with our side to the wind. And all night long the waves battered us, threatening to tear away both rudder and propeller.

The morning broke clear and cold with the surf running high. All day it took our ship's company to free ourselves from the huge chain of the *Baltic*, and all day we watched our friends on shore. Several boats from the naval fleet tried in vain to reach them. One we saw enter the surf and soon swept back, bottom up, and the sailors clinging to it. Boxes of bread and a barrel of coffee were cast over and left to drift ashore to them, and all the next night the fleet kept up an incessant fire over their heads to protect them from the enemy. Tuesday morning, the surf was quiet again. We saw the boats starting to take them away. A propeller came along and hailed us, saying they had orders to tow us to Beaufort. Our rudder was broken. Other boats were to take our comrades, and before they had embarked, we weighted anchor, and tied to another boat, were towed to this place.

                          Yours truly,
                          Hyde (Newspaper)[139]

Tuesday, December 27th

About 8 o'clock, the surf having to a degree subsided. The troops on shore were taken off and embarked. Our vessel, being disabled, was taken in tow by the propeller *John Rice* and at 5 o'clock were left off Beaufort entrance. Too late to go in that night. (Journal)

Onboard Steamer *C. Thomas*
At Sea enroute to Beaufort, N.C.
December 27th 1864

Dear Wife.

My last to you was written just as we were leaving Beaufort, N.C. last Saturday to see and serve the expedition to Wilmington. We steamed out of Beaufort Harbor about 3 o'clock pm. The sea was smooth and we reached the blockading fleet off Wilmington last Sunday morning about one o'clock. After breakfast, everything seemed so quiet that I hoped we would be allowed to enjoy a quiet Sunday, have religious worship, and take the weekdays for war's terrific work. The navy had opened upon Fort Fisher Saturday. The boat containing 200 tons of powder was exploded in the morning and the ships opened their big guns and kept up a bombardment during the day. I guess with but little effect. I am ingenuous enough to fear little was intended. Blockading has been profitable near Wilmington.

Sunday, after breakfast orders come for clearing the area and inspection at 12 noon to be ready to go ashore at one. Of course that was the last of religious worship. The whole force was at work getting ready for shore. About 2 all the boats from the fleet began to gather round us to take the land force ashore. This was a slow job as no proper ladders had been provided. At last our brigade was landed—the first ashore. And they moved up the beach towards Fort Fisher in fine style. The navy had done their work so well that no opposition was made to our landing. Meanwhile the bombardment of the fort was going on. One of the grandest scenes ever witnessed in war. Never before have so many guns been opened at once with such powerful metal on a fort. Our brigade captured some 250 Rebs and went up to the fort and one man crept up and took the flag from the parapet of the fort. All the men were now anxious to make a charge feeling that they could with little difficulty take the fort. We learned that the force inside was not large and after such a terrible bombardment, we resolved they must be greatly demoralized. It was the golden moment. Then or not at all. General Weitzel concluded it could not be done and General Curtis was ordered to fall back.

The barometer indicated the approach of a storm. As our brigade had been the first ashore, so now it was the last to embark. About dusk the surf began to rise. Soon it became impossible to get to or from shore. What a predicament to be in. Colonel Smith had ordered me to remain onboard the boat, so I had a fine chance to see and although at first disappointed, I began now to feel glad that I was left. It came on very dark. The navy was withdrawn from the fort and our boys were then about 1000 of the 2 regiments with 250 prisoners and we could not get to them nor they to us. Imagine my anxiety, the road to Wilmington was open, Fort Fisher was but three miles off. The navy could give but little aid, and they must depend upon themselves. What if a force of 3,000 should come down, form in the woods, only 4 miles back of the beach and then north, down in solid column, upon our little force. Nothing could save them from capture. We knew the enemy was not far off for we had already exchanged shot with them. Three gunboats came up and lay along the shore and all night threw shell at intervals into the woods beyond our men.

About 12 o'clock Captain Jones of the 142nd New York came onboard having for 3 hours been floating about in the harbor unable to find our ship. He got wet through in getting on the boat in the surf and told us that in all probability the rest of the brigade could not get away until the wind abated. I felt very anxious about the regiment and as I lay in my berth praying for them and unable to get asleep, about 2 o'clock I heard someone call out *Charlie Thomas* three times, and then "you're afoul of us." I jumped from my berth and as I did so there was a crash which made us shake all through and almost sent me sprawling on the floor. I ran out and saw just over our stern the huge *Baltic* and as it came, crash, and as our boat tried to get away I could hear by the grating of the propellers that we had got fouled in the anchor chain of the *Baltic*. My first impulse was to try to climb up by the *Baltic's* chain but I saw no good chance so I concluded that I must wait until the boat went down and run my chance of getting picked up. But just then the *Baltic* slipped her chains and then lurched off from us. We soon found that our hull was not damaged and as the gale increased it was certain we could not be blown ashore for we had our own anchor out and the *Baltic's* was fast around our propeller shaft. This accident was the result of clear, shear carelessness. The watch on deck neglected his duty and the result was our boat was blown by the wind back and dragged her anchor and ran onto the *Baltic*. I was not a little excited and with the anxiety for our men you may believe that I did not sleep much, no not a wink all night.

Morning broke upon us clear and beautiful. The terrible storm of the night passed away. You could see the men who had laid all the night without any protection, exposed to the pitiless tempest and helpless should the enemy come down in large force, lining the shore. And here and there a little smoke showed that they had built some camp fires. All day they lay in sight, we could neither get to them nor they to us. We sent them some provisions, shoving them on a raft through the surf. At night the gunboats ranged along the shore and all night long kept shelling the woods. I woke at sunrise this morning. It was a beautiful day. I saw that the waves had gone down. The troops were preparing to be taken off. Just then the orders came to be towed to Beaufort. Our stern post was sprung so the rudder would not turn. It took all the men on the boat all day yesterday to free ourselves from the chain of the *Baltic*. We have been sailing all day and are now rolling and pitching off Beaufort Harbor. The steamer has only the horses and two companies of the 142nd.

I expect the regiment to be along tomorrow morning. The expedition is a fizzle as I supposed it would be. Ben Butler is a very poor military chieftain, judged by what he has done. I have never had any confidence in its success from the way in which it started and then, why will military men spurn God's Sabbath as they do? I did hope that Christmas Sunday we would be permitted to rest and worship God. But no, they must go into a fight, and God has confounded their designs.

Wednesday morning. We are still pitching about Beaufort entrance. We are outside on the broad Atlantic waiting to be towed in. Last night the rudder and stern post washed off and we should have been in a terrible condition had it not been very quiet. We hope today to get in to Beaufort.

We have never had so terrible an 18 days since we came into the service. The men would be stowed in the lower hold when it was so hot that the sweat was coming off them lying and each company by turns would then have to come on deck because there was not room for all below and sometimes it was cold enough to freeze water. So they were steamed and frozen alternately. Then on the lower hold they had to lie on a lot of coal which was there for ballast. All the water allowed, part of the time, was half canteen full a day and coffee, one cup twice a day. I tell you I pity a soldier.

The big generals and their staffs sleep in comfortable quarters and carouse and drink, the poor men lie in the cold and wet and suffer. Unless God appears for us, our cause is all lost. I feel in all dangers that God is a very present help. I never so realized it.

Your affectionate Husband,

This is the anniversary of my birthday. Love to Liddy and all the Carpenters. Tell Mrs. Buddington I feel for her sufferings and that God will take care of him. I hope you had a pleasant Christmas.

Friday, December 30th

We have been now 3 days lying off the entrance. The sea running high and the wind at times blowing a gale. Yesterday Captain Jones, 142nd New York, went into the harbor in a small boat to get assistance. We are out of most everything. Hardtack and pork all that is left us. Our position is one of much peril. This morning Captain Jones returned without being able to affect anything. Only we are to be taken to Fort Monroe as soon as a boat from the harbor can come out. (Journal)

Saturday, December 31st

Today the severest gale drifted about a mile and one half. The wind went down with the sun. The regiment returned from Fort Fisher on different boats. The 30th December they were at anchor off Sewall's Point early in the morning but soon started up the river. Landed at Aiken's Landing and marched through the woods to camp which they found with some difficulty and came straggling in with no particular formation. (Journal)

> *1864 took a terrible toll on Hyde and the men of the 112th. The loss of Lieutenant Colonel Carpenter and Colonel Drake devastated the regiment, particularly Hyde. Not only were they Hyde's messmates, they were close personal friends. Hyde never forgot them. In 1866, when he wrote the 112th's regimental history, a section was included with obituaries of both men. Throughout, Hyde never lost sight of his obligations to the regiment, despite the loss of many friends. He continued to persevere and press forward providing spiritual comfort to the men of the regiment, as well as to the families back home. Appendix B provides examples of Hyde's interaction with those back home, to include those who had suffered the loss of a loved one.*
>
> *1864 did not bring an end to the war's terrible carnage. As a result of General Butler's failed attempt to take the Confederate stronghold at Fort Fisher, NC, he was relieved of command and replaced with General Alfred Terry. Terry received the same orders—seize Fort Fisher and close the Confederacy's last port along the Atlantic coast. Soon the 112th along with a great Union armada set sail to seal the fate of the Confederacy.*

4

1865

Only three days after the New Year was ushered in, the 112th received orders to break camp and proceed to Bermuda Hundred to embark upon Union transports for a second attempt to take Fort Fisher, NC.

Sunday, January 1st–Tuesday, January 3rd

Today about 9 o'clock the *Metropolis* a large side-wheel used as a hospital boat came out [of] Beaufort, took us in tow and by 12 noon we were moving towards Fort Monroe. We have a favorable prospect. The new colors of the regiment came and were planted in front of the colonel's quarters. Commissions of Colonel Smith, Captains Fox, Sampson, Crane, Lieutenant Vorce came.[1] They were mustered the 3rd January. (Journal)

Onboard Defense Transport the *Charles Thomas* at Sea
January 1st 1865

My dear Wife,

If you have received the letter I wrote to you in Beaufort Harbor, you have probably felt all the more anxious to hear again, and perhaps are today very anxious. Of course you know that I should have written you if I could. But we have been in perilous scenes and it has been utterly impossible to communicate with shore. I have already a letter written the first of last week, which I have not been able to mail to you. In that I told you I was off Beaufort Harbor. We got there Tuesday night and a succession of severe gales, the heaviest of which was last night, has prevented us from having any communication with the shore, just think of us 5 nights and 4 days off the shore with the Shackelford Shoals not two miles off. The winds blowing towards them and ourselves without a rudder and the only hope of safety our anchor and chain cables. Had the chain parted in either gale or the anchors dragged, we would inevitably have been shipwrecked. One night I thought we could not stand it though, but yesterday the gale reached the acme of its fury and the ship fairly groaned under the terrible assaults of the wind and the waves. We however outrode the storm through the mercy of God. This morning, the side-wheel ocean steamer *Western Metropolis* came out of Beaufort and about noon we got underway. Two huge harnesses were ferried from us to the other steamer and then having lifted our anchors, we were towed away and now we are pressing northward quite slow but I hope short. The weather is very fine, and we are all so pleased to be setting our faces homeward that we can truly say "Happy New Year."

O it don't seem at all like New Year's. Here on this lovely boat, just think of it, we have been twenty three days onboard this ship. Long enough to have made a voyage to Europe and return in a steamer, and long enough for a voyage to London in a packet ship. The first seven days, I boarded with the steward at an expense of two dollars a day. The officers thought as the fare began to deteriorate in quality, we would not stand the shame and so we formed a mess and have had our regimental cook, cook for us.

At Beaufort, I got some stuff which we consumed long ago and for the last 4 days we have lived on fried hardtack for breakfast, hardtack and pork for dinner and warmed up for supper. I have not had a change of underclothing since the 7th of December. The order was to prepare for a short expedition. We supposed about ten days.

Monday, 2nd

We are having fine weather and everything appears prosperous for the termination of our voyage. We ought to be at Fort Monroe this evening at 8 o'clock. The privations and discomfort of this trip have been very great. I feel quite anxious to hear from our regiment. I wonder if the order sending us to Elmira will come. Only think since I left Fort Monroe, I have not had a single letter from you. Nearly 20 days without a mail. It is the hardest of all. We got a paper of the 20th while lying off Beaufort and since then all the outer world is a blank to us. We can begin to realize the tedious of captivity as prisoners of war. But it is not worthwhile to complain. I dreamed last night of seeing you twice. God grant it may be the augury of a happy greeting soon.

Wednesday morning, January 3rd

I have just reached Fort Monroe and am finishing this in Major Ludwick's room at the hospital. We had a delightful day yesterday. The sea was smooth as glass and we got inside of the light ship about 9 pm. I am I trust truly grateful to God for his preserving goodness. I hear the regiment has gone up the James River. We follow today or by evening. I will write you as soon as I get to the front.

Yours very truly,
William

Monday, January 2nd

Evening 8 o'clock anchored inside the light boat in Hampton Roads. Rumors of another move began to be rife. (Journal)

Monday, January 2nd–Thursday, January 5th

Steamer *Charles Thomas* at sea
January 2nd 1865

My last was closed abruptly, as well as written badly. The deck of a steamer rolling about is a poor place for writing. Thank God, we are at length freed from our perilous position, and with a fair wind comparatively smooth sea and in tow of a staunch ship, making our way to Hampton Roads. I hope soon to be able to congratulate Colonel Smith and the regiment generally on their failure to get to Richmond via Wilmington. A rough time they must have had of it while ashore.

The quartermaster, myself and the sick men, as well as the cooks were ordered to remain onboard until sent for. The colonel did not even take any rations with him, evidently expecting either to return to ship that night or we would all be ordered ashore. All that we have heard since is that our regiment was entirely free from casualties, and that they were all safely embarked during the forenoon of the 27th.

God grant it all true, and that the regiment may be spared any more excursions along the Atlantic coast in the winter season, unless it be towards New York. The few of us who remained on shipboard had anything but a pleasant time. The propeller that towed us towards Beaufort dropped us just at nightfall outside the bar, with the wind blowing us directly towards the shoals of Cape Lookout. We lay there four days and five nights, encountering a succession of gales, which prevented any communication, whatever with the harbor.

During the first night a severe squall set us rolling, and we were waked up about midnight by a tremendous thumping. We thought at first that it was another collision; then feared it was the ship drifting on the shoals. But soon learned it was our rudder and stern post completely broken off and dashing against the side of the ship. The ship's crew were turned out and all the rest of the night engaged in securing the rudder and taking it on deck. With the constant rolling and various noises there was little sleeping done onboard that night.

Wednesday morning a tug came out from the harbor and told us the *Western Metropolis* was to tow us into Fort Monroe, and would be out about noon. Noon came, but no ship. The surf on the bar was so heavy that she could not get over. Another night must be spent in the same disagreeable situation as the last. On a lee shore without a rudder; our only hope is the chain and anchor. I wedged myself with blankets into my bunk so that I could not roll with the lurches of the ship and got a very comfortable night's rest. The next day no notice was taken of us from the shore and in the afternoon Captain Jones, of the 132nd started in the small boat for the harbor.[2] It was a perilous voyage, and though a small tug started to bring him back towards evening it did not dare to venture and turned back. So the third night we spent as those before, only now we had no small boat in case of trouble. But there is nothing like getting used to danger, and we slept quite well in spite of the tossing of the ship.

The next morning a tug came out with Captain Jones, and informed us that there was no pilot who would take us in or the *Metropolis* out with such a sea running over the bar. But that probably the next day we would be relieved. Friday night was the quietest we had experienced, but Saturday morning, with the rising sun, a gale came up equal in fury to the one of the week before, and blowing directly towards the shoals. The ship rolled and pitched and tumbled, every timber, at times, seemed to shake and now and then as some huge wave struck her full in the bow, we could feel the recoil as the anchor yielded to the strain. We dragged some during the day, perhaps half a mile, but about midnight the gale was over. The wind had chopped round, and New Year's Day broke upon us clear and cold and the tumult of the sea was assuaged.

The *Metropolis*, a large side-wheel steamer, used for a hospital boat, came out about nine o'clock, and after various delays a couple of large hawsers were stretched from ship to ship and by noon we were on our way to Fort Monroe. We all long to see the New York papers to find out what excuse is made for this miserable fizzle. Probably it will be said that it was ascertained that there was an immense land force at Wilmington, and that there were more men inside the fort than we had, etc., etc. But all who approached the fort believe it might have been taken, and the fact that about a thousand men of our brigade, were allowed to remain unmolested thirty-six hours on shore shows that there was no very effective force at hand.

January 3rd. We reached Hampton Roads last evening and cast anchor inside the "light ship." Our passage from Beaufort has been very pleasant. The sea smooth and no accident.

"The Red Herring Butler Expedition" is over. The boys call it the Red Herring Expedition on account of the large quantities of this nutritious delicacy issued in place of salt pork, to the troops. We have learned that our regiment went up the James River last Thursday, to their old camp, and that our camp and garrison equipage, stored at Norfolk, has been sent for. This looks like winter quarters in Virginia.

Having no celebration of either Christmas or New Year's, the officers onboard the *Charles Thomas* thought proper to close our voyage with a grand New Year's supper. I give you the bill of fare, from which you can imagine the state of our larder.

Bill of Fare
1st Hard Tack—*au naturel*.
2nd Red Herring—Peeled by a short Dutchman.
3rd Chocolate—Served in a large stew pan, without milk.

4th Five small onions—raw.
Dessert
Molasses Candy—Made of brown sugar dissolved.

These viands, devoured with the hearty relish of hungry men, were well seasoned with good humor and kindly feeling, the only condiments onboard, and are they not the best too. In spite of the many discomforts and sufferings of this excursion, there are many pleasant reminiscences of the kindly courtesies and good feeling shown in various situations. Many pleasant friendships formed with the gentlemanly officers of the 142nd New York, who were with us.

January 5th. We reached our old camp last night about ten o'clock. What was our amazement at Bermuda to hear that our regiment had gone down the river that day on another expedition under command of Major Generals Ord and Terry. Our division commander, General Ames, ordered all of us shipwrecked soldiers to our old camp to await orders. We have not had a change of clothing for 28 days and feel that a clean shirt would be a decided luxury. What General Grant thinks of the late exploits of General Butler is best indicated in the resumption of the expedition under another commander.[3] (Newspaper)

Hyde

Tuesday, January 3rd

This morning vessel moved near shore. Went ashore in small boat and up to the hospital. Pm were transferred to small river steamer and after moving up the James to Newport News, anchored for the night. Orders to be ready to move at 11 am. Moved about noon and halted for the night in the woods near Bermuda Hundred. Colonel Smith, Captains Fox, Sampson and Crane and Lieutenant Vorce were mustered before leaving. (Journal)

Wednesday, January 4th

Arrived at Bermuda Hundred where we found the regiment had this morning embarked on *Thomas Collyer* for Fort Monroe to take transports. It seems that General Grant not satisfied with the result of the 1st Fort Fisher expedition, determined to send another under command of Major General Terry to consist mainly of the same troops with the addition of the 2nd Brigade, 1st Division. Captain Carleton, of General Ames' staff, ordered us to the fort to remain until sent for.[4] At night it snowed and the morning of the 4th was one of great discomfort. About 9 moved down to landing, went immediately onboard the steamer *Thomas Collyer* and arriving at Fort Monroe at evening, they were at once transferred to the steamer *Atlantic,* in which the whole brigade was embarked. (Journal)

Perry Vorce enlisted at Westfield, New York, as a sergeant in Company E, 112th New York Volunteers. He mustered out with regiment on June 13, 1865, at Raleigh (courtesy U.S. Army Heritage and Education Center [USAHEC]).

Thursday, January 5th

Last evening about 10 o'clock we reached Chapin's Farm and went into our old quarters. They were at the fort drawing new clothing and rations. (Journal)

Camp 112th Regt N.Y. Vols.
Near Chapin's Farm
Thursday, January 5th 1865

My dear Wife,

The date of this will show you that I am again in the old camp. I wrote you from Fort Monroe and then mailed a letter I had written at sea. I sent you at least one, if not two, letters from Beaufort, South Carolina when we put in there after the first gale. I think you must ere this have received those letters. When I got back last evening, I found six letters from you waiting for me here, the last written the 24th of December. I felt very sad to learn that you had been, and were still, so troubled with cough. When this cruel war is over, I will take you to a milder climate than the Lake Shore. I was grieved at the conduct of the disaffected portion of the church and society. They have lost a good man in losing Mr. Willard and I fear that it will be very difficult for any man now to come in and reconcile matters.

I hope that dear little Freddy got a Christmas present from his Pa, though you did not mention it. I hope too that you have made your purchase before this. You say you wonder that I did not send letters to you from Fort Monroe, I was there so long. Why I certainly did send you two, and we were there from Friday pm until Monday night, from the 10th to the 13th. From that time until the 3rd of January we were completely buried to the world. I finished my last with pencil in major, now Lieutenant Colonel Ludwick's room at the Chesapeake Hospital. That afternoon we were transferred from the *Charles Thomas* to a small river steamer. There were 15 men of the 112th and about 130 of the 142nd New York. We had our usual luck for we got started very late and could not get above Newport News before night and while lying there a gale burst upon us and we had it thump, thump all night. But morning came clear and cold and at 3 o'clock we were off City Point. About 4 we got to Bermuda and then to our amazement learned that the expedition had again started for Wilmington. We passed some steamers loaded with troops quite early in the morning, but did not know what regiment was there. I was directed by General Ames to go to camp and remain until sent for. I should have been glad to go back and be with the regiment were it not that I had been just 4 weeks without any change of clothing. I intend to have a good gay old wash and clean up and then I shall be like myself again. I presume I shall find it very dull here until I join the regiment. God grant that they may all be preserved unharmed.

I wish you a happy New Year with all my soul. I hope that in the close of the year we may be once more in our own dear house. I think I should be highly honored as the principal of the Dunkirk High School.

Mr. Shelton's dose for cold is just the thing. I sometimes take it, only I use hot whiskey and water. The only thing we can get here.

Well dearest, keep up good heart. Better days are coming. If we made a fizzle at Wilmington, still there are the splendid successes of Sherman and Thomas.[5]

All will yet turn out right.

Truly as ever,
William

Everybody is down on Butler. Grant has had a court of inquiry.

Friday, January 6th–Saturday, January 7th

Some 50 recruits came for the regiment from the rendezvous at New York. A very poor lot as a whole. Some can't speak or understand a word of English. Others are lame and too foolish. On the sixth they set sail for Wilmington. That night high wind which the next day increased to a gale. (Journal)

List of recruits (Journal)

1. Robert Anderson
2. Lewis Newbury
3. Michael Deych
4. James Briggs
5. Jacob Walder
6. James Moose
7. Henry Cody
8. John Kurtz
9. Bernard McGee
10. John Curtis
11. Conrad Vehring
12. Henry Reynolds
13. Adrian VanHouten
14. Charles Stuart
15. Charles H. Wilson
16. Charles Woodbridge
17. Jacob Groschwiller
18. William Mahear
19. Alexander Waldenberger
20. Patrick O'Donnell
21. James Wilson
22. Charles Swartz
23. P. Bagley
24. Charles Knapp
25. Ferdinand Schlick
26. Matthew Malloy
27. Peter Almasher
28. William Schmidt
29. John Considine
30. George W. McIntosh
31. Matthew Flynn
32. John Troy
33. George E. Terry
34. William Gloede
35. William Collins
36. Philip Smith
37. Charles Shaver
38. Frank Fancy
39. William O'Neil
40. George W. Shirley
41. George Fath
42. William Racine
43. Joseph Burdon
44. Baptist Jerome
45. Samuel W. Hudson
46. John Locheler
47. Valentine Breyer
48. Louis Kramer
49. Thomas Kelly
50. Paul Ignatz
51. Emil Gerard
52. William O'Brien
53. Peter Bolin
54. Denis Belanger
55. Stephen Lafrican
56. William A. Beck
57. Cyrpus A. Marcon
58. Jaquis Sansonci
59. Byron Stickney
60. Patrick Durken
61. Patrick O'Brien

Monday, January 9th

New lieutenants assigned to duty in various companies. (Journal)

Camp 112th N.Y. Vols.
Chapin's Farm Va
January 9th 1865

Dear Wife,

I have not had a letter since the one you wrote December 26th. The mail has probably been stopped at Fort Monroe and either sent down to the troops on the expedition or delivered to them at the fort, if they did not leave before this morning. We have not heard a word from the regiment and have been almost utterly cut off from the outer world. True, we got New York papers 3 or 4 days old but not letters.

Keep on writing, however, for before you receive this, all things will be again established in the ancient channel.

I am very lonesome and could easily be homesick. I feel greatly worried about your health. If I knew you were well, I should feel easier. Do not omit any care or medicine necessary to your recovery. I trust by the mercy of God we shall be restored to each other by another summer.

We had over 30 deserters come into our lines yesterday or rather last night. If this Wilmington expedition proves a success or if it does not, I think the rebellion must give out with exhaustion soon.

Their condition is terrible. They are not at all prepared for a severe winter. As to the 112th coming to Elmira, I am glad you have looked at it in the light you have. I myself think it very uncertain, and indeed almost hopeless. We have no claim to exemption from further field service which might not be urged with equal prompting, nay greater by at least 20 other New York regiments, and as to going there to recruit, we have had lately, recruits enough sent to us to muster our officers. It is very probable too that very soon a general system of exchange will be agreed upon, which will obviate the necessity of keeping a prison camp at Elmira. The government is calling for 300,000 more men and a large part of that force will be raw, requiring all the old force in the field to give it steadiness.

Our regiment is today worth 3 new regiments and it is of more value to [the] government than it has been at any time since it was organized.

I can't believe that to gratify Governor Fenton even the War Department would allow the regiment to go to Elmira the remainder of this term of service and simply to go then through February and March would, it seems to me, be a great expense to government, for no corresponding benefit and too at a time when the government has no money to spare. I still hope we shall soon be in garrison somewhere, and when we are, I shall certainly have you with me. Yesterday, I preached at the Christian Commission tent to a very good audience and today I have met with an old acquaintance, formerly from Maine, who is chaplain of the 23rd United States Colored Infantry, 25th Army Corps. His name is Parkinson.[6] He married a college friend of mine, Miss Griffin of Brunswick. I was very glad to hear from her. They now have their home in Vermont. We have a pleasant circle of chaplains about here. Mr. Palmer (Methodist) of the 142nd New York was with me during the Wilmington expedition, and is certainly one of the best men I have met in the army. We messed together and I have found a new friendship in him.

I have turned doctor lately. There is no doctor here and we have some sick men. I prescribe for them and help take care of them. Thus, I try to make myself useful. My own health is excellent. I did not even contract a cold, notwithstanding all our exposure. I saw the Richmond papers say the gale we experienced was one of the severest on the coast for years. I do hope the present expedition will be more successful than the last. I think there must be a hard fight going on while I am writing this about ten miles off for the cannonading is heavier than any I have heard for a fortnight.

Captain Talcott has a very violent cold [and] had strong threatenings of fever two nights ago. I did not like alone to undertake his case and sent a man to a regiment for a surgeon who only did for him what I could have done as well. Since then I have taken him under Dr. Hyde's care. He is doing well.

                                    Your very loving husband,
                                    William L. Hyde

Please send me in your 3 next letters a 5 dollar greenback in each letter. I am clean out. William

Wednesday, January 11th

                                    Camp 112th Regt N.Y. Vols.
                                    Near Chapin's Farm
                                    January 11th 1865

My dear Wife,

I received yesterday your letter of the 5th and I assure you that though you complained in the commencement of it, of dearth of news, the letter was as cold water to a thirsty soul. You must have received both my letters written from Beaufort, though you do not mention them in this. Probably you had spoken of them in the last letter previous which I have not as yet received. I presume it has gone on to Wilmington with the regiment. I understand that they intercepted the mail at Fort Monroe and took with them the letters. Before this you are again hearing from me regularly. I wish there was more of interest in this region to employ my pen about but there is nothing. We have had 52 recruits sent to the camp and some of them are "draft" foolish and 2 of them the poorest specimen of New York City rascals. Some of them are German—some French—some Irish. There are about 20 of them sick with various kinds of diseases. A surgeon comes over daily and I have to put up their prescriptions. Yesterday, I received a letter from Captain N. S. Scott requesting me to procure the forwarding of the remains of a sergeant in his old company who was killed last summer near Petersburg.[7] This will take me to Bermuda day after tomorrow probably.

It is very lonesome here without the regiment. The roads are awful. Imagine Dunkirk as it would be in the early spring without sidewalks and you can imagine the depth of mud in the roads about here, but the byroads through the woods are intolerable. We had a very severe storm Monday night lasting through Tuesday. The rain poured down in torrents and the wind threatened to tear up everything. Day and night the wind chopped around and it was cold and the fly over my tent was somewhat loose and flapped about gaily. I was waked up 20 times I guess. Today the sky has been charming. I should go about some but the weather and traveling do not invite.

My horse has passed through the trials of the late expedition much better than most of the others. He is tough as oak. I hope he won't be sent on another. Colonel Smith's horse is quite sick and one of the public horses in the regiment so much injured that he will have to be shot. The quartermaster's beautiful little filly is badly bruised, had a swelling on her thigh as big as the crown of my hat. I think it will easily be cured. There is very little that is new with us. We get the New York papers. Evening before last there was an alarm on the picket line and quite rapid firing for a time. The long roll was sounded and in a soaking rain the men were all roused out to man the breastworks. There is no snow now about here though there was quite a little amount last week. Enough to make slosh.

I would like much to hear some of the interesting lectures you have the privilege of listening to this winter. I feel so sorry for the Willard's and so vexed at the conduct of the Jule Williams faction that I don't want to speak to those folks again.

I sometimes get disgusted with the church and ministry in general. There is too much of the spirit of the world and the devil in their conduct. When I get through with the army I shall decide whether to serve my master in the ministry of the church or in the ministry without the church. How much I do pity Mrs. Cobb, poor woman, what a sad case. I knew when at home that she was often under the influence of drink. It is sad but sin makes of this a very dark world. I was interested to hear from Jane and shall write her soon.

Love to Fred. Send Harry's letter along.

Your affectionate Husband,
William L. Hyde

Thursday, January 12th–Friday, January 13th

After lying off Beaufort Harbor 3 days, about 8 o'clock morning of the 12th the fleet left for Federal Point. They lay off during the night and on the morning of the 13th the vessels moved towards land, the gunboats shelling the shore to cover their approach of the landing of the troops. About 4 o'clock the whole command was on shore. That night threw up a defensive line quite across the peninsula from the ocean to Cape Fear River. (Journal)

Saturday, January 14th

They finished up their works and moved towards Fort Fisher. Threw up another line three fourths of a mile in advance of the first and the colored troops seized a picket boat. (Journal)

Sunday, January 15th

The bombardment of the fort which was somewhat vigorous yesterday was opened with redoubled fury. Our troops early commenced operations. Four companies were detailed as sharpshooters and pioneers.[8] These moved up, making for themselves temporary covers in the sand. The fort was reinforced from Wilmington in the morning. About 2 o'clock the brigade was formed in line. They were to rush for the bastion. The 117th on the right entered first. The fighting was desperate from traverse to traverse until about 10 pm when Abbott's Brigade having come in, a general assault was ordered.[9] As the charge was about to commence, the white flag was displayed and the fort surrendered. That night our regiment was moved back to the advance line of earthworks. Early in the morning a mine was exploded within the fort and more than 100 men were killed. The loss fell heaviest upon the 169th and 115th New York whose regiments were in that quarter of the fort. Colonel Smith was mortally wounded yesterday. He lies today in a wooden building used as a hospital under the influence of chloroform to enable him to bear the pain. (Journal)

The casualties in our regiment were (Journal)

January 14th
James B. Hosier	Company D	Wounded in thigh
Artemus Hall	Company K	Fracture of right arm, amputated
Daniel Nichols	Company K	Wound in right thigh
James Rhoades	Company H	Contusion of thigh

All wounded by a shell thrown from the pirate *Chickamauga* as our troops were advancing up the beach.

January 15th
Colonel John F. Smith		Bullet through body, mortally wounded, died 17th
Captain J. Q. A. Hollister		Slightly wounded, bullet through fleshy part right arm

Killed
Aaron Hill	Private	Company A
Paul Horvath	Private	Company C
Leonard L. Dodge	Private	Company E
Hiram Hayden	Corporal	Company F
Joseph Button	Corporal	Company F
William Thornton	Private	Company F
Henry Bowen	Private	Company F
William Raspus	Private	Company F
Lewis Comstock	Private	Company H
Samuel Kenniston	Private	Company H
Emrelu Bushnell	Private	Company H
Samuel Mount	Corporal	Company K

Wounded
Hiram E. Rice	Sergeant	Company E	Hand
Emmet Blanding	Corporal	Company E	Right shoulder
Andrew Anderson	Private	Company E	Hip
Peter Aversolt	Private	Company E	Right shoulder
Charles Kearn	Private	Company E	Hand and side
John Page	Private	Company E	Leg
George Strauss	Private	Company E	Left arm
Peter J. Peterson	Private	Company E	Lungs
Horace Eames	Private	Company F	Knee
John Eames	Private	Company F	Left foot
Hilary Wentz	Private	Company F	Left arm
Chauncey Deland	Private	Company F	Shoulder
Chalmers Hammond	Private	Company F	Breast
Gambol Bradley	Private	Company F	Arm
James R. Spaulding	Private	Company F	Left thigh
Albert C. Jones	Sergeant	Company H	Right hand

Nehemiah Davis	Private	Company H	Right foot
Stephen D. Taber	Private	Company H	Leg
James T. Hamilton	Private	Company I	Left arm
Oliver Little	Private	Company K	Groin
John Tunnell	Private	Company K	Foot
Mike Himelin	Private	Company K	Right leg
B. F. Brazee	Sergeant Major	Field & Staff	Contusion, right leg
W. W. Seeley	Sergeant	Company A	Gunshot, face
W. Heaton	Private	Company B	Gunshot, face
J. Springer	Corporal	Company D	Right thigh
[James B.] Green	Private	Company D	Right thigh
George H. Whitford	Private	Company D	Contusion, shell
Philip Decker	Private	Company D	Arm
John Esselink	Private	Company D	Right arm

Wednesday, January 18th

Colonel Smith died this noon about 12 noon. (Journal)

At or near Chapin's Farm about half mile from the fortifications. In a tent walled with logs, before a blazing fire of pitch pine, seated in my camp chair at Quartermaster Shaw's desk, a candle burning at 4 o'clock pm.

Evening of the 18th January
Anno Domini 1865

My dear Wife,

This being here without the regiment is very dull business and that is not the worst of it. If I was at all certain that we were to be here then or somewhere else by and by, I should settle down to something and be happy. But the uncertainty of where we are to be and whether we are to have any winter quarters or not, I can't enjoy. And just now we are harrowed with uncertainty as to the whereabouts of the regiment and what losses they have suffered. We have had a telegram from Fort Monroe that our forces captured Fort Fisher by storm and that we have General Whiting and Colonel Lamb as prisoners with 1,000 men of the garrison.[10] It was, I imagine, a magnificent affair and reflects great credit upon those engaged in it, but am harrowed with anxiety about the regiment. We know that all the brigade commanders in our division are wounded: Colonel Bell, Colonel Pennypacker and General Curtis.[11] General Curtis is only slightly wounded. The telegram says our losses were not large. But if, as I hear, General Curtis led the charge, our brigade stood the brunt of the battle and met with the heaviest loss and I am confident that our regiment must have been sadly cut up. Still I will not borrow anxiety but hope that my

Hiram E. Rice enlisted at Ellery, New York, as a corporal in Company E, 112th New York Volunteers. Wounded at Cold Harbor and Fort Fisher, he mustered out with regiment on June 13, 1865, at Raleigh.

worst fears may not be realized. I would give $25 of my next pay to be with them. I have my fears now that we shall be ordered about the time you are reading this to join our little regiment at Wilmington or thereabouts.

It will be they come here or we go there. I have now no expectation of going to Elmira. The new call will place a number of green regiments in the field. They will do all the guarding prisoners, etc., old soldiers will be kept out in the field.

I dread the sea voyage to that place. I do not dread the danger of the sea for most of our transport vessels are good staunch ships. I mean those that go to sea. But the anxiety about moving, the delay and trouble and the risk of my horse and baggage, I do dread. But we must take things as they come in war.

I rode last Monday near 40 miles on horseback. I started out about 9 am and rode to City Point, crossing the James on the pontoon bridge at Aiken's Landing and the Appomattox on the pontoons at Broadway Landing. From City Point I rode up to Pitkin Station about a mile from the front then back across the pontoons and down to Bermuda Landing and from the landing up to camp. It will not fall much short of 40 miles and I got back about 8 o'clock pm. The last hours ride was very dark and the roads most of the distance were execrable. I made this journey for the purpose of seeing to the disinterment and removal of the remains of Phillip McEvoy, Company C, who was killed last summer at Petersburg. My long journey was unavailing for the regulations have lately been changed in regard to the removal of remains. All embalmers have been ordered to leave and surgeons are to be detailed at the various general hospitals to embalm and keep for friends who will be likely to call for them, the bodies of soldiers and officers. My horse, I thought must be tired when I got through. But the next morning, when led out, he jumped and kicked as if he had been kept up a week. The man who used to take care of him for Captain Baker says, "You can't tire him. The only trouble the captain ever had with him was on their charges, the horse would always start to go through the southern confederacy and it was almost impossible to stop him." His disposition was not at all improved on the boat. He had six horses on him at one time all of them either treading on him or sprawled across him and he has been cross ever since. He came very near getting his left eye gouged out. But he is just as good as ever. I should have you send me a box immediately were I sure the regiment would come back here. Soon as I know where it is to be, I shall send.

If you have seen the *Herald* of the 14th and 16th you will see that Butler is not justified by Grant and Porter places him very unfavorably.

Love to Freddy.

Very affectionately,
Your husband

I called on a Union family near Petersburg Monday. A Mr. Rushmons Haden, very agreeable call. They have a very large farm, were wealthy. I then heard that A. H. Steams came through the lines last Sunday. They think the Confederacy is so nearly played out they had better cave in at once. We hear all sorts of rumors of peace and evacuating Richmond.

Thursday, January 19th

Skirmishing on road to Wilmington. (Journal)

Sunday, January 22nd

Camp 112th N.Y.
Chapin's Farm Va
January 22nd 1865

My dearest,

I am sitting this Sabbath afternoon in my comfortable tent writing to you. We have had a very stormy unpleasant week. I think yesterday was one of the rainiest days I have ever seen. It poured in torrents all day. In the morning the trees were covered with icicles and the ground was so icy that you could walk with difficulty. I wanted to go to Bermuda but was prevented by the rain. You can't imagine how nervous I have felt all the week about the regiment. The way Captain Talcott and 8 men came to be here. Colonel Smith sent him as soon as the regiment reached Fort Monroe from the 1st Wilmington expedition, with 8 men to Norfolk, to get our extra baggage, stove and etc., for winter quarters, taking it for granted that our brigade, after so much tossing about, would at length be permitted to go into winter quarters.

This squad did not get back until after the quartermaster and I with some sick men and the cooks had returned and you know that the vessel in which we were was disabled and did not get to Fort Monroe as soon by a week as the rest of fleet. Then there were 20 or 30 of those who went in the first expedition who were unable to go on the second by reason of colds, etc. Then we had 52 recruits come. That's how we happen to be here and the regiment away. If the whole corps had gone we should have been sent down but as only detachments from the corps went, we have to await the progress of events and the development of General Grant's plans. Perhaps all the force, but first what is required to man the fort, will be ordered back here.

Billy Clute went with the regiment, and his wife probably has heard from him.[12] At all events I have heard no ill of him. Bulham is not chaplain. He went out for three months to play chaplain, write letters and get up a steam and when the three months were over, found cute house and an abode in a civilized land rather more to his mind than lying in the wet under canvas. So Bliss' address is St. Joseph Post Office, Susquehanna County, PA. I feel sorry to hear of Mrs. Holstering's death. She was a noble woman, a true friend of the soldier. She devoted herself to doing good and God has I trust taken her to the home of those, who like Christ, give themselves to doing good to others.

Now my dear I must tell you about our regiment. It was in the hottest of the fight at the storming of Fort Fisher. Our brigade indeed was the first to enter the fort. They captured three hundred men on entering, turned some howitzers they found upon the enemy and by rapid and desperate attempts in half an hour had possession of three of the huge bomb proofs which were each of them about as large as Mrs. Carpenter's whole yard. They commenced the most desperate struggle known in this war or any other for the possession of the rest of the fort. Each of these bombproofs was a fort in itself and there were nine of them.

Our division took 7 by separate assaults in a contest lasting from 3 to 10 pm. A struggle unequaled in the history of war. Before dark every commanding officer in General Ames' Division had fallen. Colonel Bell, commanding the 2nd Brigade, fell early. Colonel Smith, while gallantly leading on our regiment, was hit by a minnie bullet in the bowels in nearly the same place Colonel Drake was hit at Cold Harbor and survived the night. Colonel Pennypacker, 72nd Pennsylvania, was hit before dusk, Colonel Moore and Lieutenant Colonel Lyman of the 203rd Pennsylvania, his brigade were killed.[13] General Curtis of our brigade, was hit about dusk, and the regiments lost heavily in men the 117th New York, [lost] 93; the 142nd [lost] 72; ours [lost] 41; the 3rd New York [lost] 23.[14] This loss is but a bit of a regiment.

I can't learn any minute particulars. The awful sublimity of the terrific struggle could only be appreciated by those witnessing it. The Rebel gunboats and Forts Caswell and Buchanan poured their fire into the fort after our troops entered. Admiral Porter's invincible fleet fired over two hundred cannons kept up one continuous fire upon the Rebel Forts Buchanan and Caswell and into the position of Fort Fisher held by the Rebs.

About dusk, it seemed a question whether the 2nd Division alone could take the fort. General Terry ordered Abbott's Brigade of the First Division forward into the fort. They entered the fort but before and just as the grand charge was about to be ordered, the white flags appeared and the 2nd Division had the honor of its capture and Curtis' Brigade of the desperate fighting. It was said when the men charged over ramparts nearly as high as the eaves of Mrs. Carpenter's house they would rush down after discharging their pieces and such men as had not been killed and did not surrender were immediately knocked down with the butt of the muskets. These bombproofs where like this [A diagram was drawn] each of the concluding one half acre of ground, the side wall, 20 feet high in this form [A diagram was drawn]. The first with the adjacent works covered a mile in length. O why could I not have been there? This is the bitterest trial of my military life. I have not been able to learn any particulars. I saw today Lieutenant Ross of General Curtis' staff, who told me what I have written.[15] More next time.

Affectionately,
William

I can't learn the names of the men, only Colonel Smith killed. Captain Hollister slightly wounded.[16] No other officers' names given. Poor Smith. He gave me his two watches the last expedition when he went ashore. I have not seen him since. How very sad are the experiences of this war.

Tuesday, January 24th

142nd and 3rd New York sent to Smithville and Fort Caswell to do garrison duty. (Journal)

Wednesday, January 25th

All Ripped Up
January 25th 1865

Dear Wife,

The orders foreshadowed in my last have come for the regimental baggage to be sent to Wilmington. Today we go to Deep Bottom where we expect to embark. The 108 men, however, who are here will remain a few days.

There is some reason to suppose that Richmond is being evacuated and I understand a larger force will move tomorrow out on the right of our lines. The 2,000 men of our division who are here will have to guard the picket line while the force is gone out and then they go.

The quartermaster and I go to the regiment unless we are stopped at Fort Monroe. I am tired and sick of this tumbling about. I hope a day of rest will come for us soon.

I rode to Bermuda yesterday on business and such a ride. It rained for one half of last week and up to Sunday morning and then Monday it poured. Yesterday the Rebel rams came down the James River as far as Dutch Gap and Lee had planned a grand demonstration all around. He was to send the ironclads down to City Point clearing everything out of the river and demolishing our works at City Point and Bermuda Hundred. Meanwhile the army was to attack us on all sides. But we were too vigilant. The battery near Dutch Gap sunk one of their ironclads the first fire. Two others got aground and had the monitor in the river not been out of gear, they would both have been destroyed. It was a finely laid plan but it did not work and they lost two or three hundred men captured. I don't know what is on the checkerboard for the next move but I guess when Sherman is heard from, Grant will move. I think that something is up at Richmond for the cars have for over a week been running incessantly.

I forgot to mention in my last that your lovely five dollar bill reached me safely and I am thankful. I have not got my Monday's letter yet, the one you write Thursday. The ice in the Chesapeake here interfered with the boats from Baltimore. But it will come in time. If I don't get it here I shall at Wilmington. I sort of dread the journey to Wilmington. I have no fear of disaster. But journeying on government transports is horrid. Some 20 men came to this regiment this evening, who went with the expedition, were taken sick and did not go on shore. Why they were not kept at Fort Monroe is a mystery to me. But they came and report that Colonel Smith was alive on Tuesday after the battle and was some better. Lieutenant Ross, aide to General Curtis, told me he died the next day. I have written Mrs. Smith a letter of condolence. I think that the news of his death is reliable. The men on the boat could not know only from rumor and if wounded in the bowels there is little hope that he could survive.

I got yesterday a letter from him written at sea. He sent me some indebtedness listings of his in the regiment. Officers were owing him and he wanted me to collect and send to Mrs. Smith, also all his personal effects. He had felt all summer that he would die if he went out to battle. I will write more going down river.

Very affectionately,
William

I have just received yours of the 18th with $10 in it.

Sunday, January 29th

Jones Landing
January 29th 1865

My dear Wife,

We have been having very cold weather lately for this climate. I presume this is the reason why we do not get away. All our camp and garrison equipage as well as officers' personal baggage is held waiting for boats. Mr. Shaw and I are very comfortable. We have a large cooking range belonging to one of the companies, set up between two tents to keep warm, but the regiment or rather detachment is having a hard time. They are turned out of camp and are in the woods about 3 miles from here. It seems very hard. But we hope every hour that orders will come for us to take transports. The only drawback is there are now no transports at City Point. I can well imagine from our own experience the past fortnight what weather you have been having north, awfully deep snows and lately freezing cold. Well after every winter comes a spring. Let us hope that its flowers shall bloom over the grave of rebellion. I think I did not tell you that I wrote some letters to the Jamestown papers concerning the Wilmington expedition. I think I shall continue to write weekly.

I won't write for either of the Dunkirk papers. I don't fancy them. George, I despise and the other is a copperhead concern. I wrote Mrs. Smith last week a letter of condolence and yesterday I went to Bermuda Hundred and expressed the effects Colonel Smith left here to Jamestown.

Thus the associates of the earlier days of the regiment are passing away. Not a captain in the regiment who was captain at the time of its setting out, not a first lieutenant who was a lieutenant then, not a second lieutenant. All our 2nd lieutenants were then in the ranks and most of our captains were 2nd lieutenants and sergeants when the regiment came out. Ludwick I hear, has been mustered lieutenant colonel and has gone down to Fort Fisher. The regiment will all rejoice to have him made a full colonel. All of my original mess are dead or out of service.

All of my mess of a year since are also gone. Shaw and I seem to be alone in our experience of unchangeableness.

The James was quite frozen across this morning. I saw one or two men on skates skating about on a creek near here. It is very dull indeed. No newspapers, not much mail. I hear that yesterday was the last day the 2nd Division mail was to come up here. It goes now to Fort Fisher. I am told that there has been an order here three or four weeks for the 112th to be sent to the state of New York as soon as returned from Wilmington. I guess that General Grant will manage to keep it in the field in spite of Governor Fenton or anybody else. I dread the job of getting to Wilmington. It is so risky moving our horses and government transports are generally very disagreeable. I think it may be quite pleasant after we get there.

I am astonished that Harry has been so dilatory about writing you. I have not yet written Mr. Wilder but must do so at once. As to church matters, so long as the colony folks think they can do the ruling and make others do the paying there will be trouble. I wish that they could be entirely thrown out of the trusteeship or else that others leave the society. I will write you when we start for Wilmington and then I want you to send me a box.

Very affectionately,
William

Monday, January 30th

117th New York detailed to duty near Fort Buchanan. Our regiment now was camped near a group of houses in the vicinity of Craig's Wharf doing a little fatigue duty, but comparatively at rest. (Journal)

Wednesday, February 1st

The baggage of the regiment is at Jones Landing. The recruits and others in the old camp are waiting transports to go to Fort Fisher. (Journal)

Thursday, February 2nd

We left this afternoon onboard steamer *Thames* for Fort Monroe and Federal Point. We have been waiting orders a fortnight. It is understood that the ice has delayed us. There has been a great dearth of coal at Fort Monroe. The horses of the division remain. (Journal)

Onboard Steamer *Thomas*
James River enroute to Wilmington
February 2nd 1865

Dear Wife,

Again on the move. Yesterday morning I was at Bermuda Hundred, and thought it was our destiny to wait one or two days longer. We moved from Jones Landing to Bermuda the day before. It was a beautiful day. The quartermaster had been promised trains sufficient to draw all his stuff by 7 o'clock. We, however, were too well acquainted with the laggard way of teamsters to be very much in a hurry. So we slept until 7 on our bed, which was boxes to keep us off the ground, some hay on top of them, to be turned over to the mules after it had done duty under us. One army blanket and comfortables were numerous enough to keep us warm.

When we got up, Yorker our little Dutch cook, had a good fire in a camp stove and was just stirring up the buckwheat batter in a stove pan. We had an excellent breakfast soon spread: coffee with sugar and milk, fried liver and fried pork, potatoes, and a bountiful supply of the choicest kind of buckwheat cakes. There is no cook at the St. Nicholas that can beat Yorker on the buckwheat question. Then came the taking down our house, rolling up our blankets, tying up camp chairs, packing saddlebags and boxing up the stove. All which was done by the men in about half an hour and we made an extra fire of the wood left and put round it our logs waiting for the trains. About noon trains came sufficient to take all we had, save three loads. There were 12 loads of luggage belonging to the regiment, for Colonel Smith had ordered all which was stored at Norfolk up to the front.

We rode down to Bermuda in a grand cavalcade. Our brigade quartermaster is an immense man, weighs near three hundred and has a great deal of the military air about him. The contrast between him and Shaw who is about the size of Joe Nelson is quite striking. After getting to Bermuda and finding no transports, we just put up a tent and stove and in half an hour were living again. Yorker was cooking nice black beans and soft biscuits and we eat and were filled.

Just as we were eating, Shaw's cousin, a clerk in a store in Jamestown, came in. He had come on business with a man who used to belong to the regiment. It made a pleasant addition to our situation to hear once more about home and friends. They went off to City Point and I read the last *Herald* and by and by after getting tired, went to bed. Later morning (Wednesday) got up in pretty good spirits. Yorker had the pork and potatoes fixed and was just cleaning the fry pan for the buckwheat. We washed and I shaved and made my toilet with a little more than usual care, for I wanted to ride over to Point of Rocks Hospital.

Ernest Shaw declared our buckwheat's could not be beat. Indeed they ought to be good, I gave three dollars for a 25 lb sack of the flour. Breakfast over. Old Frank saddled and I mounted accompanied by the two Shaws. Frank was in high spirits and pranced and cantered as if he was going on a charge. It was the most beautiful of mornings and seemed like early May was with us. The sun shown with mild brilliancy and I looked about to see the birds, but the birds were not around. When I got over to the hospital, I found about a dozen of our men. Charley Price among them. He was waiting to be sent to Fort Monroe. He is all out of kilter, too much whiskey. I spent some very pleasant hours with my friend Taylor who is now detailed as chaplain at the hospital.

I shall make out a newspaper article on that visit. I dined at the Christian Commission rooms with Doc Tressler of Westfield. Then I felt like riding round the fortifications to view for the last time, the places where we had camped so many times during the earlier part of the campaign. Everything was changed. Comparatively few troops were there. All of them heavy artillery. I rode on to the bank of the James and saw the wreck of the steamer that was sunk the other day. Saw where the ram *Fredericksburg* being pushed through the obstructions and at a distance on the other side the first outline of our defenses. I hoped we would have got into Richmond in this but alas I must leave the department without seeing it. When I got back to the landing about four, all was busy bustle. A transport had come and our baggage and stuff was being put onboard as fast as could be. Our men with detachment from 4 other regiments, making about 400 in all, were to go, the horses to be left to follow and on some other boat. So Billy Coy and Fisher and Jim Shaw with those others stayed to take care of the horses.[17] I found Yorker had a dinner of steak and cornbread for me. I was hungry and eat it with a relish, and then roll up blankets, strike tent and in ten minutes, our little cart was moving with all our goods down to the pier. About sundown we were all aboard the steamer *Thomas*, and moving down two miles below City Point, where we anchored for the night.

In about two hours, we shall be at Fort Monroe and then take Colonel Ludwick and Major Dunham aboard and then over for Fort Fisher. You can direct as usual until I write you. I got a letter from Harry, little lazy Rogers. He was "very sorry" he had not written before.

Very affectionately,
William L. Hyde

I received Mrs. Johnson's letter about Frank Wheeler. Frank was with the regiment unharmed when I last heard. People must remember that the men have not been able to write for two months past.

Saturday, February 4th

We have been at Fort Monroe 24 hours. Left this afternoon for Federal Point. We have [a] detachment from 5 regiments. Colonel Ludwick, Captain Dunham found us here. The baggage and camp equipage of the regiment is onboard. (Journal)

Fort Monroe
February 4th 1865

Dear Frank, *(Editor's note: It appears that Hyde used the name "Frank" as a name of endearment for his wife, Francis Elizabeth Hyde.)*

We are this pleasant afternoon about leaving for Fort Fisher. It is probable that we shall be there in two days. I would like you to make up for me, as soon as convenient, a box of all good things to eat and direct it to my address W. L. Hyde, Chaplain, 112th New York Volunteers.

Near Wilmington, N.C.

You may, if you please, put into it a ruled memorandum book of size a little less than this sheet with leather cover, black morocco and a cap.

Colonel Ludwick, Captain Dunham go down with us. Captain Hollister is here at the hospital and will go home soon. His wound is not bad. He promises if possible to come and see you.

O how I long today for wings to fly and see you. I wrote Harry yesterday.

My love to all friends. I feel the strongest assurance that all will be well with us and that I shall be on my way home as soon as the term of service expires.

Yours lovingly
William

Sunday, February 5th

Those onboard *Thames* quite seasick. (Journal)

Monday, February 6th

We reached the blockade station in the night. This morning we rounded the Point. The vessel touched on the bar. Colonel, captain and myself landed in a small boat and came up to the regiment. The night was very rainy. The colonel and party stopped in a log house belonging to Dr. Mead. He got quite thoroughly wet. (Journal)

Tuesday, February 7th

Tuesday, a very rainy day. All officers' baggage, which was landed last evening, was wet through. (Journal)

Thursday, February 9th

Headquarters 112th Regt N.Y. Vols.
Federal Point near Wilmington
February 9th 1865

My dear Wife,

You see by the date where I am. We sailed from Fort Monroe the Saturday I wrote to you and had a very commonplace and uninteresting voyage. I was just enough seasick as to lose all appetite and have a very severe headache. Colonel Ludwick, however, was very sick, Captain Dunham somewhat so. We had an awful set of desperados onboard. Ludwick found them running riot when he came onboard. He had to tie two of them up, when the others quieted down. They were recruits and had got some whiskey at Fort Monroe, which put more of the devil into them than was either polite or pleasant. We had, however, enough of our old men to rely on in case of emergency. If General Curtis had been onboard, he would probably have shot one of them and thrown him overboard. Did I tell you I spent a part of the evening I was at the fort with General and Mrs. Curtis. The general has entirely lost his left eye but was in good spirits and kept me laughing all the time. He is a rough boy, course and hearty. Mrs. Curtis, as is so often the case, is quite gentle, talks seldom and I think is very good looking, which the general is not. There have been scores of ladies to see the man who lived through the thickest of a seven hour fight.

As soon as he can safely leave Hampton, they are going to Alexandria. We reached the anchorage of the blockading fleet early on Monday morning and about 9 o'clock crossed the bar and entered the mouth of Cape Fear River, passing very near Fort Fisher and quite around 3 sides of it so that we had opportunity to view the scene of the terrible abash on the sea face by the navy. When within a quarter of a mile of land, Colonel Ludwick, Captain Dunham and myself went ashore in the small ship's boat. It was a damp gloomy morning. We had to walk about 22 and a half miles up the beach and past all the fortifications before we reached the regiment.

Our welcome was very hearty and we found those who were here in excellent health and very much improved by the quiet they have enjoyed since the fall of the fort. We were made comfortable in a little old log hut, formerly graced by some venerable Uncle Tom and Aunt Phyllis. It was Dr. Mead's quarters. It had the usual capacious fireplace at one end and a good blazing pile of wood made some show and more comfort. We dined on hard bread, pork and coffee, the three staple delicacies of the army and the only food to be had fresh now. There were chickens and pigs within a space of four miles when the army first landed, but as the boys say "they're played out." The last squeal and the last cackle long since uttered. In the afternoon it began to drizzle and at night, as our camp stuff was not landed, about 6 of us was piled onto the floor of the cabin for the night. It rained hard and the old leaky roof began to drizzle and soon it rained about as hard inside as it did out. We all were waked up by rain in our faces or on our feet and some got up and built up a fire. Lud and I wrapped our blankets closer around us and resolved to lay it out. We spent about an hour joking with each other and then picking out the places where the least rain fell, all was quiet. You would have laughed at our eating breakfast with the doctor in the morning. They had two tin plates and two tin dippers. So the doctor invited his distinguished guest to eat first. Lud and I fared sumptuously on hardtack fried in pork, fried pork itself and coffee very black, very strong with only sugar. You must know in our mess we buy canned milk by the dozen. But the scene after breakfast was the most ludicrous. It rained great guns and the roof seemed to only make it worse. We had a huge fire in the fireplace, put on our overcoats to keep off the rain and Lud, Dunham, Mead and I stood around the fire, each with a pipe in mouth smoking hard and looking at each other. After a pause of some 15 minutes, in which the smoke had been rolling out our mouths in clouds, we all broke out into a simultaneous hearty laugh, while I preferred to sing "what shall we do when the war breaks the country."

I was so anxious about any personal baggage, which had spent the night on the beach, that I started in the rain with the quartermaster sergeant and walked 2 and half miles, sometimes the water nearly were at the tops of my high boots. Well suffice it to say everything was wet through, valises, boxes and all. And about noon it cleared up. This afternoon and yesterday we spent it drying it but it is in bad shape. I had some boots that cost $11 and other things to the value of about $20 stolen from a box onboard the boat. I fear my horse was out in the gale of that night and expect to receive him pretty nearly stove up. So goes the war. The 23rd Corps, Schofield's, have just landed and then will be fifty thousand men here in a few days.[18] I'll bet on lively times soon as Sherman approaches.

Adieu for this time.

Most affectionately your husband,
William L. Hyde

Saturday, February 11th

Saturday morning. General Terry's forces move to the front, up Federal Point. General Schofield's troops moving into our defensive works. There was skirmishing all along the line. The heaviest was in front of Paines' colored division.[19] Our division lost one captain (Scott, 48th New York) killed and two or three wounded.[20] Our position was in the center. Our regiment had our man, Albert C. Bond, Company B, wounded.[21] The extreme right, consisting of Abbott's Brigade, 1st Division, moved around on the beach and captured some prisoners and a line of works. In front of our division was a deep morass, which it was almost impossible to cross, commanded by their works. It was found too that the works in front of Paine were too strong to attempt. (Journal)

Sunday, February 12th

Our division at night fell back behind some earthworks thrown up during the day and continued there during the following day. About 3 pm Sunday, orders came to move toward Fort Buchanan. It was the design to take our right, the 117th New York, up to Masonboro Inlet in steamers with a pontoon train, which we were to lay and defend while the rest of the force crossed there, thus flanking the enemy's strong position. We were at the extremity of the point about 5 pm. A strong piercing chilly wind arising. It was thought best not to attempt to lay the bridge that night. The regiment returned to camp. Few will ever forget the march up. We were almost blinded by the sand which the wind blew full in our faces. We got to camp and then remained until Tuesday afternoon. (Journal)

Monday, February 13th

Headquarters 112th Regt N.Y. Vols.
Near Fort Fisher N.C.
February 13th 1865

Dear Wife,

I was gladdened yesterday by the receipt of your letter of the 2nd February, enclosing Harry's also. I wrote him a few days since and sent him a present of 35 cents. I think he improves in calligraphy and some in spelling. For one of his age, he writes very well. I hope he will do well. I have never one moment regretted that I sent him to Stamford. I want to keep him at school as long as it will be profitable to him. I shall not send for any more money at present, as I can get off Colonel Ludwick or Captain Dunham what I shall need before pay day. There will be six months due me the last of this month. I owe considerable as my expenses have been very large, but hope to be able to send you $400 of it. We may, however, only get paid for four months. If so I shall send you $250. I hope you won't worry about money but use what you want and trust to get more when that is gone. I have no plans for a place of residence after leaving the army. I think I would like to settle somewhere south. Whether I shall continue in the ministry or not is uncertain. I shall not leave it, however, unless forced to do so. But I think I ought to never again to settle in a place like Dunkirk.

I hope you will enjoy your week's housekeeping. I was very much delighted to hear that Lizzie Fullagar had found the Savior. She is a charming girl. I wrote Nannie after I got Mother's letter. I wrote a commonplace letter about matters and things in general and I hope it will do good. I invited her to write me. I shall never write her again unless she does or unless she makes some apology for not.

We are expecting hourly to move. Friday morning the regiment was under orders and to move by land. I was obliged to burn all your letters and every other paper that I could spare. Our horses not being here, the baggage was to be left and we all go on foot. The point arrived at was Wilmington. We did not strike tents, however, until Saturday around 6 o'clock when the regiment moved about five miles and came to an impassible morass behind which was the strongest kind of works. The colored division of General Paine was on our left. We were and are part of General Ames on the right.

We skirmished some but made no serious attempt against the fortifications. I went out with the regiment and at night came in again. I had rather walk twice five miles than lay down on the ground in February. It has been regular winter weather; ice makes in our tents and at times the wind comes down from old Chautauqua and makes everything howl. It is said to be an uncommonly severe winter for this climate. Sunday morning I was almost sick for I wet my feet Saturday and went with them wet all day. You know my feet are the most vulnerable part of me. I, however, started out for the regiment about 10 o'clock and was so exceedingly weary when I got to them that though the day was charming, I could not hold service. So I lay down behind a log wrapped in my military overcoat and went to sleep. About 2, orders came to move. We were to report to Fort Buchanan on special service. We had ten miles to go most of it either over wet ground or soft sand. You may imagine the journey. We came by our old camp when the quartermaster was with the baggage and I fell out, rested an hour then swung my saddlebags over my arm and trudged on to the fort. An orderly saw me when I was about a mile from the fort and made me ride his horse.

When the sun went down the north wind sprung up and we had a regular Erie gale. Colonel Ludwick, Dunham and I curled down behind some bundles of hay. We found we were to go on transports for some point and would probably have to wade before we got through. I tell you I shrunk, but determined if Lud went, as he ought not, to go too. Well about 8 o'clock, we were allowed to go back to camp for the night. So back again 5 miles. Making for me, 20 miles of walking that day. The gale was now at its height, which was the reason we did not start in the boats. The fine sand flew like snow. It would not do to open mouths, nostrils got filled. I had to shut my eyes and whenever I opened them they would fill with sand and smart as if pricked. We got to camp as black as darkies with the black sand, washed out our eyes and then I unrolled my blankets and after heating up, went to bed and slept like a log until after 2 o'clock, when I woke up cold. There was a little place on the side where the blankets did not fit close that let in the cold. I fixed [it] and again went to sleep.

Tonight we start again I suppose. Lud stands it pretty well, but Captain Dunham is most sick today. I am well, thank God, and shall start if the regiment does. The 23rd Corps, General Schofield, is here and our duty is to go around the coast to a point, where we are to lay a pontoon bridge and thus get around the forts between here and Wilmington. Schofield marches up the beach and over the pontoons and rushes into the village. I hope to write my next [at] Wilmington.

Affectionately,
William

You can say to any of the friends of our men that they are all well. Young Bond of Fredonia got an ugly wound in the neck while on the skirmish line; the only casualty.

I felt very proud of Fred's letter. Did he write it himself? You must have guided his hand.

Tuesday, February 14th

At that time orders came to move at 3 o'clock up the beach. We moved up 2 and a half miles then filed into the woods where got supper. After supper moved out onto the beach. Our division was to lay a pontoon train cross the river and flank the enemy's position. The train of mules that drew the pontoons was not able to move them up to the point of crossing in season. About 11 at night we came within sight of the place we were to cross when the whole force turned and retraced their steps. It was an awful march that eight miles. Men dropped out constantly with exhaustion. After reaching our lines they filed into the woods for the night. It rained furiously and men in the morning awoke to find themselves in a pool of water. The colonel and staff were obliged to walk as our horses had not come to us. The colonel and myself walked in reaching camp about 4 am. (Journal)

Thursday, February 16th

> Near Fort Fisher
> February 16th 1865

Dear Wife,

When I wrote you last we were on the eve of a movement. I then thought I should be able to date my next [at] Wilmington, but alas for all calculations in war times. Tuesday we were all day waiting orders and towards night moved up the beach. We had accompanying our division a train of wagons laden with pontoon bridges. The expectation was that we were to lay them down across an inlet thus getting around some ugly works, which cover the road between here and Wilmington. We marched about eight miles and the hardest marching I ever undertook. The sand was not hard as the beach on Folly Island. It gave as we trod over it. When we started too, the wind was from the north but before we had advanced 5 miles we had it from the southeast, and every indication of a storm.

We reached the point where the pontoons were to be unloaded about half past 12 o'clock and found that several of the teams had broken down under their load and that there was a long marsh at the inlet and it would take 12 hours at least to lay the boats, which would be a fatal delay. So the command was faced about and we started to walk back. It had now got to be very warm and muggy. The sand was slippery, the men loaded down with knapsack, gun and 60 rounds of ammunition, and such a scene I hope not to witness again. Men would march til they dropped then crawl up under a sand bank and there lay. I had no horse and was carrying my saddlebags across my shoulders. I thought several times I should drop but I managed to keep up with the regiment until they had gotten inside of our picket lines.

The rain now began to pour. I sat down exhausted to rest a little, and before I got up the regiment had passed on as I suffered to camp, so I struck out for the same point. But they had gone into the woods and I found when I got back to the old camp, nothing there but the quartermaster and his guard and some men we left as unfit to go with us. I soon had a fire going and as I was pretty thoroughly wet, I dried myself and turned in. Colonel Ludwick came about the same time. He also was thoroughly exhausted. It was nearly eleven o'clock the next forenoon before we awoke. I felt as though I was seventy years old and after breakfast I went again to bed and slept several hours.

Today I feel somewhat rested, yet not altogether right. There was no need of such a march. We might have been halted often and made it much less severe. But I despair of any generals ever learning how to march troops unless they are made every three months to dismount and march themselves. We have since been quiet. I hear General Schofield is moving the 23rd Corps around on the other side of the river.

I want much to go over to Smithville and visit Fort Caswell, but I may not be able to do so. The 142nd New York and my friend Palmer is over there. We got notice yesterday of the commissions of Lieutenant Colonel Ludwick as colonel; A. Dunham as lieutenant colonel; and J. S. Mathews as major, also several commissions of 1st and 2nd lieutenants. All our prior officers were boys when we came out.

Well time jogs on and February is most gone. The peace business has turned out just as I expected. Grant and Sherman are the true peacemakers, with old Farragut and Porter. We are to have a spring campaign and I hope this will wind up the fighting. I got your letter of the last of January yesterday.

I must close hurriedly.

> Very affectionately your husband,
> William L. Hyde

I will write Fred next week.

Friday, February 17th

The regiment lay in the woods until Friday the 17th when it, with the division, was moved down to Fort Buchanan to report on the other side to General Cox who was moving on Fort Anderson from the west side of the Cape Fear.[22] A furious cannonading against the fort was kept up during the latter part of the day by the gunboats in the river. The regiment crossed in the night to Smithville by steamer. (Journal)

Saturday, February 18th

About 10 o'clock, the morning of the 18th, moved up to the left and above Fort Anderson. The bombardment of the fort by the fleet was kept up all day and at night. (Journal)

Sunday, February 19th–Wednesday, February 22nd

In the morning the divisions of the 23rd Corps moved up to charge the fort and found it deserted by all but a few stragglers. About fifty were taken prisoners. Captain Dunham who was sick when the regiment left and myself went up to Fort Anderson in the steamer *General Howard* and waited there until the regiment moved into the fort about evening. We lay down expecting before morning to be placed in boats and moved across the river. (Journal)

> Near Fort Anderson, N.C.
> Sunday PM
> February 19th 1865

My dear Wife,

This is one of the loveliest days of winter. The air is somewhat chilly but the sun shines bright and clear.

Evening before last our regiment was moved from Federal Point where we had been since the capture of Fort Fisher over to Smithville, a rural village on the Cape Fear side.

It appeared like rain and I had no means of conveying my blankets other then to carry them myself. So I thought I would not go before Saturday morning. Saturday morning I had to wait for Captain Dunham who had come in half sick from the front.

It was 10 o'clock before we started and when we got to Fort Buchanan at the extreme of the point it was nearly 12. We waited there all the afternoon for a boat to take us across the river. No boat was going and as we supposed General Ames was to follow General Schofield up the river road towards Wilmington. We feared our walk might be more than we cared to bargain for. Especially as we knew we could not reach Smithville before dark.

Moreover a mail had come for the regiment and I was very anxious to hear from you. The result of a counsel held was that we had better move up to camp and try a fresh start this morning.

I could then take the mail belonging to the regiment out to them. This morning I was up bright and early and walking out to the beach. There was severe bombardment of Fort Anderson, a Rebel work up the river on the Cape Fear side, all day yesterday and the 23rd Corps, General Schofield's, moved from Smithville by land. This morning early the troops charged upon the fort and got possession of it without any difficulty, General Hoke having withdrawn his forces during the night.[23] We got 50 prisoners who were glad to give themselves up and the fort with 9 heavy guns mounted in it. It is a fort about as large as Wagner but not quite as elaborate and strong. Sill I wonder that it should have yielded so easily as not a single gun was dismounted. I think they are somewhat short of ammunition and mean to save all their strength for a desperate struggle near Wilmington. Our division, I suppose, were sent to occupy a road which it was supposed the Rebs would try to move up, in case of giving up the fort. It is said, however, that they all crossed the river.

This morning they left the line of works on our Fort Fisher side of the river which the negros fell off a week ago and got repulsed and now the fleet has moved six miles further up towards the doomed city. I think we shall like General Schofield. He maneuvers his men finely. I believe we lost only three or four men of the 23rd Corps yesterday during the skirmishing. They say the general is famous for moving his men in positions so as to carry his points with small loss of men. When we got to Fort Buchanan this morning there was a rumor that our regiment with the rest of the division was up near Fort Anderson 15 miles from Smithville. There was a boat just starting to come up here and I told Dunham that I was not over and above elated at the prospect of a 15 mile walk when we could probably find the regiment by sailing up to the fort. So we concluded to try the *General Howard* a stern wheel steamer, born in Portland, for moving up to Sebago Lake but transferred to this department for Uncle Sam's use.

Twenty minutes brought us to the wharf at Fort Anderson. We made all inquiries but could learn nothing of the division. The fort, however, is a fine sight. The 23rd Corps was in it and in order to avoid a bad place along the Cape Fear Road to Wilmington, they are expecting to be taken across the river here on small boats and small steamers. We have just heard that our division is about an hour's march from here and we have made a great gain by taking the boat.

Wednesday

We are in Wilmington and I am now sitting in a regular house at a table finishing this letter.

We came together at Fort Anderson Sunday night and Monday morning. Every man put across the river in boats, marched all day Monday and at night bivouacked in a sort of swamp. Tuesday we moved about a good deal and at night had laid down got two hours sleep when we were started up with the report the enemy was massing on our right to attack us. We marched three hours and took position in rear of Abbott's Brigade of the 1st Division. We laid down about 4 am and slept sound for two hours. I was very sick yesterday. In fact was not fit to start when I started from the fort. I had a strong tendency to chills and diarrhea. Yesterday, I had violent diarrhea and dysentery not at all aided by sleeping in swamps on the ground.

The last time we were started out to march it did not seem as though I could move a step, but I did and I believe the effort I made was a good thing, for in the morning I was better. I feel now quite well. While we were eating breakfast this morning an orderly came in saying Wilmington was evacuated last night. We soon had orders to prepare to arm and about 9 o'clock we were drawn up in line about a mile out of Wilmington. Our brigade waited there until eleven meanwhile General Terry with Paine's negros and Abbott's Brigade had moved on rapidly to catch what stragglers they could.

About an hour after General Ames, with the 2nd and 3rd Brigades, marched through the town on to the railroad 5 miles distant and half an hour after our brigade moved through the town. It would have amused you to witness the scene. Our fine band struck up one of their liveliest airs and a motley group of all classes and sizes and shades of color came through the street. The negros in the highest glee cheering and singing and dancing, shaking each other by the hands. "Oh, bless de Lord." "We are glad to see you." And some pert ladies turned up their noses, but most of the secesh Rebs well covered behind their blinds.

We are now in the outskirts of the village waiting orders. I will write you more about it next time.

> Very affectionately,
> William L. Hyde

Monday, February 20th

The boats, however, did not take us until 5 am, when we moved up 5 miles and then were landed in small boats from the navy. After landing on the east side, we moved continuously forward joining General Terry's advance. Paine's Division and Abbott's Brigade in front of the main defensive works around Wilmington. There was some skirmishing in the afternoon and a charge attempted by the colored troops was repulsed. (Journal)

Tuesday, February 21st

There was much changing of position today. Most of our regiment was on picket. Portions skirmishing. At night we were moved behind some defenses, the excessive caution of General Terry, leading him to suppose the enemy were massing on our right, to drive us back. Early in the small hours of the night a colored driver of an ordnance train came in and informed General Terry that Wilmington was evacuated, yet such was the tardy movement of troops, that it was 10 o'clock before General Terry entered town. (Journal)

Wednesday, February 22nd

The assault of the colored troops on the evening of the 20th should have been successful. There we should have taken many prisoners and some of our returned prisoners of war. General Terry, with Paine and Abbott and two brigades of Ames' Division, went on to [the] northeast, 10 miles beyond Wilmington and there encountered the rear of the enemy's column who, having a strong position disputed their further advance. Our brigade on entering, passed through the town and along the New Berne Road, crossing a creek and pitching camp in a field near Camp Whiting. Our procession through the town was hailed with the most enthusiastic demonstrations of delight by the negros and some Union people. We found some of our own prisoners were in a most wretched plight. The living and the dead lying side by side. (Journal)

Friday, February 24th

Stragglers came in, in great numbers among them many of our returned prisoners. (Journal)

> At Fort Fisher
> Friday, February 24th 1865
> 5 o'clock am

Dear Wife,

I have just got up, built a fire in the stove and must write you a few lines at least before leaving for Wilmington again. I came down from Wilmington for the purpose of getting some rations and also to direct the quartermaster what things to send up. There was much uncertainty at [what] drives him, as to my finding a boat coming down. So I did not make any preparation, did not even take my overcoat, but walked down to see, when I found the *Eliza Hancock* was lying at the wharf ready to take Colonel Dodge and a medical director to the Point.[24] Without asking anybody's permission, I stepped onboard and after waiting an hour the boat put off.

I guess it is years since Wilmington looked as lively in the harbor, as it does now. Shipping of all kinds are there. All, of course, in the employ of Uncle Sam. Fifteen gunboats were among the crowds. Three large transports were at different wharfs discharging the hard bread, pork and beans and whiskey which Uncle Sam's boys fight for. There was all about the wharf a crowd of women, children, niggers, all sizes and colors, looking on in wonder to see so many vessels and so much life and activity. Everything in the place is as yet unsettled. It has been a place of large business. The place does not look like any southern city that I have seen. It is not as compact as Norfolk, not as regular as Jacksonville. It has same elegant public and private residences. Large numbers of the stores in the city are closed. The others do no business. The blockade business, vast as it was, all in the hands of the government and a few horrid men.

I have not yet called at any private residences in the city but have conversed with citizens and have yet to meet one who does not seem pleased with the change. I will accept some from the country whose looks betaken meek submission while they plead for guard to their property and their negros.

We get things pretty reasonably. Eggs 50 cents a dozen, milk 25 cents a quart, etc. I propose to do some visiting next week. When I got here I found my horse had gotten here and waiting 2 hours at the wharf. I was gladdened by the sight of him, fat as a hog and not a scratch on him. No more foot padding now. Frank will you believe it. I shall have to have a new suit of clothes or rather a new dress coat soon. My coat you sent me I have to wear common and my other is all soiled. Tell Little Fred Pa has not forgotten his promise to write, but I will have to wait for a little leisure. Very soon there will be a regular steamer between New York and Wilmington. Then you will get your mails. I presume we shall have to wait two weeks for our transportation and rations and then off for Raleigh. The works about Wilmington are decidedly strong. That we got them with so little loss, the Rebs are getting out of fight.

I rode up the Point this morning with the quartermaster train, we move to the regiment.

Your affectionate Husband,

Sunday, February 26th

Wilmington, N.C.
February 26th 1865

Dear Wife,

A week ago I wrote you from the walls of Fort Anderson. Today we are reposing in Wilmington. It is a rough, stormy, unpleasant day, though not cold. We are too far from [the] city to hold service there and it is too wet here. If it clears off before evening, I shall try to get the regiment together. The day after I wrote you from Federal Point, quartermaster and I rode up. It was a very chilly and rainy morning and it continued to rain most of the day. Our little mule cart and the other horses of the regiment were along. We moved very slowly at first but often getting the cart well on the road, we rode ahead and made one or two calls on the way. One family was a strong Union people who had suffered every kind of indignity from the Rebs before they left. They had all their chickens, hogs and cattle stolen and even the meal pillows and such things from their house. The lady told me before Christmas she paid $4 a pound for flour, $45 a pound for coffee and $25 a pound for sugar. They have been about starved. They are very kind to our sick soldiers.

We reached Wilmington about 2 o'clock in the pm and found everything as we left it. The cart and mule did not get along until morning. The horses were too tired to make the whole journey. I have a nice little mule. It is owned by one of the men. He can't get it fed so he gives it to me and when I get through the service, I am to give it back to him. The boys are calculating to confiscate a cart [from] the first arrant Rebel they come across and they won't have to go far here. So I shall have the means of transporting my bedding and valise without being indebted to [the] government. The colonel and I will have our things moved in my cart. The quartermaster and Lieutenant Colonel Dunham will have theirs in stores. I wish we could stay a time in Wilmington. It is a very pretty place and it would be grand to have a slight rest before the spring. I do not expect it, however, for we have already had a day to send in our estimates for clothing and transportation needed.

Well I am glad Grant does not mean to let the Rebs rest but intends to drive every army on until he envelopes Lee in his meshes. A citizen here told me that he stood by and saw them burying our dead before the evacuation and that one man was actually put into the grave before the breath had left his body and covered with the rest. I had heard this told twice but not by one who was looking on and saw it. I have also heard from so many that I can't help believing it, that there were some 8 of our very sick and dying men in one cabin when they set fire to this, with other buildings and they were burned to death. It seems too awful for belief.

I am hoping daily for a letter from you and think I must have some at division headquarters five miles off.

All our baggage and camp equipment came up this afternoon. We are going to move soon. I think, may all conspire to end this sad war as soon as possible.

With fond love,
Your Husband

(*Continued letter*) Monday morning. I did not get my letter started last evening as I intended. I rode up to the regiment in the afternoon; camp all broken up and the regiment a mile nearer the landing in the woods. This is preparatory to embarkation. Our delay in getting away is owning to the ice closing up Baltimore and the Delaware River so that coal for the use of the boats cannot be obtained. It is very unpleasant waiting here so long. I am glad you are able to do something for the wives of the absent soldiers. You can't do too much. I have just been over this morning to Point of Rocks. There is a large hospital there and they calculate to be able to accommodate 6,000 patients. I had a very pleasant interview with Den Kessler of Westfield, who was a very warm friend of Colonel Drake. He is there as a delegate of the Christian Commission. We had an excellent meeting at the Christian Commission Chapel at this landing last evening.

I long to see our dear boys and proclaim to them the glad tidings of salvation.

I presume we shall have a pleasant place at Fort Fisher. It is said our regiment is to be assigned to duty within the fort.

Oh if only the officers could have their families there with them I should be glad to go. I would have you and Fred come down to me.

Who knows? There is no doubt in my mind that we are nearing the final scene of the great struggle.

Lee may have a Waterloo in reserve for him, but Grant has him and he will bide his time to strike.

I feel very hopeful my confidant, that the end is approaching. We have had no pay since I sent you that draft last October. I hope you have enough to get along with. It is very expensive living in the army especially when one has to travel on army transports.

Very truly and affectionately,
William L. Hyde

Monday, February 27th–Tuesday, February 28th

Today a large number of prisoners of war brought into the city. Among them Adjutant Hedges of our regiment taken the 16th of May and Captain Casler, 154th New York, visited us.[25] The condition of the prisoners returned beggars all description. They all tell the same story of cruel treatment and starvation. (Journal)

Thursday, March 2nd

Today Hedges and Casler left for the north. (Journal)

Friday, March 3rd

Efforts are being made to muster some of our officers. (Journal)

Wilmington, N.C.
March 3rd 1865

My dear Wife,

I have not received a letter from you for more than a week. The mails are very irregular. It is owing no doubt to the fact that our division and brigade are at present quite scattered. A part of the brigade is at Smithville and Fort Caswell, a part here. The rest of the division has been ten miles further up the road towards Fayetteville. We are expecting them into Wilmington today.

Yesterday our eyes were gladdened by the sight of some of our returned officers and men, among others Adjutant Hedges. He is in good health and looks well. We had him and a Captain Casler, 154th New York, at our quarters all night. The story of their experiences is very rich and racy. Being officers they had privileges, which privates do not enjoy. Hedges has had two quite serious spells of sickness, but got through with them safely. They were subjected to every sort of indignity and insult at times. When Hedges was captured in May, he was taken to Libby Prison. There he was deprived of all his money. They telling him that it would be recorded and given back to him. His sword, belt, etc., were taken from him before he left the ground where he was captured. He was sent to Danville, from there to Macon, thence to Savannah, thence to Charleston, then Columbia. At Columbia they had three tunnels dug through by which they expected to escape and get to Sherman. When Sherman reached Columbia, so as to open his guns upon the place, the last trains with prisoners were leaving.

Captain Casler had some very nice bone work, which he had carved. He was a prisoner 20 months, having been taken at Gettysburg. The captain said that he intended to work out several other pieces, but he bought a file at Columbia for which he gave ten dollars. They let him keep it 3 or 4 days when the same man of whom he bought it came and took it away from him saying that he was ordered to do so by the authorities. This was probably a lie for the sake of getting it to sell to somebody else. There was a lieutenant colonel who executed some elegant carving in bone. One piece was our Savior on the cross. It was a perfect gem. There were also several other pieces. He would not have taken $500 for the cross. It was intended for a gift to his mother but the Rebs took it away from him and took his file and all.

Samuel P. Hedges enlisted at Charlotte, New York, as a sergeant in Company B, 112th New York Volunteers. He was captured at Drury's Bluff, Virginia, and mustered out with regiment on June 13, 1865, at Raleigh (courtesy U.S. Army Heritage and Education Center [USAHEC]).

On the fourth of July, they had a celebration. They had secretly manufactured a flag. They had a magnificent band and had two or three songs, which were composed among themselves. When they raised the old flag, they shouted and danced about it and the Reb lieutenant ordered out all his guard and coming into the prison enclosure said that the flag must come down. At first they bellowed it should not and were so excited they probably would have been fired into. At last one, cooler than the rest, said take the flag down and hide it. To this they agreed and had the other part of their celebration without it.

Poor Sam was often in utter despair of being exchanged but Captain Casler kept up his spirits. When he got here he was rather dilapidated. We fixed him up in shape and the colonel and Captain Dunham lent him money to go on his way rejoicing.

The cruelty our prisoners suffer has never been exaggerated. They suffer for food more than for anything else. Though they are not half clad.

We have again been mustered for pay, but when we shall get any is more than I can tell. I suppose you have sent me a box and if so, it will no doubt be here shortly. I understand that the express will be ready to deliver articles in a few days. We add to the variety of our dish here, eggs and nice milk.

I long exceedingly for the day when the regiment is discharged and I retire to civil life. I am heartily sick of this kind of life. There is very little that I can do just now and I can't bear to be so useless.

We are not likely to remain here longer than until the 15th March. I think by that time we shall be in Raleigh or elsewhere in this turbulent scene. North Carolina will come into the Union soon as she is released from the terror of Rebel bayonets.

I wish you was here to ride about Wilmington. General Terry has of course given to General Hawley, his chief of staff, the post of commander in Wilmington and the 7th Connecticut, his old regiment, is provost guard. If the 112th New York were provost guard, you would be here in less than three weeks. I hear there is a huge mail in the city. So by the evening I shall get a letter from you.

Very affectionately,
William

Saturday, March 4th

Rainy. Ellis, Hawley, Pennock, Aplin mustered as officers.[26] (Journal)

Sunday, March 5th

Wilmington, N.C.
March 5th 1865

My Dear Wife,

We are still encamped about a mile outside Wilmington on the New Berne Road, so called. Our quarters are quite comfortable considering the fact that we are expecting to move every day, which prevents us from making any improvements not absolutely essential to present comfort. I anticipate for the regiment a severe campaign this spring and summer. All our visions of "a soft thing" which we have hoped for are vanished. General Cox's Division of the 23rd Corps and another

Alfred O. Ellis enlisted at Portland, New York, as a private in Company G, 112th New York Volunteers, and mustered out with regiment on June 13, 1865, at Raleigh.

division of the same are moving today to cooperate with Sherman. We expect by the 8th or 9th to be on the same path. Since we came here, we have been very busy straightening out our regimental business, which had got somewhat behind.

Hawley was yesterday mustered 2nd lieutenant and Alfred O. Ellis, 1st lieutenant.[27] Hedges has been recommended by Colonel Ludwick for captain. Two individuals have been commissioned in this regiment who are in other regiments. Henry F. Brown of Jamestown, an old soldier in the 72nd now 120th New York has a commission in our regiment.[28] They say he will make a good officer, but we have so much material for good officers and have so good an opinion of our deserts that we do not much relish the incoming of a stranger to occupy the place of one of our men.

It is unaccountable to me why your letters do not come. I received one last Thursday dated the 15th. I have received all before this date. I was much pleased with Harry's letter. He certainly improves. You must exercise your judgment in regard to letting him come home.

I don't see why the paymaster does not visit us. There is six months pay due all of us and some men have not been paid for more than a year. I am not disposed, however, to be severe on the government. This war is an enormous affair and the army almost unwielding. It will all come down right in the end. I wish I knew what I am to do after I get through with the army. I suppose it will take some time to get out my history of the 112th Regiment. Then I must settle into some business, east, west, north or south. It is possible I may not go into the ministry again, though I should prefer doing so if I can support my family.

Monday morning. Yesterday I rode down to the town in the morning and attended church with the colonel at St. James Episcopal. Chaplain Chapman, 169th New York, led service and preached. It seems it was [the] 1st Sunday in Lent. I really enjoyed entering a sanctuary once more after so long an absence. The audience was mostly composed of officers. There were, however, some citizens and ladies even. It looked human and civilized to see ladies in a congregation.

In the afternoon, I held service with the regiment in the open air. Just think of it, while you were shivering over your little airtight stove or bundled up with 3 or 4 cloaks in the old ark at Dunkirk, I was standing out of doors and the men were all sitting on boards and whatever they could find. My hymn books were not to be found, so I lived off "Thine earthly Sabbath, Lord" etc. and we had singing. It was rather cool. The men had to keep their overcoats on. But they were all glad to have [a] meeting. We have had many warm days since we came here. But yesterday and this morning a fire on the hearth feels good.

As I write, the 23rd Corps is marching by on the New Berne Road. They have just the kind of weather for a march. They are rough fellows, the Army of the Ohio, and make much noise as they go by. They have been here about a fortnight and have got clothed up and remitted and now they are off to take part in the great struggle, which is coming off this spring.

I hope that the decisive battle may not be deferred too long for I am anxious to see the thing through. I must go down this morning and try to do something for our poor, sick, exchanged prisoners. We detailed 25 men from our regiment yesterday to take care of them and 75 from the brigade.

About half our regiment is now away from camp on various details. But when the word comes, they will all be summoned back and off we go. Frank Wheeler is very sick in hospital. You tell Mrs. Wheeler he was left at the Point when we came here. I fear he will die, though he has a very strong constitution. He is discouraged and neglects himself. I have done what I could for him.

Very truly your affectionate husband,
William L. Hyde

Monday, March 6th

Ticknor and Vorce mustered as captains. (Journal)

Wednesday, March 8th

Mr. Wiggins, sutler, came with cargo of sutler's stores. (Journal)

Thursday, March 9th

I have taken in hand the sole care of postal matters. Commissions for Lieutenant Colonel Ludwick, as colonel; Captain Dunham as lieutenant colonel; Mathews as major; Brazee as 1st lieutenant, came 3 days since. (Journal)

Wilmington, N.C.
March 9th 1865

Dear Wife,

Just after my last to you a large mail came bringing me 3 letters from you. One of them contained the express receipt. I shall expect the box soon. We have not been moved from here as I anticipated when I last wrote. The 23rd Corps went on without us and I think it will be at least two weeks now before we can move. We have no transportation train as yet and must have one before we can proceed far into the country.

There is a great lack of transports at this place. The war operations along the coast have called into service a vast fleet of boats and railroads.

We hear that Sherman's quartermaster was in here the other day and went immediately to Beaufort. It may be that our division will have the little job furnished it, of guarding a supply train from this point out to him. It is understood that he is at or near Fayetteville.

I got a letter from Harry at the same time I received yours. The young gentleman very kindly invites me to invest "$4.50 his own money" in a hand sled which one of his playmates has to sell.

I am afraid the boy's business abilities are not fully expanded. The probability is that somebody who knows sleds are not used in the summer wants to sell him one at a trifling discount.

I am writing this morning before breakfast with my coat off and doors all open. The weather is very mild. Japonicas, hyacinths, and violets all in bloom. The small farmers around are plowing and planting. We have frequent showers mostly in the night.

I called yesterday to see the Reverend Mr. Hepburn, protestant minister, here who has been quite sick.

He boards with a Mr. Cassidy, who is a very fine gentleman, and has a very accomplished lady for a wife. They are Union people and say they hope that the night of terror to which they have been so long subjected is over. I think there is more real joy in Wilmington over our successes than in any place south I have visited.

The ladies of the Union people have been very kind to our returned prisoners. They have made clothing for them and given them, even to depriving of themselves. I heard one lady say to a man who was apologizing for their treatment of our prisoners. "Sir, hanging is too good for those wretches. I would shut them in a cage and starve them to death."

This cruelty to our prisoners will do more to unhinge the South than any other single thing.

We are still pleasantly situated and I am in good health and hope to continue so. The doctor has prepared me a flask of bitters which I take every day.

There are at present, symptoms of a heavy rain. If it does not rain, I am going to visit the hospitals today if I can stand the stench.

Your affectionate husband,
William L. Hyde

Friday, March 10th

Examined the mortuary record at Fort Fisher. Thompson, Company H; Thompson, Company B; Norton Dowd, Company I; Private O'Brien, Company H and Coonrod, sick, Company D.[29] (Journal)

Sunday, March 12th

Service in morning at Presbyterian Church, in the afternoon with the regiment in open air. (Journal)

Wilmington, N.C.
March 12th 1865

Dear Wife,

How I long this pleasant Sabbath afternoon for the society of those I so much love. How I wish you, Fred and Harry were here to enjoy the delicious warmth of this bright sun shining day. We had last night quite a sharp white frost but the Sabbath opened beautifully serenading me of George Herbert's "Sweet day, so calm, so bright, so cool, the bridal of the earth and sky. The dew shall weep, they fall tonight. You thou must die."[30] I hope you have quite recovered the tone of your system and that you are enjoying yourself as well as circumstances will allow. I am reinforced that you have the religious enjoyment of which you speak and that you find Christ precious to you in your loneliness. He is truly the shadow of a great rock in a weary land to them who flee to him.

I had a very pleasant call with Colonel Ludwick at the house of a Mr. Cassidy last evening. Mr. Hepburn, the Presbyterian minister of the place, boards there. Poor man, he has been quite sick and his family are away. They live at Chapel Hill, N.C. He was a professor in the University of North Carolina when the rebellion broke out and continued there until they had to disband the college, the students having almost all left. Since then he has preached in various places and came here to stay a year—a year ago last Christmas. He was to have returned to them soon after Christmas but the taking of Fort Fisher laid an embargo upon all citizens traveling and now he can't go to them because he would run the risk of being impressed in the Reb army. He says he is almost in an agony of suspense, fearing the Rebs will sweep through Chapel Hill and take everything from his family. He is, however, firm in his convictions that the Union cause will triumph and that he shall be able very soon to travel to his home over a free North Carolina.

This Mr. Cassidy's father is a Scotchman and immigrated 60 years ago and was a resident of Bath, Maine. Immigrated from Bath in 1817 and came to Wilmington. They are ship builders. This man about my age is a ship owner and was engaged in quite an extensive ship building and mercantile business when the war broke out. They live in a very pleasant house and have one or two beautiful children. Mrs. Cassidy and some other ladies, before our troops came, when our prisoners were brought here, had their pity so excited that they took baskets of coffee and porridge and bread, etc. to give them and the officers drove them away and would not let them give them a thing. She said she gave them a piece of her mind and when coming home met some higher officers to whom she vented her indignation more fully. She now has several sick returned prisoners come to her house every day and she gives them medicines and has clothed and fed them and says she is gratified to say that they are doing well. I tell you my heart warms towards such people.

We spent a very pleasant hour and half and Mr. Stephen urged me to preach for him today to which I assented. I enjoyed it much. The Pen Church is a large new brick edifice and will hold as many as Dr. Clark's church in Buffalo. There were a large number of naval and military officers present and more citizens then I expected to find. Religion, however, is at a low ebb in this community. They have given up on all hopes of sustaining churches before the close of the war.

They could not the past winter sustain either a Sabbath school or a prayer meeting in a church, which will accommodate a thousand people.

Last eve, the 142nd New York and 3rd New York Regiments came from Smithville to join us. This I presume is a preliminary to another move. But the move cannot occur till the last of this week, for we have no trains. I understand a large train has gone out to meet Sherman.

We are all cheered by the constant inflowing of good news. Early capture in the valley and Sherman moving on with resistless power from the south. Schofield in this region. Lee will soon be hemmed in and if his troops behave as bad as they do in front of Richmond, he may wake up some morning to find himself without an army. I would not wonder if the rebellion fairly drizzled out and doubt really if there is to be much more severe fighting.

My horse is in grand spirits and the colonel and I have some pleasant rides most every day. I have been round the hospital among the returned prisoners. They are in a deplorable plight but improving.

Very affectionately,
Your husband

Monday, March 13th

Day warm and pleasant. The 13th Indiana returned from Fayetteville which they left at 6 o'clock last evening. Sherman is there. The 169th New York and 48th New York ordered out with 3 days cooked rations. (Journal)

Between March 14th–March 19th (Partial entry)

… the colored troops. They pillaged and destroyed without stint. About 5 pm reached Kenansville, a very pretty village, the county town of Dugan County. Rode up with Colonel Ludwick to the house of the teacher of our academy, a Mr. Clements. He had been stripped of everything by the colored troops. Moved on 3 miles and came to another hole. The rear of the train could go no further. Animals tired out. We halted, and about 11 pm had eaten supper and laid down. About 12, orders came for the regiment to leave the train, move on four miles to where the brigade was, draw rations and be ready to move at 6 am. We slept about 2 hours. (Journal)

Monday, March 20th

Moved at half past 6 o'clock and by noon crossed the railroad at Mount Olive Station. Moved thence west and north about 8 miles and halted for the night. This point is about 18 miles from Goldsboro. Weather warm, men very weary and footsore. Just before halting, crossed a wretched mud hole in a swamp, saw animals mired which could not be extricated. Heard firing this evening. Surgeon Washburn on General Ames' staff obliged to take an ambulance. (Journal)

Tuesday, March 21st

This morning we moved about 7 o'clock. Our course nearly west, little north. Soon after starting we crossed the swamp again, passing through a long and unpleasant water hole when the men went in up to the waist. We moved about 8 miles and halted near Cox Bridge which the Rebels had burned. Here again we met Sherman's men. Major Graves, on General Terry's staff, reported to General Sherman about 5 miles distant.[31] We are near the place of Slocum's fight.[32] Dr. Washburn quite sick, rode all day in ambulance. (Journal)

Wednesday, March 22nd

Last evening Paine's Division laid the pontoons of Sherman's army and made ready for his forces to cross the River Neuse. We heard the particulars of Slocum's fight, which was very severe. We repulsed 8 charges of the enemy. General Sherman this afternoon called on General Terry. (Journal)

Thursday, March 23rd

A very high wind. Foraging party went out with wagons. They encountered on the Raleigh Road, 3 miles out, Wheeler's Cavalry and had a spirited skirmish.[33] Three of our men were captured, Walder, Company B, Mercer, Company I and [blank].[34] About half past 6 this morning, General Sherman rode by our camp on his way to Goldsboro. Slocum's army passed over the river on the pontoons near Cox Bridge, and Howard's further down at Falling Waters. Their train has been all day passing. We are to remain here until all are safe at Goldsboro. (Journal)

Saturday, March 25th

We moved out at 6 am. Our division in advance and our regiment in rear of [the] division. Surgeon Washburn was so sick he had to be moved in an ambulance. I rode with him all day. Also Mr. Manwarring, nurse.[35] We crossed the swamp as before. Then moved down the Wilmington and Weldon Railroad to Faison's Station. Moved the surgeon into a house near the railroad. We feared the faint but his symptoms this evening are very favorable. We found here detachments of Kilpatrick's Cavalry.[36] They were in the Fayetteville fight. (Journal)

Sunday, March 26th

Our brigade changed position this morning. We understand we are now to remain here and rest till Sherman gets all his supplies and is ready for a new campaign. We hope also to be refurnished and paid. There are very strict orders about leaving camp and foraging. (Journal)

Wednesday, March 29th

We received the first of the week lists of 270 recruits or substitutes assigned to the regiment. Today we received 209 of these men. (Journal)

Thursday, March 30th

Lieutenant Colonel Ludwick, Captain A. Dunham were today mustered in accordance with their commissions as colonel and lieutenant colonel of the regiment. The recruits received this time are a much superior class to those received in January at Chapin's Farm. All our companies are now full. (Journal)

> Headquarters 112th Regt N.Y. Vols.
> Faison's Station
> Wilmington and Weldon Railroad
> March 30th 1865

My dear Wife,

I received yours of the [blank] March last evening. The first I had received since leaving

Wilmington. I find sometimes the severe difficulty in making up a letter of which you speak. I have nothing to write. But when on the march, I can generally pick up enough. I must write Harry at once. I have neglected the poor boy too long. I want him to stay with Aunt Mildred until my term of service is over. If it was near winter and his year was out I think I would have him with me. But of course I would not dare to run the risk in the summer time. I feel very happy and safe having him there. I trust the discipline through which he is passing will be of benefit to him. Perhaps you had better dispose of whatever is lying loose around Dunkirk belonging to us. I mean bedsteads, chairs, etc., keeping anything you wish to preserve as keepsakes or for association. I think too, as soon as warm weather comes on, you had better begin and visit your friends east or go and stay with Harry for a season, unless you prefer to stay in Dunkirk. I want you to do this summer just what will be the most pleasant and agreeable to you. If you prefer Dunkirk, stay there. If you would be happier in visiting, do so. If you wish to go to Saratoga or Newport, do so. You have my passport to any or all places where you would most pleasantly spend your time.

I am glad today to report Dr. Washburn is decidedly on the gain. He does not sit up and is very feeble but he is quite rational and we hope if he has no drawback that he will soon be better and able to go north. I am quite strong and think my prospects for standing the campaign good. I do not believe we are to have much more of hard fighting. Sherman is now with Grant and the president at City Point. I think the rebellion is pretty nearly played out. If you could see the country as I see it, you would think so. I don't know what the inhabitants will do for food next fall and winter.

The country is overrun and the people dare not plant. The soldiers take everything they have above their immediate needs.

Their men can't be made to fight as they once did and if they only knew as much as now, they would not fight at all. Just now a gust of wind came and ripped up the pins of our tent. I went to fasten them and came back to my letter. It was gone. I hunted the tent, could not find it. Went out, saw something white flying in the direction of Goldsboro, ran about a quarter of a mile, [or less and] sure enough, it was this precious document, seeking you in the wings of the wind.

Send my kindest regards to all our friends. I shall write Dr. Rogers tomorrow. I expect my box will be forwarded from Wilmington before I leave here.

I am full of hope and good spirits. Oh for a little cozy quiet house, this is my greatest desire. But may we all to live as to have a home in Heaven. Ludwick is full colonel, Dunham [a] lieutenant colonel, Mathews [a] major, etc. We have 290 recruits. Our regiment is now larger.

                                             Truly your affectionate husband

Friday, March 31st

                    Chaplain's Monthly Report
                  112th Regiment New York Volunteers

Headquarters, 112th Regiment New York Volunteers
In the Field, Faison's Station, N.C.

March 31st 1865

Brigadier General L. Thomas
Adjutant General

General,

I have the honor to report that on the first day of March 1865, this regiment was in camp at Wilmington, NC. On the fifteenth (15) day of the month, General Terry's forces of which our regiment forms a part, moved up towards the River Neuse in a line nearly parallel with the Wilmington and Weldon Railroad reaching Mount Olive Station on the noon of the

20th, when we moved across and in a northwesterly direction, to Cox Bridge on the Neuse River. We remained there until the morning of the 25th, when were moved back to Faison's Station on the Wilmington and Weldon Railroad where we are now encamped. On the 29th, we received 209 recruits to the regiment raising our aggregate up to the maximum.

On the 31st, Lieutenant Colonel Ludwick was mustered colonel and Captain A. Dunham lieutenant colonel, in accordance with commissions received from the governor of the state of New York.

The general sanitary condition of the regiment is good. Twenty-seven were sent to hospital during the month, which includes all thought unable to bear a march. Four have died at hospital during the month.

The general moral condition of the regiment remains unchanged.

During the month, services have been held but once on account of the exigencies of the service rendering it impracticable.

Very respectfully,
Your obedient servant,
William L. Hyde
Chaplain
112th New York Volunteers

Monday, April 24th

Monday, April 24th 1865
Raleigh, N.C.

Dear Frank,

How I wish you were here to enjoy this beautiful weather and beautiful scenery. Raleigh is the most beautiful of all the town or cities in the south, which I have seen. The streets are very wide, the shade trees abundant. The houses have an ancient and aristocratic look. There is nothing of the parvenue about the place. You feel as you travel around that there is solid comfort in the arrangements. Besides here is the state house larger and more imposing than that in Augusta Maine with something such a front and in the green fronting the building a bronze statue of Washington. There is a large insane asylum on one hill and a deaf and dumb asylum in another section. The finest church is the Episcopal, a stone structure on one side of the square opposite the Capitol. All the churches are in the vicinity of the Capitol. The Baptist Church is the next finest to the Episcopal. The Presbyterian appears to have stood for ages gazing wonderingly at the rampant growth about it. It is the oldest plainest structure in the town. I had service in camp yesterday morning and in the afternoon went into the city and attended the Presbyterian. There was a chaplain from the 17th Corps who officiated. The service was understood to be for the soldiers and there were but few citizens there. The singing was quite good. Some ladies sung which made it very pleasant. We have had a great time on reviews the past week. The 10th Corps was reviewed Thursday, the 23rd Friday, the 20th Saturday, and today the 17th. I would give much if you could have seen the display. Generals Sherman, Howard, Slocum, Schofield, Logan, Blair, Geary, Carr, Thomas, Terry and all the lesser lights with their staffs making in all several hundred mounted men seated on horseback in regular rank in the yard of the Capitol and the troops passing in the street in front. Today Generals Grant and Meade are here. I did not know it or I should have gone up town. I hear that Johnston's terms of surrender are not accepted and tomorrow the Army moves after him. We hoped that he would be wise enough to surrender without giving us further trouble. This will delay us in getting home. I never was so restless myself and never saw the regiment so restless as they are now. They all feel that as the fighting is over they ought to be permitted to go home. If we are to stay here this summer and I knew it, I would have you come on. But I hope before the 4th of July to be permitted to go to you. I received your letter of the 12th Sunday pm. I was pleased with all of it, your visit to Westfield, etc. The paymaster is here but will only pay us for 4 months to December 31st. I shall not be able to send you only about $250 of it. My expenses last fall while travelling about were enormous often times $3.00 per day for board. The government will in a few days owe me 4 months more pay. My horse is in fine condition and gay as a lark. If you were here, I would buy a light horse for you to ride. I laugh at your visions of a southern home. I pity anybody who has to live south for some years to come.

I think I shall be better contented to live north than ever. Still this is a beautiful climate and country and where a man can control his choice, in which a minister cannot, he might find very desirable places to exercise trade or profession or particularly farming.

Love to Fred,
William L. Hyde

Thursday, April 27th

Camp 112th Regt N.Y. Vols.
Raleigh, N.C.
April 27th 1865

To my darling Wife,

Your ancient and venerable husband did not have to start off in a hurry yesterday morning. The regiment was under marching orders Monday night for Wednesday and Monday night we were ordered to be up at four, break camp and move out at six o'clock. But just as we were eating our delicious pork and hardtack, washed down with raw coffee, we had orders to wait further orders before breaking camp. And then after a reasonable delay, we had word that there would be no movement that day and then at night, we heard that Johnston was about to surrender. And now we know that he has surrendered. I guess he had not a very large and enthusiastic crowd to surrender and concluded to run no risk. If there had been a fight, there would not have been many if any prisoners taken. The army had made up its mind to exterminate as they went along. The death of the president has exasperated us to the utmost.

I really have serious thoughts of trying to get you here. I can be detailed if I am willing and possibly I will be willing or not willing as chaplain of the Pettigrew General Hospital here. I think you would have good health here. Raleigh is up among the hills. It is a beautiful place about as large as Gardiner, Maine or rather Hallowell. I have not seen anything south I like so well. If I am forced to go there, I shall make it a condition that you be permitted to come down, just as soon as the remainder of the army leaves. General Terry has taken command of the district of North Carolina, and I know he thinks well of me and would grant me the favor of your company.

As to my duties in the hospital, I should be as well off as I am now. I should have certain specified hours for my visits and no marching. I think it would be as good a place as any to spend the remainder of my time of service in. And if I am to settle anywhere south of New York State, I want it to be Maryland or North Carolina. But I beg of you not to talk this matter round yet until you hear from me again. I may not be detailed. I have not yet mentioned the matter to Colonel Ludwick. If I thought there would be a hospital here for several years I might think quite seriously of such a detail as a matter of interest to me after I had got through with the army.

You would be charmed with Raleigh. I never ride through that beautiful street, leading from the governor's house to the Capitol, without thinking how I should enjoy it to have you with me on a nice little pony cantering by my side.

I feel as though I should soon be with you somewhere. I sent to Mr. Fullagar $200 to be paid to your credit. I could not possibly send more. We were only paid to December 31st. There are four months more pay now due and I shall have to live on my friends unless I get some pay soon.

If I go with the hospital, I shall be able to draw my pay more regularly.

The boys did not send home large amounts of money this time. Only about $7,000 in all. They think they are going north soon and want some to spend. John Hunt sent his wife I think fifty dollars.[37] Her brother got his money in a bill and I guess did not send home any. He is rather a hard boy, but a very quiet, good, clever soldier while kept away from liquor.

I feel happy and cheerful tonight. I have just returned from hospital, Lieutenant Horace Allen and Lieutenant Pennock are both quite sick. Allen is not alarmingly sick but has a regular typhoid fever. His symptoms are better than they were this morning. We have a pretty good camping place here. But when the rest of the army leaves, I think we shall have one much better.

Colonel Dunham has been in talking about having his wife come down. She is in Jamestown, with one boy, 5 years old and is situated much as you are sometimes. She has a home and sometimes none. Now at a tavern and now with her friends. We all shall know in a few days what is best. The probability is that within three weeks railroad communication will be established between here and Richmond and so on to Washington. Good night and pleasant dreams.

Horace F. Allen enlisted at Jamestown, New York, as a 1st sergeant in Company A, 112th New York Volunteers. He mustered out with regiment on June 13, 1865, at Raleigh.

Truly affectionately,
William L. Hyde

Monday, May 1st

Chaplain's Monthly Report
112th Regiment New York Volunteers

Camp 112th Regiment New York Volunteers
Raleigh, N.C.

May 1st 1865
Brigadier General L. Thomas
Adjutant General

General,

I have the honor to submit the following report of the moral condition and general history of this regiment for the month of April 1865.

During the month the regiment has been encamped just outside the City of Raleigh.

The moral condition is exhibited in the fact that very few cases of the infliction of punishment among the enlisted men have occurred.

None of the officers have been under censure or arrest.

Religious services have been held during two Sabbaths of the month in camp circumstances having rendered impracticable holding them the other Sabbaths.

The Chaplain has spent the other Sabbaths at the hospital of the Tenth Army Corps.

Very respectfully,
Your obedient servant,
William L. Hyde
Chaplain
112th New York Volunteers

Friday, May 19th

Raleigh, N.C.
May 19th 1865

My dear Wife,

I received your letter mailed the eleventh yesterday, just one week after it was mailed. This will show you that the mails are becoming more direct and regular.

I do not think that I have lost but two letters during my three years in the army. I mean but two from yours. I have received the little memo book Harry sent, and what is more I have just received the box you sent so long ago. I knew it would come at some time. The contents, well most of them, were in good condition. The tin cans were in some instances imperfectly sealed, so that I lost a can of peaches, one of tomatoes and leaking on the dried beef, I lost that. Yorker thinks the rest is all good. We have made way a can of peaches already. I hope the can will prove good.

I am looking impatiently for the day when I can enjoy all the good things of the table with you. We do not know when we leave and probably will not till about the time but I think that by the first of June we shall turn our faces northward.

I shall let you know everything in due season. The prospect is that we march through Richmond and perhaps Washington. It will be a long march, but we shall enter upon it with zeal and confidence, as it will be towards home.

I am going to write Dunham today about my uniform suit. I must have one soon and I shall hope to get Captain Russ to bring it to me. I shall be very careful of it so as to have it in good shape to wear when I get home.

I wondered why you did not mention the letters I sent you by Captain Russ, but it was hardly time for him to reach Dunkirk. Probably you got them Saturday. He has a thirty day leave of absence and will return early in June.

John Hunt promised to call and see you, also some others. We have just changed camp and are now located in a beautiful grove and I hope will not have to move again until we move toward home.

I am now quite near the hospital. About as far as from Mrs. Carpenter's to the locomotive works. Horace Allen goes home this morning and takes these letters along with him. I received day before yesterday a long and very touching letter from Mrs. Washburn. I pity her and all who suffer from this war. I shall send this to Stamford. I am very glad you are to go there. I think you will make yourself happy with the boys and I shall expect to see you soon. You had better find what days the mail leaves and what days it reaches Stamford and we will arrange our time of writing to correspond.

With love to Harry and Fred
W. Hyde

Only think of Jeff Davis in petticoats. If I were round I would turn in bloomers after this. Poor Jeff. The boots betrayed him. Thank God he is caught.

Saturday, May 27th

Camp 112th Regt N.Y. Vols.
Raleigh, N.C.
May 27th 1865

Dear Wife,

I am sorry you did not get the letter, as it is evident you did not write before Captain Russ started, in which I thought it so risky that I should not wish you to come here to Raleigh. At all events you had better have acted on your judgment and gone to Stamford, for you know that I would have been perfectly satisfied even if I had fixed my mind upon your coming here. I am sorry that you were disappointed in not receiving the usual letter written Thursday. I was overwhelmed with work last week and had not vigor to write. It rained two or three days last week very hard, Friday or Saturday. Friday there was a terrible thunderstorm. I pitied the poor sick fellows under canvas but today it is delightful, the air just cool enough. I think the extremes here are as great as with us at the north. The climate is milder but the changes from hot to cold weather are as great within 24 hours.

The mortality in the hospital has been very great. We have lost over a hundred men since we took those buildings.

We are now thoroughly renovating them, removing and burning up old bedding and purifying the walls and floor thoroughly and moving fever patients into tents. Fevers are much more successfully treated in tents than in wooden buildings. The reason is the air circulates more freely and the poison does not collect and fix itself on everything, as it does in a building.

I have the general charge of the whole hospital. Three other chaplains assist in visiting the wards of which there are 20. I have but four wards under my own peculiar charge. These I calculate to visit carefully twice a week and go through them every day. If any are in trouble or likely to die, I devote most time to them. I never calculate at any one time to spend more than an hour in the wards, because I find that it is not safe to breathe such an air too long. Though it is seldom, except near fever patients, that there is any offensive odor. We have some 50 contraband employees in and about the hospital besides nurses. There are 20 women in the kitchen and washing departments.

There is one surgeon in charge and eight assistant surgeons employed in the buildings. The hospital was called the finest in the southern Confederacy.

The Lord help the poor fellows elsewhere. It was in a horridly filthy condition and when we came there were over 300 sick Rebels. At present there are but 35. They received my visits as chaplain very kindly and are always glad to see me. I think not one of them but what is glad the war is over. Though most of them have no enthusiasm for the old Union.

They know they are whipped and it guiles them to acknowledge it. But that will soon pass away. They could not be driven into war again. The most of them that are left are suffering from wounds. I pity them. What a future! Wounded in the service of a rebellion against a government that was always only too lenient. Without means of support, dragged into a war whose object was to build the chains more rigidly about poor slaves. They will have no governmental aid in the future. I hope that associations in the south will provide homes for the disabled and that the support of these will be forced upon them whose property supported the rebellion. I think if I were sure of a hospital being kept up here I should be willing for a year or two to be a hospital chaplain. I could rent a house within a quarter of a mile. It is very healthy here. The land is high and rambling, the water good, all the streams are flowing. No stagnant marshes anywhere about. The only trouble would be society, which would soon be forthcoming. But the prospect is that the hospital will soon be abandoned and everything moved north. I am anxious for the time to come. I want to be with you and the children. I have ordered Dunham, in case my clothes cannot be sent by Russ or some man coming here, to be sent to Reverend G. D. Downey, agent, Christian Commission for me by express. I hope to hear from you at Stamford. May God keep you and the dear children in health. My regards to Mr. and Mrs. Wilder. I have had prayers in the wards, preaching at 10 at hospital, preaching at 2 in camp, 3 communions in the church in Raleigh and prayer meeting this evening.

Truly and affectionately,
William L. Hyde

Wednesday, May 31st

Camp 112th Regt N.Y. Vols.
Raleigh, N.C.
May 31st 1865

My dear Wife,

I received two letters from you today, the 21st and 25th. I felt much comforted at the calm, trustful, confident tone of your letters. You feel just as I would wish and I feel more secure and less anxious. Indeed my anxious feelings are only temporary. I sometimes look on the blue side of things which is not healthy.

I know we shall be taken care of somehow. I am very glad you invested the hundred in government securities. I wish I had ten thousand in them. If I had acted on my own judgment instead of that of Bookstaver, I should not have to sell my house when I did and the parish could have had it now for a parsonage. I hope they will succeed in obtaining it. I have joyful news for you. The order from the War Department mustering out our regiment is now here. It may take two or three weeks to complete the papers, but it will be done soon. So that you need not count on a very long stay at Stamford. I think I shall let Harry stay there till we get settled. Could you make the arrangement, in case the regiment should go to Jamestown, to leave Fred at Stamford. I should not want to stay in Jamestown and Dunkirk but a few days. Then I would return with you to Stamford and we all go east together. I do not make any calculations ahead. The future is uncertain. The orders that have come out since I began this letter leads me to think that the regiment will be mustered out here and be paid either at Hart Island near New York City or at Norfolk.

I presume I cannot get transportation for my horse beyond Baltimore unless we go from New Berne by propeller to New York. If I cannot, I shall ride him through to Chautauqua.

Some of the military men here want me to take a post chaplaincy. I would not hesitate, if I could choose my post, but I would be obliged in that case to go where I was sent and very likely I might not get into a climate that you could live in.

I see Mr. Whittlesey retaining his commission as major and has gone to Mississippi as one of the commissioners for the freedmen, appointed by General Howard.[38]

I suppose I might easily get into some business of the same kind if I chose to do so. I want much to get this letter off to you this morning. Yesterday was the 1st of June and the National Fast.[39] Services were held on the state house grounds at Raleigh, and we had a brigade service at 6 o'clock pm. I addressed the brigade and we had band music and religious exercises. At the close, I made a jest at parting address to the brigade, which evidently took very well.

I was very tired after it was over and went to bed early and had a grand sleep. We have got in the way of playing backgammon and dominoes here. Chaplain Palmer and I sat down after supper and I wiled away an hour. Backgammon was about all I was up to. I think with a curb, you could ride Frank. He is getting to be very manageable and is as handsome and spirited as ever.

We are in a most restless state here. Everybody is on tip too. We are ordered to be mustered out and yet the mustering officer says it will take them weeks to get the papers ready. The order specifies all whose term expires the 30th of September. My time is not out until the 10th of October and I am afraid I may be obliged to make a special request. I am going to see the officer today about it.

I never shall cease to feel grateful to Dr. Rogers for his kindness to you. Also to Carrie. She is quiet but she is kind. I received the stamp you sent. You speak of an expression in Nannie's letter about your weak eyes. I understood it. You wrote something about reading fine point about President Lincoln's funeral or else being out in the sun, and that your eyes were suffering from the effects.

I want you to continue to write me until I give you directions to stop.

You will be informed of any change in the program for the future. Our return will probably be considerably delayed.

I can't bear the suspense. I want it over. Never have I felt so restless and every officer is in the same condition.

I must close or fail [to send off] the mail.

Affectionately your husband,
William L. Hyde

Love to the boys.

Thursday, June 1st

Headquarters, 1st Brig. 2nd Div. 10th A. C.
Raleigh, N.C.
June 1, 1865

Circular

Today having been appointed by the President of the United States as a day of "humiliation and mourning." Divine Service will be held at 6 o'clock pm on the brigade color line under the direction of Chaplain W. L. Hyde, 112th New York Volunteers.

Officers and men will wear their side arms.

By order of
Colonel A. M. Barney
142nd New York Volunteers
Commanding, Brigade

Sunday, June 4th

Camp 112th Regiment New York Volunteers
Raleigh, N.C.
June 4th 1865

My dear Wife,

If you ever were so tired that your whole frame fairly throbbed, you can imagine how I am tonight. I was at the hospital from 9 to 12. Preached in camp at 2, went to hospital and through 3 wards, now at 4. Then attended the burial of 6 soldiers who had died and have just eaten my supper. After supper I am going up to a prayer meeting.

I ride up and back so that I have no fatigue of walking. I have not heard from you since yours of the 25th. I suppose you did not write until you left for Stamford. I hope you were not deluded by the reports of the regiment having been ordered to New York. For although there are orders here for the regiment to be mustered out immediately, it will take two or three weeks time to do it. I have no hopes of getting home before July, if as early.

But I am going to be patient and not worry in the least. My health is improving. I get cherries and eggs now. Once in a while get real cow's milk so that I am not confined to the dry coarse food we have been existing upon. I find it makes a great difference with me. We have two Philadelphia ladies at the hospital. They are real ladies, warm hearted, Christian women who have done an untold amount of good. One of them, a young widow lady, Mrs. Beck, is in a very critical condition. She has a gastric trouble, which I fear is the result of imbibing animal poison and there is danger of either ulcerations or typhoid fever setting in. Mrs. Harris, the other lady, says that she has an obstinate trouble of the bowels and they both feel that they must leave as soon as possible. But poor Mrs. Beck is too feeble today to leave.

We hope that she may be able, early in the week, to get away. Oh what exciting times we are having. Nothing talked of but how to get home. All the men discussing the probabilities of how long we are to remain here. Every officer here read and repeated the various orders relative to discharging troops until he knows to a word what they are and then all officers are busy as bees working on the rolls of their companies. Men are coming daily from different points out of the department to the regiment to be mustered out with it Monday. We hear all sorts of rumors as to time when and place where. The mustering officer says we are to be mustered out here and to be paid here. If so, it will be very difficult getting our horses home. It will cost $75, I think, unless some of the boys want to ride, though I shall ride myself, with others through Richmond to Washington. I hope, however, we will be able to get transportation to New York by paying a small price. The only thing that now stands in the way of the immediate muster out of the regiment is the rolls and the mustering officer who is slower than cold tar.

About 200 men are to be sent away from the hospital tomorrow, some to Wilmington and others to New Berne. I expect Captain Russ back this week and with him my clothes. I am sorely in need of some good clothes and shirts. Why I have been this month, wearing out my thick woolen shirt and I have no other. I have a pair of cotton drawers, badly torn, but it is warm enough to do without them.

If the regiment should go to New York City, I shall come direct to Stamford. I could take a steamer to Catskill Landing and having my horse with me, I could ride through to Stamford in a day or two, horseback.

If the regiment goes to Elmira, I think I shall have my horse sent to Jamestown and I shall go immediately the other way to you.

Then we will go to Maine or wherever, we think best. If the government pays me the three months extra pay, I have about $1,000 coming to me.

I received your letter of the 29th this morning. I hope you found three letters at Stamford waiting for you.

Truly, etc.
William L. Hyde

Thursday, June 8th

Camp 112th Regt N.Y. Vols.
Raleigh, N.C.
June 8th 1865

My dear Wife,

The closing scenes of our sojourn in Raleigh are close at hand. The 112th New York are already on their way. The 117th are to be mustered out this afternoon. Tomorrow (Friday) we are to dissolve our partnership with Uncle Samuel and probably will have the opportunity of being citizens before night. We are to move by way of Weldon to City Point and then take transportation for New York. I believe the government gives us transportation to Hart Island. If so, probably the regiment will scatter as soon as paid. If we go to Jamestown to be paid off, we shall have a grand reception no doubt. It will take four days to march from Weldon to City Point. We can't march [in] such weather as this more than 15 to 20 miles a day. Before you receive this we shall be on the march. You will not get another letter from me dated Raleigh. I presume the next you hear will be by telegram from New York or letter from City Point, Virginia. If we go direct to Elmira and Jamestown, I think your best way will be to wait my writing. If I should wish to tarry only a day in Jamestown just now, it would not be worth your while to leave Stamford and go there only to return again immediately. So make no plans. If we should stay at Hart Island a week, I should have you come down to the city. In case I send for you to come to Jamestown, you had better make arrangements to leave Fred and Harry both. I feel nervous at the thought that my face, in the good providence of God, is to soon to be turned home. Three years of such life as I have lived has left its mark upon me. I am older. I have seen misery in almost every conceivable form. I know more of men than before, and I hope am better prepared in something to appreciate the blessings of a quiet home.

I know not what the Lord has in store for me, but I trust his goodness. You must know that I had a real fight about my horse. He was stolen from a post in the street one day when I was downtown and I thought I never should see him again. I had bills posted and an advertisement in the papers. But a man came in with him the next day. He was found out on the Holly Springs Road. When found he was loose but a negro had been seen riding him a while before. Probably he got alarmed and fearing detection, left him. I assure you I was glad enough to see him come back.

It would have amused you to see the men of the regiment. They formed a circle around him and hurrahed and I really believe were as glad to see him as if he had been a lost child. Many a terrible threat had been uttered against the man who should be found having stolen him. We got back just in time for faithful Fisk to take [him] along on the road with the other horses. We are to go by rail to Weldon or Gaston, but the horses will have to be sent by the traveled road because there is not transportation sufficient to accommodate horses and men on the cars. Several of our officers are very nervous, fearing they may be forced to remain in the service. Our recruits go into the Forty-Seventh New York. Some of the young officers will have to go with them. George Dixon fears he will have to stay. I guess he has cause for it. George makes a fine appearing captain. I don't think he takes the care of his company he ought to. He is too boyish. Captain Ticknor, I presume, will have to stay. He is a first rate officer. I could remain if I wished to do so and may be forced to remain a few weeks, volsus-volsus.[40] But I think I have some strings, which I could pull, even in case they wanted to keep me, that would be effective. I have not a single plan beyond getting back to you. I think I shall go east before attempting to get settled again, but I may conclude to make an effort first to get planted before I go to rambling.

I expect Captain Russ with my clothes tonight or at least as soon as tomorrow morning. If not, I shall meet him somewhere or get them sometime. I don't worry about them. I paid $25 to get my horse back and it cost $12.50 to advertise. But $37.50 is not $200. Oh time fly, fly. I want the hour of return to come speedily.

Friday morning. The mail leaves at 10 o'clock. I thought I would delay sending this letter to the last moment. We shall hardly get mustered out before Monday. I hear the mustering officers have not clerks enough to do all their necessary business in time. I would write all day today and till midnight to be able to get away one day sooner. Well it will not be long at the longest. We do not yet know what officers have to stay. The weather is beautiful, very warm in the middle of the day. The mornings and nights are delightful. I have not heard of a single case of wanton outrage in any part of South Carolina since the war was over. I think the prospects of returning, quite and very flattering.

The negros, when properly used and instructed, do not seem to be disposed to any lawlessness and there are no idlers allowed to live in that trade.

Lovingly your husband,
William L. Hyde

It is thought we shall go from City Point to New York City and thence on to Buffalo.

Sunday, June 11th

Sabbath pm
Raleigh, N.C.
June 11th 1865

My dear Wife,

We are not yet on our way as I told you in Thursday's letter. I thought we should be at this time. It is a large job to untie all the red tape with which we have been bound for three years past. We are now expecting to be mustered our tomorrow and to start for City Point the next day. You need not write again to me until you receive further directions. I shall leave word to have any letters that may come within 4 days of our leaving sent to Fort Monroe, care of the Christian Commission, simply directed to Reverend William L. Hyde. Captain Russ is expected here tonight or tomorrow. He may be delayed longer, but I hardly think beyond that time. If he comes before I go, I shall be glad. If not, I shall have my clothes forwarded directly to Fort Monroe if they come within 4 days and to New York City if they are longer delayed.

I have such good success in getting things sent me. I do not fear they can be lost.

I hope to see you before two Sabbaths more have passed. How pleasant it will be to go to church together! How pleasant to have Fred and Harry with us. How pleasant to sit down and sing the old familiar home tunes. I had worship today under the trees. It was quite warm. This is the last time I shall ever meet the regiment at Sunday service in the field. I felt an inspiration for the services for the circumstances. This forenoon, I went to the Presbyterian Church and heard a young minister preach a very ordinary sermon. It did seem so pleasant to hear female voices in the singing.

The weather here is delicious. It is very warm in the sun, but under the trees nothing can be more dreamily delicious than this climate. I would not object to living in the old "North State" if there was anything I could do in the way of my profession. I should want plenty of northern friends if I settled here or anywhere south. We do not get mail and papers here with the regularity I would expect. The mail comes by way of the canal from Norfolk to New Berne and it takes sometimes three days to make the passage.

I guess somebody is sneaking piles of money out of the government using these old boats.

I see Orrin Stevens, Captain Stevens' son and young Davidson of Forestville, both of them railroad conductors. They run from Raleigh to Morehead City. Lieutenant Hawley has the appointment here of military conductor and I have no doubt he will get a grand position on some of these roads, if he will take it. The government retains him for three months longer. There are four lieutenants and two captains held. Dixon and Russ are the captains. Dixon, however, has resigned and may succeed in getting out. I see the New York City people are making fools of themselves and showing themselves as rowdies and disagreeable as ever. The reception of General Grant was a great ovation and must have been to the general a great bore. I believe I have seen all the great generals, except Thomas and Sheridan.[41]

I find the boys are very impatient here. They all want to be moving on to their homes. Well it will soon come. Enjoy all you can at Stamford. I presume now I shall send for you to come to Chautauqua. Perhaps taking both the boys with you and perhaps leaving Harry there still. I must make him some nice gift. What shall it be? If you should have occasion to write me as soon as you get this, you can direct to me without regiment, simply W. L. H., Care of A. J. Manley, Esquire, 14 Warren Street, New York City. I may be in New York long enough to run up there.

The probabilities are that we should be landed in Jersey City and take the railroad direct to Buffalo. If you wish, you and Fred can start for Buffalo on the receipt of this to board there somewhere until I can.

Very affectionately,
William

Love to the boys.
They shall have a good time on my return.

> Two days after writing this letter home, Chaplain Hyde and the majority of the regiment were mustered out of military service and began the slow journey back to their families and the Empire State.[42] After thirty-three months as the regimental chaplain, providing spiritual and physical comfort to those in need, William L. Hyde's war was finally over.
>
> Hyde returned to his family and eventually settled in Dunkirk, New York, for approximately one year before moving to Ripley, to take up the position as pastor for the local Presbyterian Church. Between 1871 and 1874, he was pastor for the Presbyterian Church in Sherman, New York. Afterwards, for reasons unknown, Hyde switched his profession to the field of education, becoming a school principal in Ovid, NY and later a teacher at a private school in Jamestown. He also did editorial work for the Jamestown Journal and served in the ministry as a supply clergyman.

In 1885, twenty years after the war, Hyde applied to the government for a disability pension for injuries suffered during the Bermuda Hundred Campaign. As a testament to Hyde's service with the 112th, seven former regimental officers supported Hyde's request, paying him the greatest tribute when they wrote "that he came to the regiment physically sound and capable of great endurance, as was shown by his constant and multifarious labors for the good of the regiment, in and beyond the line of his duty; that in camp or on the march, in the hospital, or on the field of battle, he was ever found in the place of duty; untiring in his efforts to promote the morals, or to mitigate the sufferings of his comrades, or to do the thousand nameless acts of kindness which touched some human need."[43]

Chaplain Hyde answered his last roll call at 4:15 pm on July 31, 1896, and passed into eternal rest. At his funeral service, held at the Jamestown First Presbyterian Church, over 150 Union veterans of the late war attended. As Hyde's remains lay in state, his casket was draped with an American flag and upon the flag rested a closed Bible.

Appendix A: Mortuary Records

The following company mortuary reports were transcribed from Hyde's original reports. The names, dates, locations, and causes of death have been corrected or added, when necessary, using a combination of the Annual Report of the Adjutant General of the State of New York for the Year 1903; Registers of the 107th–113th Regiments of Infantry, Hyde's regimental history of the 112th and the service records from the National Archives.

The original report covering the Field and Staff element of the regiment was missing from Hyde's papers and has been reconstructed by the editor using Hyde's report format. A legend is provided to assist in determining the rank of each soldier.

Rank Abbreviations

Col	Colonel
Corp	Corporal
LtCol	Lieutenant Colonel
Mus	Musician
Ord Sgt	Ordnance Sergeant
P	Private
Sgt	Sergeant
Surg	Surgeon
1st Sgt	First Sergeant
1st Lt	First Lieutenant
2nd Lt	Second Lieutenant
RQM	Regimental Quartermaster

Mortuary List of Field and Staff, 112th New York State Volunteers

Name	Rank	Date of Death	Location of Death	Cause of Death
Franklin Waters	RQM	Oct 3, 1863	Beaufort, SC	Died of disease
Elial F. Carpenter	LtCol	May 18, 1864	Bermuda Hundred, Va	Wounds received in action
Jeremiah C. Drake	Col	June 2, 1864	Cold Harbor, Va	Killed in action
Hiram Vorce	Ord Sgt	June 23, 1864	Petersburg, Va	Killed in action
John F. Smith	Col	Jan 18, 1865	Fort Fisher, NC	Wounds received in action
Charles E. Washburn	Surg	Apr 10, 1865	Magnolia Station, NC	Died of disease

Mortuary List of Company A, 112th New York State Volunteers

Name	Rank	Date of Death	Location of Death	Cause of Death
Russell H. Dean	P	Dec 16, 1862	Suffolk, VA	Fever

Name	Rank	Date of Death	Location of Death	Cause of Death
Henry H. Peck	P	Jul 3, 1863	White House, VA	Fever
Enos C. Hunt	Sgt	Nov 7, 1863	Jamestown, NY	Diarrhea
George Simpson	P	Mar 31, 1864	Jacksonville, FL	Pyemia
Willard Cass	P	May 6, 1864	Beaufort, SC	Died of disease
Abram Danforth	P	May 16, 1864	Near Fort Darling, VA	Killed in action
Samuel S. Staples	P	Jun 1, 1864	Cold Harbor, VA	Killed in action
Horace W. Barber	Corp	Jun 8, 1864	White House, VA	Wounds received in action
Edward Shelters	P	Jun 10, 1864	Hampton, VA	Wounds received in action
John Marvin Arthur	P	Jun 16, 1864	Washington, DC	Wounds received in action
Samuel G. Sherwin	1st Lt	Jun 28, 1864	Near Petersburg, VA	Killed on duty
Lauren Arnold	P	Jul 6, 1864	Near Petersburg, VA	Killed on duty
Michael Dolan	P	Aug 26, 1864	Hampton, VA	Malarial fever
Charlie W. West	P	Sep 29, 1864	Chapin's Farm, VA	Killed in action
Wesley Bennett	P	Oct 26, 1864	10th A. C. Hospital	Typhoid fever
Thomas Brown	P	Jan 3, 1865	Salisbury, NC	Died of disease
Lyman H. Stoddard	Corp	Jan 13, 1865	Salisbury, NC	Died of disease
Aaron Hill	P	Jan 15, 1865	Fort Fisher, NC	Killed in action

Mortuary List of Company B, 112th New York State Volunteers

Name	Rank	Date of Death	Location of Death	Cause of Death
Henry W. Smith	P	Oct 22, 1862	Suffolk, VA	Fever
Hugh O. Jones	P	Nov 15, 1862	Suffolk, VA	Diarrhea
William C. Chamberlim	Corp	Nov 23, 1862	Suffolk, VA	Fever
Theron Reed	Corp	Nov 29, 1862	Suffolk, VA	Fever
William S. Hart	P	May 1, 1863	Fredonia, NY	Fever
James Alverson	P	Jul 12, 1863	Portsmouth, VA	Fever
Henry A. Benjamin	P	Sep 14, 1863	Folly Island, SC	Heart disease
Norman Cook	P	Sep 27, 1863	USS *Arago*	Diarrhea
Daniel B. Thayer	Mus	Oct 14, 1863	Fort Schyler, NY	Diarrhea
Aldo D. Weatherwax	P	Oct 24, 1863	Folly Island, SC	Fever
Lawrence W. Rolph	P	Nov 5, 1863	Beaufort, SC	Diarrhea
John A. Gilbert	Sgt	Nov 10, 1863	Fredonia, NY	Diarrhea
Daniel S. Barhite	P	Dec 13, 1863	Ellington, NY	Diarrhea
Kies Tracy	Corp	Mar 14, 1864	Stockton, NY	Chronic Diarrhea
Milton E. Phillips	P	Apr 5, 1864	Jacksonville, FL	Diphtheria
Squire H. Shaw	Corp	Jun 3, 1864	Cold Harbor, VA	Wounds received in action
John W. Palmeter	P	Jun 20, 1864	Washington, DC	Wounds received in action
John K. Post	P	Jun 21, 1864	Washington, DC	Wounds received in action
George T. Westly	P	Oct 27, 1864	Near Deep Bottom, VA	Wounds received in action
William W. Story	P	Oct 28, 1864	Near Deep Bottom, VA	Wounds received in action
Walter J. Hart	Corp	Oct 29, 1864	Near Deep Bottom, VA	Wounds received in action
Andrew A. Sprague	P	Dec 7, 1864	Jones Landing, VA	Died of disease
Roswell W. Graves	Corp	Dec 7, 1864	Charlotte, NY	Abscess on lungs
Simon Bigalow	P	Dec 10, 1864	Salisbury, NC	Starvation
Charles E. Fisk	P	Dec 10, 1864	Salisbury, NC	Starvation
Eber W. Starr	P	Dec 31, 1864	DeVall's Bluff, AR	Died of disease
Mason C. Thompson	P	Feb 23, 1865	Fort Fisher, NC	Fever
Addison Dalrymple	P	Feb 27, 1865	Fort Fisher, NC	Typhoid fever
John S. Edgar	P	Apr 1, 1865	Faison, NC	Fever
George W. Giffin[1]	P	Sep 29, 1864	Salisbury, NC	Died of disease
George W. Clough	P	Jun 4, 1865	Raleigh, NC	Fever
J. Wesley Shaw	P	Jul 30, 1865	Petersburg, VA	Killed

Mortuary List of Company C, 112th New York State Volunteers

Name	Rank	Date of Death	Location of Death	Cause of Death
Ira A. Knowlton	P	Oct 13, 1862	Suffolk, VA	Fever
Charles H. Barhite	Corp	Oct 29, 1862	Suffolk, VA	Dysentery
Malcom W. Gage	P	Dec 13, 1862	Suffolk, VA	Measles
George A. Watson	Sgt	Jan 30, 1863	Deserted House, VA	Wounds received in action
George E. Squires	P	Feb 26, 1863	Suffolk, VA	Dysentery
Sumner Boss	P	Sep 2, 1863	Folly Island, SC	Fever
Darius VanVliet	P	Oct 15, 1863	Fort Schuyler, NY	Diarrhea
Samuel S. McKee	P	Oct 17, 1863	Folly Island, SC	Fever
John H. Scott	P	Oct 22, 1863	Beaufort, SC	Disease of head
James G. Walrod	P	Oct 29, 1863	Beaufort, SC	Diarrhea
Thomas W. Frink	P	Nov 3, 1863	Beaufort, SC	Diarrhea
Barton Merritt	P	Dec 17, 1863	Folly Island, SC	Fever
David Mills	P	Jan 3, 1864	Beaufort, SC	Diarrhea
Frederick B. Scott	P	Jan 13, 1864	Folly Island, SC	Fever
William B. Sharp	P	Jan 18, 1864	Folly Island, SC	Dysentery
Franklin Harrington	P	May 16, 1864	Proctor's Creek, VA	Wounds received in action
Joseph Barna	P	Jun 1, 1864	Cold Harbor, VA	Killed in action
Robert Erath	P	Jun 1, 1864	Cold Harbor, VA	Killed in action
James M. Potter	Corp	Jun 1, 1864	Cold Harbor, VA	Killed in battle
Simeon L. Allen	Corp	Jun 1, 1864	Cold Harbor, VA	Killed in battle
David S. Crowell	Corp	Jun 1, 1864	Cold Harbor, VA	Killed in battle
Henry Mann	P	Jun 14, 1864	Hanover, NY	Chronic diarrhea
Philip McEvoy	Corp	Jun 30, 1864	Near Petersburg, VA	Killed on duty
Lewis Scofield	P	Jul 1, 1864	Washington, DC	Wounds received in action
Daniel E. Bullock	P	Sep 29, 1864	Chapin's Farm, VA	Killed in action
John Smith	P	Sep 29, 1864	Chapin's Farm, VA	Killed in action
Henry Warner	P	Sep 29, 1864	Chapin's Farm, VA	Killed in action
Albert J. Weaver	P	Sep 29, 1864	Chapin's Farm, VA	Killed in action
Walter A. Coonrod	P	Oct 27, 1864	Darbytown Road, VA	Killed in action
Franklin Bullock	P	Oct 27, 1864	Darbytown Road, VA	Killed in action
Willard Kiny	Corp	Nov 6, 1864	Cherry Creek, NY	Wounds received in action
John M. Myers	P	Dec 5, 1864	Salisbury, NC	Disease
James Stafford	P	Dec 10, 1864	Hampton, VA	Wounds received in action
Paul Horvath	P	Jan 15, 1865	Fort Fisher, NC	Killed in action
William McLaughlin	P	Mar 20, 1865	Annapolis, MD	Disease contracted in rebel prison
Henry H. Pierce	P	Apr 8, 1865	Willet's Point, NY	Erysipelas

Mortuary Record of Company D, 112th New York State Volunteers

Name	Rank	Date of Death	Location of Death	Cause of Death
Daniel M. Waite	Corp	Oct 19, 1862	Suffolk, VA	Marasmus
David Hagius	P	Nov 18, 1862	Suffolk, VA	Pneumonia
James Lewis	P	Dec 26, 1862	Suffolk, VA	Fever
Edwin B. Leach	P	Aug 10, 1863	Portsmouth, VA	Congestive fever
Charles Neil	Corp	Aug 28, 1863	Folly Island, SC	Inflammation bowels
John Tezepher	P	Sep 25, 1863	Folly Island, SC	Inflammation bowels
F. S. Lanning	Sgt	Oct 7, 1863	Folly Island, SC	Heart disease
Richard W. Gleason	Corp	Nov 7, 1863	Harmony, NY	Chronic diarrhea
Benjamin F. Hurlburt	Corp	Jun 1, 1864	Cold Harbor, VA	Killed in action
Homer Austin	P	Jun 1, 1864	Cold Harbor, VA	Killed in action
James A. Doig	P	Jun 1, 1864	Cold Harbor, VA	Killed in action
James G. Kean	P	Jun 1, 1864	Cold Harbor, VA	Killed in action
Isaac P. Miracle	P	Jun 1, 1864	Cold Harbor, VA	Killed in action
Philip Mark	P	Jun 1, 1864	Cold Harbor, VA	Killed in action

Appendix A

Name	Rank	Date of Death	Location of Death	Cause of Death
Henry Findley	P	Jun 2, 1864	Cold Harbor, VA	Killed in action
Martin Eddy	P	Jun 6, 1864	Cold Harbor, VA	Wounds received in action
Irvin E. Braley	P	Jun 12, 1864	Hampton, VA	Wounds received in action
Gardner R. C. Williams	Sgt	Aug 9, 1864	Fort Monroe, VA	Wounds received in action
Stephen Heath	Corp	Sep 29, 1864	Chapin's Farm, VA	Killed in action
John Johnson	P	Nov 13, 1864	Hampton, VA	Wounds received in action
Hiram Dickson	P	Jan 18, 1865	Hampton, VA	Wounds and diarrhea
John Springer	Corp	Jan 18, 1865	Fort Fisher, NC	Wound and diarrhea
John Esselink	P	Feb 7, 1865	Hampton, VA	Gunshot wound
Conrad Sicke	P	Feb 24, 1865	Fort Fisher, NC	Lung fever
Sylvester E. Chapin	P	Mar 27, 1865	Wilmington, NC	Fever

Mortuary Record of Company E, 112th New York State Volunteers

Name	Rank	Date of Death	Location of Death	Cause of Death
Andre William Matteson	Sgt	Oct 27, 1862	Suffolk, VA	Fever
Hollister H. Peck	Corp	Dec 4, 1862	Suffolk, VA	Fever
Spencer Manley	P	Dec 29, 1862	Suffolk, VA	Fever
Ellery C. Belden	P	Jan 4, 1863	Suffolk, VA	Fever
Frank M. Crosgrove	P	Jan 25, 1863	Suffolk, VA	Fever
Albert Baker	Corp	Apr 16, 1863	Suffolk, VA	Killed in action
A. J. Boyden	P	Jun 29, 1863	Hampton, VA	Fever
Thomas Sparkes	P	Jul 24, 1863	Portsmouth, VA	Diarrhea
George R. Atkinson	P	Jul 25, 1863	Portsmouth, VA	Diarrhea and fever
Peter Lawson	P	Oct 8, 1863	Folly Island, SC	Dysentery
Daniel B. Thayer	Mus	Oct 14, 1863	Folly Island, SC	Chronic diarrhea
Augustus E. Phetteplace	P	Oct 21, 1863	Fort Schuyler, NY	Dysentery
Charles Harmon	P	Oct 23, 1863	Folly Island, SC	Gastric fever
Horace A. Edwards	P	Oct 27, 1863	Beaufort, SC	Diarrhea
Horatio N. Bowers	P	Nov 24, 1863	Folly Island, SC	Diarrhea
Charles H. Bushee	P	Dec 8, 1863	Folly Island, SC	Diarrhea
Henry Eslor	P	Dec 24, 1863	Beaufort, SC	Diarrhea
Galen Cluxton	P	Dec 29, 1863	Beaufort, SC	Diarrhea
Charles P. Young	P	May 6, 1864	Hilton Head, SC	Diarrhea
Nathan Edmonds	P	Jun 1, 1864	Cold Harbor, VA	Killed in action
Hamilton Lenox	P	Jun 1, 1864	Cold Harbor, VA	Killed in action
John Stowell	P	Jun 1, 1864	Cold Harbor, VA	Killed in action
John Tewinkle	P	Jun 1, 1864	Cold Harbor, VA	Killed in action
John Wienman	P	Jun 1, 1864	Cold Harbor, VA	Killed in action
John C. Eddy	P	Jun 1, 1864	Cold Harbor, VA	Missing in action
F. J. Ruhling	Sgt	Jun 18, 1864	Hampton, VA	Wounds received in action
Hiram Vorce	Sgt	Jun 28, 1864	Near Petersburg, VA	Killed on duty
Levi J. Knapp	P	Jul 3, 1864	Philadelphia, PA	Wounds received in action
Addison P. Green	P	Jul 20, 1864	Washington, DC	Wounds received in action
Henry C. Dayton	P	Jul 20, 1864	Halstead, NY	Chronic diarrhea
William Tewinkle	P	Sep 22, 1864	Philadelphia, VA	Died of disease
John B. Spencer	P	Sep 26, 1864	Mayville, NY	Died of disease
Cornelius M. Tiffany	P	Sep 28, 1864	David's Island, NY	Chronic diarrhea
John Carleson	P	Oct 27, 1864	Boydton Plank Road, VA	Killed in action
Leonard L. Dodge	P	Jan 15, 1865	Fort Fisher, NC	Killed in action
Peter J. Peterson	P	Jan 15, 1865	Fort Fisher, NC	Wounds received in action
Andrew Anderson	P	Jan 16, 1865	Fort Fisher, NC	Wounds received in action
Andrew Bennett	P	Feb 16, 1865	Salisbury, NC	Disease

Left: Gardner R. C. Williams enlisted at Clymer, New York, as a corporal in Company D, 112th New York Volunteers. He died from wounds received at Petersburg, Virginia. *Right:* Samuel O. Wilcox enlisted at Chautauqua, New York, as a private in Company H, 112th New York Volunteers. He died of disease at Suffolk, Virginia.

Name	Rank	Date of Death	Location of Death	Cause of Death
Charles M. Carr	P	Apr 14, 1865	Wilmington, NC	Fever
William F. Onley	P	Apr 19, 1865	Wilmington, NC	Fever
Emmet C. Blanding	P	May 20, 1865	Beaufort, NC	Wounds received in action
Simon Beyer	P	Sep 30, 1865	Salisbury, NC	Disease
John P. McDonald	P	Nov 18, 1865	Salisbury, NC	Disease

Mortuary Record of Company F, 112th New York State Volunteers

Name	Rank	Date of Death	Location of Death	Cause of Death
Franklin W. Daniels	P	Oct 20, 1862	Suffolk, VA	Fever & dysentery
Gilman Bartlett	P	Dec 28, 1862	Suffolk, VA	Fever
Marshal C. Dean	P	Mar 22, 1863	Suffolk, VA	Fever
John J. Losee	P	Apr 11, 1863	Suffolk, VA	Fever
Jared Ploss	P	Nov 24, 1863	Harmony, NY	Diarrhea
Charles J. Winchester	Corp	Dec 17, 1863	Folly Island, SC	Diarrhea
Michael O'Brien	Corp	May 24, 1864	Hospital, City Point, VA	Wounds received in action
Charles H. Baker	Sgt	Jun 1, 1864	Cold Harbor, VA	Killed in action
Sylvester M. Hart	P	Jun 1, 1864	Cold Harbor, VA	Killed in action
Algernon D. Hazard	Corp	Jun 7, 1864	White House, VA	Wounds received in action
Woodley W. Booty	P	Jun 13, 1864	Washington, DC	Wounds received in action
Silas Tiffany	P	Jul 27, 1864	Near Petersburg, VA	Fever
Joseph F. Hall	Sgt	Aug 12, 1864	Jamestown, NY	Consumption

Name	Rank	Date of Death	Location of Death	Cause of Death
Judson F. Geer	P	Aug 19, 1864	Washington, DC	Wounds received in action
John Peters	P	Sep 17, 1864	Steamer *Cosmopolitan*	Fever & dysentery
Joseph H. Button	Corp	Jan 15, 1865	Fort Fisher, NC	Killed in action
Hiram Hayden	Corp	Jan 15, 1865	Fort Fisher, NC	Killed in action
Henry Bowen	P	Jan 15, 1865	Fort Fisher, NC	Killed in action
William Thornton	P	Jan 15, 1865	Fort Fisher, NC	Killed in action
William Raspus	P	Jan 15, 1865	Fort Fisher, NC	Killed in action
David Broadhead	P	Feb 18, 1865	Federal Point, NC	Fever
John E. Eames	P	Mar 17, 1865	Fort Schuyler, NY	Wounds received in action
Cornelius VanGeen	P	Apr 7, 1865	Wilmington, NC	Fever

Mortuary Record of Company G, 112th New York State Volunteers

Name	Rank	Date of Death	Location of Death	Cause of Death
Lester Merriman	P	Oct 29, 1862	Suffolk, VA	Fever
Harvey Potter	P	Oct 31, 1862	Suffolk, VA	Fever
Frank L. Wilson	Sgt	Nov 3, 1862	Suffolk, VA	Fever
Paul Squimer	P	Dec 15, 1862	Suffolk, VA	Fever
William Johnson	P	Jul 29, 1863	Portsmouth, VA	Fever
Frank C. Bullock	Corp	Aug 31, 1863	Folly Island, SC	Fever
Samuel P. Bloomfield	P	Oct 1, 1863	Hampton, VA	Fever
Christian Russ	P	Oct 11, 1863	Folly Island, SC	Fever & dysentery
Nash Abbot	P	Oct 18, 1863	Beaufort, SC	Diarrhea
Caleb H. Schaffer	P	Nov 23, 1863	Folly Island, SC	Diarrhea
William Baldwin	Corp	May 3, 1864	Dunkirk, NY	Diarrhea
Charles W. Lawrence	P	May 6, 1864	Hilton Head, SC	Diarrhea
Orrin S. Camp	P	May 24, 1864	Bermuda Hundred, VA	Killed on duty
William Laine	P	Jun 1, 1864	Cold Harbor, VA	Killed in action
William Pease	P	Jun 1, 1864	Cold Harbor, VA	Killed in action
Almond Ploss	P	Jun 1, 1864	Cold Harbor, VA	Killed in action
Thomas Binns	P	Jun 1, 1864	Cold Harbor, VA	Killed in action
Gilman Shirley	P	Jun 1, 1864	Cold Harbor, VA	Killed in action
Dewitt C. Tew	P	Jun 1, 1864	Cold Harbor, VA	Killed in action
Fred Bartmann	P	Jun 2, [3rd] 1864	Cold Harbor, VA	Wounds received in action
Henry Baldwin	P	Jun 18, 1864	Hampton, VA	Wounds received in action
Robert Henry	P	Jun 25, 1864	Near Petersburg, VA	Killed on duty
James Cahall	P	Jun 25, 1864	Philadelphia, PA	Wounds received in action
James A. Dwyer	P	Dec 29, 1864	City Point, VA	Heart
William Dupledge	P	Mar 28, 1865	Faisons Station, NC	Fever

Mortuary Record of Company H, 112th New York State Volunteers

Name	Rank	Date of Death	Location of Death	Cause of Death
John G. Mayborn	P	Nov 10, 1862	Suffolk, VA	Fever
Marcus Vanness	Corp	Nov 11, 1862	Suffolk, VA	Inflamed bowels
Walter S. Risley	p	Dec 17, 1862	Suffolk, VA	Measles
Charles H. Tucker	1st Sgt	Apr 14, 1863	Suffolk, VA	Wounds received in action
Henry Hayes	P	Apr 22, 1863	Hampton, VA	Diphtheria
James Davis	P	May 15, 1863	Carrsville, VA	Killed in action
Julius Stebbins	P	May 31, 1863	Suffolk, VA	Diphtheria
Samuel O. Wilcox	P	Jul 5, 1863	Hampton, VA	Diarrhea
George Thompson	P	Sep 25, 1863	Black Island, SC	Killed on duty
George W. Ellis	P	Oct 12, 1863	Folly Island, SC	Dysentery
Perry Heath	P	Oct 18, 1863	Folly Island, SC	Fever
B. S. Ferguson	P	Oct 24, 1863	Folly Island, SC	Dysentery
Conrad H. Mertz	P	Oct 25, 1863	Fort Schuyler, NY	Diarrhea

Name	Rank	Date of Death	Location of Death	Cause of Death
James Combs	P	Nov 1, 1863	Beaufort, SC	Diarrhea
Orwell Whitney	P	Nov 11, 1863	Washington, DC	Diarrhea
Loyal Allen	P	Nov 24, 1863	Folly Island, SC	Fever
William W. Lenox	P	Nov 31, 1863	Folly Island, SC	Fever
Isaac D. Miles	P	Dec 2, 1863	Beaufort, SC	Chronic diarrhea
William C. Keyes	Sgt	Jun 1, 1864	Cold Harbor, VA	Killed
Robert L. Coe	Corp	Jun 1, 1864	Cold Harbor, VA	Killed
John E. Freeman	Corp	Jun 1, 1864	Cold Harbor, VA	Killed
Nelson L. Wallace	P	Jun 1, 1864	Cold Harbor, VA	Killed
Chester S. Hannum	Sgt	Jun 2, 864	Cold Harbor, VA	Wounds received in action
William F. Smith	P	Jun 21, 1864	Washington, DC	Wounds received in action
William H. Weatherly	P	Jul 19, 1864	Hampton Hospital, VA	Killed
Roland D. Abbey	P	Sep 29, 1864	Chapin's Farm, VA	Killed
Robert Adkins	P	Sep 29, 1864	Chapin's Farm, VA	Killed
Charles Donaldson	P	Sep 29, 1864	Chapin's Farm, VA	Wounds received in action
Wallace Appleby	Corp	Sep 29, 1864	Chapin's Farm, VA	Killed
Henry B. Cushing	P	Sep 29, 1864	Chapin's Farm, VA	Killed
John A. Delain	P	Sep 29, 1864	Chapin's Farm, VA	Killed
Samuel Hull	P	Oct 27, 1864	Darbytown Road, VA	Killed
William H. Hubbard	P	Nov 5, 1864	Hampton, VA	Wounds received in action
Lewis Comstock	P	Jan 15, 1865	Fort Fisher, NC	Killed
Samuel Kenniston	P	Jan 15, 1865	Fort Fisher, NC	Killed
Emrelu Bushnell	P	Jan 15, 1865	Fort Fisher, NC	Killed
Patrick O'Brien	P	Mar 1, 1865	Fort Fisher, NC	Fever

Mortuary Record of Company I, 112th New York State Volunteers

Name	Rank	Date of Death	Location of Death	Cause of Death
Henry A. Duncan[2]	P	Oct 7, 1862	Suffolk, VA	Peritonitis
David M. Smith	P	Nov 14, 1862	Suffolk, VA	Fever
Charles E. Teed	P	Nov 23, 1862	Suffolk, VA	Measles
John C. Taylor	P	Feb 14, 1863	Suffolk, VA	Fever
William W. White	P	Apr 24, 1863	Suffolk, VA	Fever
James Apthorp	P	Aug 20, 1863	Fredonia, NY	Fever
Reed W. Cummings	P	Sep 12, 1863	Folly Island, SC	Fever
Eddy A. Hewes	Mus	Sep 27, 1863	Folly Island, SC	Heart disease
William J. Pierce	P	Oct 19, 1863	Folly Island, SC	Gastric fever
Charles E. Duncan	P	Nov 2, 1863	Folly Island, SC	Gastric fever
Cornelius W. Parker	Corp	Nov 24, 1863	Beaufort, SC	Diarrhea
Charles E. Wilson	P	Dec 12, 1863	Folly Island, SC	Diarrhea
John S. Williams	Sgt	Feb 1, 1864	Folly Island, SC	Erysipelas
Joel Tarbell	P	Feb 17, 1864	David's Island, NY	Chronic diarrhea
William Apthorp	P	Feb 17, 1864	Fredonia, NY	Diarrhea
Noble Doty	P	Jun 1, 1864	Cold Harbor, VA	Killed
H. J. Sweet	Corp	Jun 4, 1864	Rochester, NY	Chronic diarrhea
Fred A. Pierce	P	Jun 7, 1864	White House, VA	Wounds received in action
Asa A. Sweet	P	Jun 25, 1864	Near Petersburg	Killed
Norton Dowd	P	Jan 27, 1865	Fort Fisher, NC	Congestive chills
Hiram L. Smith	P	Apr 9, 1865	Wilmington, NC	Heart disease
Samuel Apthorp	P	Nov 2, 1864	Salisbury, NC	Diarrhea
George Apthorp	P	Nov 13, 1864	Salisbury, NC	Diarrhea
George W. Clute	P	Jan 2, 1865	Salisbury, NC	Chronic diarrhea & starvation
John A. Bockstanz	P	Apr 8, 1865	Wilmington, NC	Fever
George W. Kenada[3]	P	Apr 13, 1865	Hampton, VA	Chronic diarrhea
Joel A. Fisher	P	May 9, 1865	Hampton, VA	Fever

Mortuary Record of Company K, 112th New York State Volunteers

Name	Rank	Date of Death	Location of Death	Cause of Death
Richard Rockwell	P	Oct 22, 1862	Suffolk, VA	Fever
Albert Losee	P	Oct 23, 1862	Suffolk, VA	Fever
Warham S. Foot	P	Oct 27, 1862	Suffolk, VA	Fever
Otis A. Mason	P	Jan 9, 1863	Suffolk, VA	Fever & measles
James S. Corbet	P	Feb 2, 1863	Suffolk, VA	Fever
Frank Bronson	P	Feb 26, 1863	Suffolk, VA	Dysentery
Everett Shattuck	P	Jul 20, 1863	Suffolk, VA	Fever
Nelson Gage	P	Sep 13, 1863	Suffolk, VA	Fever
Marion Gardner	P	Oct 30, 1863	Folly Island, SC	Fever
Alfred Barber	P	Nov 11, 1863	Folly Island, SC	Diarrhea
Daniel A. Blanding	P	Nov 20, 1863	St. Augustine, FL	Diarrhea
Risley Cole	P	Feb 20, 1864	David's Island, NY	Dysentery
Carlos Smith	P	Apr 3, 1864	Ellington, NY	Diarrhea
Silas Phillips	P	May 13, 1864	Hilton Head, SC	Diarrhea
Loren White	Sgt	Jun 1, 1864	Cold Harbor, VA	Killed
Edwin T. Goodwin	Sgt	Jun 1, 1864	Cold Harbor, VA	Killed
Avery R. Gould	Corp	Jun 1, 1864	Cold Harbor, VA	Killed
Theodore Burr	P	Jun 19, 1864	Cold Harbor, VA	Wounds received in action
Samuel Bush	P	Jun 26, 1864	Near Petersburg, VA	Killed
Henry Hull	2nd Lt	July 3, 1864	Washinton, DC	Wounds received in action
Henry Sutton	P	July 18, 1864	Point of Rocks, VA	Fever
William Ferrin	P	Aug 1, 1864	New Orleans, LA	Chronic diarrhea
Smith Peacock	Corp	Aug 3, 1864	Point of Rocks, VA	Died of disease
John Guiles	P	Aug 15, 1864	Hampton, VA	Wounds received in action
George F. Mount	1st Lt	Aug 25, 1864	Bermuda Hundred, VA	Wounds received in action
F. W. Harris	P	Oct 27, 1864	Darbytown Road, VA	Killed in action
William Wilson	Corp	Nov 5, 1864	Jones Landing, VA	Wounds received in action
Samuel V. Mount	Corp	Jan 15, 1865	Fort Fisher, NC	Killed
Lyman Briggs	P	Apr 24, 1865	Buffalo, NY	Disease of the heart

Appendix B:
Dear Chaplain Hyde

The following war-dated letters were written to William Hyde while he served as chaplain with the Chautauqua Regiment. Although some of the letters are from former military comrades, most were written from relatives of soldiers who had served with Hyde and the 112th New York Volunteers.

Letter after letter, the writer offers Hyde their heartfelt appreciation for his kindness, caring and ministering to their ill or dying soldier. During the course of the war, Hyde's regiment suffered the loss of 327 soldiers, due to combat wounds, deaths or illness. These letters represent only a fraction of the correspondence between Chaplain Hyde and those grieving families back home.

Camp of the 72nd Regiment near Alexandria [VA]
October 3rd 1862

My Dear Sir,

On receipt of your letter of the 30th instant last evening, I was very much surprised to learn that you had concluded to go with the 112th and not with us and sincerely hope that there may yet be some mistake about the matter that will cause you to adhere to your original intention of casting your lot with this regiment.

I can assure you sir that a most unanimous welcome awaits you here and that we have endeavored to forward matters as speedily as circumstances would admit in order that the place might be secured to you. General Taylor had already made arrangements for a young man from his locality but we persuaded him to give way and allow you to receive the appointment instead. I am a little astonished at the alacrity of the military committee and also the officers of the 112th Regiment when they knew we were endeavoring to make place for you. Our little handful of men is gradually increasing and already number near 600 and even more convalescing from diseases and wounds to make up near 200 more so that with the recruits we are receiving it will not be long before the regiment will again be close on to the maximum in numbers. If circumstances have so changed that you cannot come with us I can assure you sir that you have our heartfelt wishes for your success and prosperity with the 112th or wherever you may go.

Our friend the major is at present acting brigade general but will probably be relieved in a few days when we hope and expect to find him bonafide colonel of our regiment.

I regret to have to inform you that Captain Abell had the misfortune to break his leg the day before yesterday by his horse falling over another captain's horse, which had fallen immediately in front of him.[1]

All is quiet in our vicinity.
Please remember me to Dr. Smith and oblige.

Yours Cordially,
C. K. Irwin[2]
To
Reverend W. Hyde
Dunkirk
Chautauqua County, NY

I would say that Captain Abell's case is not a bad one, as it is only a simple fracture of the shinbone a few inches above the ankle. The captain will probably go home in a few days to remain 4 or 5 weeks recruiting.

> *Irwin obviously expected Hyde to muster as the chaplain with the 72nd New York Infantry. He does not hide his disappointment with the officers of the 112th in their quest to acquire Hyde as their chaplain. Three months after this letter, Reverend William R. Eastman mustered into service as chaplain with the 72nd.*

Sherman [NY]
November 20th 1862

Mr. Hyde
Dear Sir,

I received your kind letter last Saturday evening, which truly afforded me comfort in this time of deep affliction. It is great comfort to know that my husband had good care and surgical attendance, and also that he had kind friends there that cared for his precious soul. I feel very grateful to you for your kind and faithful care for his best interests. The life of the body is very precious, but that of the immortal soul is far more precious. The body of my dear husband now lies in the silent grave and I trust his ransomed spirit has taken its flight to the realms of bliss. It is indeed heartrending to part with a loved companion and especially under such aggravating circumstances. If I could have watched over him as he laid upon his dying couch and listened to his last words it would have been a great consolation to me now but even this was denied me. Oh the horrors of war; this accursed thing. How many precious lives it has already cost. How many hearts are now bleeding at every pore for their loved ones. And when will the end be. God only knows. But may He overrule all these events to our good both individually and nationally and may peace soon be proclaimed is my earnest and daily prayer.

Dear Sir, I thank you for your kind sympathy which you expressed for me and my dear little children which are now left without a father's care. I feel that our loss is a very heavy one but I trust it will be but a little while before we shall be reunited in heaven where there will be no more partings and where sin can never enter.

We have not heard from Brother Thomas since John died.[3] We fear that he is sick being so exhausted with care and sorrow. If he is, I hope some one of his friends there will write to us immediately.

We can never reward you for your kindness but great will be your reward in heaven. I hope you will try to comfort the dear brother in his affliction and point him to the Savior and may God bless him and you is my prayer.

Yours with great respect,
Hannah E. Mayborn[4]

Dunkirk, Chautauqua County [NY]
December 20th 1862

To the Honorable Reverend Mr. W. L. Hyde
Dear Sir and Friend,

I received your respected letter of the 15th instant on the 20th of the same month in safety; but when we knew the meaning about it, our parents' hearts burst out in sorrow and affliction, which you can sympathize with. Never can our hearts more be shocked as by the loss of our beloved son, P. Squimer who, in the bloom of his life, has exchanged the present with the eternal.[5] O may the God of hosts grant to receive our son in his heavenly kingdom and that his angels may bear him in the lap of our father Abraham.

Dear Sir, Mr. Hyde! We, the afflicted and bereaved parents, give our warm thanks for your care, and pain you had taken to nurse him as much as was in your power. The God of peace be your rewarder now and evermore.

We give also thanks to you for the speedily writing to us and inform us of his death, and as we understand in your letter the describing of his nursing. We are fully satisfied that there was good care for him when he was in the hospital.

Yea, it is indeed a hard blow for our hearts, though still we humble ourselves to the will of our Creator and obey His commandments.

Now dear friend, we once more give our thanks for your pain you have taken to our son, and herewith I remain your ever beloved friend with all respects,

P. Krayger

N. B. Sir! Receive the best respects of the writer, who is very much cast down at the death of Paul, because it reminds me very often to my brother who is in the 3rd Excelsior Regiment, and was in battle at Fredericksburg.[6]

Your beloved friend,
Leonard Stroyer

Please to give my respects to William Kloet and tell him I received his letter of the 7th and I will answer very soon.[7]

L. Stroyer

Excuse the writer, as he is no Yankee to write English letters. Good bye!

Dunkirk, Chautauqua County [NY]
December 27th 1862

To the Reverend W. L. Hyde
Dear Sir and Friend,

Yours of the 23rd has come to our hands in safety and reached us yesterday and I am ready to answer him. In the first place, I let you know, and am glad to state that we are all usually happy and healthy. God be thanked for this treasure, which is unpayable to the human race.

As I understand your letter, you want to know how old the age of our son Paul was when he died. As far as that concern, I will write you it as far as possible. When he closed his eyes he was 18 years, 9 months and 2 days.

Further I thank you once more for the pain and trouble you have taken for us on the case of our son, P. Squimer and we pray that the heavens may bless you as well as every soldier in the army. That peace may soon follow, which will bring so many afflicted hearts into an everlasting joy. May the God of hosts grant to hear our prayers and bring this rebellion soon to an end.

Now friend, as we do not know much news, we will close for the present, and put in all our sorrow, our trust in Him who is the rewarder of all our good.

Receive the best respects from my wife and all the children and herewith I remain your humble friend and servant.

With all love to you,
Peter Krayger

Kiantone [NY]
January 3rd 1863

Dear Chaplain and Friend,

I think I may truly call you my friend. When I take into consideration the kindness and attention which I received at your hands while at Suffolk in the case of the discharge for Edward Jones and the interest which you manifested in his care, I think I can justly call you my friend and also the friend of the soldier.[8] (And by the way they need friends, I have found out, if anybody does.) When I first saw you at Suffolk, it was one pleasant evening. I passed by your tent and saw two young men sick in your quarters. Although there was a hospital close by provided for the sick, you had converted your own private quarters into a hospital and as I passed and looked in upon the fevered cheeks of those poor fellows, I thought I read from your countenance (and don't think I was mistaken) that you left your friends and dear ones at home and went into an enemy's country to serve your God and your country and that you was determined to do so to the best of your abilities and when I returned to my home and related the circumstances to my friends and more particular, to the father of Jones (the boy discharged), he said the U.S. government for once has got the right man in the right place and would to God that all the army officers were like him. I think I can say amen to that.

I hear sad stories about the health of the 112th Regiment. Hope they are not all true. If so, God pity them. Although there is a great many around you, you must be very lonely at times thinking of home and the dear ones so far from you. But God is able to bear you through all these trials and troubles and it is my heart's desire and sincere prayer that he will do it and when the war is over (and God speed the day) bring you safely home to the bosom of your beloved family.

Hoping to hear from you frequently. I remain
Yours truly,
G. S. David

Freehold [NY]
January 6th 1863

To William L. Hyde, Chaplain
112th Regiment New York State Volunteers

Dear Sir,

Your letter of the 27th December bearing the sad tidings of the death of my brother James Lewis of Company D, came to hand on the 3rd instant.[9] It was rather a hard blow for us. Yet I can say (although I am led to mourn the loss of a near and dear brother) thy will O' Lord be done. I have many times prayed that if it was consistent with the Lord's will that my brother might return home once more. But all my hopes in that are cut off. Yet I have another hope still greater than all earthly hopes. That is of great consolation to me. I have a hope that reaches beyond this veil of tears. That I shall meet that brother in the paradise of God where there will be no more war, tears or death!

I tender you my sincere thanks for your kindness in pointing my brother to the Lamb of God. I have long prayed for that Brother, and I think not in vain. Now may the God of Heaven give you wisdom to instruct the soldier and lead you to His Kingdom.

Yours very truly,
H. S. Lewis

P. S. I wish you to see Captain Curtis of Company D and ascertain if he has received my letter. If he has not, please tell him that I have concluded to let the body of my brother remain where it is now buried and place a set of tombstones at his grave.
H. S. Lewis

Westfield [NY]
January 6th 1863
Reverend William L. Hyde
Dear Sir,

When you left Dunkirk to join the regiment in Suffolk, among the many packages for the soldiers with which anxious friends overloaded you, was one for my brother George Dixon.[10] To apologize for that troubling a stranger whose benevolence was already sufficiently taxed, is one motive I have for addressing you. If before you finish reading my note, you discover that I have another, I am sure you will not blame me.

The package contained a rubber blanket. At that time, you remember, the regiment had only the shelter tent, and we were very anxious that George should have his blanket. We were informed that the Express was not at all reliable beyond Washington. Indeed, that the company did not undertake to carry beyond that city. This was a mistake, as we soon afterward learned. But we credited it, and what to do we did not know, for our poor boy we feared was suffering. So when we heard that you would in a few days go to join the regiment, not considering that half of Dunkirk and Fredonia would ask similar favors, we sent the package to you, with the request that you would be so good as to take it. We are exceedingly obliged to you for your kindness in doing so, but are really ashamed of having asked it, and I have ever since wished to apologize.

George is the only surviving son of an old man seventy-five years of age and the only brother of two sisters. I need not tell you how constant is our solicitude for him. How daily and hourly our hearts go out after him. He is only nineteen years old, thoughtless, pleasure loving, and irreligious. O, it was hard to let him go away to temptation, suffering and probable death, knowing that he was without the grace of God, the only sure defense and support!

I ask for him, sir, your Christian sympathy and your prayers. We know not for what purpose he was sent into the army. Perhaps some peril or suffering incident to a soldier's life, may so affect his heart that your friendship, if you will extend it to him, may be blessed to him as no other teaching or influence has been.

You will perhaps wonder that I, a stranger, should so write to you. But although you do not know me, I have heard much about you, from Mrs. Skinner and Mrs. Massey, and know what manner of man I address. So although I remember that my brother is only one of a thousand who have equal claim upon your kind regard, I have ventured to prefer my petition for him. I assure you, sir, that numbers in Westfield whom you do not know, whose friends are connected with the 112th Regiment "thanked God and took courage" when they heard of your appointment as chaplain, and they continually pray that strength may be given you for your self-denying labors, and that the Master whom you serve, will abundantly reward you for them.

Yours truly,
Caroline P. Dixon

⁂

Fredonia [NY]
March 16th 1863

My dear Chaplain,

 I am in receipt of your favor of the 5th instant. In the matter of difference with the quartermaster, the major (Carpenter) had the same cause of complaint that I had excepting the promise made to me by the quartermaster to command the old a/c in the next settlement which he now blandly declines to do on the grounds that "the old a/c is settled." He is welcome to all the consolation he can derive from such gyrating deception.

 The $3.99 is justly due from me and no more. It is more justly the money of Lieutenant Colonel Carpenter than any other member of that mess. If he will receive it, please pay it to him. If not, use it for the benefit of the boys of the 112th. The sword belt, if not sold, you may send to me if you have the opportunity. I am exceedingly anxious to hear that Surgeon Boyd is convalescent. I have been anxious for him but I trust the Lord will spare him for future usefulness in this sad world, many years longer.

 We were pleased (wife and I) to learn that you and your men were enjoying yourselves in our old quarters. I should have been better pleased if you had the whole of it. The vandal spirit, which sometimes crops out of the authority which rank confers for higher objects, is so sickening as to beggar description.

 When I left Suffolk I lost a gold pen and it is barely probable that I put it into the box containing the gloves I sold to you. Have you seen it?

With kindest regards to all. I am yours
Very truly,
F. A. Redington[11]

⁂

Westfield [NY]
October 22nd 1863

To Chaplain Hyde
My Dear Chaplain,

 With a heart overwhelmed with grief and sadness, I now address you at this time. Your kind and sympathetic letter was received on the 14th announcing the death of my beloved husband, which almost broke my heart.

 In that letter you tell of Mr. Waters' trust in Jesus; of his "willingness to die"; of his reliance on his Savior, that he felt that Jesus Christ was a complete and all sufficient Savior.[12] No words can express to you how precious are those words to me. What consolation to a bereaved heart. How could I be reconciled to his departure if I had no hope that he was not saved through the precious Savior his only hope.

 I am sorely afflicted, but God in his mercy doeth all things well. In love He chasten not wittingly. But it is hard for me to say "Thy will be done, O' Lord." I am deprived of one of the best of husbands dearly beloved by me. My children of a kind and indulgent father, one that was ever ready to render any self denial for the happiness of his family. In sickness, he was the only one that could always know just what I wanted to make me comfortable. Always ready to confer a favor on and to my happiness. Always frank, generous and kind; attentive to all of our wants, every wish granted if in his power. He was very refined in his tastes, a lover of music and oh how much shall I miss the music of his flute, which was a pleasure to all to hear. And to where shall I go for counsel and advice, that was always given so cheerfully. But alas, he is no more, he is gone. O' I cannot realize that I shall see his face no more. It is a distracting thought. And my only consolation is to go to my blessed Savior and I am sure he will be my support through all of my trials.

Words can never express my gratitude to you for your Christian guidance and kindness to Mr. Waters while upon a bed of suffering and death. It fills my heart with anguish to think of the weeks and days of agony and distress he endured, and no wife that would have so fondly and quickly gone to him.

Did he not think it cruel that he was permitted to stay there on that desolate island with no relative to administer to him the care and comforts which are so necessary to the sick? It almost breaks my heart to think he might not have died if I had insisted upon some friend going for him when I received your first letter. Nearly all of the letters I received when he was first taken said that he was improving and I had so much hope that I should see him soon. From what Mr. Marvin said to me, that it never occurred to me that it was necessary that some friend should go for him.[13]

Mr. Hyde you mention in one of your letters that Mr. Waters had two letters from Westfield and you advised to his not reading until the morrow. I cannot but fear that one of those letters caused my dear Franklin deep sorrow and I reproach myself with the thought that I have been the cause of hastening on his disease and perhaps its fatal termination. It was written in a fault finding spirit and I am sure it was anxiety for his goal and I am conscious that I grieved his kind and tender spirit while upon a sick bed. If I could but know that he forgave me. Will you please write me all of the particulars for I cannot but feel that I have committed a great wrong?

I thank you for your sympathy and Christian consolation. Your letters have been a great satisfaction in great distress. They have comforted the broken spirit.

Did Mr. Waters make any of his wishes known in regard to his family or his two sons? Did he not leave one message for his disconsolate wife?

I have trespassed upon your time. I know and I presume I have written altogether too much about myself. I hope you will pardon me, for I hardly know what I write. My mind is so bewildered.

George Parmlee called today and I gave him a list of articles I wish you to have if they are of any use to you, or dispose of them as you think best.[14] The horse, saddle and bridle I wish to have sold. The bedding, sheets, etc., appropriate as you please. I have sent you an inventory of articles at Folly Island. I shall send my order for the articles at Beaufort. I received a letter from my brother that went on to Beaufort, he had arrived at [Nailsack] today.

From your afflicted friend,
E. Waters
[Eliza Farnsworth Waters]

Office of U.S. Christian Commission
Pawnee Landing
Folly Island, SC
April 13th 1864

Reverend W. L. Hyde
Chaplain
112th New York Volunteers

Dear Brother,

Yours of the 2nd April was received, too late to reply before you would leave Jacksonville for your contemplated visit home however. I marked your box of books, "care of Christian Commission, Hilton Head" and forwarded it yesterday. I also wrote to them, to keep the box until you shall call for it.

I was rejoiced to hear such good news from your meetings. I hope the spirit of God will abide with you and your meetings, and very many be eternally benefitted. I read an extract of your letter to my meeting and it gave much pleasure.

The meetings in the Christian Commission tent commenced about the time you left here, have been well sustained by the attendance and assistance of members of the 117th, 89th, and 3rd New York Regiments. The Lord by his Holy Spirit has reclaimed some and revived others and converted others. Praise be His name! I cannot express to you, dear brother, how wonderfully the master has guided and aided me in these labors, exceeding my expectations. So limited was my faith. To Him be all, all the glory!

There are today, indication of changes, still farther, among the remaining troops near Pawnee, orders have been received (it is said) to prepare for a move. The particulars are unknown. I expect to remain by divine permission until June or July. Your other property here in Christian Commission tent, bunk frame, stove, table and top case, are safely on hand.

Please let me hear from you again.

Yours Respectfully and affectionately,
Charles A. Roundy
Delegate, U.S. Christian Commission

Portland [NY]
April 13th 1864
Reverend W. Hyde
Dear Sir,

I address you as a perfect stranger but I hope not a stranger at the throne of grace, for we all have the same Father in Heaven to go to in our afflictions if we come humbly at the foot of the cross. He is ever ready to hear and answer our petitions. You may think strange in my writing to you but when I tell you I have a very dear son in the 112th Regiment of which you are their spiritual guide and if it is not asking too much of you, I want you to watch over him and give him such advice as he needs away from home, where he has no father and mother to counsel and advise with. If my dear boy had been a Christian, it seems as if I could have given him up for then, if he did not live to come home, I should live in hopes of meeting him where parting would be no more. But to think of my only son being in the army and unprepared to meet his God in peace at any moment is enough to break a mother's heart.

I often think if we had been more faithful, as we both promised to be when we gave him to God in baptism when he was a helpless babe, he might have been a Christian long ago. But I feel as if I was a poor, weak mortal unable of myself to do anything. But I do hope by the help of God, my husband and I will be able to pray for our dear son that God would give him a heart to pray for forgiveness of his sins and give a new heart that he may enjoy religion. I think it would be such comfort to him in his lonely hours away from home. My son's name is Darwin Buel.[15] He is in Captain Chaddock's company. He has not been there but a few weeks. We got the first letter from him last night since he got to the regiment and it was very joyfully received. I assure you, if it would not be taxing you too much, we should like to hear from you whenever it is convenient and hear how Darwin gets along. I suppose you have a great many such requests as to loved friends. But we feel as if we had a share in your sympathy. May God bless you in your labor of love for the soldiers, is the prayers of Darwin's father and mother. Any time Darwin is not able to write too, I hope you will do it for him. Please accept these few lines from Darwin's mother, hoping you may be the means in the hands of God of doing him a great deal of good.

Truly your friend,
Mrs. J. B. Buel
Portland
Chautauqua County, NY

Conewango [NY]
August 2nd 1864

Reverend Mr. Hyde
Sir,

Your kind letter announcing the death of our brother Samuel was duly received.[16] We were grateful to you for informing us of his death. You stated that his effects were in the hands of the orderly Mr. Button. I have neglected to send for them, not knowing how to get them. If you or Mr. Button would be to the trouble to put up such of them as you think best and send by Express to Randolph, Cattaraugus County, NY it would oblige us very much. We should be glad of his papers and small articles. His clothes that are partly worn, you may give away if they will do anybody any good. He wrote to us some time ago that he had left his watch with a Mr. Abel D. Brooks, an eclectic physician, who was sick and going, he thought, to the general hospital. If you can get it or inform us how to get it, we should be very grateful. If he had any money by him, use it to pay the Express charges. If not, send them without paying and we will pay it when they come.

Yours respectfully,
Milton Bush

Westfield [NY]
August 21st 1864

Dear Chaplain Hyde,

Your kind letter of the 5th was very gratefully received. It came at the close of a day of unusual sadness. All my days are sad now a gloomy shadow has fallen on all my pleasant things. But this had been darker than usual. I had been with the children for a Sunday school picnic on the shore of the lake, where every tree and rock and breaking wave reminded me of the past; and the joyousness of the happy throng made my loneliness almost unendurable. I shun such scenes alone and at home with my children, I can better bear our great sorrow. But the letter came after we returned and I sat thinking over all the experiences of the day. And feeling that if after it all I could only receive a letter from him whose absence I mourn. I could be resigned and cheerful. And so God sends alleviations in my most trying hours—he knows how dear a letter from the 112th would be. And how consoling the sympathy of my husband's friend.

I am sorry to learn of your continued ill health. Is it not your duty to come home? Your life is too valuable to be lost, even in so good a cause.

I pray your dear family may never have occasion to reproach themselves when too late- as I do myself- that the entreaties for the return of the absent are not more urgent. But perhaps all that could be urged would make no difference with your division.

Westfield Church is yet without a pastor. O' how delighted I should be if yourself and family would come here, provided the arrangement would please you.

Mr. Muzzy is in town and I think is very anxious of returning to his previous position here.

Colonel Smith sent me the speeches you [provided] in your letter and they are to be published in our paper this week. It is gratifying to hear our beloved dead remembered we cannot do too much to keep their memory bright. I cannot endure to see the grass grow over my dear one's grave. I want it kept as posh as though made but yesterday. So shall his memory ever be to me.

I wish I could tell you how very near heaven seems, now that my husband is there, it's so near that I sometimes am sure he hears me when I tell him, in my anguish, how dark my way is and how heavy my burden and desolate and empty is my life without his companionship—and O' how I long for an audible expression of his sympathy. It will be but a little while and the portals will open for me. May I be prepared to enter in and be permitted to enjoy with him and all as have loved him, an unending life of joy.

The $30 I do not need at present. Do not send it until perfectly convenient. Whenever I can in any way repay you for your many, many acts of kindness, I shall be happy to do it. Please let me know how I can serve you.

At one time you spoke of sending that saddle, did you do so? I have not received it. I think there must be a box of bedding stored with the regimental baggage at Norfolk belonging to my husband. If so, I should be glad of it if it can be obtained after the campaign. If Charley Higgins is yet in the regiment perhaps he would attend to sending it home.

I hope you will pardon me for not answering your letter of July 1st and your last more promptly-it has not been because they are unappreciated-but I dread so much to sit down to write-such a crowd of heart and proper crushing thoughts rush into my mind. I cannot write calmly or satisfactorily. Please remember me to any who care to be remembered by me. I feel an interest in the dear 112th and write again soon.

Yours in affection,
Clara W. Drake[17]

Jamestown [NY]
October 22nd 1864

Dear Chaplain,

Your very welcome letter, which you wrote me in Fort Monroe, came to hand yesterday. And I need not tell you how glad I was to hear from you and to know that you were still numbered with the living. Myself and children are usually well, but oh how lonely. How much I think about you. How much our regiment has suffered. How much longer will this cruel war continue. Poor Major Ludwick. How sorry I feel for him. I hope he will recover. I think if a soldier can only live, arms and legs are of little account. If my dear husband could only live without an arm or leg either one how glad I should have been.[18] Every day I live, I feel my loss more and more. Dear man. I believe he is happy in heaven, but oh how can I give him up yet. I know he is not lost, only gone before, waiting for me to come to him and bring my little children with me, which I am striving to do. Looking to God for help.

Elial F. Carpenter and his wife Julia in a photograph likely taken at Camp Suffolk, Virginia, during the winter of 1862–1863 (courtesy U.S. Army Heritage and Education Center [USAHEC]).

Chaplain, you do not know how hard it is. And God grant you may never know what my poor heart does. I am living all alone with my children and expect to. And I can tell you it looks dark to me as I look into the future. But I must trust in God. He doeth all things well. I received the 90 dollars from Captain Dunham and was very glad to get it. It being the first money I have received since the death of my husband. Captain Curtis never has been to see me since he came home, nor has not paid me. My lawyer wrote him a letter but he does not seem inclined to pay me. Well, if he thinks it will do him more good that it would a widow and fatherless children, he is welcome to it. I think it strange that he does not come and see me. I saw Mrs. Rouse yesterday. Her family is well. Remember me in much kindness to my friends. Is Colonel Smith with the regiment now? I hope he will be made to take command and stay with the regiment. Chaplain, can't you come home? Do come. I want to see you so much. I think you have been in the army long enough. Captain Palmeter's wife visited me last week. She gets along nicely. Write me soon.

Yours in great haste,
Julia A. Carpenter

Westfield [NY]
October 31st 1864

Dear Chaplain Hyde,

Your favors of the 12th and 14th instant were duly received also the $20.00. I feel under great obligation to you for your kindness to me and mine. Everything you have done has been perfectly satisfactory to us-the best that could have been done in the case. It is not enough for me to say I thank you, nor does it seem appropriate to try to cancel a debt of gratitude with money but if you please I would like to know what your expenses on our account have been that I may at least make that up to you.

Surgeon Hall has settled with me for the horse paying $100.00. I had many bitter tears when I saw the noble horse without his dearly loved master and it was hard for me to give him up-but like harder trials must be endured.

The bedding and other things, especially that chair, I regret losing-if Colonel Smith has that he will certainly send it to me if he is the gentleman I think him. He told me about it when he was here and said he would have it sent if it was in the box-but added that he had one just like it! I will write and see what he says about it-of course, not telling him what I have heard from it since his return to the regiment. It is a little matter but as a relic of the past I should prize it "above rubies."

Please excuse this hastily written note, and believe me
Your friend,
Clara W. Drake

Jamestown [NY]
March 16th [1865]

Chaplain Hyde
Dear Sir,

To feel we have friends who will not forget us in the hour of trial is indeed a comfort and the sympathy they give is a cordial to the stricken heart of the mourner.

Without these words of cheer and God's promise, I must have fallen under the crushing weight of woe. I shall long remember your acts of kindness and the mention you make of my husband's excellences as a friend and as a commander.

His untiring care of his men and his wish to influence them for good has always been his aim. This I have known. And at this time to hear from you that his efforts were appreciated, gives me pleasure. And in some slight degree softens the anguish which fills my heart.

The children are too young to know their loss. But to me the future seems dark. Our home is desolate.

Hoping you may be spared to your wife and little ones.

I am your friend,
L. Smith

Chaplain,

I hope you have disposed of the colonel's horse to advantages and without trouble to yourself. I supposed he had two horses or a horse and a mule.

Will you see Stafford and take up a note he holds against the colonel. The amount I have forgotten. When was the regiment last paid?

Yours,
Lottie Smith[19]

Ogdensburgh New York
27th March 1865

My Dear Chaplain,

I am at last honored with the receipt of your very interesting letter and history of affairs in the old brigade of February 17th 1865. Allow me to congratulate you upon coming out of so many hardships and perils with such fine spirits as you possessed at the time of writing your letter.

Had I more leisure, I could give you some interesting and amusing accounts respecting what I have seen amid the dangers, excessive kindness of friends not the least of these, I have passed through since and saw you at Fort Monroe.

It will be enough to say that "I still live" and what is better in a much healthier and sounder state than six weeks ago. I still suffer much from dizziness and probably shall for some little time.

I leave for Fortress Monroe April 1st. Please say to Colonel Ludwick that I will stop in Albany and see Governor Fenton respecting his regiment and do all in my power to obtain men to fill it up.

I do not believe he will have any trouble in a new muster unless the surgeon refuses to pass him a proper certificate in which case he can obtain an order from the Secretary of War.

There can certainly be no difficulty unless the mustering officer objects to the medical certificate. Mrs. Curtis desires to be remembered. Wishing yourself and the regiment all the happiness and pleasure it is possible to crowd into a soldier's life.

I am very sincerely yours.
N. Martin Curtis[20]

Newton M. Curtis served with the 16th and 142nd New York Infantry. He was wounded at Fort Fisher four times, losing his left eye. He received the Medal of Honor for his actions at Fort Fisher.

W. L. Hyde
Chaplain
112th New York Volunteers
Ellenville [NY]
June 6, 1865
From Mrs. Louisa Reed[21]

To Mr. Hyde
Sir,

I received your communication of the 25th announcing the death of my dear husband only three days after I first heard of his illness. He said he had typhoid fever but was better and wanted me to send a friend after him to bring him home. He did not say when I must send [him] and I was advised to wait to hear from him again. And as the letter had been written ten days [ago,] I expected to hear from him the last of the week and went to the [post] office and one was given to me. The handwriting was strange. I hastened home [and] gave it to his sister for I had not the power to open it. The contents of that letter I can never forget. I was looking to a few days or weeks at most between his last letter and his return to his home, but now all time separates him from those he loved and who loved him. I would have given up my little ones, much as I loved them, if I could have kept him, but my Father in Heaven knew best what to do. I do not wish to murmur at his will, but I find myself almost frantic. I cannot think calmly or reason as clearly as I could under other or lesser trials, for he was my earthly all. I am alone in the world, no relations but his to claim as mine. But I have still as ever a kind Father in Heaven, who still comes for me and mine and I am striving to sink into his will. I want to make my family [an] unbroken one in Heaven.

I shall always remember your kindness to my dear Husband. I am so thankful that death found [him] prepared and surrounded by Christian friends who could cheer and comfort him in the absence of his own loved ones, who would have given all they even owned to have heard one word from his own lips. While you live, your name will not be forgotten by me or his parents and sisters. I pray that you may return to your own home in safety and health to enjoy that peace which has cost so many lives and whenever you are called to return your soul to the God that gave it, you may have the blest assurance that you have done what you could.

It is his Father's wish to have his body brought home if is possible. What do you think of it and if it can be got, how much would it cost? And could he be sent without our sending someone after it? Are they not someones that are to come to New York that could bring it with them? If you think it can, please let me know the cost and it will be sent to you. Is there anything of Oliver's that you have? I wish you would express it to me. Also if it is not too much to ask, please find out how his account stands with the regiment, as regards [to] his pay. For I shall have to make a statement to the lawyer that will take my business to settle. Hoping soon to hear from you.

I remain yours,
Respectfully L. R.

Fredonia [NY]
June 16th 1865

Dear Chaplain Hyde,

I want to add my thanks to Mother's for your brotherly care for dear Father in his last sickness and your exceeding kindness to us in our deep sorrow. There can never be another to whom our thoughts will turn so gratefully as to you. It is indeed a consolation to us to know that he was watched over so tenderly and anxiously. But oh, Chaplain Hyde, if only we could have been with him! If he might but have reached home and kissed me once more and called me "dear child," as he used to do! He had passed through so many dangers and had so nearly served his three years that I was sure he would be spared to us. I counted the months and weeks before he would come; over and over again I pictured to myself our meeting. We had scarce a thought or a plan that was not intertwined with the thought of his return. Oh how can we bear the disappointment! It seems such a long, weary life before us and I am so young that I may have to live a long time, you know. But I cannot be thankful enough that I am the eldest. I have enjoyed my Father's love and care longer than my little brothers and being older, had shared more of his confidence and received a different kind of love from theirs. He told me himself that he loved me better than he did anyone else in the world, except Mother. And I can remember him so well. There is nothing in our house which does not recall to me some word, or look, or smile. The house is as he made and left it. The furniture as he used it. I can almost see his quick step in the streets. I turn to his seat in church, in the prayer meeting, in the Sabbath school. The trees, the books, the favorite airs I used to play for him, indeed, a thousand things bring sweet memories with which nothing would tempt me to part. Oh, why must I lose such a Father just as I was old enough to begin to appreciate him? It is sad to have one's young life so darkened. Has this cloud a silver lining? Poor Mother grieves night and day and refuses to be comforted. Father would say as he has said so often, "Be a comfort to your Mother, dear child," and so I hope I shall be. But there is no one to take Father's place.

Rumors have been rife here that the 112th was on its way home, and would be mustered out very soon. To come so near such joy as we expected, and then to lose it! There will be nobody, dear Chaplain Hyde, out of your own family, who will welcome you home more heartfully than me.

We were much troubled by what you said of your ill health. But hope by this time you are well again. Please thank dear Dr. Morris, in my name, for his kindness and sympathy and most of all for the true regard which he showed for my beloved Father. I am thankful that he could have had such friends as Dr. Morris and yourself. When you reach home, we hope to see you often and learn from your own lips many things about dear Father, which our hearts long to know. Till then, and ever, I hope you will regard me as a friend for my Father's sake.

Lucy M. Washburn[22]

Jamestown [NY]
February 25, 1866
Chaplain W. L. Hyde
Dear Sir,

I received your letter last week and have answered your questions as near as I can and I believe all but the date of the company being full and that is as near as I can ascertain. I am grateful for the interest you felt in my deceased husband.[23] He always felt a deep interest in you and felt that he had evidence of your esteem for him. He spoke of you in his last sickness and remarked to me, you were one of the best men that lived in the world. He prized his friends very highly. I feel that an apology is due you for not answering your very kind and sympathizing letter, after the death of my very dear husband. It was a consolation to me to know that I was remembered by his friends in time of sorrow and grief. I cannot express the anguish and sorrow of heart I have felt, since the death of my dear husband. It is truly sad and lonely in our quiet home. He was always cheerful through his long and tenacious sickness. Never thought his suffering too great. He was happy and peaceful and realized most of the time what was passing around him, until his spirit ascended to God who gave it. O how sad the thought that he never can return to our home again to cheer it with his presence and fill the vacant chair. I will not tax you with my troubles. I shall be very happy to see you here at my home when you come to Jamestown and I hope your wife can come too. Give my kind regards to her. I will make it as pleasant as I can for you. I sent an obituary notice of my husband's death to you but I don't know whether you got it or not. I will send it [again] if I have one to spare. Accept my kind regards for you and family.

Respectfully yours,
Mrs. J. G. Palmeter

Chaplain Hyde
Reverend W. L. Hyde
Dear Sir,

    I have never forgotten your kindness to my brother while in the army. Nor did my departed Mother, who always remembered you with gratitude. And it was her request that I should present you with something that you could regard as a small token of our remembrance of past favors and obligations.

    Had thought of a book but deeming it probable that a gift of that kind might be duplicated in your own library. I beg your acceptance of the enclosed, accompanied with kindest regards for yourself and family.

Yours truly,
Mary A. Prendergast[24]

Appendix C:
The Union Soldier

by William Lyman Hyde

The Union Soldier as I knew him eleven years ago[1]

On the 31st day of May 1864, the 3rd Brigade, 2nd Division, 10th Army Corps was resting near White House, Va awaiting the arrival of parts of the force re it should move out to join the Army of the Potomac now getting into position for another assault upon the entrenchments around Richmond. Grant had been fighting hard since the crossing of the Rapidan [on] the 4th and had already lost over 25,000 men in a campaign of 26 days. This obliged him to recruit his weakened forces from every available quarter. Ben Butler being bottled up at Bermuda Hundred with the Army of the James, Grant thought best to order Smith's Corps the 18th with a division of the 10th to come to his help.[2] The 112th Regiment did. The 112th Regiment New York Volunteers was the 1st regiment of this brigade. This was a country regiment of the same class as your own 126th recruited from the towns and villages of the southwestern most county of the state. It was in this regiment that I became acquainted most thoroughly with the Union soldier. The soldier however of 1864 was somewhat different from the same soldier in 1862. Then he was a raw recruit fresh from the farm or the shop. In many cases, utterly unacquainted with any portion of the big world a hundred miles distant from his rural home.

We all know with what consideration a new recruit was treated in those dark days when soldiers were sorely wanted, and everybody who hadn't gone was anxiously considering how somebody else could be procured to go for him. The man who enlisted was pitied by everybody, men who had never known or noticed him now gave him a hearty shake and applauded his patriotism. Ladies showered bouquets and sweetest smiles upon him. He began to feel himself a hero in advance and walked the street with a consciousness that everybody was looking at him and with an air that seemed to say, "Well things down South have gone bad thus far but wait till I get down there. Little Mac and I'll settle this small lark in about 2 months." When the new regiments went forth that fall from their places of enlistment, what shouts and huzzas attend them, amid the tears and adieus of mothers and sisters. On the way they were feasting at halting places with lavish generosity and for a few days, he was in more danger from loyal pie and cake than from rebel bullets.

But what a change awaited him so soon as [he] got within the precincts of Washington as anywhere south of the mythical Mason and Dixon line. Then he began to feel the grip of military rule and the grip was hard. Accustomed to freedom and consideration at home he now found himself a mere machine every motion to be regulated according to that pattern prescribed in the teachings or the regulations blue book called the service. He couldn't lie abed when he felt particularly tired after reveille without being assigned a berth in the guard house. He goes some fine morning burdened with some outrageous grievance, to the tent of the captain who was an old neighbor, and [with] cap on head begins, "I say Jim, that's all sour" and was met with an impervious "stop sir, hold your tongue, when you wish to address me, take off your hat sir, assume the position of a soldier and wait till I ask you to speak." He turns on his heel and goes out. He doesn't know what it means. It wasn't in his enlistment papers. He thought he enlisted to put down rebellion, but as one said to me he finds that he enlisted to keep his gun barrel higher, his shoes blacked and to take off his hat to that – idiot lieutenant.

From the plum cake and ham sandwiches of his faring he now has rations, good wholesome hardtack, the boxes are marked N. A. Boston. He vows it means Noah's Ark and Boston was old Noah's darkey cook. He used to sleep on a bed, now he sleeps on the ground or pine brush, if he can get it, with a cotton handkerchief over him. He must spring at the assembly call, rub his eyes open, buckle on his accoutrements and pack his gear and be in line in 5 minutes. Every turn he takes he hears some harsh voice of command or reprimand, and feels hedging his every step the iron hand of military law. What wonder that he was annoyed, irritated, exasperated every day a vast deal of grumbling and could pour out of his mouth fearful expletives.

But the soldier of 64 was toughened up. He knew what to expect, hard knocks, the arrogance of power, sickness, marches, all that human limbs are capable of enduring. Stand through rainy nights and days on the picket line, lie down and sleep after a long wet march, fight all day and march all night, at the word of command faltering not to dash across the sloshing field to capture rifle pits, or drive the enemy from his defenses. In 1864, the weakly and sickly had gone to hospitals, the chicken hearted had most of them got out of service and we had left, of the thousand men who went out, 600 hardy men at this 30th of May, diminished in number by about 100 laid out in the disastrous fight at Drewry's Bluff.

At four o'clock in the afternoon the bugle of a battery nearby sounded the assembly and soon after the drum summoned the brigade to move out on the New Castle Road. We were in the rear of Smith's 18th Corps command, knew nothing of our destination save only that we were to be added to the already famous Army of the Potomac. The morning had been showery, and the air of the evening was dank and heavy with not a breath of wind stirring. It was a Virginia road and what soldier that doesn't know about them. And is there any marching more vexatious, tedious, wearing to strength and spirits than to be the rear guard of a large advancing column. March a few rods and halt. Boys [that] don't fall out shall move in a minute. But 15 paces, then forward and march again 10 minutes and halt. Don't fall out boys, don't fall out. But it don't go this time, the men sink down in their tracks or by the roadside, hardly seated when from the head of the regiment we hear the word forward. And so it goes, into the night until at midnight after marching 8 hours we have moved 9 miles. The horses in the battery ahead give out and we can move no farther. Just as we move into an open field the rain begins to fall and we listen to its patter upon the fly beneath where we seek shelter and rest. At four o'clock the brigade is roused up. Hundreds of little fires are soon gleaming sending up their smoke and men gather about them to make their coffee. Some holding their pork to the fire on their ramrod, others crunching it between soaked hard bread, others are frying it in a half canteen. It must be done quick for we were to move at ½ past 4 and so we did promptly with a repetition of the slow tedious march of the nights before. Save that at 9 o'clock we had a halt of an hour near a little stream that empties into the Chickahominy. And at 12 pm we were at the famous Stone House and Tavern which enjoys the soubriquet of Cold Harbor. Here we rest more than an hour to let the rear of Wright's 6th Corps, which had come from another opposite direction, pass on to the battlefield, then fall in.[3] What an afternoon! What a march! Hot without a breath of air. The road ground by wheels, hoofs and feet to an [illegible] powder and inches deep rose in clouds, as the column passed by completely enveloping the men. So completely covering clothes and face that all were of one color. So deep the dust upon the faces of the men that face and blouses were of one color. And down the faces coursed the heavy sweat furrowing channels, giving to all that comical look that men would roar with laughter in spite of the choking dust. And here comes along the way of the regiment. "Bill says he just look at Sam, Virginny soil 10 inches deep all over his face and all furrowed out for potatoes, every furrow running right down into his mouth." We move only about 3 miles. At 4 o'clock pass the headquarters of General

Wright. A brief halt then on right a skirt of woods. And now up rides General Brooks and says to the colonel commanding the brigade, "Put your men into position at once."[4] The general is impatient to open. The line moves on. I remain with the surgeon to prepare for the approaching harvest of wounded men. How still it is, not a sound from any quarter. To the left of where we are, on ground slightly rising, is a light battery. As we are conversing, the surgeon and I, a puff of smoke rises then whang whang. Immediately from hundreds of cannons blaze forth the fires of death. Along the whole line the prolonged rattle of musketry. Just over that little ridge the play of death, the draw of destruction is already opening. This battle of the 1st of June is not the historical Battle of Cold Harbor. The only object of this was to secure possession of a position around which Grant could swing his army for an assault upon works farther to the left. Two corps were engaged in this. Though terribly cut up they were sufficiently successful for the object of the general. The story of the charge will read like a multitude of others. In front of our brigade after passing though the skirt of woods is an open field. The advanced trenches across its farther extremity. This is crossed. In face of a galling fire the 1st works are carried, and behind them the men are formed for an assault upon the 2nd line. A few reach this, but cannot hold it. The deadly fire mows them down and having lost half their number, they fall back to the line already taken and hold this. Out of the 500 men of our regiment with whom I had marched an hour ago, 260 lay stretched in death or gasping, maimed or torn, were giving to the soil their blood. The brigade commander and half the regiment commanders lay dead or dying. And some, oh fearful word, were missing. What untold agony of uncertainty or terror lay in that ominous word missing. What visions does imagination conjure up of Rebel prisons and hospitals, of slow lingering torture, of limbs needlessly sacrificed, of Andersonville and Salisbury with their slow starvation and prolonged tortures. How many a wife and mother would have felt the certain news of death a relief to that harrowing wearisome uncertainty, that made the hours of the day heavy with shadow and filled the hours of the night with direct phantoms of torture. Two days afterwards and the flower of the Army of the Potomac was hurled against one of the strongest positions ever held for defense and 7000 men in one short half hour lay dead or dying.

But we turn from this scene to the hospital a short distance from the main road at least a mile from the battlefield and well sheltered behind a ridge sloped on 3 sides toward a ravine. A cluster of young stretched along the ravine and on the farther side of the field was skirted with woods. This was the field hospital. Its canvas covering the overarching sky, itself one vast ward. Its beds the naked earth. Down the ravine a little distance a single canvas stretched over a pole supported by two stakes formed the operating tent. 4 crotched stakes supporting two 8 foot poles, and covered with the sides of hardtack boxes formed the operating table upon where many a brave man was to be stretched in the endeavor to save life by the sacrifice of limb. Beside this table was the hospital chest. Its cover open and supported by stakes and upon it in grave array the saws, the knives, the bandages, the threaded needles, the chloroform and sponges and towels, a basin and pail of water and nearby walked the surgeon to and fro endeavoring to calm his nerves for the trying duties soon to devolve upon him.

And now the wounded begin to come. Some able to hobble in themselves or supported by a comrade, holding on to his broken arm; another shattered in both legs and brought in on a stretcher; another shot through the body for whom there was a few lingering hours of suffering ere the soldier's last sleep. All the evening they are brought along until at nightfall along two sides of the field they lie in long parallel rows: windrows of that fierce harvest of death. Some are ghostly from loss of blood, others bearing on their faces the lines of extreme agony, no coward cries and shrieks, but let me tell you bearing their sufferings with heroic fortitude worthy of the men who had dashed into the cannon's jaws at the call of duty. These stretched upon the ground with no covering, no food, no shelter from the damp dews of night. There they must lie till morning brings them help or death musters them out. And this long array of the maimed and dying was but a part of that fearful carnage. All night long burial parties are out scouring the field, covering with earth the dead and bringing off the wounded.

No more hopeless task was ever committed to a few then the care of this prostrate multitude.

We did what we could, but it seemed only like throwing in a few straws to stay this mighty flood of mortal agony. Two hours after midnight I paired around with the assistant surgeon for the last time to carry cordials or opiates or water to any most needy. My friend carried with him a lantern. As we reached the outer row of our prostrate comrades at the top of the rise, not a sound was heard, save now and then from some quarter a low moan as if of pain. Not a moving form could be seen. There was a glimmer of light from far down the ravine near the surgeon's quarters, all else dark, cold, still as though we stood within the portals of some vast tomb. We hear nearby a rustle and going there we ask, "What can we do for you?" "O I am so cold" is the response. What could we do gladly, would we have given the poor fellow our last blanket, but alas we have none for ourselves. Our horses are we know not where. We go out a little way toward the battlefield hoping to find one dropped. But in vain, all we can do for him is to gather up a few pieces of a broken cot and lay them over his stomach. Alas we knew not that it was the chill of rapidly approaching death. Utterly exhausted, we return to the tent below. We find a surgeon wrapped in a blanket on the ground, we turn him over and unroll him and then shrink down by his side but not to sleep. But every soldier knows that this is a mild picture compared with some after scenes of battle. Think of a disastrous route and these poor fellows lying all along the woods where they fell, the pouring rain making pools of water around where they lay. Think of the sufferings of those wounded, hurried from the battlefield in army wagons over corduroy roads. No my picture is a mild one of the horrors of the after fight.

There ended the night, the morning broke secure and bright, balmy with heaven's choicest colors, as though no battle had left upon nature its dreadful scars. At four o'clock we were up and on our way to the colonel commanding [the] brigade who had been brought in the night before with a mortal wound. Soon an order came to me to take charge of a detail of men, examine the field, select out the dead, take charge of their effects and then bury them. There they lay all around mingled with the living. 50 stalwart men. We took their names as we found them, all but one who had no mark. We carefully collected what we found about their persons, in little bundles marked them to send home. We pinned upon their clothes their name and then they were borne away, just over the ridge into a contiguous field. Did you ever witness a burial in camp? It is a sad scene. No mother near to kiss the brow, no sisters to lay flowers, no father to look tenderly through his tears, no coffin even to enshroud the form. Usually the drum corporal leads the procession of comrades with a solemn dirge. Here no drum was heard. Only ½ the usual escort is at hand. The chaplain and the working party alone are here. We mark every grave with the only piece of board there is, the short service, the prayer, the earth to earth. All but one. That one is unknown. Quote Longfellow.

Amid all this scene of mortal war lay my ever beloved commander the gallant Drake, who fell standing upon the works his men had taken and with mortal wound was borne from the field. A true Christian hero, if he must die, how fit a place amid the wreck of that splendid brigade who 12 hours before he had cheered on over the rough slashing, across the open plains into the teeth of death.

But why recount these harrowing scenes, scenes full of mortal anguish, scenes which sent their thrills of anguish to every quarter of the land. It is said that the slaughter of Cold Harbor, the 3rd of June made a vacant place in almost every county of every state in the United States. Why dwell upon it. I'll tell you why. I want you never to forget that what of peace and quiet you enjoy today, you owe it to those fallen heroes who gave their blood to cement a republic shattered by rebellion. Among the tender and touching of the war was that of the Eastern man, drafted in one of the calls for troops. Who having a large and young family felt that he could not go. Just then came a young man who offered to be his substitute; he was accepted and went. After a period of service, he fell wounded and was taken to a hospital, while he lay there, the man whose place he filled came down, nursed him while living, buried him when he died and placed at the head of his grave a stone with the inscription he died for me.

Everyone of us living today in the only free republic which has, since the memory of man, ever stood the test of an internal strife so terrific; each one of us today, enjoying our peaceful homes, our peaceful avocations, each one of us looking upon the grave of a soldier whether we knew him or not, whether a man of the East, West, North or South, whether born in America, England, France, Germany, or Ireland, each night say with truth, this man died for me.

When after the surrender of Lee, fighting all ended, my regiment was stationed at Raleigh, NC engaged in various duty. I volunteered my services as chaplain to the General Hospital where several hundred men were lying. Meeting their soldiers from every part of the Union, passing among them daily to cheer them in their recovery or minister to them the offices of religion, I learned to look at men not through theological spectacles, but to see beneath the outer incrustations which defile our humanity to the true deep soul of manhood and to hold in higher reverence the simpler virtues of common men. A belief then took firm hold upon me, a belief not shaken by and mere recent experiences, that while the Republic nourished such children, she need never despair of a perpetuated existence.

And now comrades, my friends, fine ladies and maidens, even the soldier's friend in all his dark days of toils and anguish, let us go hence to yonder resting place of the dead, to scatter afresh upon their graves the revels of spring, the tokens of her resurrection from the winter grave. Let us lay these final tributes of remembrance upon mounds that cover their prostrate forms and as we do so, let us in the spirit of those words of our martyred President see to it that we here dedicate ourselves anew to the enlarging, [adoring] and perpetuating the work for which they died. Let us, as we hold the country's dead defenders in hallowed memory, labor to perpetuate those institutions for whose preservation they fought, to the end of time.

> The earth is hallowed where their feet have trod
> The day is blessed whose sun triumphant rose
> Their tribute paid to freedom and to God
> Their life exchanged for fame's sublime repose.[5]

Hyde's military service was a pivotal point in his life. The comradeship and bonds developed with his brother officers and enlisted men during the war remained with him for the rest of his life. Throughout his postwar years, he remained active with various veteran organizations, to include the Grand Army of the Republic and the Military Order of the Loyal Legion.

Appendix D:
Ships Referenced by Hyde

The information provided for this section was extracted from the following sources:

- *The Army's Navy Series. Dictionary of Transports and Combatant Vessels Steam and Sail Employed by the Union Army, 1861–1868* by Charles D. Gibson and E. Kay Gibson.
- *Dictionary of American Naval Fighting Ships.* Vol. 1. By the United States Navy Department.
- *Handbook of the United States Navy: A compilation of all the principal events in the history of every vessel of the United States Navy from April 1861 to May 1864* by B. S. Osbon.

Arago: A schooner borrowed by the Union Navy from the United States Coast Survey during the American Civil War. She was outfitted as a gunboat and used by the Union Navy as a picket and patrol vessel on Confederate waterways. After the war, she rejoined the Coast Survey and served until 1881.

Atlantic: A 2,860-ton sidewheel steamer built by the New York Shipbuilder, William H. Brown in 1849. Purchased by the Collins Line of New York, the *Atlantic* made her first transatlantic trip from New York to Liverpool, England on April 27, 1850. During the Civil War, she was chartered by the Federal army to transport soldiers.

Baltic: A sidewheel steamer built in 1850 for transatlantic service. She was repeatedly chartered by both the army and navy during the Civil War. In 1864 she was utilized as a hospital ship and transported wounded soldiers from City Point, Virginia, to medical facilities at Newport News, Virginia.

Benjamin DeFord: A 1,090-ton steamer also known as the *Ben DeFord*. Built by the Bethlehem Steel Company of Wilmington, Delaware, in 1859. She was built for the Merchants and Miners Transportation Company and was delivered for service in March 1860. Chartered by the War Department in 1861 and purchased in 1864. Used throughout the war for transporting soldiers, supplies and mail.

Brooklyn: A wooden screw sloop of war launched in 1858 by Jacob A. Westervelt and Son in New York City. Her war record includes duty with the West Gulf Blockading Squadron, service on the Mississippi River, action against New Orleans, Vicksburg and Mobile Bay. During her service at Mobile Bay, she was struck 40 times by Confederate batteries and suffered 11 men killed and 43 wounded. The Navy decommissioned her on May 14, 1889.

Canonicus: A 1,034-ton, United States Navy Ironclad, with a single turret containing two guns. Built by Harrison Loring at South Boston and launched on August 1, 1863. Her war record included service with the James River Flotilla, North Atlantic Blockading Squadron, both assaults upon Fort Fisher and with the South Atlantic Blockading Squadron. During the second assault on Fort Fisher, she received thirty-six hits from Confederate batteries and twice had her flag shot away.

Charles Thomas: A screw-steamer chartered by the Quartermaster Department on December 29, 1863. On March 10, 1864, the army purchased the steamer at Philadelphia, Pennsylvania. In December 1864, she transported the 112th New York to participate in the first assault against Fort Fisher, North Carolina.

Chickamauga: Originally the Southern blockade-runner *Edith,* she was purchased by the Confederate Navy and refitted as the CSS *Chickamauga.* Armed with three rifled cannons and a crew of 120 officers and men, she was placed into service on October 28, 1864. After the evacuation of Wilmington, North Carolina, the CSS *Chickamauga* sailed up the Cape Fear River where her crew sank her.

Convoy: A screw steamer purchased by the Quartermaster Department on July 1, 1863 for use as a troop transport ship.

Cosmopolitan: A sidewheel steamer used as a troop transport ship during the expedition to the Savannah River in 1862. Served as a hospital ship during the action against Fort Wagner and Charleston, South Carolina, in 1863. Supported operations at Jacksonville, Florida, in 1864. Carried supplies to Sherman's army during the Carolina Campaign of 1865.

Cossack: A sidewheel steamer purchased by the United States Army on November 27, 1861. The *Cossack* transported Union soldiers in support of General Burnside's attack on Roanoke Island, North Carolina, in 1862. She also moved elements of the army to South Carolina, Florida and Texas.

Daniel Webster: A sidewheel steamer employed by the Quartermaster Department to transport soldiers and supplies. She was used in support of the Peninsular Campaign of 1862 and the expedition to Port Royal, South Carolina. She was also used by the Sanitary Commission to transport wounded soldiers to Boston, Massachusetts.

Eliza Hancock: Also known as the *Eliza Hancox.* A 347-ton sidewheel steamer chartered by the army in April 1864 for operations on the Pamunkey River, Virginia. Used to supply General Sherman during his movement from Savannah, Georgia, into North Carolina. Participated in the second assault upon Fort Fisher, North Carolina, in January 1865 by ferrying soldiers ashore from the larger transports. She was also used to evacuate Union soldiers wounded at Fort Fisher.

Ericsson: A 1,902-ton steamer utilized by the army during the expedition to Port Royal, South Carolina.

Escort: A sidewheel steamer chartered by the War Department to transport troops and cargo. Records indicate she was chartered between February and May 1863 and later purchased by the Quartermaster Department on June 18, 1863, at New York City.

Fredericksburg: A Confederate ironclad, the CSS *Fredericksburg* was active along the James River throughout 1864 and into early 1865. Just prior to the fall of Richmond, the CSS *Fredericksburg* was destroyed in order to prevent her capture by Union forces.

General Howard: A 158-ton sternwheel steamer chartered by the army to supply General Sherman's army during their sweep through Georgia, South Carolina and North Carolina. Saw action at the second assault upon Fort Fisher, North Carolina, and was one of the first supply ships to ascend the Cape Fear River to support operations against Fayetteville, North Carolina.

General Lyon: A screw steamer. One of the transports used to carry Union soldiers from City Point, Virginia, to New York City to guard against civil unrest and a Confederate threat from Canada. The *General Lyon* also took part in both assaults against Fort Fisher, North Carolina. In addition to transporting Union soldiers into the fight, the *General Lyon* also carried released Union prisoners of war from Wilmington, North Carolina, north to freedom and medical care.

Hellen Getty: A steamer, she was built by Henry Willink in Savannah, Georgia, in 1858. During the war she was used by the army to transport troops and equipment.

John Brooks: A sidewheel steamer chartered by the army throughout the war. Ship used as transport for troops and supplies. The *John Brooks* also served as an army mail steamer to City Point, Virginia.

John Rice: A screw steamer purchased by the Quartermaster Department on February 25, 1864. Primarily used as a troop transport.

Malvern: A sidewheel steamer originally known as the *William G. Hewes*, she was built in 1860 by Harlan and Hollingsworth Company in Wilmington, Delaware. On April 28, 1861, the governor of Louisiana ordered the ship seized and placed her into Confederate service as a blockade-runner. After the Union capture of New Orleans, she shifted operations between North and South Carolina and was renamed the *Ella and Annie*. On November 8, 1863 the USS *Niphon* recaptured her. Outfitted for war service, she was commissioned by the United States Navy in February 1864 and saw service with the North Atlantic Blockading Squadron and participated in the Wilmington expedition against Fort Fisher, North Carolina. She was decommissioned on October 24, 1865.

Maple Leaf: A passenger and freight steamer, launched in Canada in 1851. Chartered by the Quartermaster Department at a rate of $550 per month, she was in service until April 1, 1864, when she was destroyed by a Confederate mine. She sank in the St. John's River, Florida, with much of the personal belongings and camp equipage from the 13th Indiana Infantry, 112th New York Infantry and the 169th New York Infantry.

Mary Washington: A steamer chartered by the army throughout the war as a troop transport.

Monitor: A sidewheel steamer in support of the Richmond Campaign.

Morgan: An 863-ton, sidewheel steamer that was partially armored and served as a Confederate warship. Built in Mobile, Alabama, between 1861 and 1862. The *Morgan* participated in the naval battle of Mobile Bay on August 5, 1864. She survived the war and was surrendered to the United States Navy on May 4, 1865.

Pawtuxet: A sidewheel steamer launched by the Portsmouth, New Hampshire Navy Yard on March 19, 1864. Her war record included service with the North Atlantic Blockading Squadron and both assaults upon Fort Fisher, North Carolina. She was decommissioned at New York on June 15, 1865.

Saxon: A 413-ton propeller steamer, built in Brewer, Maine, in 1861. She was chartered by the War Department to transport Union soldiers and supplies.

Star of the South: A screw steamer chartered by both the army and navy throughout the war. Used primarily as a troop transport for the army and for a short period the navy employed her as a patrol vessel.

Thames: A 590-ton steamer, chartered to transport troops in support of the Peninsular Campaign and the second assault upon Fort Fisher, North Carolina.

Thomas Collyer: A sidewheel steamer chartered as a troopship. She supported amphibious operations along the Neuse River in North Carolina, and the evacuation of Union forces from Washington, North Carolina.

Thomas Powell: A steamer chartered for use as a hospital ship for the Army of the James.

Wabash: A steam screw frigate, she was launched at the Philadelphia Navy Yard on October 24, 1855. At the outbreak of war, she served as the flagship of the Atlantic Blockading Squadron. She participated in General Butler's amphibious assault at Hatteras Inlet, North Carolina, and afterwards was designated as flagship for the South Atlantic Blockading Squadron. After a brief refit in October 1861, she spearheaded the Federal attack on Port Royal, South Carolina. The USS *Wabash* also participated in both assaults against Fort Fisher. She was decommissioned at Boston, Massachusetts, on February 14, 1865.

Western Metropolis: A steamer chartered by the Quartermaster Department from December 1863 until January 1865. Used as a hospital ship to evacuate wounded during the Richmond Campaign of 1864.

Westfield: A sidewheel steamer purchased by the navy from Cornelius Vanderbilt in November 1861. Supported Admiral David Porter's Mortar Flotilla and served as a costal survey ship along the lower Mississippi in preparation for Union assaults upon Forts Jackson and St. Philip, Louisiana. The *Westfield* also saw service at Galveston, Texas, where she was destroyed by the Union navy to prevent her capture by Confederate forces.

Chapter Notes

Introduction

1. Phisterer, Frederick, *New York in the War of the Rebellion 1861 to 1865*, pp. 43–54.
2. War Department, General Order No. 49, Section No. 9, Washington, August 3, 1861.
3. Correspondence from New York Adjutant General's Office to Major J. T. Sprague, United States Army, October 10, 1862. United States National Archives, William L. Hyde's pension file.
4. Adjutant Selden E. Marvin's letter of November 6, 1862, and printed in the *Jamestown Journal* newspaper, November 21, 1862.
5. American Historical Society, *History of Chautauqua County, New York and Its People*, Vol. II (Boston, New York, Chicago: 1921), p. 331.

Chapter 1

1. Foster's Provisional Brigade comprised the following infantry regiments: 13th Indiana; 6th Massachusetts; 112th and 130th New York. Between October and December 1862, the following Pennsylvania infantry regiments were added: 58th, 165th, 166th, 167th and 176th.
2. Major General John J. Peck. A New Yorker by birth, a graduate of the United States Military Academy and was a veteran of the Mexican War. On September 22, 1862, Peck received command of all Union forces in Virginia, south of the James River.
3. Battery L, 4th United States Artillery.
4. Battery D, 4th United States Artillery.
5. Although Drake protested to Governor Morgan (New York), the issue was referred back to the army via Generals Dix and Peck. In the end, Drake received an admonishment and was still required to provide soldiers to serve with various artillery batteries.
6. Elial F. Carpenter, Field & Staff, 112th. Initially served with the 49th New York and was mustered into the 112th as a major on October 30, 1862. Promoted to lieutenant colonel, January 13, 1863. Died of wounds received at Drury's Bluff, Virginia, on May 18, 1864. Drury's Bluff is also referred to as Drewry's Bluff.
7. Brigadier General Henry W. Wessells served as a brigade commander in the IV Army Corps at Suffolk, Virginia. He was wounded during the Peninsular Campaign at Seven Pines and took part in the operations in North Carolina. He was captured at Plymouth, North Carolina, and later exchanged.
8. Israel Vogdes, Brigadier General of Volunteers, West Point Class of 1837. Captured defending Fort Pickens, Florida, in 1861 and exchanged in August 1862. Took part in Charleston Harbor operations and later placed in command of the defenses for Norfolk and Portsmouth, Virginia.
9. *Dunkirk Union*, published in the paper dated December 31, 1862. Although some dates of death differ from the Annual Report of the Adjutant General of the State of New York for the Year 1903; Registers of the 107th–113th Regiments of Infantry, I elected to present the dates as noted in the newspaper article.
10. Moloch is a Semitic rooted word meaning "king." It has been used figuratively in English literature to refer to a person or thing demanding or requiring a very costly sacrifice.
11. 1st Battalion New York Sharpshooters.
12. Brigadier General Francis B. Spinola. The brigade consisted of the 132nd, 158th and 163rd New York infantry regiments.

Chapter 2

1. The 2nd Provisional Brigade was commanded by Colonel Alfred Gibbs and consisted of the following infantry regiments: 112th and 130th New York, and 58th, 175th and 177th Pennsylvania.
2. 1st New York Mounted Rifles.
3. Chaplain Addison J. Whitaker, 11th Pennsylvania Cavalry.
4. Doctor Henry Rogers was a physician from Dunkirk, New York.
5. Chaplain John W. Hanson, 6th Massachusetts Infantry.
6. Private Francis G. Powers, Company D, 112th. Discharged for disability on May 4, 1863.
7. Private Otis A. Mason, Company K, 112th. Died from typhoid fever at Suffolk, Virginia.
8. Privates Francis G. Powers, Company D, 112th and James Davis, Company H, 112th. Davis was killed at Carrsville, Virginia, on May 16, 1863.
9. Captain Enoch A. Curtis, Company D, 112th.

Wounded at Cold Harbor on June 1, 1864, and discharged for disability on September 15, 1864. 1st Lieutenant Lewis Andrews, Company F, 112th. Discharged for disability on December 8, 1862.

10. Assistant Surgeon Edson Boyd, Field & Staff, 112th. Discharged for disability on November 9, 1863.

11. "Thy word have I hid in mine heart, that I might not sin against thee." (King James Version).

12. Refers to Lieutenant Colonel Frederick A. Redington, Field & Staff, 112th. Resigned due to ill health.

13. Assistant Surgeon Jeffrey R. Thomas, Field & Staff, 112th. Discharged for disability on December 20, 1862.

14. Louis Colman, dry goods merchant from Dunkirk, New York.

15. Private Julius B. Hewes, Company I, 112th. Served as Chaplain Hyde's assistant. Brother of Private Eddy A. Hewes, Company I, 112th.

16. Galatians 6:7 (KJV).

17. Private Frank M. Crosgrove, Company E, 112th. Died from typhoid fever at Hampton, Virginia.

18. Job 19:25–26 (KJV).

19. Isaiah 38:1 (KJV).

20. Mark 4:39 (KJV).

21. Entry most likely refers to Sergeant Ammon B. Cobb, Company I, 112th or Private Grant Cobb, Company A, 112th.

22. Private Charles L. Norton, Company G, 112th.

23. Captain John G. Palmeter, Company H, 112th. Wounded at Cold Harbor on June 1, 1864, and died of wounds on August 1, 1864.

24. Lieutenant Colonel Cyrus J. Dobbs, 13th Indiana Infantry.

25. Private George A. Watson, Company C, 112th.

26. Refers to skirmish at Deserted House, Virginia, also known as Kelly's Store. According to Hyde's regimental history, it was the first battle in which the 112th was actively engaged. Hyde also refers to it as the battle of the Blackwater.

27. Dr. Wright provided this letter to the newspaper *Fredonia Censor*. It was published on February 4, 1863.

28. Brigadier General Michael Corcoran in command of the 1st Division, VII Corps. As colonel, commanded the 69th New York Infantry, part of the famed Irish Brigade. Killed at the age of 36, when his horse fell upon him and fractured his skull.

29. Private Warren Smith, Company C, 112th. Wounded at Cold Harbor, Virginia, on June 1, 1864. Captain Naham S. Scott, Company C, 112th. Discharged for disability on May 24, 1864.

30. Sickness and disease took its toll on the Chautauqua Regiment. Hyde recorded in his regimental history that when they left Suffolk, "No regiment had buried so large a number of men as the 112th." In the regiment's mortuary records maintained by Hyde, are the names of forty-four soldiers who succumbed to illness while at Suffolk. Mortuary records can be found in Appendix A.

31. Sergeant Samuel G. Sherwin, Company A, 112th. Promoted to 2nd lieutenant on January 11, 1863 and to 1st lieutenant on December 28, 1863. Killed at Petersburg, Virginia, on June 28, 1864.

32. Private Russell H. Dean, Company A, 112th. Died of typhoid fever on September 15, 1863.

33. Private Gilman Bartlett, Company F, 112th. Died of typhoid fever on December 28, 1862.

34. Captain Joseph S. Mathews, Company F, 112th. Promoted to major on April 9, 1865.

35. Private John Lawson, 7th Company, 1st Battalion New York Sharpshooters. Died of disease on December 20, 1862.

36. John Ericsson, Swedish-American inventory and mechanical engineer. Designed the navy's first ironclad ship, the USS *Monitor*.

37. *Chautauqua Democrat*, January 14, 1863, Vol. X, No. 578, p. 2. The article was dated erroneously as January 30, 1863. It is assumed the correct date of the article should read January 3, 1863.

38. 1st Lieutenant Alfred Dunham, Company A, 112th. Promoted to captain on January 11, 1863, and to lieutenant colonel on January 31, 1865. Wounded in action at Darbytown Road, Virginia, on October 27, 1864.

39. Psalms 32:8 (KJV).

40. Newspaper published in Chautauqua County, New York, from 1860–1868.

41. Major John F. Smith, Company A and Field & Staff, 112th. Promoted to lieutenant colonel and later to colonel of the regiment. Died on January 18, 1865 from wounds received at Fort Fisher.

42. 1st Lieutenant and Adjutant Selden D. Marvin, Field & Staff, 112th. Mustered out of the 112th on September 13, 1863, to receive promotion to major and paymaster in the United States Army.

43. Mark 10:38 and Matthew 20:22 (KJV).

44. Daniel Tompkins Van Buren served as a captain in the 20th New York State Militia and with the United States Volunteers, Adjutant General Department. Brevetted to brigadier general on March 13, 1865 for faithful and meritorious service during the war.

45. Private John C. Taylor, Company I, 112th. Died from typhoid fever on February 14, 1863 at Suffolk, Virginia.

46. Private Oliver A. Nichols, Company D, 112th. Promoted to corporal on October 23, 1864.

47. Private Hiram Dickson, Company D, 112th. Wounded at Hatcher's Run, Virginia, and again at Chaffin's Farm, Virginia. Died from amputation of the leg on January 18, 1865 at Hampton, Virginia.

48. Private William R. Pelton, Company D, 112th. Transferred to the United States Army, Signal Corps on July 20, 1863.

49. Private Asahel Hulit, Company E, 112th. Discharged for disability on May 26, 1863.

50. Sergeant Frank B. Brazee, Company A, 112th. Promoted to sergeant major on October 11, 1864, 2nd lieutenant on January 5, 1865 and 1st lieutenant on January 6, 1865.

51. Chaplains D. Henry Miller, 15th Connecticut Infantry and Silas Cummings, 4th Rhode Island Infantry.

52. Captain Isaac B. Bowdish, Commissary of Subsistence, United States Volunteers. Was killed in a railroad accident while onboard a commissary train traveling from Norfolk to Suffolk, Virginia.

53. Sergeant Charles H. Tucker, Company H, 112th. Wounded while on picket duty on April 13, 1863. Died of wounds on April 14, 1863 at Camp Suffolk, Virginia.

54. Corporal Albert Baker, Company E, 112th. Killed in action at Suffolk, Virginia.

55. Major General Henry W. Halleck, General-in-Chief of the United States Army. Nicknamed "Old Brains."

56. Privates John J. Munson, Company E, 112th and George W. Heath, Company D, 112th. Both soldiers were captured while on picket duty. They were exchanged and returned to duty with the regiment on October 20, 1863.

57. Hyde's regimental history recounts that on May 13th Negro laborers, who were tearing up rails for the Federal army, dropped their tools and scattered when Rebel artillery frightened them.

58. Private James Davis, Company H, 112th. Killed in action at Carrsville, Virginia.

59. Dr. Daniel W. Hand began his military service with the 1st Minnesota Infantry as an assistant surgeon. In 1863, he was assigned as Medical Director of United States Forces at Suffolk, Virginia. While traveling outside of Suffolk, he was ambushed by a group of Confederate guerrillas, captured and sent to Libby Prison. He was later returned as part of a prisoner exchange.

60. Captain William H. Chaddock, Company B, 112th. Discharged for disability on November 25, 1864.

61. Private James G. Walrod, Company C, 112th. Died of disease on October 27, 1863.

62. Private Leroy Lord, Company C, 112th. Transferred to the Veteran Reserve Corps on January 9, 1865.

63. Privates William A. Barhite, Company B, 112th; Darius Van Vliet, Company C, 112th; Franklin E. Kinphenger, Company D, 112th, and Conrad H. Mertz, Company H, 112th. Unable to determine complete identification for Smith, Baldwin and Thayer.

64. Possibly Assistant Surgeon James W. Applegate of the 11th Pennsylvania Cavalry.

65. Private David Mills, Company C, 112th. Died of disease on January 3, 1864.

66. Private Albert M. Wigtman, Company B, 112th.

67. Private Delos D. Richardson, Company I, 112th.

68. Private Augustus Green, Company D, 112th.

69. Private Charles W. Mount, Company C, 112th. Transferred to the Veteran Reserve Corps on May 31, 1863.

70. Private Augustus E. Pheteplace, Company E, 112th. Died of disease on October 21, 1863 at Fort Schuyler, New York.

71. Possibly Musician Abner D. Smith, Company A, 112th.

72. The Christian Commission, organized in the early days of the war, focused on the religious and spiritual needs of the soldiers and worked in cooperation with the army and navy chaplains. The commission often augmented the military chaplains with hard to get religious materials such as bibles, prayer books and hymnals. For the soldier in the field, the commission often provided letter writing materials enabling the soldiers the means to communicate with their families back home. Refers to Chaplain David J. Lee, 166th Pennsylvania Infantry.

73. Chaplain Joel W. Eaton, 169th New York Infantry. Discharged for disability at Folly Island, South Carolina, on August 20, 1863.

74. Frank is the name of Chaplain Hyde's horse.

75. 166th Pennsylvania Infantry.

76. William Henry Fitzhugh Lee, son of Confederate General Robert E. Lee. Served in the Confederate army and rose from the rank of captain to major general. As a colonel, commanded the 9th Virginia Cavalry.

77. Colonel Samuel P. Spear, commanded the 11th Pennsylvania Cavalry, also know as Spear's Cavalry.

78. William Bookstaver, a lawyer in Dunkirk, New York.

79. Rumford College was located in King William County, Virginia. It was a private school for boys and a preparatory school for William and Mary College. It was established in 1804.

80. During this period, the 112th was assigned to Foster's 2nd Brigade, 1st Division, 7th Army Corps. On July 20, 1863, Brigadier General George W. Getty was given command of the Department of Virginia and the 7th Army Corps.

81. Zachary Taylor, "Old Zack." Born in Barboursville, Virginia, in 1784. Served as 12th President of the United States from 1849 to 1850, when he suddenly died at the age of 65. Taylor had six children, one of whom, daughter Sarah Knox Taylor, married future Confederate President Jefferson Davis. His only son, Richard "Dick" Taylor, served in the Confederate army and rose to the rank of lieutenant general.

82. First Families of Virginia. Term used to refer to the socially prominent and prosperous families of colonial Virginia.

83. Colonel David W. Wardrop commanded an independent brigade that included the 99th and 118th New York Infantry regiments.

84. Describes the attempt to burn South Anna Bridge, Virginia.

85. Private Henry H. Peck, Company A, 112th. Died of typhoid fever on July 3, 1863 at White House, Virginia.

86. Generals Erasmus D. Keyes and George W. Getty were part of the Union operations on the Peninsula to draw Confederate soldiers away from General Robert E. Lee and the Army of Northern Virginia invasion into Pennsylvania.

87. Captain Patrick Barrett, 72nd New York Infantry. Died on May 6, 1862 from wounds received at Williamsburg, Virginia.

88. New York City Draft Riots, July 13–16, 1863. Caused over a million dollars worth of property damage and the death of at least a dozen citizens. Union soldiers were called upon to crush the riots and did so, killing or injuring over 1,000 rioters.

89. 1st Lieutenant George W. Barber, Company G, 112th. Promoted to captain, May 18, 1864. Discharged for disability October 4, 1864.

90. A *New York Times* correspondent reported that on Sunday, July 12, 1863, 2nd Lieutenant Alanson L. Sanborn of Company B, 1st United States Colored Troops was confronted by Dr. David M. Wright, a secessionist. While Sanborn was marching his soldiers down Main Street, Norfolk, Wright shouted to Sanborn that "he was a damned cowardly son of a bitch." Sanborn halted his soldiers and confronted Wright, where upon Wright shot Sanborn twice with a Colt revolver. Sanborn was killed and Wright was taken into custody by Lieutenant Colonel Hugh C. Flood of the 155th New York Infantry and later turned over to the provost marshal for trial.

91. Commanded by Captain Phineas A. Davis. The battery was also known as the 7th Battery, Massachusetts Light Artillery.

92. Surgeon Charles E. Washburn, Field & Staff, 112th. Commissioned on October 27, 1862. Died from typhoid fever on April 10, 1865 near Faison's Station, North Carolina.

93. Hyde was very fond of his sons, Henry Warren Hyde and Frederick William Hyde. At the time of this letter, Henry was 10 years old and Frederick was 6. The Hyde's had a third son, Wallace, who died in infancy prior to Hyde joining the 112th.

94. Dodge's Rifles was another name for the 1st New York Mounted Rifles. The regiment was initially commanded by Colonel Charles C. Dodge.

95. Captain Phineas Stevens, Company G, 112th. Discharged for disability on February 11, 1864.

96. Corporal Harvey D. Harter, Company F, 112th. Wounded at Cold Harbor on June 1, 1864 and promoted to sergeant on February 13, 1865.

97. 1st Lieutenant George S. Talcott, Company C, D & I, 112th. Promoted to captain on October 12, 1864.

98. Captain Charles H. Oley, Company I, 112th. Discharged for disability on November 28, 1864.

99. *Christian Mirror*, published weekly in Portland, Maine, from 1822–1899.

100. Corporal William Aplin, Company F, 112th. Promoted to sergeant on October 27, 1863, and to 2nd lieutenant on June 13, 1865.

101. Private Thaddeus K. Furman, Company F, 112th.

102. "There is a way that seemeth right unto a man: but thee end thereof are the ways of death." (KJV).

103. 1st Lieutenant Alexander M. Lowery, Company H, 112th. Discharged August 22, 1863, at Folly Island, South Carolina.

104. Captain Gurdon L. Pierce, Company C, 112th. Killed at Cold Harbor, Virginia, on June 1, 1864.

105. Corporal Charles Neil, Company D, 112th. Died of disease on August 28, 1863, at Folly Island, South Carolina.

106. Captain Daniel Ferguson, Company K, 169th New York Infantry. Wounded at Cold Harbor, Virginia, and killed at Fort Fisher, North Carolina. The funeral referenced is for Corporal Charles D. Frisbie of the 169th New York Infantry. A New York newspaper, the *Troy Daily Times,* reported on September 15, 1863, that Corporal Frisbie was shot through the heart by a sharpshooter, while working in the trenches before Fort Wagner, Morris Island, on the 28th and instantly killed. His son, Private James Frisbie, also with the 169th, died of disease while the regiment was at Suffolk, Virginia, in May 1863.

107. "So teach us to number our days, that we may apply our hearts unto wisdom." (KJV).

108. Private Frank C. Bullock, Company G, 112th. Died of fever on August 31, 1863. Prior service with 9th New York Cavalry.

109. Letter courtesy of Emory University, Atlanta, Georgia.

110. Private Egbert C. Vanscoy, Company E, 112th.

111. Private Nelson Gage, Company K, 112th. Died of fever on September 13, 1863 at Folly Island, South Carolina.

112. James 5:16 (KJV).

113. Private Augustus Green, Company D, 112th. Served as a hospital steward in May 1865.

114. Private Bernard McGee, Company B, 112th. Hyde might have confused Private McGee with Private Samuel S. McKee. According to the NY Adjutant General Reports, McGee did not enlist until December 19, 1864.

115. Could be Private Loyal Allen or Private Orrin S. Allen. Both enlisted August 22, 1862 and served in Company H, 112th.

116. Isaiah 6:5 (KJV).

117. Private Adoniram J. Oviatt, Company D, 112th. Promoted to corporal on May 1, 1865.

118. Private Reed W. Cummings, Company I, 112th. Died of typhoid fever.

119. Acts 21:14 (KJV).

120. Private John Tezepher, Company D, 112th. Died from inflammation of the bowels on September 25, 1863.

121. Private Sumner Boss, Company C, 112th. Died from typhoid fever on September 2, 1863.

122. Major General Quincy A. Gillmore. Commanded Department of the South and the X Army Corps from June 12, 1863 until May 1, 1864.

123. Chaplain Homer H. Moore, 2nd South Carolina Colored Infantry. Regiment also known as the 34th United States Colored Infantry.

124. Chaplain John Crabbs, 67th Ohio Infantry. Promoted from private to chaplain on January 15, 1862. Resigned on July 7, 1864.

125. Boatner's *Civil War Dictionary* states the mission of the Sanitary Commission was to "do for the soldiers what the government did not do, and this included raising the hygienic standards of the camps and diet, caring for the wounded, coordinating the program to send food and supplies to the soldiers, and compiling a directory of the sick and wounded in army hospitals."

126. Hyde was mistaken with the officer's name. The correct name is Lieutenant Robert Scott, Company D, 13th Indiana Infantry. Scott died on September 10, 1863 at Folly Island from acute dysentery.

127. Lieutenant Colonel John M. Wilson, Field & Staff, 13th Indiana Infantry. Later service with the 155th Indiana Infantry.

128. Captain Ephraim A. Ludwick, Company K,

112th. Wounded at Chaffin's Farm and later promoted to colonel of the regiment.

129. Private Jared Ploss, Company F, 112th. Died of disease on November 24, 1863.

130. I was unable to determine the identity of Private Apthorp, as there were four soldiers in the regiment with the same last name. Elliott is Private William Elliott, Company B, 112th. Discharged for disability on September 14, 1864.

131. Private Henry A. Benjamin, Company B, 112th. Died from heart disease on September 12, 1863, at Folly Island, South Carolina.

132. Quartermaster Frank Waters, Field & Staff, 112th. Died of disease on October 3, 1863, at Suffolk, Virginia.

133. Hyde recorded the wrong company for Mount. After an extensive review of the 112th service records at the National Archives, I think Hyde is referring to 1st Lieutenant George F. Mount of Company K. George was recorded as "Absent sick at Hilton Head, August 11, 1863." He returned to the regiment sometime in later September 1863. Mount was killed in action at Bermuda Hundred, Virginia, on August 25, 1864.

134. Corporal Thomas A. Rhodes, Company F, 112th. Transferred to United States Signal Corps on March 12, 1864.

135. Private Kies Tracy, died of disease on March 14, 1864; Private Norman F. Cook, died of disease onboard the *Arago* on September 27, 1863; Private Henry J. Sweet, given a sick furlough on September 15, 1863; Private Benjamin F. Gossett; Sergeant Enos C. Hunt, died of disease at Jamestown, New York, on November 7, 1863; Private William McElroy, captured and paroled.

136. Private George Thompson, Company H, 112th.

137. "Blessed are they that dwell in thy house: they will be still praising thee." (KJV).

138. Private Eddy A. Hewes, Company I, 112th. Brother of Private Julius B. Hewes, Company I, 112th.

139. "Blessed are they that dwell in thy house: they will be still praising thee." (KJV).

140. 2nd Lieutenant George W. Fox, Company G, 112th. Discharged on November 4, 1863.

141. 2nd Lieutenant Leonard C. Alden, Company D, 55th Massachusetts Infantry. Died of disease on October 5, 1863, at Hilton Head, South Carolina.

142. Private Henry Huber, Company G, 112th. Transferred to 3rd New York Infantry on June 13, 1865.

143. I am unsure of Chaplain Harris' identity. Possibly one of the Beaufort hospital chaplains.

144. Chaplain James Wells, 11th Maine Infantry.

145. Private Christian Russ, Company G, 112th.

146. "Blessed are those who dwell in your house; they will be still praising thee." (KJV).

147. "For there is one God and one mediator between God and mankind, the man Christ Jesus." (KJV).

148. Private George W. Ellis, Company H, 112th. Died of disease on October 12, 1863, at Folly Island, South Carolina.

149. Private Perry Heath, Company H, 112th. Died on October 18, 1863, from typhoid fever at Folly Island, South Carolina.

150. Private John Wright, Company G, 112th. Promoted to corporal on April 23, 1864. Wounded at Cold Harbor, Virginia, on June 1, 1864.

151. Sergeant George H. Dixon, Companies A, C & G, 112th. Promoted to 1st sergeant on March 18, 1863, 2nd lieutenant on May 31, 1864, 1st lieutenant on October 13, 1864, and to captain on April 24, 1865. Transferred to the 3rd New York Infantry on June 13, 1865.

152. Captain Josiah M. Lucas, United States Volunteers, Commissary Department.

153. Major Edmund J. Porter, United States Volunteers, Paymaster Department.

154. Private Charles Harmon, Company E, 112th. Died on Folly Island, South Carolina, at the age of 44.

155. "Now then we are ambassadors for Christ, as though God did beseech you by us: we "pray you" in Christ's stead, be ye reconciled to God." (KJV).

156. Private Daniel A. Blanding, Company K, 112th. Died on November 20, 1863, at St. Augustine, Florida.

157. Private John H. Scott, Company C, 112th. Died of dysentery onboard the steamer *Cosmopolitan* on October 22, 1863.

158. Hyde must be referring to casualties from regiments other than the 112th. During this period, the majority of casualties for the 112th came from typhoid fever rather than from contact with Confederate forces.

159. Naaman, a leper, commander of the Army of Syria and King of Aram and healed of leprosy.

160. Jesus comforts his disciples. "Let not your heart be troubled. Ye believe in God, believe in me also." (KJV).

161. Chaplains Ova H. Seymour, 157th New York Infantry; J. F. Crippen, 117th New York Infantry; Robert F. Kabus, 107th Ohio Infantry; and William L. Hyde, 112th New York Infantry.

162. Captain John W. M. Appleton, 54th Massachusetts Infantry. Wounded at Fort Wagner, South Carolina, on July 18, 1863.

163. Chaplain Henry Hill, 3rd New Hampshire Infantry.

164. "But when Herod heard thereof, he said, It is John, whom I beheaded, he is risen from the dead." (KJV).

165. Private Franklin Cramer, Company I, 112th. Discharged for disability on November 11, 1863, at Folly Island, South Carolina, and Private Charles R. Bliss, Company F, 112th.

166. Corporal John A. Gilbert, Company B, 112th. Promoted to sergeant on June 23, 1863, and discharged for disability on November 10, 1863; Private Mathew Hogges, Company K, 112th. Discharged November 11, 1863; Private John Wanshis, Company H, 112th. Discharged for disability on November 16, 1863; Private Dexter S. Fowler, Company F, 112th. Discharged for disability on November 14, 1863; Private Locklin Lowell, Company I, 112th. Discharged for disability on November 3, 1863; Private Leland A. Kirk, Company B, 112th. Discharged on November

10, 1863; Private William F. Onley, Company E, 112th. Died on April 19, 1865, at Wilmington, North Carolina; Private Nash Abbot, Company G, 112th. Died November 18, 1863, at Beaufort, South Carolina; Private Henry Eslor, Company E, 112th. Died of disease on December 24, 1863, at Beaufort, South Carolina; Private William J. Pierce, Company I, 112th. Died of disease on October 19, 1863, at Folly Island, South Carolina; and Private Henry H. Pierce, Company C, 112th. Died on April 8, 1865, at Grant Hospital, Willetts Point, NY.

167. Private Alfred Barber, Company K, 112th. Died on November 11, 1863, at Folly Island, South Carolina.

168. Acts 26:28 (KJV).

169. Mark 10:46–52 (KJV).

170. Brigadier General John T. Sprague, Adjutant General of the State of New York, from 1861 until 1865. Prior service as a United States Marine in 1834.

171. Private Caleb H. Shaffer, Company G, 112th. Died of disease on November 23, 1863, at Folly Island, South Carolina.

172. Ann Eliza Pratt, secretary for the Fredonia Soldier's Aid Society. Wife of Daniel J. Pratt, professor of ancient languages.

173. Corporal Cornelius W. Parker, Company I, 112th. Died of disease on November 24, 1863, at Beaufort, South Carolina.

174. Hyde misspelled his name. Private Jacob Polder, Company F, 112th. Wounded June 1, 1864, at Cold Harbor, Virginia.

175. *Fredonia Censor*, December 30, 1863, Vol. XLIII, No. 46, p. 2.

176. Privates Horatio N. Bowers, Company E, 112th and Loyal Allen, Company H, 112th. Both soldiers died of disease on November 24, 1863, at Folly Island, South Carolina.

177. Mary A. Allen, wife of Private Loyal Allen, Company H, 112th.

178. *Mayville Sentinel*, January 27, 1864, Vol. XXX, No. 15, p. 3.

179. John 4:14 (KJV).

180. Psalm 107:31 (KJV).

181. I Kings 18:21 (KJV).

182. 2nd Lieutenant Samuel P. Hedges, Company B & C, 112th. Captured near Drewry's Bluff, Virginia, on May 16, 1864.

183. 2nd Lieutenant Charles A. Kimberly, Company E & B, 112th. Wounded at Chaffin's Farm, Virginia, on September 29, 1864, and discharged for disability on March 23, 1865.

184. Chaplain Edgar T. Chapman, 169th New York Infantry.

185. "Saying, Where is he that is born King of the Jews? For we have seen his star in the east, and are come to worship him." and "When Herod the king had heard these things, he was troubled, and all Jerusalem with him." (KJV).

Chapter 3

1. 1st Lieutenant Robert A. Corbett, Company D, 112th. Wounded at Cold Harbor, Virginia, on June 1, 1864. Discharged for disability on October 17, 1864.

2. 2nd Lieutenant George W. Edmonds, Companies C & H, 112th. Killed at Darbytown Road, Virginia, on October 27, 1864.

3. The *North American Review* was established in Boston in 1815 and was the first literary magazine published in the United States.

4. Barton's Brigade was commanded by Colonel William B. Barton. The brigade consisted of the following infantry regiments: 47th, 48th and 115th New York, 76th Pennsylvania, and the 3rd and 4th South Carolina Colored Infantry.

5. Lieutenant Colonel Edward W. Smith, United States Volunteers, Adjutant General Department. Received brevetted promotions to colonel and brigadier general.

6. Brigadier General John P. Hatch and Brigadier General Truman Seymour. Hatch was wounded earlier at South Mountain, Maryland, and Seymour was severely wounded leading his division in the attack against Fort Wagner on July 18, 1863. Seymour was later captured during the fighting at the Battle of the Wilderness in Virginia.

7. On April 1, 1864, while crossing the St. Johns River in Florida, the *Maple Leaf* struck a Confederate mine and sank in shallow water. Hyde describes the loss on page 71 of his regimental history: "Valuable company books and papers, which would have been of essential service in preparing the statistical records of the regiment, as well as the tents and other property of the regiment, were lost."

8. Major General Benjamin Butler. Commanded the Army of the James until relieved by General Grant in January 1865. Resigned his commission on November 30, 1865. Elected to Congress in 1866 and in 1882 was elected governor of Massachusetts.

9. Brigadier General George F. Shepley commanded the District of Eastern Virginia in May 1864. He was earlier commissioned as colonel of the 12th Maine Infantry. After the capture of New Orleans, General Butler appointed him military governor of Louisiana.

10. Brigadier General Adelbert Ames served as commander of the 20th Maine Infantry, earned the Medal of Honor for action at 1st Bull Run, commanded a brigade at Gettysburg and participated in the assault at Fort Fisher.

11. Brigadier General Charles A. Heckman commanded Heckman's Brigade. He was twice wounded during Burnside's North Carolina Expedition in 1862. He was wounded for a third time at Port Walthall, Virginia, on May 7, 1864, and later captured near Drewry's Bluff, Virginia, on May 16, 1864. During this period, he commanded the 1st Brigade, 2nd Division, XVIII Corps. The brigade consisted of the following infantry regiments: 23rd, 25th and 27th Massachusetts; 9th New Jersey; 55th Pennsylvania; 89th, 148th and 158th New York; and the 10th New York Heavy Artillery.

12. Private William Foy, Company A, 112th.

13. Private Edward Shelters, Company A, 112th. Wounded at Drewry's Bluff, Virginia, on May 16, 1864. Died of his wounds on June 10, 1864.

14. Brigadier General Godfrey Weitzel served as

the Chief Engineer for the Army of the James during this action at Drewry's Bluff, Virginia. In September 1864, he assumed command of the XVIII Corps and in November of the same year was given command of the XXV Corps. He and his Corps participated in the failed attempt to capture Fort Fisher in December 1864 and were thus reassigned when Butler was relieved of his command.

15. *Fredonia Censor*, June 1, 1864, Vol. XLIV, No. 16, p. 2. Hyde's original letter to the *Dunkirk Journal* seems to be lost to the ages and is the reason I am using the excerpt from the *Fredonia Censor*. Hyde is describing the 112th actions during the Battle of Drewry's Bluff, Virginia.

16. Corporal Michael O'Brien, Company F, 112th. Died of wounds on May 24, 1864, at Bermuda Hundred, Virginia.

17. Private Henry Bowen, Company F, 112th. Killed at Fort Fisher on January 15, 1865. Private Levi S. Brownell, Company G, 112th.

18. Surgeon John J. Craven. Served as surgeon with the 1st New Jersey Infantry and then joined the United States Volunteer Medical Staff in September 1861.

19. *Jamestown Journal*, June 3, 1864, Vol. XXXVIII, No. 52, p. 2.

20. Private Orrin Camp, Company G, 112th.

21. 2nd Lieutenant Horace F. Allen, Company A, 112th.

22. *Dunkirk Journal*, June 10, 1864, Vol. XV, No. 5, p.1.

23. Private George H. Evens, Company I, 112th.

24. Captain Henry A. Johnson, Company F, 13th Indiana Infantry.

25. 2nd Lieutenant William H. Potter, Company D, 112th. Discharged for disability on September 28, 1864.

26. Major General Horatio G. Wright, commanding the VI Corps at Cold Harbor, Virginia.

27. I Corinthians 15:57 (KJV).

28. Colonel John McConihe, commanded the 169th New York Infantry Regiment. Killed in action at Cold Harbor, Virginia, on June 1, 1864. Brevetted to the grade of brigadier general for his service at Cold Harbor. Nathaniel B. Sylvester in his *History of Rensselaer County, New York*, writes McConihe's last words at Cold Harbor were: "Cease firing; fix bayonets and charge again. Dress up the colors—don't leave the colors!"

29. Letter courtesy of the Library of Congress, Washington, D.C. George W. Patterson was a New York Republican whose political career lasted from 1832 until 1879. He served as a member of the state's assembly, as lieutenant governor and was also elected to the United States House of Representatives, representing New York's 33rd district.

30. The Battle of Proctor's Creek is also known as the second battle of Drewry's Bluff.

31. See June 9th 1864, entry from *Westfield Republican*.

32. Corporal Horace W. Barber, Company A, 112th. Died of wounds on June 8, 1864.

33. 2nd Lieutenant Henry Hull, Company K, 112th. Wounded at Cold Harbor on June 2, 1864. Died of wounds on July 3, 1864 at Cold Harbor, Virginia.

34. Corporal Francis G. Wheeler, Company G, 112th. Died from disease onboard the *General J. K. Barnes* on April 11, 1865.

35. The following Company G, 112th casualties noted in this entry are all as a result of the fighting at Cold Harbor, Virginia: Private Charles Gantcher; Sergeant Chauncey W. Hawley, promoted to 1st sergeant on October 12, 1864, 2nd lieutenant on January 4, 1865, and to 1st lieutenant on April 19, 1865; Private William Pease; Private Gilman Shirley, Private Charles Pecor, captured at Cold Harbor and later paroled. He was mustered out of service on June 24, 1865, at New York City; and Private William R. Laine, killed at Cold Harbor on June 1, 1864.

36. Hyde is referring to the 72nd New York Infantry, known as the "3rd Excelsior." The regiment was one of five infantry regiments that made up the Excelsior Brigade. Five companies within the 72nd New York were from Chautauqua County. Charles K. Irwin served as the regiment's surgeon and mustered out with the regiment near Petersburg, Virginia, on June 19, 1864; Samuel Bailey, mustered in as a sergeant major and was later promoted to 1st lieutenant, he was wounded at Williamsburg, Virginia, on May 5, 1862, and promoted to captain on September 26, 1862. He mustered out with the regiment on June 20, 1864. Private Henry C. Stillman mustered into service for three years on September 2, 1862, was transferred to the 120th New York Infantry on June 23, 1864, and was mustered out of service at Washington, DC, on June 3, 1865.

37. Commissary Sergeant Otis W. Shelton, 72nd New York Infantry.

38. I Corinthians 15:57 (KJV).

39. The battle for Cold Harbor devastated the ranks of the 112th regiment, both emotionally and physically. The loss of Colonel Drake right after losing Lieutenant Colonel Carpenter, at Drewry's Bluff, was a formidable blow to the regiment. The number of casualties at Cold Harbor varies between Civil War sources. Hyde did attempt to give an account of the regiment's losses. Although his mortuary reports only documented those soldiers killed, within his letters and journal he did attempt to identify those wounded in action. According to William F. Fox's book *Regimental Losses in the American Civil War*, Fox notes the 112th suffered: 28 killed, 140 wounded and 12 missing. The Union army's staggering losses for Cold Harbor would mount to approximately 12,700 (killed, wounded and missing). Years after the war, when Grant wrote his memoirs, he wrote, "I have always regretted that the last assault at Cold Harbor was ever made."

40. *Westfield Republican*, June 22, 1864, Vol. X, No. 11, p. 1.

41. Colonel Alexander Piper commanded the 10th New York Heavy Artillery and Colonel Martin N. Curtis assumed command of the 2nd Brigade, 3rd Division, XVIII Corps. In January 1865, as a brigadier general, Curtis led a brigade during the second assault upon Fort Fisher and was wounded four

times during the action. For his bravery and leadership at Fort Fisher, he was later awarded the Medal of Honor.

42. 2nd Lieutenant Clarence Crane, Company I, 112th. Promoted to 1st lieutenant on July 23, 1864, and to captain on November 29, 1864. Mustered out with the regiment on June 13, 1865, at Raleigh, North Carolina.

43. Lieutenant Colonel Thomas W. Hyde, 7th Maine Infantry. Cousin to Chaplain William Hyde. Commissioned into the 7th Maine as a captain and rose to the rank of lieutenant colonel. Earned the Medal of Honor for his heroic actions at Antietam, Maryland. On August 21, 1864, he transferred to the 1st Maine Veteran Infantry and was promoted to colonel. On April 2, 1865, he received a brevet promotion to brigadier general.

44. Major General William F. "Baldy" Smith, commanded the XVIII Corps. The corps was attached to General George Meade and the Army of the Potomac during the action at Cold Harbor, Virginia.

45. Corporal Joseph W. Buffman, Company G, 112th. Wounded at Cold Harbor and discharged for disability, January 17, 1865.

46. I Corinthians 15:57 (KJV).

47. Private Austin H. Stafford, Companies B & K, 112th.

48. Major James A. Colvin, 169th New York Infantry. Promoted on November 9, 1864, to lieutenant colonel and mustered out with the regiment on July 19, 1865, at Raleigh, North Carolina.

49. Surgeon Benjamin F. Goodrich. Enlisted as a hospital steward with the 9th New York Cavalry in 1861. In April 1862, he was promoted to acting assistant surgeon in the United States Army and assigned to the battalion of United States Engineers attached to the Army of the Potomac. During the fall of 1864 he resigned from the army to practice medicine in Jamestown, New York. He later engaged in the manufacturing of India-rubber goods and started the well known "B. F. Goodrich Company."

50. Journal entry abruptly ended and sentence was incomplete.

51. Assistant Surgeon Charles Mead and Quartermaster Warner D. Shaw. Both officers served with the Field & Staff element of the 112th.

52. Colonel Louis Bell, 4th New Hampshire Infantry. He took command of 3rd Brigade, 2nd Division, X Corps on June 20, 1864. Died on January 16, 1865, from wounds received at Fort Fisher.

53. Major General Edward O. C. Ord. As commander of the XVIII Corps, was wounded during the assault upon Fort Harrison, which was part of the Richmond defenses. In January 1865, he took command of the Army of the James and the Department of North Carolina. Brigadier General John W. Turner commanded the 2nd Division, X Corps.

54. Private James D. Findley, Companies K & H, 112th. Discharged for disability.

55. Privates Robert Henry, Company G, and Asa A. Sweet, Company I, killed in action at Petersburg, Virginia, on June 25, 1864.

56. Private Julius M. Shaw, Company B, 112th.

57. 1st Lieutenant William H. Shaw, Field & Staff, 112th. Also served as regimental quartermaster.

58. Private Benjamin Vandewark, Company A, 112th.

59. Hyde is referring to 1st Lieutenant Robert A. Corbett, Company D, 112th. Wounded at Cold Harbor on June 1, 1864, and promoted to captain on September 13, 1864. Discharged for disability on October 17, 1864.

60. Private Samuel Bush, Company K, 112th. Killed at Petersburg, Virginia, on June 26, 1864.

61. Hyde's mortuary reports document Vorce and Sherwin being killed on June 28, 1864, and McEvoy on June 30, 1864.

62. 1st Lieutenant Herman Sixby, Company E, 112th. Wounded on July 30, 1864, at Petersburg, Virginia. Discharged for disability on February 3, 1865.

63. Hyde is referring to Commissary Sergeant Otis W. Shelton, 72nd New York Infantry.

64. Corporal Bartholomew F. Myers, 120th New York Infantry. Promoted to sergeant on January 1, 1865. Also served with the 72nd New York Infantry.

65. Hyde is referring to 2nd Lieutenant Horace F. Allen, Company A, 112th.

66. Hyde is referring to the Ladies' Aid Society of Dunkirk, for which his wife served as secretary.

67. Copperheads refers to Northern Democrats who opposed Lincoln's war policy and sought a reconciliation with the South through a negotiated peace.

68. *Sketch of the Life of Colonel J. C. Drake* by George W. Patterson and William L. Hyde. This pamphlet is available at the Patterson Library at Westfield, New York.

69. Private Silas N. Toles, Company G, 112th. Promoted to corporal on November 12, 1864, and to sergeant on March 6, 1865.

70. Private Albert C. Fisk, Company I, 112th.

71. Brigadier General Alfred H. Terry. Commanded the X Corps during operations against Petersburg and Richmond, Virginia. Participated in the first assault against Fort Fisher as part of General Butler's command in December 1864. Commanded the second and successful assault, capturing Fort Fisher in January 1865. Promoted to major general on January 16, 1865. During the Indian Wars, Terry was in charge of the Department of Dakota.

72. Chaplain William H. Taylor, 48th New York Infantry. On page 92 of his regimental history, Hyde writes, "There were, the second week in July, twenty-seven of the regiment in a camp hospital established for slight cases, and twenty had been sent back to [the] general hospital. This out of a total of 355 present for duty."

73. Private G. Wilton Lewis, Company G, 112th. Wounded at Petersburg, Virginia, on July 26, 1864. Discharged for disability on October 18, 1864.

74. The *History of Charles the Bold, Duke of Burgundy in Volumes One and Two*, by John Foster Kirk. Published by J. B. Lippincott & Company, Philadelphia, Pennsylvania, in 1864.

75. Private William S. Carpenter, Company D, 112th. Wounded at Petersburg, Virginia, on May 16, 1864.

76. By the end of 1864, Hyde's opinion of the value and fighting capabilities of black soldiers has a drastic change. His description of their courage and valor at Cold Harbor and throughout the Petersburg campaign gives credit to their service to the Union.

77. Letter courtesy of Navarro College, Corsicana, Texas.

78. 1st Lieutenant Lyman J. Parker, Companies C & I, 112th. Promoted to captain in Company C on July 23, 1864. Wounded at Chaffin's Farm, Virginia, on September 29, 1864, and discharged for disability on December 23, 1864.

79. Refers to Admiral David G. Farragut's victory at the Battle of Mobile Bay, Alabama, on August 4, 1864.

80. Brigadier General William W. Averell, Union cavalry commander. Participated in the Shenandoah Campaign of 1864 with General Philip Sheridan.

81. Major General John A. Dix. Noted for suppressing the New York City draft riots of 1863.

82. Corporal Francis J. Goodrich, Company I, 112th and Private Egbert C. Vanscoy, Company E, 112th.

83. Major General George G. Meade commanded the Army of the Potomac, and Major General Winfield S. Hancock commanded the II Corps.

84. Colonel Joseph R. Hawley, commander of the 2nd Brigade, 1st Division, X Corps. Served as regimental commander for the 7th Connecticut Infantry and was promoted to brigadier general on September 13, 1864. On September 28, 1865, he received a brevet promotion to major general for his service during the war.

85. Possibly a European institution; the name and location isn't known.

86. Major General Gouverneur K. Warren, commander of the V Corps, Army of the Potomac. Hero of Gettysburg for his defense of Little Round Top.

87. Sergeant Major Alroy A. Ticknor, Field & Staff and Companies A & B, 112th. Promoted to 1st lieutenant of Company A on August 22, 1864, and to captain of Company B on November 28, 1864. Prior service with the 49th New York Infantry.

88. Major General David B. Birney. Selected by General Grant to command the X Corps but fell ill from malaria and died in Philadelphia, Pennsylvania, on October 18, 1864.

89. Wallie refers to Wallace E. Hyde, Chaplain Hyde's second son. Born March 17, 1855 and died on October 4, 1856.

90. Private Charles Koepke, Company G, 112th.

91. Lieutenant Colonel Zina H. Robinson, 9th Maine Infantry.

92. 1st Lieutenant George F. Mount, Company K, 112th. Killed at Bermuda Hundred on August 25, 1864. Hyde misspells Captain Augustus M. Erwin's name in both his regimental history and his journal as Ewing. Erwin was wounded at Bermuda Hundred on August 25, 1864. He transferred to the 48th New York Infantry on June 9, 1865.

93. Private Augustus Neil, Company D, 112th. Captured at Bermuda Hundred, Virginia, on August 25, 1864. Exchanged prisoner of war on May 15, 1865, and Private Thomas Brown, Company A, 112th. Captured near Petersburg, Virginia, on August 25, 1864. Died as a prisoner of war at Salisbury, North Carolina, on January 30, 1865.

94. Private Levi E. Tenny, Company G, 112th. Transferred to the 3rd New York Infantry on June 13, 1865.

95. The *Dunkirk Weekly Journal*, September 9, 1864, Vol. XV, No. 18, page 2.

96. Possibly refers to Mrs. Jeremiah Drake's letter dated August 21, 1864. See Appendix B.

97. Private Albert J. Weaver, Company C, 112th. Killed at Chaffin's Farm, Virginia, on September 29, 1864. Private Newell B. Richardson, Company C, 112th. Wounded at Cold Harbor on June 1, 1864.

98. Chaplain Report courtesy of the National Archives.

99. Brigadier General Lorenzo Thomas, Adjutant General of the Army, 1861–1869.

100. Privates Andrew J. Simmons and Solomon W. Whitford of Company D, 112th. Both wounded on September 2, 1864, at Petersburg, Virginia.

101. 1st Lieutenant Herman S. Fox, Companies F & H, 112th. Promoted to captain on August 25, 1864.

102. These soldiers all died from typhoid fever: Private Michael Dolan, Company B on August 26, 1864; Corporal Smith Peacock on August 3, 1864; and Private John Peters, Jr. on September 17, 1864.

103. Private Deloss Robbins was wounded at Chaffin's Farm, Virginia, on September 27, 1864, and Private Charles H. West was killed there on September 29, 1864.

104. Chaplain Lucius L. Palmer, 142nd New York Infantry.

105. Private Nehemiah Davis, Company H, 112th. Wounded at Petersburg, Virginia, on September 21, 1864 and at Fort Fisher, North Carolina, on January 15, 1865.

106. On September 14, 1864, Confederate Major General Wade Hampton led a cavalry force of approximately 3,000 soldiers on a daring raid behind the Union lines. The objective of the raid was to capture cattle in order to feed the Rebel army defending Petersburg and Richmond. With minimum casualties, Hampton's force drove over 2,000 head of cattle back into the Confederate lines.

107. Private Robert L. Bronson, Company D, 112th.

108. Colonel Rufus Daggett, 117th New York Infantry. Prior service with the 14th New York Infantry. Promoted to brigadier general by brevet on January 15, 1865.

109. Surgeon Charles M. Clark, 39th Illinois Infantry.

110. Chaplain Report courtesy of the National Archives.

111. Chapin's is also known as Chaffin's.

112. Corporal Ebenezer Skellie, Company D, 112th. Wounded on September 29, 1864, at Chaffin's Farm, Virginia.

113. Sergeant Alfred O. Ellis, Company G, 112th. Color Sergeant, promoted to 2nd lieutenant on October 17, 1864, and to 1st lieutenant on January 4, 1865.

114. *Jamestown Journal*, October 14, 1864, Vol. XXXIX, No. 19, p. 1.
115. Letter courtesy of Navarro College, Corsicana, Texas.
116. Brigadier General August V. Kautz. Commanded cavalry operations for the XXIII Corps during the Petersburg and Richmond campaigns. Brevetted to major general on February 14, 1865. Prior service as colonel of the 2nd Ohio Cavalry.
117. Chaplain Thomas L. Ambrose, 12th New Hampshire Infantry. Wounded at Petersburg on July 24, 1864. Died of his wounds at Fort Monroe, Virginia, on August 19, 1864.
118. Private Frank R. Case, Company A, 112th. Case must have returned to the regiment, records show that he mustered out with his company at Raleigh, North Carolina, on June 13, 1865.
119. Chaplain Charles C. Tiffany, 6th Connecticut Infantry.
120. Private George T. Westly, Company C, 112th. Killed in action at Darbytown Road, Virginia, on October 27, 1864.
121. Corporal William Wilson, Company K, 112th. Wounded on October 27, 1864, at Darbytown Road, Virginia. Died of his wounds on November 5, 1864.
122. Psalms 139:23 (KJV).
123. Private Charles Price, Company G, 112th.
124. Horatio Seymour, twice governor of New York (1853–1854 and 1863–1864). Democratic candidate for the 1868 presidential election. Lost to the Republican, Ulysses S. Grant.
125. The Freedmen's Aid Society was founded in 1861 by various religious groups to provide teachers and schools in the South in an effort to raise the standard of education for former slaves. In March 1865, The Freedmen's Bureau was established as part of the War Department to provide aid to freed slaves during the Reconstruction Period.
126. Corporal Walter J. Hart, Company B, 112th. Wounded at Darbytown Road, Virginia, on October 28, 1864. Died of wounds on November 29, 1864.
127. Chaplain Report courtesy of the National Archives.
128. Private Morgan Phillips, Company B, 112th.
129. Private John M. Wood, Company G, 112th.
130. Reuben E. Fenton. New York Democrat, twice elected to governor of New York (1864 and 1866). Also served as a United States Senator from New York between 1869 and 1875.
131. On the night of October 26, 1864, Navy Lieutenant William B. Cushing led a daring raid upon the Roanoke River to attack the Confederate ironclad *Albemarle* located near Plymouth, North Carolina. Using a spar torpedo, Cushing was successful in sinking the Rebel ironclad in about six feet of water. The Confederates were able to recover the ship's munitions and cannons and put them to use in the defense of Plymouth. Cushing received the thanks of Congress for his exploit. His brother, Army Lieutenant Alonzo Cushing, was killed on the third day of fighting at Gettysburg; and 151 years later, he received the Medal of Honor for his heroic actions.
132. Chaplain Report courtesy of the National Archives.
133. Private Martin J. Stafford, Company A, 112th.
134. Admiral David D. Porter. Supported Grant and Sherman during the Vicksburg Campaign of 1863 and led the navy component in the successful attack against Fort Fisher in 1865.
135. *The Days of Shoddy*. A novel of the great rebellion in 1861, written by Henry Morford and published by T. B. Peterson & Brothers, Philadelphia in 1863.
136. Old Hundredth, also known as the Doxology, composed by Louis Bourgeois in 1551.
137. Colonel Albert M. Barney commanded the 1st Brigade, 2nd Division, X Corps. Also served as the colonel of the 142nd New York Infantry. Received a brevet promotion to brigadier general on March 11, 1865.
138. Captain William A. Jones, 142nd New York Infantry. Promoted to major on December 3, 1864 and to lieutenant colonel on January 25, 1865.
139. *Jamestown Journal*, January 20, 1865, Vol. XXXIX, No. 33, pp. 1–2.

Chapter 4

1. Captain David Sampson, Company K, 112th.
2. Captain Ervin A. Jones, Company F, 132nd New York Infantry. Also saw service with the 3rd and 99th New York Infantry.
3. *Jamestown Journal*, January 20, 1865, Vol. XXXIX, No. 33, p. 2.
4. Captain Charles A. Carleton, United States Volunteers Adjutant General Department. Prior service with the 12th New York State Militia and the 4th New Hampshire Infantry. Breveted to lieutenant colonel for his actions at Fort Fisher, North Carolina.
5. By January 1865, Major Generals William T. Sherman and George H. Thomas, "the Rock of Chickamauga," had taken Atlanta, Nashville, and virtually destroyed all Confederate capability to continue fighting in the West. The Union push was now focused towards destroying Joseph E. Johnston's Confederates in the Carolinas.
6. Chaplain Royal Parkinson, 23rd United States Colored Infantry.
7. Captain Naham S. Scott, Company C, 112th. Discharged for disability on May 24, 1864.
8. Pioneers were soldiers who performed construction and engineering tasks for the army.
9. Abbott's Brigade was the 2nd Brigade, 1st Division, XXIV Corps, commanded by Colonel Joseph C. Abbott. The infantry regiments within the brigade were: 6th and 7th Connecticut, 3rd and 7th New Hampshire and the 16th New York Heavy Artillery.
10. Confederates Major General William H. C. Whiting and Colonel William Lamb were both wounded and captured while defending Fort Fisher. Whiting served as the district commander, which included Wilmington and the Cape Fear defenses. Lamb commanded the immediate garrison at Fort Fisher, which included North Carolina infantry and

artillery units and elements from the Confederate Navy.

11. Colonel Galusha Pennypacker commanded the 97th Pennsylvania Infantry during the second assault upon Fort Fisher. In the course of the war, he was wounded five times. For his actions at Fort Fisher, he was awarded the Medal of Honor. While recovering from the wound he received at Fort Fisher, he was promoted to brigadier general—one month before his twenty-first birthday.

12. Private George W. Clute, Company I, 112th. Captured near Chaffin's Farm, Virginia, on August 25, 1864. Died while in captivity at Salisbury, North Carolina.

13. Colonel John W. Moore and Lieutenant Colonel Jonas W. Lyman, both killed during the 2nd assault upon Fort Fisher, North Carolina.

14. Brigadier General Newton M. Curtis, commanded 1st Brigade, 2nd Division, XXIV Corps during the 2nd assault upon Fort Fisher. Previously, he commanded the 142nd New York Infantry. Received the Medal of Honor for his actions at Fort Fisher, where he was wounded four times.

15. 1st Lieutenant George W. Ross, 117th New York Infantry.

16. Captain John Q. A. Hollister, Company E, 112th.

17. Wagoner William S. Coy, Company D, 112th and Wagoner James Shaw, Company A, 112th. Unable to determine the first name of Fisher.

18. Major General John M. Schofield, commanded the XXIII Corps. Schofield's Corps was moved from service in Tennessee to North Carolina to link up with Major General William T. Sherman's army.

19. Brigadier General Charles J. Paine commanded the 3rd Division, X Corps. The 3rd Division was made up of three brigades, each with three regiments of colored infantry.

20. Unable to identify a Captain Scott with the 48th New York Infantry.

21. Private Albert C. Bond, Company B, 112th. Wounded at Cold Harbor on June 2, 1864. Discharged from a hospital in York, Pennsylvania, on June 16, 1865.

22. Major General Jacob D. Cox. As a major general, Cox commanded the District of Ohio in 1863. During the Atlanta Campaign, he commanded a division in the XXIII Corps and in 1865 he served alongside Major General John A. Schofield when the XXIII Corps linked up with Sherman's Army as it swept into North Carolina.

23. Confederate Major General Robert F. Hoke commanded a division in support of the defenses of Fort Fisher, North Carolina.

24. Colonel George S. Dodge, United States Quartermaster Department. Received a brevet promotion to brigadier general for valuable service in the movement against Fort Fisher, North Carolina.

25. Captain Benjamin G. Casler, 154th New York Infantry. Captured at Gettysburg on July 1, 1863.

26. 1st Lieutenant Francis E. Pennock, Company I, 112th. Wounded at Chaffin's Farm, Virginia, on September 29, 1864.

27. 1st Lieutenant Alfred O. Ellis, Company G, C & D, 112th. Promoted to color sergeant on November 21, 1863.

28. Henri Le Fevre Brown, 72nd and 120th New York Regiments. Medal of Honor recipient for the Battle of the Wilderness, May 6, 1864.

29. Unable to identify Thompson of Company H and Coonrod of Company D. Private Mason C. Thompson, Company B, died from fever. Private Norton Dowd, Company I, died from congestive chills. Private Patrick O'Brien, Company H, died from fever.

30. Quote is from George Herbert's poem "Virtue." Herbert was a 17th Century English poet and Anglican priest.

31. Major Eugene E. Graves, United States Volunteers. Served on General Terry's staff as aide de camp. Also had prior service with the 8th and 13th Connecticut Infantry Regiments.

32. Major General Henry W. Slocum commanded the XIV and XX Corps that made up the left wing of General Sherman's "March to the Sea" and the Carolina Campaign.

33. Major General Joseph Wheeler. Confederate cavalry officer, wounded three times during the war. Captured in May 1865, sent to Fort Delaware, Delaware, and released in June 1865. Served in the United States Army as a major general of volunteers during the Spanish American War.

34. Privates Jacob Walder, Company B, 112th and Charles Mercer, Company I, 112th.

35. Private Carlos F. Manwaring, Company F, 112th.

36. Major General Hugh J. Kilpatrick commanded Sherman's cavalry in the "March to the Sea" and Carolina campaigns.

37. Corporal John J. Hunt, Company G, 112th.

38. Eliphalet Whittlesey served as chaplain with the 19th Maine Infantry, United States Volunteers, and the 46th United States Colored Troops during the war.

39. A National Fast Day/National Day of Prayer has occurred in this country since it was established by the Second Continental Congress in 1775. Most Presidents have made proclamations for a day of national prayer and/or fasting, including President Lincoln during the Civil War.

40. Latin term meaning transitive.

41. Major General George H. Thomas and Major General Philip H. Sheridan.

42. All of the regiment's members whose term of service date expired on October 1, 1865, were mustered out of service at Raleigh, North Carolina, on June 13, 1865. Recruits who had recently joined the regiment were consolidated with the 3rd New York Infantry and remained in the field at Raleigh for additional duty. The 3rd New York Infantry was mustered out of service at Raleigh, North Carolina, on August 28, 1865.

43. Affidavit from William L. Hyde's pension file at the National Archives, Washington, DC. Document dated November 14, 1885.

Appendix A

1. The military service record at the National Archives lists his name as George W. Griffin and states that he died from a gunshot wound on the battlefield at Chaffin's Farm, Virginia.
2. Also listed as Private Alba Harry Duncan. Hyde notes on page 205 in his regimental history that Duncan was the first death of the regiment.
3. The military service record at the National Archives lists his name as George W. Kennedy.

Appendix B

1. Captain Caspar K. Abell, Company D, 72nd New York Infantry.
2. Surgeon Charles K. Irwin, 72nd New York Infantry.
3. Private Thomas Mayborn (Maybourne), Company H, 112th. He was on detached duty with the 7th Massachusetts Battery Light Artillery at the time his company mustered out of service in 1865. Private John Mayborn, Company H, 112th. Died of disease at Suffolk, Virginia, on November 10, 1862.
4. Hannah E. Mayborn was the wife of Private John G. Mayborn of Company H, 112th. Private Mayborn died from typhoid fever at Suffolk, Virginia, on November 10, 1862.
5. Private Paul Squimer enlisted into Company G, 112th on August 13, 1862. While encamped at Suffolk, Virginia, he contracted typhoid fever and succumbed to the disease on December 15, 1862.
6. Private George Stroyer, 72nd New York Infantry. He was wounded at Gettysburg, Pennsylvania, and also served with the 120th New York Infantry.
7. Wagoner William Kloet, Company G, 112th.
8. Private Edward P. Jones, Company D, 112th. Discharged for disability on November 24, 1862.
9. Private James Lewis, Company D, 112th. Died of disease at Suffolk, Virginia, on December 6, 1862.
10. Corporal George H. Dixon, Companies G, C & A, 112th. Promoted to sergeant on March 5, 1863; 1st sergeant on March 18, 1863; 2nd lieutenant on May 31, 1864; 1st lieutenant on October 13, 1864; and to captain on April 24, 1865. Also served with the 3rd New York Infantry.
11. Lieutenant Colonel Frederick A. Redington, Field & Staff, 112th. Discharged for disability on January 14, 1863.
12. Captain Franklin Waters, Company E, 112th. Also served as the regimental quartermaster. Died of disease at Suffolk, Virginia, on October 3, 1863.
13. 1st Lieutenant & Adjutant Selden E. Marvin, Field & Staff, 112th. Mustered out of the 112th on September 13, 1863 to take a commission as major and paymaster in the United States Army.
14. Sergeant George F. Parmlee, Company G, 112th. Discharged at Folly Island, South Carolina, on September 22, 1862.
15. Private Davis J. Buel enlisted on February 24, 1864, for a period of three years with Company B, 112th. He transferred to the 3rd New York Infantry on June 13, 1865, and was mustered out of service at Raleigh, North Carolina, on August 28, 1865.
16. Private Samuel Bush was forty-one years of age when he enlisted to serve three years with Company K, 112th on August 30, 1862. On June 26, 1864, he was killed in action at Petersburg, Virginia.
17. Wife of Colonel Jeremiah C. Drake, Field & Staff, 112th. Drake died of wounds received at Cold Harbor, Virginia, on June 2, 1864.
18. Wife of Lieutenant Colonel Elial F. Carpenter, Field & Staff, 112th. Carpenter died of wounds received at Drewry's Bluff, Virginia, on May 18, 1864.
19. Wife of Colonel John P. Smith, Field & Staff, 112th. Smith fell, mortally wounded, while leading the 112th in an assault upon Fort Fisher, North Carolina, on January 15, 1865. He died from his wounds on January 18, 1865.
20. Major General Newton M. Curtis. Curtis commanded the 1st Brigade, 2nd Division, XXIV Corps in the second assault upon Fort Fisher, North Carolina, on January 15, 1865. For his exploits at Fort Fisher, he was awarded the Medal of Honor.
21. Letter regarding Private Oliver T. Reed, Company A, 3rd New York Infantry. Reed died from typhoid fever on May 24, 1865. This is another example of Chaplain Hyde providing assistance to families other than those of the 112th.
22. Daughter of Surgeon Charles E. Washburn, Field & Staff, 112th. Washburn died of typhoid fever near Faisons Station, North Carolina, on April 10, 1865.
23. Mary A. Palmeter, wife of Captain John G. Palmeter, Company H, 112th. Palmeter died of wounds received at Cold Harbor, Virginia, on August 1, 1864 at Jamestown, New York.
24. After researching the Chautauqua County census records for 1860, I believe Mary Prendergast is the sister of Private Charles F. Prendergast of the 9th New York Cavalry.

Appendix C

1. The title of this document indicates it was written circa 1875 and perhaps presented to members of the Grand Army of the Republic.
2. Major General William F. "Baldy" Smith commanded the 18th Army Corps as part of the Army of the James, at Cold Harbor and during the early phase of the Petersburg Campaign.
3. Major General Horatio G. Wright, a veteran of the Army of the Potomac since Gettysburg, commanded the 6th Army Corps during Cold Harbor.
4. Major General William T. H. Brooks commanded the 1st Division, 18th Army Corps during Cold Harbor and Petersburg.
5. A verse from a poem, *In Memoriam, Gettysburg, July 1–4, 1863*, published in *Poems of the Republic* by William O. Bourne in 1864.

References and Sources

Manuscript Collections

William Lyman Hyde Papers. The Pearce Civil War Collection, Navarro College, Corsicana, TX.

William Lyman Hyde Papers. Jim Quinlan Collection, Alexandria, VA.

George Washington Patterson Papers. United States Library of Congress, Washington, DC.

Civil War Collection. Emory University, Atlanta, GA.

Primary Sources

Hyde, William L. *History of the One Hundred and Twelfth Regiment N.Y. Volunteers.* Fredonia, NY: W. McKinstry, 1866. Reprinted by Higginson, Salem, Mass., 1998.

Official Army Register of the Volunteer Force of the United States Army for the Years 1861, 1862, 1863, 1864, 1865. 9 vols. Washington, DC: Adjutant General's Office, 1865. Reprinted by Ron R. Van Sickle Military Books. Gaithersburg, MD, 1987.

United States Army Heritage and Education Center. Military Order of the Loyal Legion of the United States (MOLLUS) Civil War Collection. Massachusetts Photograph Collection. Carlisle, PA.

United States Census Bureau. Census Records 1860 and 1865. National Archives, Washington, DC.

United States Department of the Interior. Pension and Military Service Records. National Archives, Washington, DC.

War of the Rebellion: Official Records of the Union and Confederate Armies. 128 vols. Washington, DC: Government Printing Office, 1880–1901.

Newspapers

Chautauqua Democrat
Dunkirk Journal
Dunkirk Union
Dunkirk Weekly Journal
Fredonia Censor
Jamestown Journal
Mayville Sentinel
Westfield Republican

Secondary Sources

Allardice, Bruce S. *More Generals in Gray.* Baton Rouge: Louisiana State University Press, 1995.

Barrett, John G. *The Civil War in North Carolina.* Chapel Hill: University of North Carolina Press, 1963.

Bates, Samuel P. *History of Pennsylvania Volunteers, 1861–1865.* Harrisburg, PA: Singerly, 1869. Reprinted by Broadfoot, Wilmington, NC, 1993.

Billings, John D. *Hardtack and Coffee: The Unwritten Story of Army Life.* Boston, MA: George M. Smith, 1887. Reprinted by Corner House, Williamstown, MA, 1993.

Billingsley, A. S. *From the Flag to the Cross; or Scenes and Incidents of Christianity in the War: The Conversions, Prayers, Dying Requests, Last Words, Sufferings and Deaths of Our Soldiers, on the Battlefield, in Hospital, Camp and Prison; and a Description of Distinguished Christian Men and Their Labors.* Philadelphia: New World, 1872.

Boatner, Mark M. *The Civil War Dictionary.* New York: David McKay, 1959.

Brown, Henri Le Fevre. *History of the Third Regiment Excelsior Brigade 72nd New York Volunteer Infantry.* Jamestown, NY: Journal Printing, 1902.

The Congressional Medal of Honor. Chico, CA: Sharp and Dunnigan, 1988.

Downs, John P., Fenwick Y. Hedley, et al., eds. *History of Chautauqua County New York and Its People.* Vol. 2. Boston: American Historical Society, 1921.

Dyer, Frederick H. *Compendium of the War of the Rebellion.* Des Moines, IA: Dyer, 1908. Reprinted by Morningside Bookshop, Dayton, OH, 1979.

Fallon, John T., United States Adjutant General's Office. *List of Synonyms of Organizations in the Volunteer Service of the United States During the Years 1861, 62, 63, 64, and 65.* Washington, D.C.: Government Printing Office, 1885.

Faust, Drew Gilpin. *This Republic of Suffering:*

Death and the American Civil War. New York: Vintage Books, Random House, 2008.

Fox, William F. *Regimental Losses in the American Civil War*. Albany, NY: Brandow, 1898. Reprinted by Morningside House, Dayton, OH, 1985.

Gragg, Rod. *Confederate Goliath: The Battle of Fort Fisher*. New York: Harper Perennial, 1991.

Gibson, Charles Dana, and E. Kay Gibson. "The Army's Navy Series." *Dictionary of Transports and Combatant Vessels Steam and Sail Employed by the Union Army, 1861–1868*. Camden, ME: Ensign Press, 1995.

Hanson, John W. *Historical Sketch of the Old Sixth Regiment of Massachusetts Volunteers: During Its Three Campaigns in 1861, 1862, 1863 and 1864*. Boston, MA: Lee and Shepard, 1866.

Heitman, Francis B. *Historical Register and Dictionary of the United States Army 1789–1903*. Washington, D.C.: Government Printing Office, 1903. Reprinted by Olde Soldiers Books, Gaithersburg, MD, 1988.

Hunt, Roger. *Colonels in Blue: Union Army Colonels of the Civil War: The New England States: Connecticut, Maine, Massachusetts, New Hampshire, Rhode Island and Vermont*. Atglen, PA: Schiffer, 2001.

Hunt, Roger. *Colonels in Blue: Union Army Colonels of the Civil War: New York*. Atglen, PA: Schiffer, 2003.

Hunt, Roger. *Colonels in Blue: Union Army Colonels of the Civil War: The Mid-Atlantic States: Pennsylvania, New Jersey, Maryland, Delaware and the District of Columbia*. Mechanicsburg, PA: Stackpole Books, 2003.

Hunt, Roger, and Jack R. Brown. *Brevet Brigadier Generals in Blue*. Gaithersburg, MD: Olde Soldiers Books, 1990.

Maine Association. "In Memoriam," *The Maine Bugle*, Vol. 4 (January 1897): 93–94.

Massachusetts Adjutant General, comp. *Massachusetts Soldiers, Sailors, and Marines in the Civil War*. Brookline, MA: Riverdale, 1935.

Navy Department. *Dictionary of American Naval Fighting Ships*. Vol. 1. Washington, D.C.: U.S. Government Printing Office, 1959. Reprinted with corrections 1979.

New York. *Annual Report, of the Adjutant General of the State of New York: 1861–1865*. Albany, NY: Wynkoop, Hallenbeck, Crawford, 1893–1905.

Osbon, B. S., comp. *Hand Book of the United States Navy: Being a Compilation of All the Principal Events in the History of Every Vessel of the United States Navy, April 1861 to May 1864*. New York: Trubner, 1864.

Phisterer, Frederick, comp. *New York in the War of the Rebellion 1861 to 1865*. Albany, NY: Lyon, 1912.

Rhea, Gordon C. *Cold Harbor: Grant and Lee, May 26–June 3, 1864*. Baton Rouge: Louisiana State University Press, 2002.

United States Army Heritage and Education Center, Civil War Photographs Digital Collection, Carlisle, PA.

Warner, Ezra J. *Generals in Blue: Lives of the Union Commanders*. Baton Rouge: Louisiana State University Press, 1994.

Warner, Ezra J. *Generals in Gray: Lives of the Confederate Commanders*. Baton Rouge: Louisiana State University Press, 1993.

Wiley, Bell Irvin. *The Life of Billy Yank: The Common Soldier of the Union*. Baton Rouge: Louisiana State University Press, 1978.

Wilt, Richard, ed. *New York Soldiers in the Civil War*. Bowie, MD: Heritage, 1999.

Index

Numbers in ***bold italics*** indicate pages with photographs.

Abbey, Roland D. 130, 136, 239
Abbott, Joseph C. 196, 199, 206, 210, 211, 274n9
Abbott, Nash 55, 238, 270n166
Abell, Casper K. 241, 242, 276AppBn1
Adkins, Robert 136, 239
Alden, Leonard C. 50, 269n141
Allen, Horace F. 74, 101, 108, ***224***, 225, 271n21, 272n65
Allen, Loyal 57, 239, 268n115, 270n176
Allen, Mary A. 57, 270n177
Allen, Orrin S. 136, 268n115
Allen, Simeon L. 78, 235
Almasher, Peter 193
Alverson, James 234
Ambrose, Thomas L. 145, 274n117
Ames, Adelbert 66, 97, 175, 182, 191, 192, 199, 207, 209, 210, 211, 219, 270n10
Anderson, Andrew 196, 236
Anderson, Robert 193
Andrews, Lewis 14, 266n9
Angel, Mr. & Mrs. 162
Aplin, William 43, 215, 268n100
Appleby, Wallace 136, 239
Applegate, James W. 25, 267n64
Appleton, John W.M. 54, 269n162
Apthorp, George 124, 239
Apthorp, James 239
Apthorp, Samuel F. 124, 239
Apthorp, William 239
Arnold, Lauren 234
Arnold, Milo 140
Arthur, John M. 78, 234
Atkinson, George R. 236
Austin, Homer 78, 235
Austin, Palmer 82
Averell, William W. 273n80
Aversolt, Peter 196
Ayres, Doctor 19

Baber, Lieutenant 134
Bagley, P. 193
Bailey, Samuel 86, 271n36
Baker, Albert 23, 236, 267n54
Baker, Charles H. 79, 237

Baldwin, Henry 79, 238
Baldwin, William 238
Ball, James 136, 150
Barber, Alfred 55, 240, 270n167
Barber, George W. 37, 113, 114, ***127***, 267n89
Barber, Horace W. 78, 85, 234, 271n32
Barhite, Charles H. 235
Barhite, Daniel S. 234
Barhite, William A. 25, 267n63
Barna, Joseph 78, 235
Barney, Albert M. 179, 228, 274n137
Barrett, Mrs. 36
Barrett, Patrick 267n87
Bartlett, Gilman 18, 237, 266n33
Bartmann, Fred 79, 83, 238
Barton, William B. 63, 270n4
Beauregard, Pierre G.T. 73
Beck, Mrs. 228
Beck, William A. 193
Beecher, Eli C. 79
Beecher, Henry W. 117
Belanger, Denis 193
Belden, Ellery C. 236
Bell, Louis 96, 197, 199, 272n52
Bellows, Mr. 103
Bellows, Mrs. 98, 112, 170
Benjamin, Henry A. 48, 234, 269n131
Bennett, Andrew 124, 235
Bennett, Wesley 234
Benz, Conrad 12
Beyer, Simon 124, 237
Bigalow, Simon 136, 234
Binns, Thomas 238
Birney, David B. 119, ***120***, 126, 131, 133, 137, 138, 140, 273n88
Bisset, William 153
Blair, Francis P. 222
Blanding, Daniel A. 53, 240, 269n156
Blanding, Emmet C. 196, 237
Bliss, Charles R. 55, 269n165
Bloomfield, Samuel P. 238
Bockstanz, John A. 239
Bolin, Peter 193
Bond, Albert C. 78, 206, 275n21

Bookstaver, William 109, 227, 267n78
Booty, Woodley W. 79, 237
Boss, Sumner 47, 235, 268n121
Bourne, William O. 276AppCn5
Bowdish, Isaac B. 22, 266n52
Bowen, Henry 70, 196, 238, 271n17
Bowers, Horatio N. 57, 236, 270n176
Bowers, Mr. 57
Boyd, Edson ***14***, 15, 22, 151, 266n10
Boyden, Andrew J. 236
Bradley, Gambol 196
Braley, Irvin E. 78, 236
Brazee, B. Frank ***22***, 139, 197, 217, 266n50
Breyer, Valentine 193
Briggs, James 193
Briggs, Lyman 240
Broadhead, David 238
Bronson, Frank 240
Bronson, Robert L. 131, 273n107
Brooks, Abel D. 249
Brooks, Stillman 78
Brooks, William T.H. 258, 276AppCn4
Brown, Henri L. 275n28
Brown, Henry F. 216
Brown, Thomas 78, 123, 124, 234, 273n93
Brownell, Levi S. 271n17
Brownell, Sherman 70, 74
Buchanan, William H. 153
Bucklin, Willard 79
Buddington, Mr. & Mrs. 38
Buel, Darwin 248
Buel, Davis J. 276n15
Buel, Mrs. J.B. 248
Buffman, Joseph W. 79, 83, 90, 272n45
Bullock, Daniel E. 130, 136, 235
Bullock, Franklin 44, 45, 47, 152, 235, 238, 268n108
Bunker, George 162
Burdon, Joseph 193
Burns, Thomas 79
Burnside, Ambrose E. ***13***, 95
Burr, Theodore 80, 240

279

Index

Bush, Milton 249
Bush, Samuel 98, 240, 249, 272*n*60, 276*n*16
Bushee, Charles H. 236
Bushnell, Emrelu 130, 196, 239
Butler, Benjamin F. *65*, 66, 67, 72, 73, 85, 97, 109, 119, 122, 123, 131, 144, 159, 166, 168, 169, 173, 176, 178, 181, 186, 187, 191, 192, 256, 270*n*8, 270*n*9, 271*n*14, 272*n*71
Button, Joseph H. 196, 238

Cahall, James 238
Camp, Orrin S. 74, 238, 271*n*20
Cander, Charlie 112
Carey, George L. 79
Carey, John A. 79
Carleson, John 153, 236
Carleton, Charles A. 191, 274*n*4
Carpenter, Elial F. 8, 18, *29*, 32, 38, 39, 40, 41, 43, 44, 48, 49, 50, 52, 54, 58, 59, 66, 67, 68, 69, 70, 71, 73, 74, 82, 84, 87, 89, 92, 104, 142, 187, 233, 246, ***250***, 265*ch*1*n*6, 271*n*39, 276*n*18
Carpenter, Fannie 168
Carpenter, Julia 114, 125, 149, 156, 169, 199, 200, 225, ***250***, 251, 276*n*18
Carpenter, Mr. 112, 155, 156
Carpenter, William 68, 69, 109, 272*n*75
Carr, Alonzo 80
Carr, Charles M. 237
Carr, Joseph B. 222
Carrie, Dr. S. 122
Case, Frank R. 53, 147, 164, 274*n*118
Casler, Benjamin G. 213, 214, 215, 275*n*25
Cass, Willard 234
Cassidy, Mr. 217, 218
Chaddock, William H. 24, 37, 48, 50, 61, 62, 63, 67, **69**, 73, 75, 81, 86, 89, 92, 94, 97, 105, 107, 114, 120, 130, 155, 248, 267*n*60
Chamberlim, William 11, 234
Chapin, Sylvester E. 78, 236
Chapman, Edgar T. 56, 59, 83, 85, 146, 149, 173, 216, 270*n*184
Christy, Herbert 80, ***81***
Clark, Charles M 135, 139, 141, 273*n*109
Clark, Dr. 218
Clark, Joel B. 135
Clark, Luman A. 136
Clough, George W. 234
Clover, Elizabeth 6
Clute, George W. 124, 199, 239, 275*n*12
Cluxton, Galen 236
Cobb, Ammon B. ***16***, 17, 136, 150, 266*n*21
Cobb, Grant 266*n*21
Cobb, Mrs. 93, 98, 103, 195
Cody, Henry 193
Coe, Robert L. 79, 239
Coffee, Thomas 82
Cohall, James 79, 83
Cole, Risley 240

Coleman, Mr. 36, 93
Collins, William 193
Colman, Louis 15, 266*n*14
Colvin, James A. 92, 272*n*48
Combs, James 53, 239
Comer, Charles 24
Comstock, Lewis 196, 239
Considine, John 193
Cook, Norman F. 49, 234, 269*n*135
Coonrod, Walter A. 136, 153, 235
Cooper, Nathan L. 136, 149
Corbet, James S. 240
Corbett, Robert A. 61, 78, 98, 148, 149, 166, 270*n*1, 272*n*59
Corcoran, Michael 17, 25, 27, 37, 266*n*28
Cox, Jacob D. 209, 215, 275*n*22
Coy, William S. 203, 275*n*17
Crabbs, John 47, 268*n*124
Cramer, Franklin 55, 269*n*165
Crandall, Harry 82
Crane, Clarence A. 89, ***90***, 94, 108, 119, 138, 155, 180, 188, 191, 272*n*42
Crane, Dr. 52
Craven, John J. 72, 271*n*18
Crippen, J.F. 54, 269*n*161
Crosgrove, Frank M. 16, 236, 266*n*17
Crowell, David S. 78, 235
Cummings, Reed W. 46, 47, 239, 268*n*118
Cummings, Silas 22, 266*n*51
Curtis, Enoch A. 14, 35, 36, 58, 59, 66, 78, 83, 129, 245, 251, 265*ch*2*n*9
Curtis, John 193
Curtis, Mrs. 204, 205, 252
Curtis, Newton M. 89, 92, 94, 95, 96, 97, 101, 126, 143, 144, 145, 152, 154, 164, 165, 166, 167, 168, 175, 178, 179, 181, 182, 183, 185, 197, 199, 200, 201, 204, ***252***, 271*n*41, 275*n*14, 276*n*20
Cushing, Alonzo 274*n*131
Cushing, Henry B. 79, 136, 239
Cushing, William B. 169, 274*n*131

Daggett, Rufus 134, 138, 273*n*108
Dalrymple, Addison 234
Danford, Abraham 68, 69, 234
Daniels, Franklin W. 10, 237
Daniels, George B. 10
Darby, Levi 82
David, G.S. 244
David, Nehemiah 129, 197
Davis, A.M. 25
Davis, Captain 152, 154
Davis, Edwin 80
Davis, Harvey 68, 69
Davis, James 14, 24, 238, 265*n*8, 267*n*58
Davis, Jefferson 7, 157, 225, 267*n*81
Davis, Nehemiah 273*n*105
Davis, Phineas 38, 268*n*91
Dayton, Henry C. 236
Dean, Jesse 12
Dean, Marshal C. 237

Dean, Russell H. 12, 18, 233, 266*n*32
Decker, Philip 197
Delain, John 136, 239
Deland, Chauncey 196
Dennison, Ferdinand W. 80
Denton, Egbert G. 136, 149, 150
Deych, Michael 193
Dickens, Charles 182
Dickson, Harvey 21
Dickson, Hiram 21, 74, 136, 236, 266*n*47
Dix, John A. ***113***, 114, 127, 166, 168, 265*ch*1*n*5, 273*n*81
Dixon, Caroline P. 246
Dixon, George H. 53, 175, 230, 231, 245, 269*n*151, 276*n*10
Dobbs, Cyrus J. 17, **64**, 266*n*24
Dodge, Charles C. 40, 268*n*94
Dodge, George S. 211, 275*n*24
Dodge, Leonard L. 196, 236
Doig, James A. 78, 235
Dolan, Michael 129, 234, 273*n*102
Donaldson, Charles 239
Doty, Noble 80, 239
Douglas, Mrs. 173
Dowd, Norton 218, 239, 275*n*29
Downey, G.D. 226
Drake, Clara W. 85, 98, 99, 103, 114, 123, 125, 146, 167, 250, 251, 273*n*96, 276*n*17
Drake, Jeremiah C. 5, 6, 8, 16, 25, 28, 29, 32, 33, 34, 36, 38, 39, 40, 45, 48, 49, 50, 51, 52, 53, 54, 55, 59, 62, 64, 65, 66, 67, 69, 71, 72, 73, 74, 75, ***77***, 78, 81, 82, 83, 84, 86, 87, 88, 89, 91, 92, 93, 95, 97, 100, 103, 107, 155, 160, 161, 187, 199, 213, 233, 259, 265*ch*1*n*5, 271*n*39, 272*n*68, 276*n*17
Duncan, Alba H. 10, 276*appA*n2
Duncan, Charles E. 239
Duncan, Henry A. 239
Dunham, Alfred 19, 24, 58, 59, 66, 101, 119, 138, 140, 146, 149, 152, 155, 157, 158, 165, 203, 204, 205, 206, 207, 208, 209, 210, 213, 214, 217, 220, 221, 222, 251, 266*n*38
Dunnewald, John 136
Dupledge, William 238
Durken, Patrick 193
Dutcher, Edward A. 80, ***81***
Dwight, Captain 91
Dwyer, james A. 238

Eames, Horace 196
Eames, John 196, 238
Early, Jubal 133
Eastman, William R. 242
Eaton, Joel W. 267*n*73
Eddy, George W. 136
Eddy, John C. 79, 236
Eddy, Martin 78, 236
Edgar, John S. 234
Edmonds, Charles 79
Edmonds, George W. 62, ***151***, 152, 154, 155, 164, 165, 270*n*2
Edmonds, Mrs. 154
Edmonds, Nathan 236

Index

Edwards, Horace A. 53, 236
Eells, Moses 82
Elliott, William 48, 269n130
Ellis, Alfred O. 139, **215**, 216, 273n113, 275n27
Ellis, George W. 52, 238, 269n148
Emmons, Mr. 47
Erath, Robert 78, 235
Ericsson, John 19, 266n36
Eslor, Henry 55, 236, 270n166
Esselink, John 196, 236
Eveleth, Henry 130
Evens, George H. 74, 271n23
Everson, Mr. 52
Ewing, Augustus M. 122, 273n92

Fancy, Frank 193
Farragut, David G. 113, 118, 208, 273n79
Fath, George 193
Felton, Egbert W. 136, 149
Fenton, Reuben E. 148, 155, 166, 168, 170, 173, 175, 194, 201, 252, 274n130
Ferguson, Benjamin S. 238
Ferguson, Daniel 44, 268n106
Ferrin, Samuel A. 136
Ferrin, William 240
Findley, Henry 78, 236
Findley, James D. 97, 272n54
Fink, John 79
Fisher, Joel A. 239
Fisk, Albert C. 105, 121, 130, 272n70
Fisk, Charles E. 136, 175, 234
Fisk, Mr. 90, 157
Fitch, Marlow 79, **80**
Flood, Hugh C. 268n90
Flynn, Matthew 193
Follett 73
Foot, Warham S. 10, 240
Forbes, Mr. 148, 162
Foster, John G. 38
Foster, Robert S. **7**, 8, 12, 29, 33, 38, 53, 55, 62, 64, 65, 66, 111, 152, 154, 172, 265ch1n1
Foster, Seth 153
Fowler, Dexter S. 55, 269n166
Fox, George W. 51, 54, 135, 269n140
Fox, Heman S. **128**, 188, 191, 273n101
Fox, William F. 271n39
Foy, William **67**, 68, 270n12
Frank (horse) 28, 32, 97, 100, 101, 104, 132, 133, 141, 142, 144, 151, 171, 203, 227, 267n74
Frank, Martin 52
Freeman, John E. 80, 239
Frink, Thomas W. 235
Frisbie, Charles D. 268n106
Frisbie, James 268n106
Fritts, Benjamin 78
Fullager, Lizzie 206
Fullager, Mr. 106, 145, 223
Furman, Thaddeus K. 43, 268n101

Gage, Charles B. 11
Gage, Judson 136, 149, 150
Gage, Malcom W. 11, 235
Gage, Nelson 46, 240, 268n111
Galloway, John 79
Gantcher, Charles 79, 83, 271n35
Gantcher, Mrs. 86
Gardiner, R.H. 30
Gardner, George W. **135**
Gardner, John S. 78
Gardner, Marion 240
Gawn, Henry K. 82
Geary, John W. 222
Geer, Judson F. 79, 238
Gerard, Emil 193
Getty, George W. 33, 36, 37, 267n80
Gibbs, Alfred 265ch2n1
Giffin, George W. 136, 234
Gilbert, John A. 55, 234, 269n166
Gillmore, Quincy A. 47, 49, 50, 54, 55, 59, 61, 66, 73, 106, 268n122
Gilvin, Isaiah 129
Gleason, Richard W. 235
Gloede, William 193
Goodrich, Benjamin F. 92, 272n49
Goodrich, Francis J. 114, 155, 170, 273n82
Goodwin, Edwin T. 80, 240
Gossett, Benjamin F. 49, 269n135
Gould, Avery R. 80, 240
Gould, Myron 136
Graham 46
Graham, Benjamin 50, 51
Graham, William 5
Grant, Ulysses S. 7, **8**, 13, 60, 65, 75, 90, 95, 96, 98, 101, 102, 103, 104, 106, 107, 109, 115, 118, 120, 121, 125, 128, 129, 132, 134, 154, 169, 170, 191, 192, 198, 199, 200, 201, 208, 213, 221, 222, 231, 256, 258, 273n88, 274n124, 274n134
Graves, Eugene E. 219, 275n31
Graves, Roswell W. 234
Green, Addison P. 82, 236
Green, Augustus 25, 46, 267n68, 268n113
Green, James B. 197
Griffin, George W. 276AppAn1
Griffin, Mrs. 194
Groschwiller, Jacob 193
Grover, Harvey B. 78, 136, 149
Guiles, John 240

Haden, Rushmons 198
Hagius, David 235
Haight, Benjamin S. 68, 69
Hall, Artemus 196
Hall, Joseph F. 237
Hall (surgeon) 251
Halleck, Henry, W 23, 267n55
Hamilton, James T. 153, 197
Hammond, Chalmers 130, 196
Hampton, Wade 273n106
Hancock, Winfield S. 116, **117**, 140, 272n83
Hand, Daniel W. 24, 267n59
Hannum, Chester S. 80, 239
Hanson, John W. 14, 15, 19, 265ch2n5

Harmon, Charles 53, 236, 269n154
Harrington, Franklin 68, 235
Harris (chaplain) 51, 269n143
Harris, Elbert L. **135**
Harris, Frank W. 152, 2450
Harris, Mrs. 228
Harris, Nancy Ann 27
Hart, Mrs. 168
Hart, Sylvester M. 79, 237
Hart, Walter J. 151, 152, 157, 234, 274n126
Hart, William S. 234
Harter, Harvey D. 40, 79, 268n96
Haskins, Ethan A. 153
Hatch, John P. 64, 270n6
Hawley, Chauncey W. 86, 170, 215, 216, 231, 271n35
Hawley, Joseph R. 116, 162, 215, 273n84
Hayden, Hiram 196, 238
Hayes, Henry 238
Hazard, Algernon D. 79, 237
Heath, George W. 23, 78, 267n56
Heath, Perry 238, 269n149
Heath, Stephen 136, 236
Heaton, William 197
Heckman, Charles A. 67, 68, 71, 72, 73, 270n11
Hedges, Samuel P. 59, 67, 68, 69, 71, 73, 213, **214**, 216, 270n182
Hegunbourg, Kate 117
Hemenger, Amasa 153
Hempsted, John K. 136
Henry, Robert 97, 238, 272n55
Hepburn (Reverend) 217, 218
Herbert, George 218, 275n30
Herrick, Elisha A. 94
Herring, Mr. 161
Hewes, Eddy A. 239, 266n15, 269n138
Hewes, Edward 50, 51
Hewes, Julius B. 15, 28, 50, 101, 115, 116, 266n15, 269n138
Hewitt, William H. 124
Heywood, Rufus 44
Higgins, Charles A. 250
Higgins, Mr. 37
Hill, Aaron 196, 234
Hill, Henry 54, 269n163
Himelin, Mike 197
Hobart, Joseph 79
Hodge, Patrick 124
Hogges, Mathew 55, 269n166
Hogins, Amos 11
Hogins, David 11
Hoke, Robert F. 210, 275n23
Hollenbeck, Addison 131
Hollister, John Q.A. 196, 200, 204, 275n16
Holstering, Mrs. 199
Holt, Marvin G. 53
Hooker, Joseph 13, 36
Horvath, Paul 196, 235
Hosier, James B. 78
Hosier, John B. 96, 196
Hosier, Sidney 136
Hotchkiss, Dewitt C. 135
Howard, Oliver O. 122, 227
Hubbard, Henry 152

Index

Hubbard, William H. 165, 239
Huber, Henry 51, 269n142
Hudson (chaplain) 54
Hudson, Samuel W. 193
Hulit, Asahel 21, 266n49
Hull, Henry 78, 82, 85, 240, 271n33
Hull, Samuel 152, 239
Hungsford, S.H. 50
Hunt, Enos 49, 234, 269n135
Hunt, John 143, 224, 225, 275n37
Hunt, Mary 14
Hunt, Mr. 117, 143
Hunt, Mrs. 86, 107, 117, 130, 143, 144, 145
Hunter, Mrs. 31
Hurlburt, Benjamin F. 78, 235
Huytink, John 78
Hyde, Clark 119
Hyde, Frederick 6, 31, 40, 93, 99, 103, 105, 109, 112, 117, 118, 121, 125, 130, 132, 146, 149, 150, 151, 156, 161, 167, 169, 170, 173, 175, 177, 192, 195, 198, 207, 209, 212, 213, 218, 223, 225, 226, 229, 231, 268n93
Hyde, Henry 6
Hyde, Henry W. 6, 40, 93, 98, 100, 103, 104, 106, 107, 110, 113, 115, 119, 125, 131, 132, 133, 146, 148, 149, 150, 156, 168, 170, 175, 177, 195, 202, 203, 206, 216, 217, 218, 221, 225, 229, 231, 268n93
Hyde, Maria 6
Hyde, Thomas 90, 272n43
Hyde, Zina 90

Ignatz, Paul 193
Irwin, Charles K. 86, 92, 242, 271n36, 276AppBn2
Ives, Henry 136

Jackson, Robert 153
Jackson, Thomas J. 13
Jerome, Baptist 193
Johnson, Henry A. 75, 271n24
Johnson, John 153, 236
Johnson, Mrs. 203
Johnson, William 238
Johnston, Joseph E. 222, 274n5
Jones, Albert C. 80, 136, 150, 196
Jones, Augustus 79
Jones, Edward 244, 276n8
Jones, Ervin A. 190, 274n2
Jones, Hugh O. 11, 234
Jones, John 68, 69
Jones, William A. 185, 187, 274n138
Judd (Reverend) 117

Kabus, Robert F. 54, 269n161
Kautz, August V. 142, 274n116
Kazer, Francis J. 136
Kean, James G. 78, 235
Kearn, Charles 196
Kelley, John 79, 83
Kelly, Thomas 193
Kelser, Myron 79
Kenada, George W. 239

Kennedy, George W. 276n3
Kenniston, Samuel 130, 196, 239
Kenniston, William 130
Kessler, Den 213
Keyes, Erasmus D. 36, 267n86
Keyes, Lyman B. 78
Keyes, William C. 80, 239
Kilburn, Robert 82
Kilpatrick, Hugh J. 220, 275n36
Kimball, Mr. 54
Kimberly, Charles A. 59, 66, **70**, 134, 135, 137, 139, 140, 141, 145, 149, 270n183
King, Ezekiel 78
King, Willard 153
Kingsland, Warren J. 78
Kinphenger, Franklin E. 25, 267n63
Kiny, Willard 235
Kirk, Leland A. 55, 269n166
Kloet, William 243, 276n7
Knapp, Charles 193
Knapp, Levi J. 79, 236
Knowlton, Ira A. 10, 235
Knowlton, William 10
Koepke, Charles 121, 273n90
Kramer, Louis 193
Krayer, Peter 11
Krayger, Peter 243, 244
Kurtz, John 193

Lafrican, Stephen 193
Laine, William R. 79, 83, 86, 92, 238, 271n35
Lamb, William 197, 274n10
Lanning Francis S. 235
Larrabee, Charles 98
Lawrence, Charles W. 238
Lawson, Charles 79
Lawson, John 12, 19, 266n35
Lawson, Peter 236
Leach, Edwin B. 235
Lee, David J. 27, 267n72
Lee, Robert E. 13, 104, 106, 118, 120, 121, 134, 139, 176, 190, 200, 219, 267n76, 267n86
Lee, W.H. Fitzhugh 30, 267n76
Lenox, Hamilton 79, 236
Lenox, William W. 239
Lervry, Alexander M. 100
Lewis, G. Wilton 272n73
Lewis, H.S. 245
Lewis, James 235, 244, 276n9
Lewis, Leewellan 153
Lewis (Reverend) 62
Lincoln, Abraham 5, 7, 13, 118, 151, 155, 161, 227, 272n67, 275n39
Link, Andrew 79, 83
Little, Oliver 197
Locheler, John 193
Logan, John A. 222
Lord, Leroy 25, 156, 267n62
Losee, Albert 10, 240
Losee, Clark 10
Losee, John J. 237
Loucks, John 79
Lowell, Locklin 55, 269n166
Lowery, Alexander M. 44, 268n103

Lucas, Josiah M. 53, 269n152
Ludwick, Ephraim A. 44, 48, 50, 51, 58, 59, 66, 69, 74, 92, 93, 94, 97, 108, 112, 116, 123, 127, 134, 135, 137, 139, 140, 141, 142, 143, 145, 146, 148, 149, 155, 157, 168, 173, 189, 192, 203, 204, 205, 206, 207, 208, 216, 217, 218, 219, 220, 221, 222, 223, 250, 252, 268n128
Lyman, Jonas W. 199, 274n13

Magorin, Penn 118
Mahear, William 193
Mahoney, John 136
Malloy, Matthew 193
Manley, A.J. 160, 161, 162, 231
Manley, Spencer 236
Mann, Henry 235
Manwarring, Carlos F. 220, 275n35
Marcon, Cyrpus A. 193
Mark, Philip 78, 235
Markham, Henry 130
Markham, Lucius 78
Marsh, Ira 136
Martin, Chapin H. 153
Martin, William E. 130, 136
Marvin, Selden D. **21**, 247, 265Intro.n4, 266n42, 276n13
Mason, John 143
Mason, Otis A. 14, 240, 265ch2n7
Massey, Mrs. 245
Mathews, Joseph S. 19, 48, 82, **86**, 92, 93, 148, 155, 165, 208, 217, 221, 266n34
Matteson, Andre W. 10, 236
Matteson, Victor M. 10
Mayborn, Hannah E. 242, 276AppBn4
Mayborn, John G. 10, 238, 276AppBn4
Mayborn, Thomas 242, 276AppBn3
McCann, Abby 39
McClellan, George B. 148
McConihe, John 82, **83**, 84, 271n28
McCoul, Frank 80
McCourt, John 175
McDonald, John P. 124, 237
McElroy, William 49, 269n135
McEvoy, Phillip 98, **99**, 198, 235, 272n61
McGee, Bernard 46, 193, 268n114
McIntosh, George W. 193
McKee, Samuel S. 235, 268n114
McLaughlin, William 78, 124, 235
Mead, Charles 94, 104, 108, 119, 175, 204, 205, 272n51
Meade, George G. 116, 131, 220, 272n44, 273n83
Mercer, Charles 80, 275n34
Merrill, John 112
Merriman, Lester C. 12, 238
Merritt, Barton 235
Mertz, Conrad H. 25, 238, 267n63
Miles, Isaac D. 53, 239
Milhouse, J.A. 44
Miller, D. Henry 22, 266n51

Index

Mills, David 25, 235, 267n65
Miracle, Isaac P. 78, 83, 235
Moore, Homer H. 47, 268n123
Moore, John W. 199, 275n13
Moose, James 193
Morehouse, Silas 153
Morgan, Edwin D. 8, 265ch1n5
Morris, Dr. 254
Morse, Hiram P. *150*
Mount, Charles W. 25, 267n69
Mount, George F. 122, 123, 126, 240, 269n133, 273n92
Mount, Samuel V. 136, 196, 240
Mulvihill, Daniel 79
Munger, Charles 78
Munson, John J. 23, 79, 128, 267n56
Murray, A.W. 11
Muzzy, Mr. 249
Myers, Bartholomew 101, 272n64
Myers, John 124, 235
Myers, Oliver C. 124

Neil, Augustus 82, 123, 124, 273n93
Neil, Charles 44, 45, 46, 235, 268n105
Neil, Mrs. 44
Nelson, Joe 203
Nelson, John 70
Nevins, Perry W. 78, 136
Newbury, Lewis 193
Newell, Thomas J. 79
Nichols, Arthur P. 21
Nichols, Daniel 136, 196
Nichols, Franklin 136
Nichols, George L. 27
Nichols, Oliver 21, 136, 266n46
Norton, Charles L. 16, 266n22

Oakes, John F. 80, *81*
O'Brien, Michael 70, 237, 271n16
O'Brien, Patrick 193, 218, 239, 275n29
O'Brien, William 193
O'Donnell, Patrick 193
Oley, Charles H. 41, 59, 108, 149, 268n98
Olmstead 24
Olto, Justin S. 21
O'Neil, William 193
Onley, William F. 55, 237, 270n166
Ord, Edward O.C. 97, 172, 191, 272n53
Ordaway, Jason 152
Oviatt, Adoniram J. 268n117

Page, John 196
Paine, Charles J. 206, 207, 210, 211, 220, 275n19
Palmer, Lucius L. 129, 137, 178, 194, 208, 227, 273n104
Palmeter, John G. 16, 28, 41, 51, 52, *77*, 78, 83, 84, 85, 92, 127, 251, 266n23, 276n23
Palmeter, John W. 78, 234
Palmeter, Mary A. 255, 276n23
Pangborn, James *130*, 150
Park, George 136

Parker, Cornelius W. 52, 56, 239, 270n173
Parker, Lyman J. 111, 135, 273n78
Parkinson, Royal 194, 274n6
Parmlee, George 247, 276n14
Paschke, John G. 78
Patterson, George W. 84, 103, 271n29, 272n68
Peacock, Smith 129, 240, 273n102
Pease, William 79, 86, 238, 271n35
Peck, Henry H. 34, 234, 267n85
Peck, Hollister H. 11, 236
Peck, John J. 7, 37, 39, 265ch1n2, 265ch1n5
Pecor, Charles 79, 86, 271n35
Peeks, Mrs. 114
Peets, Mr. 105
Pelton, William R. *21*, 266n48
Pennock, Francis E. 135, 215, 224, 275n26
Pennypacker, Galusha 1 97, 199, 275n11
Peters, John Jr. 129, 238, 273n102
Peterson, Peter, J. 79, 196, 236
Peterson, William 78
Pheteplace, Augustus E. 25, 236, 267n70
Phillips, Frederick 136
Phillips, Milton 149, 234
Phillips, Mr. 173
Phillips, Morgan 167, 274n128
Phillips, Silas 240
Phisterer, Frederick 5, 265Intro.n1
Pickett, Manhattan 82
Pierce, Fred A. 80, 83, 239
Pierce, Gurdon L. 44, 78, 268n104
Pierce, Henry H. 55, 235, 270n166
Pierce, William J. 55, 239, 270n166
Piper, Alexander *89*, 271n41
Pitt, Samuel C. 153
Ploss, Almond 79, 83, 238
Ploss, David 78
Ploss, Jared 48, 237, 269n129
Polder, Jacob 56, 270n174
Porter, David D. 176, 198, 199, 208, 274n134
Porter, Edmund J. 53, 269n153
Post, John K. 78, 234
Post, Mr. 162
Potter, Harvey 10, 238
Potter, James M. 78, 235
Potter, John 10
Potter, William H. *76*, 119, 140, 271n25
Powers, Alonzo H. 80
Powers, Francis G. 1, 265ch2n6, 265ch2n8
Powers, Joel A. 136
Pratt, Ann E. 56, 57, 270n172
Pratt, Daniel J. 270n172
Prendergast, Charles 276n24
Prendergast, Mary A. 255, 276n24
Price, Charles 38, 155, 203, 274n123
Putnam, Davis O. 136

Racine, William 193
Raspus, William 196, 238
Raymond, Israel R. *152*, 153

Redington, Frederick A. 15, 68, 69, 118, 157, 166, 246, 266n12, 276n11
Reed, C.F. 144
Reed, Louisa 253
Reed, Oliver T. 276n21
Reed, Theron 11, 234
Renne, James 153
Reynolds, Henry 193
Rhoades, James 196
Rhodes, Thomas A. 49, 269n134
Rhuling, F.J.W. 79
Rice, Francis E. 6, 28
Rice, Hiram E. 86, 196, *197*
Richardson, Delos D. 25, 267n67
Richardson, Newell B. 78, 124, 273n97
Risley, Hanson 101
Risley, Walter S. 12, 238
Robbins, Deloss 129, 135, 272n103
Robbins, Thomas 129
Robinson, Charles H. 150
Robinson, Zina H. 122, 273n91
Rockwell, Richard A. 10, 240
Rogers, Henry 14
Rogers, Dr. Henry 38, 52, 91, 103, 119, 121, 132, 148, 167, 169, 221, 227, 265ch2n4
Rolph, Lawrence W. 53, 234
Rolph, Thomas S. 79, 83
Ross, George W. 200, 201, 275n15
Roundy, Charles A. 248
Rouse, George W. 53
Rouse, Mrs. 251
Rowan, Mr. 31
Ruch, Jacob B. *152*, 153
Ruhling, Frederick W.J. 236
Russ, Christian 51, 238, 269n145
Russ, Joseph C. 56, 108, 155, 156, 225, 229, 230, 231
Russell, Enoch 129

Sampson, David 188, 191, 274n1
Sanborn, Alanson L. 268n90
Sansonci, Jaquis 193
Saunders, Mr. 42
Schaffer, Caleb H. 238
Schlick, Ferdinand 193
Schmidt, John 136
Schmidt, William 193
Schofield, John M. 205, 207, 208, 209, 210, 219, 222, 275n18, 275n22
Scofield, Lewis 78, 235
Scott, Frederick B. 235
Scott, John H. 53, 235, 269n157
Scott, Mr. 117
Scott, Naham S. 17, 26, *107*, 194, 266n29, 274n7
Scott, Robert 268n126
Scott, William W. 52
Scribner, Frank L. 80
Sears, William H. 135
Seeley, William W. 78, 197
Seymour, Horatio 168, 274n124
Seymour, Ova H. 54, 269n161
Seymour, Truman 64, 270n6
Shaffer, Caleb H. 56, 270n171
Sharp, William B. 235

Shattuck, Everett 240
Shaver, Charles 193
Shaw, Ernest 203
Shaw, James 203, 275n17
Shaw, Joseph 234
Shaw, Julius M. 98, 272n56
Shaw, Mr. & Mrs. 162, 166, 173, 175, 176
Shaw, Squire H. 78, 234
Shaw, Warner D. 112, 114, 144, 149, 153, 156, 160, 165, 166, 175, 197, 201, 272n51
Shaw, William H. 98, 151, 168, 272n57
Shelters, Edward 68, 69, 234, 270n13
Shelton, Mary 112, 125
Shelton, Mr. 192
Shelton, Mrs. 105, 149
Shelton, Otis W. 86, 92, 101, 105, 106, 271n37, 272n63
Shepley, George F. 65, 270n9
Sheridan, Philip 129, 131, 132, 133, 148, 231, 273n80, 275n41
Sherman, William T. 13, 169, 192, 200, 205, 208, 214, 216, 217, 219, 220, 221, 222, 274n134, 274n5, 275n18, 275n22, 275n32, 275n36
Sherwin, Samuel G. 17, 75, 76, 96, 98, 234, 266n31, 272n61
Shirley, George W. 193
Shirley, Gilman 79, 86, 117, 238, 271n35
Shirley, Mrs. 117
Sicke, Conrad 236
Simmons, Andrew J. 127, 273n100
Simpson, George 234
Sixby, Herman 99, **100,** 272n62
Skellie, Ebenezer 136, 139, 273n112
Skellie, William R. 153
Skinner, Mrs. 245
Skinner, William H. 79
Slayton, Charles 79
Slayton, Ezra 79
Sloan, Almon 78
Slocum, Henry W. 219, 220, 222, 275n32
Slotboom, John A. 78
Smith, Abner D. 267n71
Smith, A.W. 25
Smith, Carlos 240
Smith, David M. 11, 239
Smith, Dr. 119, 121, 175, 176
Smith, Edward W. 64, 270n5
Smith, Gideon 78
Smith, Henry W. 10, 234
Smith, Hiram 239
Smith, John 235
Smith, John F. **9,** 17, 19, 36, 37, 59, 62, 86, 89, **93,** 96, 97, 101, 105, 108, 109, 111, 112, 119, 128, 130, 132, 140, 142, 144, 149, 159, 160, 161, 162, 163, 164, 165, 166, 167, 168, 171, 178, 179, 180, 181, 185, 188, 189, 191, 195, 196, 197, 199, 200, 201, 202, 233, 249, 251, 266n41, 276n19
Smith, Joseph C. 79
Smith, Lottie 201, 252, 276n19

Smith, Philip 193
Smith, Stukley E. 136, 149
Smith, Warren 17, 78, 266n29
Smith, William F. 80, 90, 239, 256, 272n44, 276AppCn2
Sour, Nicholas 83
Sparkes, Thomas 236
Spaulding, James R. 196
Spear, Samuel P. 30, **31,** 33, 38, 40, 267n77
Spear, William A. 136
Spencer, John B. 236
Spinola, Francis B. 12, 265ch1n12
Sprague, Andrew A. 234
Sprague, John T. 55, 265Intro.n3, 270n170
Springer, John 78, 197, 236
Squimer, Paul 11, 238, 243, 276AppBn5
Squires, George E. 235
Stafford, Austin **91,** 272n47
Stafford, James 153, 235
Stafford, Martin J. **173,** 274n133
Staples, Samuel S. 78, 234
Starr, Eber W. 234
Steam, A.H. 198
Stebbins, Julius 238
Stephen, Mr. 218
Stevens, Major 163, 166
Stevens, Orrin 231
Stevens, Phineas 40, 44, 45, 52, 54, 55, 168, 268n95
Stevens, Wait J. 80
Stickney, Byron 193
Stiles, Mr. 105
Stillman, Henry 86, 105, 271n36
Stillman, Mr. 161, 162, 173
Stoddard, Lyman H. 124, 234
Stone, Martin B. 129
Stonehouse, J.B. 6
Story, William W. 151, 152, 234
Stowell, John 79, 236
Stowell, William 79
Strauss, George 196
Strong, Walter 68, 69
Stroyer, George 276n6
Stroyer, Leonard 243
Stuart, Charles 193
Stuart, Sidney P. 136, 149
Sullivan, Michael 135
Sutton, Henry 240
Swanson, William 79
Swartz, Charles 193
Sweet, Asa 97, 239
Sweet, De Loss 78
Sweet, Henry J. 49, 239, 269n135
Sweet, Theophilus H. 135
Sylvester, Nathaniel B. 271n28

Taber, Stephen D. 136, 197
Talcott, George S. 41, 59, 66, 109, 155, 160, 166, 194, 199, 268n97
Talcott, Mrs. 166
Tarbell, Joel D. 53, 239
Taylor, John C. 21, 239, 266n45
Taylor, Mr. 31, 33, 34, 37, 56, 58, 59
Taylor, William H. 108, 149, 173, 272n72

Taylor, Zachary 267n81
Teed, Charles E. 11, 239
Tenny, Levi E. 123, 273n94
Tenny, Wilson P. 79, 83
Terry, Alfred H. 106, 110, **116,** 145, 164, 187, 191, 199, 210, 211, 215, 219, 220, 221, 222, 223, 272n71, 275n31
Terry, George E. 193
Tew, Dewitt C. 79, **80,** 238
Tewinkle, John 79, 236
Tewinkle, William 236
Tezepher, John 47, 235, 268n120
Thayer, Daniel B. 25, 234, 236
Thomas, George H. 192, 222, 231, 274n5, 275n41
Thomas, Jeffrey R. 14, **15,** 266n13
Thomas, Lorenzo **126,** 136, 163, 171, 221, 224, 273n99
Thompson, Charles 153
Thompson, George 50, 238, 269n136
Thompson, Mason C. 78, 218, 234, 275n29
Thompson, Mrs. 50
Thompson, T.C. 149
Thornton, William 196, 238
Ticknor, Alroy A. 119, 217, 273n87
Tiffany, Charles C. 149, 173, 274n119
Tiffany, Cornelius M. 236
Tiffany, Silas 237
Tillotson, Jared N. 80
Toles, Mrs. 121
Toles, Newell 104, 114, 121
Toles, Silas 272n69
Tracy, Kies 49, 234, 269n135
Traver, Charles B. 79
Tressler, Dr. 203
Trot, John 193
Tucker, Charles H. 22, 238, 267n53
Tunnell, John 197
Turner, John W. 97, 123, 173, 272n53
Tuttle, William W. 53

Vader, Jacob 68, 69
Van Buren, Daniel T. 266n44
Van Buren, Jim 31
Vandewark, Benjamin 98, 272n58
Vandewark, John 135
Van Geen, Cornelius 238
Van Houten, Adrian 193
Vanness, Marcus 10, 238
Vanscoy, Egbert C. 45, 114, 268n110, 273n82
Van Vliet, Darius 25, 46, 235, 267n63
Vehring, Conrad 193
Vogdes, Israel 8, 49, 50, 62, 65, 265ch1n8
Vorce, Hiram 98, **99,** 233, 236, 272n61
Vorce, Perry 188, **191,** 217

Waite, Daniel M. 10, 235
Waldenberger, Alexander 193
Walder, Jacob 193, 275n34

Index

Wallace, Nelson L. 80, 239
Walrod, James G. 25, 235, 267n61
Wanshis, John 55, 269n166
Ward, James 130, 136
Ward, William 128
Wardrop, David W. 33, 34, 267n83
Warner, Charles O. 78
Warner, Henry 136, 235
Warner, John 136
Warner, Robert 135
Warren, Gouverneur K. 118, 120, 273n86
Washburn, Charles E. 38, 50, 52, 56, 89, 90, 91, 94, 112, 114, 116, 121, 139, 141, 149, 155, 159, **160**, 166, 167, 219, 221, 233, 268n92, 276n22
Washburn, Lucy M. 159, 161, 162, 225, 254, 276n22
Waters, Eliza F. 247
Waters, Frank 38, 48, 51, 233, 246, 247, 269n132, 276n12
Waters, Mrs. 49
Watson, George A. 17, 19, 235, 266n25
Weatherly, William H. 239
Weatherwax, Aldo D. 234
Weaver, Albert J. 124, 136, 235, 273n97
Weitzel, Godfrey 69, 73, 74, 85, 172, 185, 270n14
Wells, James 51, 149, 269n144

Wentz, Hilary 196
Wessells, Henry W. 8, 12, 265ch1n7
West, Charles W. 129, 135, 234, 272n103
Westly, George T. 151, 152, 154, 164, 234, 274n120
Whalon, Frank 79
Wheeler, Frank 86, 104, 148, 203, 216, 271n34
Wheeler, Joseph 220, 275n33
Wheeler, Mrs. 216
Whitaker, Addison J. 13, 16, 27, 265ch2n3
White, Loren 80, 240
White, William W. 239
Whitford, George 153, 197
Whitford, Solomon W. 79, 127, 273n100
Whiting, William H.C. 197, 274n10
Whitney, Orwell 239
Whittlesey, Eliphalet 227, 275n38
Wienman, John 236
Wiggens (Sutler) 217
Wigtman, Albert M. 25, 267n66
Wilcox, Samuel O. **237**, 238
Wilde, Mr. 145
Wilder, Mr. 171, 202, 226
Willard, Mr. 98, 101, 102, 121, 192
Williams, Dr. 91, 115
Williams, Gardner R.C. 236, **237**

Williams, James 124
Williams, J.B. 37
Williams, J.L. 37
Williams, John S. 239
Williams, Jule 195
Williams, Juli 30
Wilson, Charles E. 239
Wilson, Charles H. 193
Wilson, Francis 79
Wilson, Frank L. 10, 238
Wilson, George D. 153
Wilson, James 193
Wilson, John M. 48, 51, 52, 268n127
Wilson, William 153, **154**, 240, 274n121
Winchester, Charles J. 237
Wineman, John 79
Wood, John 168, 274n129
Woodbridge, Charles 193
Woodward, Levi E. 152
Wright, David M. 268n90
Wright, Dr. 17, 266n27
Wright, H.C. 121
Wright, Horatio G. 77, 95, 258, 271n26, 276AppCn3
Wright, John 53, 79, 83, 269n150
Wright, Mr. 117

Yorker, Anthony 174, 202, 225
Young, Charles P. 236